ALL COLOUR COOKERY COLLECTION

EBURY

ALL COLOUR
COOKERY
COLLECTION

OVER 600 DOUBLE-TESTED RECIPES,
EACH ONE ILLUSTRATED IN COLOUR

CRESSET EDITIONS

First published by Cresset Editions in 1994
an imprint of Random House (UK) Limited
20 Vauxhall Bridge Road
London SW1V 2SA

A catalogue record for this book is available from the British Library

ISBN: 0 09 178590 1

Photography by Sue Atkinson, Jan Baldwin, Martin Bridgdale, Laurie Evans,
Ken Field, Melvin Grey, John Heseltine, Tim Hill, Tim Imrie, James Jackson,
David Johnson, Paul Kemp, Don Last, James Murphy, Peter Myers,
Alan Newnham, Charlie Stebbings, Grant Symon, Rosemary Weller,
Andrew Whittuck, Paul Williams.

Printed and bound in Italy by New Interlitho S.p.a., Milan

COOK'S NOTES

- Both metric and imperial measures are given in the recipes in this book. Follow one set of measures only as they are not interchangeable.
- All spoon measures are level unless otherwise stated.
- All ovens should be preheated to the specified temperature.
- Microwave cooking instructions are given for some of the recipes in this book. When using these, please note that HIGH refers to 100% full power output of a 600-700 watt cooker; MEDIUM refers to 60% of full power; LOW refers to 35% of full power.

  If your microwave power output is lower than 600 watts, it may be necessary to allow longer than recommended. In any event you should always check food before the end of the cooking time, to ensure that it does not overcook.

CONTENTS

MEAT

This mouth-watering selection of meat-based dishes includes all types of meat and offal cooked in every way imaginable. From warming country casseroles to an elegant crown roast of lamb or a simply cooked, tender, juicy steak — you will be sure to find a recipe to please.

SIRLOIN STEAKS WITH MUSTARD

SERVES 4

50 g (2 oz) wholegrain mustard	30 ml (2 tbsp) chopped parsley
15 g (½ oz) plain flour	30 ml (2 tbsp) chopped thyme
four 175 g (6 oz) sirloin steaks	

1 Mix together the mustard and flour, then spread on top of each steak.
2 Line a grill pan with foil, sprinkle with the herbs and put the steaks on top. Cook under a preheated grill for 5–15 minutes, turning frequently, until the steaks are cooked to your liking. Serve at once.

——— TO MICROWAVE ———

Complete step 1. Preheat a large browning dish on HIGH for 5 minutes or according to manufacturer's instructions. Quickly put the herbs and steaks in the browning dish and cook on HIGH for 5–7 minutes.

STILTON STEAKS

SERVES 4

100 g (4 oz) Stilton cheese, crumbled	pepper
25 g (1 oz) butter, softened	four 100–175 g (4–6 oz) sirloin or fillet steaks
50–75 g (2–3 oz) walnut pieces, finely chopped	

1 Put the cheese in a bowl and mash with a fork. Add the butter and walnuts and mix in. Season to taste.
2 Put the steaks on the grill rack and season with plenty of pepper. Cook under a preheated grill for 5–15 minutes, turning frequently, until the steaks are cooked to your liking.
3 Remove the steaks from under the grill, sprinkle the cheese and nut mixture evenly over them and press down with a palette knife. Grill for a further minute or until the topping is melted and bubbling. Serve hot.

STEAK WITH CREAM SAUCE

SERVES 4

four 175 g (6 oz) fillet steaks	15 ml (1 tbsp) lemon juice
2 garlic cloves, crushed (optional)	30 ml (2 tbsp) Worcestershire sauce
salt and pepper	15–30 ml (1–2 tbsp) brandy
50 g (2 oz) butter	150 ml (5 fl oz) single cream
100 g (4 oz) button mushrooms, very thinly sliced	15 ml (1tbsp) finely chopped parsley
25 g (1 oz) onion, very finely chopped	parsley sprigs, to garnish

1 Rub the steaks with the garlic and season well.
2 Melt half the butter in a frying pan and fry the steaks over a high heat for about 2 minutes on each side to brown. If you like your steaks well done, cook for longer. Transfer to a warm serving dish and keep hot.
3 Heat the remaining butter in the frying pan and quickly fry the mushrooms and onion for about 5 minutes or until tender. Add the lemon juice, Worcestershire sauce and brandy and bring to the boil.
4 Stir in the cream and chopped parsley, bring almost to the boil, check the seasoning, then quickly pour over the steaks. Serve garnished with parsley sprigs.

JUGGED STEAK

SERVES 4

700 g (1½ lb) stewing steak, cut into 2.5 cm (1 inch) cubes	about 450 ml (¾ pint) beef stock
25 g (1 oz) plain wholemeal flour	225 g (8 oz) sausagemeat
1 medium onion, sliced	50 g (2 oz) fresh wholemeal breadcrumbs
4 cloves	30 ml (2 tbsp) chopped parsley
salt and pepper	15 ml (1 tbsp) redcurrant jelly
150 ml (¼ pint) port	

1 Toss the meat in the flour, shaking off excess, and put in an ovenprof casserole.
2 Add the onion and cloves and season to taste. Pour in the port and just enough stock to cover the meat.
3 Cover the casserole and cook in a preheated oven at 170°C (325°F) mark 3 for about 3 hours or until the meat is tender.
4 Meanwhile, mix together the sausagemeat, breadcrumbs and parsley and season to taste. With floured hands, form the mixture into eight balls.
5 Forty minutes before the end of the cooking time, stir the redcurrant jelly into the casserole. Add the forcemeat balls and cook, uncovered, until the forcemeat balls are cooked and brown. Skim off any excess fat and serve hot.

STRIPS OF BEEF IN WHISKY SAUCE

SERVES 4

15 g (½ oz) butter	75 ml (3 tbsp) whisky liqueur, such as Drambuie
700 g (1½ lb) sirloin steak, cut into strips	75 ml (3 fl oz) double cream
1 large onion, chopped	salt and pepper

1 Melt the butter in a frying pan. Add the beef strips and onion and cook for 5–10 minutes or until the beef is brown and cooked to taste.

2 Stir in the liqueur and cream. Heat gently to reduce slightly. Season to taste, then serve at once.

─────────── **TO MICROWAVE** ───────────

Preheat a large browning dish on HIGH for 5 minutes or according to manufacturer's instructions. Quickly put the butter, beef and onion in the browning dish. Cook on HIGH for 5–7 minutes or until the meat is cooked to taste, stirring frequently. Stir in the liqueur and season to taste. Cook on HIGH for 1 minute, then stir in the cream and serve at once.

BEEF OLIVES

SERVES 4

75 g (3 oz) streaky bacon rashers, finely chopped	salt and pepper
1 small onion, chopped	8 thin slices of topside beef, weighing about 700 g (1½ lb)
10 ml (2 tsp) chopped parsley	15 ml (1 tbsp) prepared English mustard
100 g (4 oz) fresh breadcrumbs	45 ml (3 tbsp) seasoned flour
50 g (2 oz) shredded beef suet	25 g (1 oz) butter
1.25 ml (¼ tsp) dried mixed herbs	30 ml (2 tbsp) vegetable oil
1 egg, size 6	450 ml (¾ pint) beef stock
1 lemon	2 medium onions, sliced

1 Mix the bacon with the chopped onion, parsley, breadcrumbs, suet, herbs and egg. Add the grated rind of ½ of the lemon and 5 ml (1 tsp) juice and season to taste.

2 Put the meat between two sheets of greaseproof paper and beat out with a meat mallet or rolling pin.

3 Spread mustard thinly over the meat, then divide the stuffing equally between the pieces. Roll up and secure with strong cotton or fine string. Toss in seasoned flour, reserving excess flour.

4 Heat the butter and oil in a shallow flameproof casserole into which all the beef olives will just fit. Add the olives and cook until well browned. Remove from the pan.

5 Stir the remaining seasoned flour into the pan residue and cook for 1–2 minutes or until lightly browned. Remove from the heat, gradually stir in the stock and bring to the boil. Season to taste, then return the meat to the pan.

6 Scatter the sliced onions over the meat. Cover and cook in a preheated oven at 170°C (325°F) mark 3 for 1½ hours.

MINCED BEEF KEBABS WITH HORSERADISH RELISH

SERVES 6

700 g (1½ lb) lean minced beef	salt and pepper
250 g (9 oz) grated onion	1 egg, beaten
135 ml (9 tbsp) horseradish sauce	plain flour, for coating
45 ml (3 tbsp) chopped thyme	150 ml (¼ pint) natural yogurt
250 g (9 oz) fresh white breadcrumbs	120 ml (8 tbsp) finely chopped parsley

1 Put the minced beef in a large bowl and mix in the onion, 90 ml (6 tbsp) of the horseradish, the thyme and breadcrumbs. Season to taste.
2 Add enough egg to bind the mixture together and, with floured hands, shape into 18 even-sized sausages. Cover and chill in the refrigerator until required.
3 Thread the kebabs lengthways on to six oiled skewers. Cook under a preheated grill for about 20 minutes, turning frequently.
4 Meanwhile, mix the yogurt with the remaining horseradish and the parsley. Serve the kebabs hot, with the sauce in a separate sauceboat.

VARIATION

For a more luxurious horseradish sauce, stir 30 ml (2 tbsp) grated fresh horseradish into a whipped mixture of 75 ml (3 fl oz) whipping cream and 150 ml (¼ pint) soured cream. Add 5 ml (1 tsp) vinegar, 2.5 ml (½ tsp) sugar and salt and pepper to taste.

BITKIS

SERVES 6

100 g (4 oz) medium oatmeal	60 ml (4 tbsp) vegetable oil
300 ml (½ pint) milk	25 g (1 oz) butter
2 medium onions, roughly chopped	25 g (1 oz) plain flour
900 g (2 lb) lean minced beef	450 ml (¾ pint) beef or chicken stock
salt and pepper	30 ml (2 tbsp) tomato purée
15 ml (3 tbsp) caraway seeds (optional)	300 ml (½ pint) soured cream
75 ml (5 tbsp) seasoned flour	parsley sprigs, to garnish

1 Soak the oatmeal in the milk overnight. Squeeze out excess milk and mix the oatmeal with the onions, minced beef and seasoning to taste.
2 Put this mixture twice through a mincer or mix in a food processor until smooth. Beat in 10 ml (2 tsp) of the caraway seeds, if using.
3 Shape in 18 round flat cakes, or bitkis. Coat with seasoned flour.
4 Heat the oil in a large frying pan, add the bitkis and cook until well browned. Place in a single layer in a large shallow ovenproof dish.
5 Melt the butter in a saucepan, add the plain flour and cook over low heat, stirring with a wooden spoon, for 2 minutes. Remove from the heat and gradually blend in the stock. Bring to the boil slowly, then simmer for 2–3 minutes, stirring. Stir in the tomato purée, soured cream and remaining caraway seeds, if using.
6 Pour the sauce over the bitkis and cook in a preheated oven at 180°C (350°F) mark 4 for about 1¼ hours or until the juices run clear. Garnish with parsley.

ITALIAN-STYLE MEATBALLS

SERVES 4

30 ml (2 tbsp) olive oil	50 g (2 oz) fresh white breadcrumbs
1 large onion, finely chopped	50 g (2 oz) Parmesan cheese, freshly grated
2 garlic cloves, crushed	1 egg, beaten
397 g (14 oz) can chopped tomatoes	20 small black olives, stoned
10 ml (2 tsp) dried mixed herbs	vegetable oil, for deep frying
10 ml (2 tsp) dried oregano	100 ml (4 fl oz) red or white dry Italian wine
salt and pepper	
450 g (1 lb) lean minced beef	

1 Heat the oil in a heavy-based saucepan, add the onion and half of the crushed garlic and fry gently for about 5 minutes or until soft and lightly coloured.

2 Add the tomatoes, half of the herbs and seasoning to taste. Bring to the boil, stirring, then lower the heat, cover and simmer for about 20 minutes

3 Meanwhile, make the meatballs. Put the minced beef in a bowl with the breadcrumbs, Parmesan, remaining garlic and herbs. Mix well, then season and bind with egg.

4 Pick up a small amount of the mixture, about the size of a walnut. Press one olive in the centre, then shape the mixture around it. Repeat to make 20 meatballs.

5 Heat the oil in a deep-fat fryer to 190°C (375°F). Deep-fry the meatballs in batches for 2–3 minutes or until lightly browned, then drain thoroughly on kitchen paper.

6 Stir the wine into the tomato sauce, than add 300 ml (½ pint) water and the meatballs. Shake the pan to coat the balls in the sauce, adding more water if necessary. Cover and simmer for 15 minutes, then season and serve.

CHINESE BEEF AND VEGETABLE STIR-FRY

SERVES 4

350 g (12 oz) fillet or rump steak, sliced into very thin strips	1 onion, thinly sliced
30 ml (2 tbsp) cornflour	1 garlic clove, crushed
60 ml (4 tbsp) soy sauce	2.5 cm (1 inch) piece of fresh root ginger, crushed
90 ml (6 tbsp) dry sherry	2 celery sticks, thinly sliced
30 ml (2 tbsp) dark soft brown sugar	1 red pepper, sliced into thin strips
30 ml (2 tbsp) wine vinegar	225 g (8 oz) mange-touts, halved
salt and pepper	
75 ml (5 tbsp) sesame or vegetable oil	

1 Put the steak in a bowl. Mix together the next five ingredients and season to taste. Pour over the steak, stir well to mix, then cover and leave to marinate for 1 hour.

2 Heat 30 ml (2 tbsp) of the oil in a wok or large frying pan. Add the onion, garlic and ginger and fry gently, stirring, for 5 minutes or until soft.

3 Heat another 15 ml (1 tbsp) of the oil in the pan. Add the celery and red pepper and fry, stirring, for a further 5 minutes or until tender but still crisp. Remove the vegetables from the pan with a slotted spoon.

4 Drain the steak from the marinade. Heat the remaining oil in the pan, add the steak and stir-fry over high heat for 5 minutes. Remove with a slotted spoon and set aside.

5 Add the mange-touts to the wok and stir-fry over high heat for 2–3 minutes. Return the steak and vegetables to the wok, then pour in the marinade and stir until bubbling and well mixed. Taste and season. Serve immediately.

BOILED BEEF AND CARROTS

SERVES 6

1.6 kg (3½ lb) lean salted silverside or brisket of beef	8 cloves
bouquet garni	2 small turnips, quartered
6 black peppercorns, lightly crushed	2 celery sticks, chopped
2 small onions, quartered	1 leek, chopped
	18 small carrots

1 If necessary, soak the meat in cold water for several hours or overnight, then rinse. Tie up into a neat joint.
2 Place the beef in a large saucepan, add just enough water to cover and bring slowly to the boil. Skim the surface, then add the bouquet garni, peppercorns, onions (each quarter stuck with a clove), turnips, celery and leek. Lower the heat and simmer very gently for about 2 hours.
3 Add the small carrots and simmer gently for a further 30–40 minutes or until the carrots are tender.
4 Carefully transfer the beef and small carrots to a warmed serving plate and keep warm.
5 Skim the fat from the surface of the cooling liquor, then strain. Boil the liquid to reduce slightly, then pour into a warmed sauceboat or jug.
6 Serve the beef surrounded by the carrots, with the sauce served separately.

SPICED BEEF

SERVES 6

1.8 kg (4 lb) salted rolled silverside	100 g (4 oz) dark soft brown sugar
1 medium onion, sliced	2.5 ml (½ tsp) mustard powder
4 medium carrots, sliced	5 ml (1 tsp) ground cinnamon
1 small turnip, sliced	juice of 1 lemon
8 cloves	

1 If necessary, soak the meat in cold water for several hours or overnight, then rinse. Tie up the meat to form a neat joint and put in a large saucepan or flameproof casserole with the vegetables.
2 Cover with water and bring slowly to the boil. Skim the surface, cover and simmer for 3–4 hours or until tender. Leave to cool completely in the liquid for 3–4 hours.
3 Drain the meat well, then put into a roasting tin and stick the cloves into the fat. Mix together the remaining ingredients and spread over the meat.
4 Bake in a preheated oven at 180°C (350°F) mark 4 for 45 minutes to 1 hour or until tender, basting from time to time. Serve hot or cold.

--- COOK'S TIP ---

If the meat has not had a prolonged salting it may not need soaking, so check with your butcher when buying. The long cooking ensures that the beef is meltingly tender.

BEEF IN WINE WITH WALNUTS

SERVES 6

900 g (2 lb) shin of beef, cut into 2.5 cm (1 inch) cubes	1 garlic clove, crushed
150 ml (¼ pint) dry red wine	5 ml (1 tsp) ground allspice
3 medium parsnips	30 ml (2 tbsp) plain flour
15 ml (1 tbsp) vegetable oil	150 ml (¼ pint) beef stock
15 g (½ oz) butter	50 g (2 oz) walnut pieces, ground
1 small onion, finely chopped	salt and pepper
	chopped walnuts, to garnish

1 Put the beef in a bowl with the wine and mix well. Cover and leave to marinate overnight, stirring occasionally.
2 Cut the parsnips into 5 cm (2 inch) lengths, about 1 cm (½ inch) wide. Drain the meat from the marinade, reserving the marinade. Heat the oil and butter in a large frying pan, add the beef, a few pieces at a time, and cook over a high heat until browned. Transfer to an ovenproof casserole with a slotted spoon.
3 Add the onion and garlic to the frying pan and fry for 5–10 minutes or until beginning to brown. Stir in the allspice, flour, reserved marinade, stock and ground walnuts. Bring to the boil, stirring constantly.
4 Pour into the casserole and add the parsnips. Season lightly to taste. Cover and cook in a preheated oven at 170°C (325°F) mark 3 for 2½–3 hours or until the meat is really tender.
5 Serve hot, straight from the casserole, sprinkled with the chopped walnuts.

BEEF AND CHESTNUT CASSEROLE

SERVES 4

45 ml (3 tbsp) vegetable oil	30 ml (2 tbsp) mushroom ketchup
1.1 kg (2½ lb) chuck steak, cubed	5 ml (1 tsp) dried mixed herbs
1 medium onion, sliced	salt and pepper
1 garlic clove, crushed	439 g (15½ oz) can whole chestnuts in salted water, drained
30 ml (2 tbsp) plain wholemeal flour	
300 ml (½ pint) dry cider	30 ml (2 tbsp) chopped fresh parsley, to garnish
300 ml (½ pint) beef stock	

1 Heat the oil in a large flameproof casserole, add the beef in batches and fry over brisk heat until browned on all sides. Remove with a slotted spoon and set aside.
2 Add the onion and garlic to the casserole, lower the heat and fry gently for 5 minutes or until soft but not coloured.
3 Return the meat to the casserole and stir in the flour. Cook, stirring, for 1–2 minutes, then stir in the cider, stock and mushroom ketchup. Bring slowly to the boil, then add the herbs and season to taste.
4 Cover the casserole and cook in a preheated oven at 170°C (325°F) mark 3 for 2 hours or until the beef is tender.
5 Ten minutes before the end of the cooking time, remove the casserole from the oven and add the chestnuts. Return to the oven to complete cooking. Taste and adjust the seasoning and sprinkle with the parsley before serving.

BEEF STEW WITH DUMPLINGS

SERVES 4

700 g (1½ lb) stewing steak, cut into cubes	3 medium tomatoes, quartered
15 ml (1 tbsp) plain flour	5 ml (1 tsp) dried mixed herbs
50 g (2 oz) dripping or lard	15 ml (1 tbsp) tomato purée (optional)
3 medium onions, diced	FOR THE DUMPLINGS
450 g (1 lb) carrots, diced	225 g (8 oz) self-raising flour
450–550 g (1–1¼ lb) potatoes, peeled and diced	pinch of salt
4 celery sticks, diced	75 g (3 oz) margarine
600 ml (1 pint) beef stock	
salt and pepper	

1 Put the meat in a plastic bag with the flour and shake until coated. Heat the dripping or lard in a large saucepan, add the meat and cook until browned. Remove the meat from the pan with a slotted spoon.

2 Add the onions, carrots, potatoes and celery to the pan and fry for about 5 minutes or until lightly browned.

3 Remove the pan from the heat and add the stock, seasoning, tomatoes, herbs and tomato purée (if using). Return the meat to the pan, bring to the boil, cover, reduce the heat and simmer gently for 2 hours.

4 To make the dumplings, put the flour and salt in a bowl, add the margarine and rub in until the mixture resembles fine breadcrumbs. Gradually mix in 75–90 ml (5–6 tbsp) water until the mixture forms a light, elastic dough. Turn on to a floured surface and knead lightly. Cut the dough into eight pieces and roll each into a ball.

5 Arrange the dumplings on top of the stew, re-cover and continue cooking for a further 20–25 minutes.

BEEF IN CIDER

SERVES 4–5

15 ml (1 tbsp) vegetable oil	25 g (1 oz) plain flour
450 g (1 lb) braising steak, cut into cubes	300 ml (½ pint) cider
225 g (8 oz) chipolata sausages, halved	5 cloves
1 medium onion, chopped	3 beef stock cubes
2 celery sticks, chopped	salt and pepper
1 Granny Smith apple, cored and sliced	10 ml (2 tsp) chopped parsley, to garnish

1 Heat the oil in a large frying pan, add the meat, sausages and onion and fry for about 10 minutes or until lightly browned.

2 Add the celery and apple and sprinkle in the flour. Stir well, then add the cider and cloves. Crumble in the stock cubes and stir well again.

3 Transfer to an ovenproof casserole, cover and cook in a preheated oven at 180°C (350°F) mark 4 for 2–2½ hours or until the meat is tender. Season to taste and garnish with parsley before serving.

BEEF IN STOUT

SERVES 4–6

15 g (½ oz) butter	salt and pepper
about 15 ml (1 tbsp) vegetable oil	30 ml (2 tbsp) plain flour
900 g (2 lb) stewing steak, cut into 5 cm (2 inch) cubes	300 ml (½ pint) stout
4 medium onions, sliced	1 bay leaf
225 g (8 oz) button mushrooms, halved	5 ml (1 tsp) soft dark brown sugar

1 Heat the butter and oil in a large flameproof casserole and cook the meat for 10 minutes or until browned all over. Remove the meat from the pan with a slotted spoon.
2 Add the onions and mushrooms to the pan, adding more oil if necessary, and fry for about 5 minutes or until softened. Season to taste, add the flour and stir well so that the flour absorbs the fat.
3 Return the meat to the pan, pour in the stout and add the bay leaf and brown sugar. Stir well to mix.
4 Cover and cook gently, either on the hob or in a preheated oven at 180°C (350°F) mark 4 for about 2½ hours or until the meat is tender.

─────── **COOK'S TIP** ───────

Stout gets its dark colour and bitterness from the roasted malt or barley used in its brewing. It makes a delicious gravy when used in a casserole and is packed with goodness.

MEXICAN BEEF TORTILLAS

SERVES 4

30 ml (2 tbsp) vegetable oil	salt and pepper
2 onions, finely chopped	350 g (12 oz) ripe tomatoes, skinned and roughly chopped
2 garlic cloves, crushed	
2.5–5 ml (½–1 tsp) chilli powder	2 fresh green chillies, seeded and finely chopped
450 g (1 lb) lean minced beef	5 ml (1 tsp) granulated sugar
30 ml (2 tbsp) tomato purée	12 hot tortillas (see below)

1 Heat the oil in a heavy-based saucepan, add half the onions and garlic and fry gently for 5 minutes or until soft and lightly coloured. Add the chilli powder and fry for a further 1–2 minutes, stirring constantly.
2 Add the beef and fry until browned. Add the tomato purée and stir to mix, then add salt and pepper to taste. Fry for a further 10–15 minutes, stirring occasionally.
3 Meanwhile, put the tomatoes in a blender or food processor with the remaining onions and garlic, the chillies, sugar and salt and pepper to taste. Work until quite smooth, then transfer to a sauceboat or jug.
4 Put a spoonful of the beef mixture on a hot tortilla and roll up. Repeat until all the beef and tortillas are used. Serve immediately, with the cold tomato sauce.

─────── **COOK'S TIP** ───────

To make 12 tortillas, mix 250 g (9 oz) plain flour with 5 ml (1 tsp) salt and rub in 40 g (1½ oz) lard. Gradually add 225 ml (8 fl oz) tepid water and mix to a dough. Knead lightly and shape into 12 pieces. Roll out thinly between sheets of waxed paper. Cook the tortillas for about 30 seconds on each side in an ungreased frying pan until speckled with brown. Stack in foil to keep hot.

BOEUF STROGANOFF
SERVES 4

700 g (1½ lb) rump steak, thinly sliced	225 g (8 oz) mushrooms, sliced
45 ml (3 tbsp) plain flour	150 ml (¼ pint) soured cream
salt and pepper	
50 g (2 oz) butter	10 ml (2 tsp) tomato purée (optional)
1 onion, thinly sliced	

1 Put the steak slices between two sheets of greaseproof paper and beat out with a meat mallet or rolling pin.
2 Trim the fat off the steak and discard. Cut the meat across the grain into thin strips. Coat the strips of steak in flour seasoned with salt and pepper.
3 Melt half the butter in a sauté pan, add the meat and fry for 5–7 minutes or until golden brown, tossing constantly.
4 Add the remaining butter, the onion and mushrooms and fry, stirring, for 3–4 minutes. Stir in the soured cream and tomato purée (if liked), and season well, using plenty of pepper. Heat through gently, without boiling. Transfer to a warmed serving dish and serve immediately.

HUNGARIAN GOULASH
SERVES 6

45 ml (3 tbsp) beef dripping or vegetable oil	397 g (14 oz) can tomatoes
3 medium onions, chopped	salt and pepper
2 garlic cloves, crushed	1 green or red pepper, chopped
1.1 kg (2½ lb) chuck steak or shin of beef, cut into 4 cm (1½ inch) pieces	550 g (1¼ lb) potatoes, peeled and cut into 2.5 cm (1 inch) chunks
15 ml (1 tbsp) paprika	2 green chillies (optional)
1.25 ml (¼ tsp) caraway seeds	

1 Melt the dripping or heat the oil in a flameproof casserole, add the onions and garlic and cook over moderate heat for 10 minutes or until the onions are soft and golden brown, stirring occasionally.
2 Add the meat and cook over high heat, stirring constantly, until browned slightly. Add the paprika, caraway seeds, tomatoes with their juice, 300 ml (½ pint) water and salt and pepper to taste. Stir well to break up the tomatoes.
3 Bring to the boil, cover and cook in a preheated oven at 170°C (325°F) mark 3 for 1½ hours.
4 Remove the casserole from the oven and stir in the chopped pepper and potatoes, adding the whole chillies if liked. Cover and return to the oven for a further 45 minutes or until the potatoes are tender. The goulash should be of a fairly thin consistency.
5 Remove the chillies, and taste and adjust the seasoning before serving.

BEEF AND SPINACH CURRY

SERVES 4–6

10 black peppercorns	6 garlic cloves, crushed
4 cloves	2.5 cm (1 inch) piece of fresh root ginger, finely chopped
2 bay leaves	
seeds of 6 cardamoms	900 g (2 lb) lean stewing beef, cut into 2.5 cm (1 inch) cubes
10 ml (2 tsp) cumin seeds	
15 ml (1 tbsp) coriander seeds	150 ml (¼ pint) natural yogurt
2.5 ml (½ tsp) chilli powder	900 g (2 lb) fresh spinach, stalks removed, or two 300 g (10.6 oz) packs frozen spinach, thawed and drained
5 ml (1 tsp) salt	
90 ml (6 tbsp) ghee or vegetable oil	
1 large onion, finely chopped	

1 Finely grind the dry spices and salt in a small electric mill or with a pestle and mortar.
2 Heat the ghee or oil in a large heavy-based saucepan or flameproof casserole, add the onion, garlic, ginger and ground spices and cook over a moderate heat for about 5 minutes or until softened and just turning brown.
3 Increase the heat and add the meat. Cook, stirring all the time, until the meat is well browned on all sides. Add the yogurt to the pan, 15 ml (1 tbsp) at a time. Cook each addition over a high heat, stirring constantly, until the yogurt is absorbed.
4 Cover the pan tightly with a lid and turn down the heat to very low. Simmer for 1½ hours or until the meat is tender, stirring occasionally.
5 Add the spinach, mix well and cook over a moderate heat for a further 5–10 minutes, stirring all the time until the liquid has evaporated. Adjust the seasoning and serve.

SPICED MINCE WITH PEAS

SERVES 4–6

30 ml (2 tbsp) ghee or vegetable oil	900 g (2 lb) lean minced beef
1 medium onion, finely chopped	226 g (8 oz) can tomatoes, chopped
2.5 cm (1 inch) piece of fresh root ginger, grated	5 ml (1 tsp) caster sugar
8 garlic cloves, crushed	10 ml (2 tsp) salt
10 ml (2 tsp) ground cumin	350 g (12 oz) frozen peas
15 ml (1 tbsp) ground coriander	45 ml (3 tbsp) chopped coriander, parsley or mint
5 ml (1 tsp) chilli powder	30 ml (2 tbsp) lemon or lime juice
2.5 ml (½ tsp) ground turmeric	5 ml (1 tsp) garam masala

1 Heat the ghee or oil in a heavy-based saucepan or flameproof casserole, add the onion and cook over a high heat for about 5 minutes or until just turning brown. Lower the heat, add the ginger, garlic and spices and cook gently for 2–3 minutes.
2 Add the minced meat, chopped tomatoes with their juice, sugar and salt. Stir well until mixed and bring to the boil. Cover and simmer for 45 minutes.
3 Stir in the peas, herbs and lemon or lime juice. Cover and simmer for 15 minutes, stirring occasionally.
4 To serve, sprinkle with garam masala. Serve hot.

STEAMED BEEF AND TOMATO PUDDING

SERVES 4–6

FOR THE FILLING	
45 ml (3 tbsp) olive oil	2.5 ml (½ tsp) dried oregano
2.5 ml (½ tsp) cumin seeds	15 ml (1 tbsp) paprika
100 g (4 oz) onion, chopped	2.5 ml (½ tsp) black pepper
100 g (4 oz) mixed red, green and yellow peppers, diced	1 beef stock cube
1 garlic clove, crushed	50 g (2 oz) mushrooms, chopped
2.5 ml (½ tsp) salt	FOR THE PASTRY
1 bay leaf	225 g (8 oz) self-raising flour
450 g (1 lb) lean minced beef	50 g (2 oz) shredded beef suet
397 g (14 oz) can tomatoes	50 g (2 oz) potato, grated
30 ml (2 tbsp) tomato purée	2.5 ml (½ tsp) salt
	2.5 ml (½ tsp) baking powder

1 Heat the oil in a pan, add the cumin and fry for 30 seconds. Add the onion and peppers and fry for 5–6 minutes. Add the garlic, salt and bay leaf. Add the beef, stir well and fry for 5 minutes. Drain the tomatoes, reserving the juice, and chop, discarding the seeds.

2 Add the tomatoes, tomato purée, oregano, paprika, pepper, stock cube and tomato juice and cook for 10 minutes. Add the mushrooms, season and cook for 5 minutes.

3 To make the pastry, mix the ingredients and gradually add about 150 ml (¼ pint) water to bind. Roll out to a 35.5 cm (14 inch) round and cut out one quarter for the lid. Use to line a greased 1.4 litre (2½ pint) pudding basin. Spoon in the meat and cover with the pastry lid. Cover with greaseproof paper and foil and steam for 1½ hours.

CURRIED MINCE AND APPLE BAKE

SERVES 4

50 g (2 oz) slice of bread, crusts removed	700 g (1½ lb) lean minced beef
300 ml (½ pint) milk	30 ml (2 tbsp) raisins
40 g (1½ oz) butter or margarine	25 g (1 oz) flaked almonds
2 medium onions, finely chopped	15 ml (1 tbsp) lemon juice
1 cooking apple, cored and chopped	salt and pepper
15 ml (1 tbsp) mild curry powder	2 bay leaves
	3 eggs

1 Put the bread in a bowl, pour in the milk and leave to soak. Meanwhile, melt the butter in a saucepan, add the onions and fry for 5 minutes or until beginning to soften. Add the apple and curry powder and fry, stirring, for a further 2–3 minutes.

2 Turn the onion mixture into a bowl and add the meat, raisins, almonds, lemon juice and salt and pepper to taste. Mix until well combined.

3 Squeeze the milk from the bread, reserving the milk, and stir the bread into the meat mixture.

4 Place the bay leaves on the bottom of a 1.1 litre (2 pint) pie dish. Fill with the meat mixture, then cover with foil. Bake in a preheated oven at 180°C (350°F) mark 4 for 35 minutes, then remove the foil and break up the meat mixture with a fork.

5 Whisk the eggs together with the reserved milk and pour over the meat, stirring gently to distribute the custard mixture evenly.

6 Return the dish to the oven and cook for a further 35 minutes or until the custard has set and the top browned.

BEEF 'MOUSSAKA'

SERVES 4–6

450 g (1 lb) aubergines, sliced	397 g (14 oz) can tomatoes
salt and pepper	300 ml (10 fl oz) natural yogurt
90 ml (6 tbsp) vegetable oil	2 eggs, size 3, beaten
2 large onions, sliced	1.25 ml (¼ tsp) grated nutmeg
1 garlic clove, chopped	25 g (1 oz) grated Parmesan cheese
700 g (1½ lb) lean minced beef	

1 Layer the aubergine slices in a colander, sprinkling each layer with salt. Cover and leave for about 30 minutes.

2 Meanwhile, heat 30 ml (2 tbsp) oil in a frying pan and fry the onions and garlic for 5 minutes. Add the minced meat and fry for 10 minutes. Add the tomatoes with their juice, season to taste and simmer for 20 minutes.

3 Drain the aubergine slices, rinse and dry well on absorbent kitchen paper. Heat the remaining oil in a separate large frying pan and cook the aubergine slices for 4–5 minutes or until lightly browned, turning once. Add more oil, if necessary.

4 Arrange a layer of aubergine slices in the bottom of a large ovenproof dish and spoon over a layer of the meat mixture. Continue the layers until all the meat and aubergines are used, finishing with a layer of aubergines.

5 Beat the yogurt, eggs and nutmeg together, season to taste and stir in half the Parmesan. Pour over the dish and sprinkle with the remaining cheese. Cook in a preheated oven at 180°C (350°F) mark 4 for 45–60 minutes.

BEEF AND RED BEAN GRATIN

SERVES 4

100 g (4 oz) dried red kidney beans, soaked overnight	225 g (8 oz) tomatoes, skinned and chopped
75 g (3 oz) butter or margarine	15 ml (1 tbsp) tomato purée
1 small onion, thinly sliced	5 ml (1 tsp) chopped fresh mixed herbs or 2.5 ml (½ tsp) dried
225 g (8 oz) lean minced beef	250 ml (9 fl oz) milk
65 g (2½ oz) plain flour	50 g (2 oz) Cheddar cheese, grated
200 ml (7 fl oz) beef stock	1.25 ml (¼ tsp) prepared English mustard
cayenne	
salt and pepper	

1 Drain the beans and put in a saucepan. Cover with water and boil rapidly for 10 minutes, then boil gently for 45 minutes or until tender. Drain.

2 Melt 25 g (1 oz) butter in a saucepan, add the onion and beef and brown over a high heat, stirring. Stir in 40 g (1½ oz) flour, the stock, cayenne, salt and pepper. Cook until very thick. Transfer to an ovenproof dish.

3 Melt another 25 g (1 oz) butter in the pan, add the tomatoes and cook for 10 minutes or until soft. Stir in the beans, tomato purée and herbs and simmer until reduced. Spread over the meat.

4 Melt the remaining butter in a clean pan and add the remaining flour. Cook, stirring, for 2 minutes. Remove from the heat and stir in the milk. Bring to the boil and cook, stirring, until thick.

5 Stir in half the cheese and the mustard and season. Pour the sauce over the bean layer and sprinkle the remaining cheese on top. Bake in a preheated oven at 200°C (400°F) mark 6 for 25 minutes or until golden brown. Serve hot.

MEAT AND POTATO PIE

SERVES 4

STEAK AND KIDNEY PIE

SERVES 4

FOR THE FILLING	
vegetable oil, for frying	300 ml (½ pint) beef stock
225 g (8 oz) baby onions	150 ml (¼ pint) red wine
1 garlic clove, crushed	salt and pepper
100 g (4 oz) button mushrooms	5 ml (1 tsp) cornflour
450 g (1 lb) stewing steak, cubed	FOR THE PASTRY
	50 g (2 oz) shredded beef suet
4 large potatoes, peeled and cut into small cubes	100 g (4 oz) self-raising flour
175 g (6 oz) carrots, sliced	pinch of salt
5 ml (1 tsp) dried mixed herbs	milk, to glaze

1 Heat a little oil in a medium saucepan, add the onions, garlic and mushrooms and fry for 3 minutes. Drain and place in a 1.1 litre (2 pint) ovenproof casserole.

2 Add the meat to the pan, a few pieces at a time, and fry until browned, then add to the casserole.

3 Add the potatoes, carrots and herbs to the casserole and pour in the stock and wine. Season well, stir and cook in a preheated oven at 170°C (325°F) mark 3 for 2 hours.

4 Fifteen minutes before the end of the cooking time, blend the cornflour to a paste with a little cold water. Stir into the casserole and continue cooking.

5 Meanwhile, to make the pastry, mix the suet, flour and salt in a bowl and gradually stir in enough water to bind. Roll out the pastry until large enough to cover the casserole and press the edges firmly on to the rim. Brush with a little milk to glaze. Return to the oven and cook at 200°C (400°F) mark 6 for about 30 minutes or until brown.

salt and pepper	150 ml (¼ pint) beef stock
200 g (7 oz) plain flour	150 ml (¼ pint) brown ale
700 g (1½ lb) braising steak, cubed	1 bay leaf
175 g (6 oz) ox kidney, cored and chopped	2.5 ml (½ tsp) dried thyme
	15 ml (1 tbsp) Worcestershire sauce
100 g (4 oz) butter	15 ml (1 tbsp) tomato purée
1–2 garlic cloves, crushed	
1 large onion, chopped	milk, to glaze
100 g (4 oz) button mushrooms	

1 Season 25 g (1 oz) of the flour, then toss the steak and kidney in the flour, shaking off and reserving any excess.

2 Melt 25 g (1 oz) of the butter in a large saucepan and lightly fry the garlic, onion and mushrooms for 3 minutes. Add the steak, kidney and reserved seasoned flour and cook for 5 minutes or until lightly browned.

3 Gradually stir in the stock, ale, bay leaf, thyme, Worcestershire sauce and tomato purée. Cover and simmer for 1¼ hours. Spoon into a 1.7 litre (3 pint) pie dish.

4 Put the remaining flour and a pinch of salt in a bowl. Rub in the remaining butter. Gradually add about 60 ml (4 tbsp) cold water and mix to form a dough.

5 Roll out the dough to 5 cm (2 inches) wider than the pie dish. Cut a 2.5 cm (1 inch) wide strip from the outer edge. Brush the rim of the dish with water and press the pastry strip in place around it. Brush with water and cover with the pastry lid. Garnish with pastry leaves, brush with milk and bake in a preheated oven at 200°C (400°F) mark 6 for 30–45 minutes or until golden brown.

MEAT LOAF WITH ONION SAUCE

SERVES 4

25 g (1 oz) butter	60 ml (4 tbsp) tomato purée
2 medium onions, finely chopped	15 ml (1 tbsp) chopped fresh mixed herbs or 5 ml (1 tsp) dried
5 ml (1 tsp) paprika	salt and pepper
450 g (1 lb) lean minced beef	1 egg, beaten
75 g (3 oz) fresh breadcrumbs	15 g (½ oz) plain wholemeal flour
1 garlic clove, crushed	300 ml (½ pint) milk

1 Grease a 900 ml (1½ pint) loaf tin, then line the base with greased greaseproof paper. Melt half the butter in a frying pan. Add half the onions and cook for 5 minutes or until soft. Add the paprika and cook for 1 minute, stirring. Remove from the heat.

2 Add the beef, breadcrumbs, garlic, tomato purée and herbs to the onions and season to taste. Stir thoroughly until evenly mixed, then bind with the beaten egg.

3 Spoon the mixture into the loaf tin, level the surface and cover tightly with foil. Stand the tin in a roasting tin and pour in water to a depth of 2.5 cm (1 inch). Bake in a preheated oven at 180°C (350°F) mark 4 for 1½ hours.

4 Meanwhile, melt the remaining butter in a saucepan. Add the rest of the onion and cook for 10 minutes or until soft but not coloured, stirring occasionally. Add the flour and cook for 1–2 minutes, stirring. Remove from the heat and add the milk, stirring constantly. Simmer for 2–3 minutes or until thick, stirring constantly. Simmer very gently for a further 2–3 minutes. Season to taste.

5 To serve the meat loaf, turn out on to a warmed plate and peel off the paper. Serve with the hot onion sauce.

BEEF WELLINGTON

SERVES 8

1.4 kg (3 lb) fillet of beef	175 g (6 oz) smooth liver pâté
pepper	368 g (13 oz) packet frozen puff pastry, thawed
15 ml (1 tbsp) vegetable oil	1 egg, beaten, to glaze
40 g (1½ oz) butter	
225 g (8 oz) button mushrooms, sliced	

1 Trim and tie up the fillet at intervals so it retains its shape. Season to taste with pepper. Heat the oil and 15 g (½ oz) of the butter in a large frying pan, add the meat and fry briskly on all sides. Press down with a wooden spoon while frying to seal well. Transfer to a roasting tin.

2 Roast the beef in a preheated oven at 220°C (425°F) mark 7 for 20 minutes, then set the beef aside to allow it to cool. Remove the string.

3 Meanwhile, melt the remaining butter in the frying pan and fry the mushrooms for about 5 minutes or until soft. Leave until cold, then blend with the pâté.

4 On a lightly floured surface, roll out the pastry to a large rectangle measuring about 33 x 28 cm (13 x 11 inches) and 0.5 cm (¼ inch) thick.

5 Spread the pâté mixture down the centre of the pastry. Place the meat on top. Brush the pastry edges with egg. Fold the pastry edges over lengthways. Place on a baking sheet with the pastry join underneath and fold the ends under the meat.

6 Decorate with leaves cut from the pastry trimmings, brush with the remaining egg and bake in a preheated oven at 220°C (425°F) mark 7 for 50–60 minutes, depending on how well done you like your beef, covering with foil after 25 minutes. Allow to rest for 10 minutes before serving.

VEAL ESCALOPES IN MUSHROOM SAUCE

SERVES 4

four 175 g (6 oz) veal escalopes	1 small onion, chopped
2 slices of cooked ham, halved	100 g (4 oz) button mushrooms, sliced
50 g (2 oz) butter	25 g (1 oz) plain flour
1 celery stick, chopped	300 ml (½ pint) milk
1 eating apple, peeled, cored and chopped	salt and pepper
25 g (1 oz) Cheddar cheese, grated	30 ml (2 tbsp) fromage frais
	celery leaves, to garnish

1 Put each escalope between two sheets of dampened greaseproof paper and beat until thin with a meat mallet.
2 Place a ham slice on each escalope.
3 Melt 15 g (½ oz) of the butter in a large frying pan, add the celery and apple and fry lightly for 3–4 minutes. Stir in the cheese.
4 Place some of the stuffing on each escalope and roll up, securing with wooden cocktail sticks or fine string.
5 Melt the remaining butter in the pan. Add the veal rolls and cook over a high heat until browned on all sides, then reduce the heat and cook for 10 minutes. Remove from the pan, place on a warmed serving plate and keep hot.
6 Add the onion and mushrooms to the pan and cook for about 5 minutes or until softened. Stir in the flour and cook for 2 minutes, then gradually add the milk, stirring continuously, until the sauce thickens, boils and is smooth. Simmer for 1–2 minutes. Season to taste.
7 Stir the fromage frais into the sauce, pour over the escalopes and garnish with celery leaves. Serve at once.

ESCALOPES FINES HERBES

SERVES 4

four 100 g (4 oz) veal escalopes	30 ml (2 tbsp) chopped herbs (parsley, chervil, tarragon and chives)
salt and pepper	60 ml (4 tbsp) double cream
45 ml (3 tbsp) plain flour	
25 g (1 oz) butter or margarine	lemon wedges, to serve
100 ml (4 fl oz) dry white wine	

1 Place the veal escalopes between two sheets of dampened greaseproof paper and beat until thin with a rolling pin or meat mallet.
2 Season the flour with a little salt and pepper and use to coat the escalopes.
3 Melt the butter or margarine in a large frying pan, add the escalopes and fry over a high heat for 1–2 minutes on each side or until browned. (You may have to fry in two batches, depending on the size of the pan.) Lower the heat and continue to cook for a further 4 minutes on each side or until tender. Transfer the veal to a warmed serving dish, cover and keep hot.
4 Add the white wine to the pan and bring slowly to the boil, stirring to scrape up any sediment left in the pan. Stir in the herbs and cream and season to taste. Simmer very gently for about 5 minutes or until slightly thickened.
5 Pour the sauce over the escalopes and serve immediately, with lemon wedges.

VEAL COBBLER

SERVES 4–6

SAUTÉED VEAL WITH COURGETTES AND GRAPEFRUIT

SERVES 4

---

25 g (1 oz) butter	225 g (8 oz) button mushrooms, sliced
1 large onion, finely chopped	30 ml (2 tbsp) soured cream
1 garlic clove, crushed	chopped parsley, to garnish
900 g (2 lb) lean pie veal, cut into 2.5 cm (1 inch) cubes	FOR THE TOPPING
	225 g (8 oz) self raising flour
30 ml (2 tbsp) paprika	pinch of salt
salt and pepper	50 g (2 oz) butter
1 red pepper, cut into rings	150 ml (¼ pint) milk
1 green pepper, cut into rings	milk, to glaze
397 g (14 oz) can chopped tomatoes	

1 Melt the butter in a flameproof casserole, add the onion and garlic and sauté for 5 minutes. Add the pie veal and cook for a further 5–7 minutes or until evenly browned.

2 Stir in the paprika, season and cook for a further 2 minutes. Add the pepper rings, tomatoes and mushrooms. Stir well and cook for 5 minutes. Cover and cook in a preheated oven at 190°C (375°F) mark 5 for 1½–2 hours.

3 Meanwhile, make the scone topping. Sift the flour and salt into a bowl, add the butter and rub in until the mixture resembles fine breadcrumbs. Gradually mix in the milk to form a smooth, soft dough. Roll out to 1 cm (½ inch) thick and cut into rounds using a 5 cm (2 inch) cutter.

4 Remove the casserole from the oven and carefully position the scones around the edge of the dish. Brush with milk to glaze, then cook, uncovered, for a final 30–35 minutes. Pour the soured cream over the casserole, avoiding the scones, and sprinkle with parsley.

---

450 g (1 lb) veal rump or fillet, in one piece	450 g (1 lb) courgettes, thinly sliced
2 grapefruit	a few saffron strands
45 ml (3 tbsp) olive oil	salt and pepper

1 Cut the veal into wafer-thin slices. Place between two sheets of dampened greaseproof paper and beat out with a rolling pin or meat mallet.

2 With a potato peeler, pare the rind off one of the grapefruit. Cut into thin julienne strips. Squeeze the juice from the grapefruit and reserve.

3 With a serrated knife, peel the remaining grapefruit as you would an apple, removing all skin and pith. Slice the grapefruit flesh thinly and set aside.

4 Heat 30 ml (2 tbsp) of the oil in a large frying pan. Add a few slices of veal and sauté for about 2–3 minutes or until well browned on both sides. Transfer to a warmed serving dish, cover and keep warm while sautéeing the remainder.

5 Heat the remaining oil in the pan, add the courgettes and sauté for 2–3 minutes or until beginning to brown. Add the julienne strips of grapefruit rind, the saffron strands and 90 ml (6 tbsp) of the reserved grapefruit juice.

6 Bring to the boil, then lower the heat and simmer for 4–5 minutes or until the liquid is well reduced. Stir in the thinly sliced grapefruit and heat through.

7 Season to taste, pour over the veal and serve.

FRICASSÉE OF VEAL

SERVES 6

900 g (2 lb) stewing veal	salt and pepper
450 g (1 lb) carrots	50 g (2 oz) butter
1 medium onion, sliced	50 g (2 oz) plain flour
15 ml (1 tbsp) chopped fresh thyme or 2.5 ml (½ tsp) dried	2 egg yolks
	150 ml (5 fl oz) single cream
150 ml (¼ pint) dry white wine	chopped parsley, to garnish

1 Cut the veal into 4 cm (1½ inch) cubes, discarding any skin or fat. Put the meat in a saucepan, cover with cold water, bring to the boil and cook for 1 minute. Strain the meat and rinse under cold running water to remove all scum. Rinse out the pan thoroughly and replace the meat.

2 Cut the carrots into finger-sized pieces and add to the pan with the onion, thyme, wine and 900 ml (1½ pints) water. Season to taste. Bring slowly to the boil, cover and simmer gently for about 1¼ hours or until the veal is quite tender.

3 Strain off the cooking liquid, make up to 750 ml (1¼ pints) with stock, if necessary, and reserve. Keep the veal and vegetables warm in a covered serving dish.

4 Melt the butter in a saucepan, stir in the flour and cook gently for 1 minute, stirring. Remove from the heat and gradually stir in the strained cooking liquid and season well. Bring to the boil, stirring all the time, then simmer for 5 minutes.

5 Mix the egg yolks with the cream. Remove the sauce from the heat and stir in the cream mixture. Return to the heat and warm gently, without boiling, until the sauce becomes slightly thicker. Adjust the seasoning and pour over the meat. Serve garnished with parsley.

SPICED VEAL WITH PEPPERS

SERVES 4

550 g (1¼ lb) pie veal	2.5 ml (½ tsp) ground cumin
15 ml (1 tbsp) vegetable oil	2.5 ml (½ tsp) chilli powder
2 medium onions, thinly sliced	1.25 ml (¼ tsp) ground cloves
2 small red peppers, thinly sliced	225 g (8 oz) tomatoes, skinned and roughly chopped
1 garlic clove, crushed	
2.5 ml (½ tsp) ground ginger	300 ml (½ pint) natural yogurt
2.5 ml (½ tsp) ground turmeric	salt and pepper

1 Trim the veal of fat and cut into chunky cubes.

2 Heat the oil in a large saucepan. Add the onions, peppers, garlic and spices and fry for 1 minute. Stir in the chopped tomatoes.

3 Turn the heat to very low and add the yogurt very gradually, stirring well between each addition.

4 Add the veal and season to taste. Cover and simmer gently for 30 minutes.

5 Uncover the pan and cook the veal for a further 30 minutes or until it is tender and the liquid has reduced. Stir occasionally to prevent the meat sticking to the pan. Taste and adjust the seasoning before serving.

VEAL IN MARSALA
SERVES 6

six 75 g (3 oz) veal escalopes	175 g (6 oz) button mushrooms, sliced
salt and pepper	90 ml (6 tbsp) Marsala
plain flour, for coating	90 ml (6 tbsp) chicken stock
60 ml (4 tbsp) vegetable oil	5 ml (1 tsp) arrowroot
50 g (2 oz) butter	lemon wedges, to serve
1 onion, finely chopped	

1 Trim each escalope to remove any skin. Place well apart between two sheets of dampened greaseproof paper and beat out until very thin, using a meat mallet or rolling pin.
2 Season the flour, add the veal and toss until coated. Heat the oil and butter in a large sauté or deep frying pan, add the veal and cook until well browned on all sides.
3 Push the veal to the side of the pan and add the onion and mushrooms to the remaining fat. Cook until browned. Add the Marsala and stock, bring to the boil and season lightly.
4 Cover the pan and cook gently for 5–10 minutes or until the veal is quite tender. Transfer to a warmed serving dish, cover and keep warm.
5 Mix the arrowroot to a smooth paste with a little water. Stir into the pan juices off the heat, then bring slowly to the boil, stirring all the time. Cook for 1 minute, adjust the seasoning and spoon over the veal. Serve with lemon.

VEAL COLLOPS
SERVES 4

four 100 g (4 oz) veal escalopes	10 ml (2 tsp) plain flour
65 g (2½ oz) butter	salt and pepper
1 small onion, chopped	pinch of ground mace
175 ml (6 fl oz) dry white wine	FOR THE GARNISH crisp bacon rolls
400 ml (14 fl oz) veal stock	button mushroom caps
5–10 ml (1–2 tsp) mushroom ketchup	lemon twists
about 15 ml (1 tbsp) lemon juice	parsley sprigs

1 Cut each escalope into two pieces and place between two sheets of dampened greaseproof paper. Beat until thin with a rolling pin or meat mallet.
2 Melt 50 g (2 oz) of the butter in a frying pan, add the veal and cook for about 2 minutes on each side. Transfer to a warmed plate and keep warm.
3 Add the onion to the butter remaining in the pan and cook for about 3 minutes or until softened but not browned, stirring frequently. Stir in the wine, bring to the boil and cook until almost evaporated. Stir in the stock, mushroom ketchup and lemon juice, return to the boil and simmer until reduced to 225 ml (8 fl oz).
4 Work the flour into the remaining butter, then gradually whisk into the stock to thicken it slightly. Season with salt, pepper and mace, taste and add more mushroom ketchup and lemon juice if necessary.
5 Arrange the collops, overlapping each other, on a warmed oval serving platter. Spoon some of the sauce down the centre of the collops, garnish and serve the remaining sauce separately.

VEAL AND KIDNEY PIE
SERVES 6

900 g (2 lb) stewing veal, cut into 2.5 cm (1 inch) cubes	40 g (1½ oz) plain flour
juice of 1 lemon	30 ml (2 tbsp) single cream
6.25 ml (1¼ tsp) dried tarragon	FOR THE PASTRY 100 g (4 oz) plain wholemeal flour
salt and pepper	225 g (8 oz) plain white flour
225 g (8 oz) lamb kidneys	225 g (8 oz) butter or margarine
350 g (12 oz) leeks	1 egg, beaten, to glaze
40 g (1½ oz) butter or margarine	

1 Place the veal in a saucepan with 900 ml (1½ pints) water, 15 ml (1 tbsp) lemon juice and 5 ml (1 tsp) tarragon. Season, cover and simmer for 1–1¼ hours.
2 Meanwhile, skin and core the kidneys and cut into bite-sized pieces. Trim and slice the leeks, rinse and drain.
3 Stir the kidneys and leeks into the saucepan. Cover and simmer for a further 8–10 minutes. Strain off the liquor and reserve. Spoon into a 26.5 cm (10½ inch) pie plate.
4 To make the sauce, melt the butter in a saucepan, stir in the flour and cook for 1–2 minutes. Remove from the heat and stir in 600 ml (1 pint) of the reserved stock. Cook, stirring, until thick. Remove from the heat and stir in 15 ml (1 tbsp) lemon juice, 1.25 ml (¼ tsp) tarragon and the cream. Season, pour over the veal and cool.
5 To make the pastry, mix the flours and rub in the butter. Gradually add about 75 ml (5 tbsp) water. Chill.
6 Roll out the pastry and use to cover the pie. Brush with beaten egg. Bake in a preheated oven at 190°C (375°F) mark 5 for about 40 minutes or until well browned.

VEAL AND HAM PIE
SERVES 8–10

450 g (1 lb) lean minced veal	2 medium onions, finely chopped
100 g (4 oz) boiled ham, minced	salt and pepper
30 ml (2 tbsp) chopped parsley	100 g (4 oz) lard
2.5 ml (½ tsp) ground mace	350 g (12 oz) plain wholemeal flour
1.25 ml (¼ tsp) ground bay leaves	1 egg yolk
finely grated rind of 1 lemon	3 eggs, hard-boiled and shelled
	10 ml (2 tsp) powdered aspic jelly

1 Grease a 1.4 litre (2½ pint) loaf tin and line the base with greased greaseproof paper.
2 Put the first seven ingredients in a bowl and add 5 ml (1 tsp) salt and 1.25 ml (¼ tsp) pepper. Mix well.
3 Put the lard and 200 ml (7 fl oz) water in a saucepan and heat gently to melt. Bring to the boil, remove from the heat and tip in the flour with 2.5 ml (½ tsp) salt. Beat well to form a soft dough. Beat the egg yolk into the dough. Cover with a damp tea towel and rest in a warm place for 20 minutes. Do not allow to cool.
4 Use two thirds of the pastry to line the prepared tin. Press in half the meat and place the eggs down the centre. Fill with the remaining meat.
5 Roll out the remaining pastry and use to cover the pie. Make a hole in the centre of the pie. Bake at 180°C (350°F) mark 4 for 1½ hours. Leave to cool for 3–4 hours.
6 Make up the aspic jelly with 300 ml (½ pint) water and leave to cool for about 10 minutes. Pour the aspic through the hole in the top of the pie. Chill the pie for about 1 hour. Leave at room temperature for 1 hour before turning out.

VEAL WITH TUNA FISH MAYONNAISE

SERVES 4–6

900 g (2 lb) boned, rolled and tied leg or loin of veal	2 cloves
300 ml (½ pint) dry white wine	200 g (7 oz) can tuna in oil, drained
1 carrot, sliced	4 canned anchovy fillets, soaked in milk for 20 minutes and drained
1 celery stick, sliced	
a few parsley sprigs	300 ml (½ pint) thick mayonnaise
2 bay leaves	
a few black peppercorns	15 ml (1 tbsp) capers, roughly chopped
salt and pepper	lemon slices, black olives and lamb's lettuce, to garnish
1 small onion	

1 Put the veal in a large saucepan and add the wine, carrot, celery, parsley, bay leaves, peppercorns and 5 ml (1 tsp) salt. Push the cloves into the onion and add to the pan. Add enough water to cover, then bring to the boil.

2 Lower the heat, cover the pan and simmer gently for 1–1¼ hours or until the veal is tender. Remove the pan from the heat and leave the veal to cool in the liquid.

3 When the meat is cold, remove from the pan, reserving the liquid, and dry with kitchen paper. Untie the meat, slice and arrange on a platter. Cover with cling film.

4 Pound the tuna and anchovies together, then stir into the mayonnaise with the capers and pepper to taste. Thin to a coating consistency with a few spoonfuls of the reserved cooking liquid, taste and adjust the seasoning.

5 Spoon the mayonnaise over the veal, then cover loosely with foil. Chill for 24–48 hours. To serve, leave the veal to stand at room temperature for 1 hour. Uncover and garnish.

PORTMANTEAU LAMB CHOPS

SERVES 4

4 thick lamb loin chops	salt and pepper
40 g (1½ oz) butter	1 egg, beaten
100 g (4 oz) chicken livers, thawed if frozen and finely chopped	50 g (2 oz) fresh wholemeal breadcrumbs
	parsley sprigs, to garnish
100 g (4 oz) mushrooms, finely chopped	

1 Using a sharp, pointed knife, make a horizontal cut in each chop, working from the outside fat edge to the bone, to form a pocket.

2 To make the stuffing, melt 15 g (½ oz) of the butter in a frying pan, add the chicken livers and mushrooms and fry for 4–5 minutes or until soft but not brown. Season to taste.

3 Leave the stuffing to cool slightly, then spoon into the cavity in the chops and secure the open edges with wooden cocktail sticks.

4 Dip the chops in the beaten egg, then in the breadcrumbs to coat thoroughly.

5 Put the chops in a roasting tin. Melt the remaining butter and pour over the chops. Bake in a preheated oven at 200°C (400°F) mark 6 for 15 minutes, then turn and bake for a further 15 minutes or until golden brown. Serve hot, garnish with parsley sprigs.

TANGY CHOPS

SERVES 4

30 ml (2 tbsp) vegetable oil	15 ml (1 tbsp) chopped fresh mint or 5 ml (1 tsp) dried
4 lamb chump chops	
salt and pepper	5 ml (1 tsp) sugar
juice and finely grated rind of 1 lemon	150 ml (¼ pint) beef or chicken stock
30 ml (2 tbsp) chopped fresh parsley or 10 ml (2 tsp) dried	

1 Heat the oil in a frying pan, add the chops and fry over a brisk heat until browned on both sides. Lower the heat and season to taste.
2 Mix the lemon juice and rind with the herbs and sugar, then spoon this mixture over the chops and pour in the stock. Cover the pan tightly and simmer gently for 30 minutes or until the meat is tender. Serve hot with the juices poured over.

VARIATION
You can vary the herbs used in this dish, depending on what is available. Fresh rosemary is, of course, the classic herb to use with lamb.

LAMB STEAKS WITH CAPER SAUCE

SERVES 4

salt and pepper	300 ml (½ pint) lamb or beef stock
four 175 g (6 oz) lamb leg steaks	
25 g (1 oz) butter	30 ml (2 tbsp) drained capers
5 ml (1 tsp) plain flour	15 ml (1 tbsp) vinegar from the capers

1 Season the lamb steaks to taste. Heat the butter in a frying pan and fry the steaks gently for 10–15 minutes or until browned on both sides, turning occasionally. Remove from the pan with a slotted spoon.
2 Stir to loosen any sediment at the bottom of the pan, then stir in the flour and cook for 1–2 minutes. Gradually add the stock, stirring all the time, then cook until the sauce thickens, boils and is smooth. Add the capers and vinegar and simmer for 1–2 minutes.
3 Return the lamb steaks to the pan and simmer for 5 minutes or until cooked to your liking. Serve hot.

SHEPHERD'S PIE

SERVES 4

700 g (1½ lb) potatoes, peeled	15 ml (1 tbsp) Worcestershire sauce
salt and pepper	90 ml (6 tbsp) chopped parsley
450 g (1 lb) cooked lamb	5 ml (1 tsp) dried marjoram
30 ml (2 tbsp) vegetable oil	
1 medium onion, chopped	50 g (2 oz) Cheddar cheese, grated
30 ml (2 tbsp) plain flour	
300 ml (½ pint) lamb or beef stock	chopped parsley, to garnish

1 Cook the potatoes in boiling salted water for 20 minutes or until tender.
2 Meanwhile, trim the excess fat from the lamb and discard. Chop the meat finely or mince coarsely.
3 Heat the oil in a frying pan, add the onion and fry for 5 minutes or until lightly browned. Stir in the flour and fry for 2–3 minutes. Add the stock and simmer, stirring, until thickened.
4 Stir in the lamb, Worcestershire sauce, parsley, marjoram and salt and pepper. Spoon into a 1.1 litre (2 pint) shallow pie dish.
5 Drain the potatoes. Mash well, then beat in the cheese and salt and pepper. Spoon or pipe over the lamb.
6 Bake in a preheated oven at 200°C (400°F) mark 6 for 30 minutes or until well browned. Serve hot, sprinkled with parsley.

VARIATION
Cottage Pie
Replace the minced lamb with minced beef and omit the marjoram and cheese for a traditional 'Cottage' pie.

LAMB CUTLETS REFORM

SERVES 4

15 g (½ oz) butter	2 blades of mace
1 small onion, finely chopped	1 bay leaf
1 medium carrot, finely chopped	4 juniper berries, crushed
	pinch of dried thyme
50 g (2 oz) lean ham, cut into thin strips	eight 75 g (3 oz) lamb cutlets
60 ml (4 tbsp) red wine vinegar	50 g (2 oz) ham, finely minced
45 ml (3 tbsp) port	50 g (2 oz) fresh breadcrumbs
600 ml (1 pint) lamb or chicken stock	1 egg, beaten
2 cloves	15 ml (1 tbsp) cornflour

1 To make the sauce, melt the butter in a saucepan, add the onion, carrot and ham strips and cook until just turning brown. Add the vinegar and port and boil until almost all the liquid has evaporated.
2 Remove the pan from the heat and add the stock, cloves, mace, bay leaf, juniper berries and thyme. Stir well and bring to the boil. Simmer for 30 minutes.
3 Meanwhile, trim the cutlets to remove most of the surrounding fat. Scrape the bone of each cutlet absolutely clean to within 2.5 cm (1 inch) of the 'eye' of the meat.
4 Mix the minced ham and breadcrumbs together. Brush each cutlet with beaten egg and coat with the ham and breadcrumb mixture. Cover and chill until required.
5 Blend the cornflour with about 30 ml (2 tbsp) water and add to the sauce. Stir well and bring the sauce to the boil, stirring continuously. Simmer until thickened.
6 Cook the cutlets under a preheated grill for 4 minutes on each side. Reheat the sauce and serve separately.

LAMB FILLET WITH REDCURRANT SAUCE

SERVES 3

90 ml (6 tbsp) soured cream	450 g (1 lb) lamb fillet
1 garlic clove, crushed	30 ml (2 tbsp) dry red wine
5 ml (1 tsp) wholegrain mustard	15 ml (1 tbsp) redcurrant jelly
salt and pepper	

1 Mix 30 ml (2 tbsp) of the soured cream with the garlic and mustard. Season to taste.

2 Put the lamb fillet in a roasting tin and spoon the garlic mixture all over. Roast in a preheated oven at 180°C (350°F) mark 4 for 30 minutes or until tender and cooked to your liking. Transfer the lamb to a warmed serving dish and keep warm.

3 Add the wine to the roasting tin, stirring in any sediment from the bottom of the tin. Stir in the redcurrant jelly. Bring to the boil, then stir in the remaining soured cream and boil for 2–3 minutes or until thickened slightly.

4 Slice the lamb and serve with the sauce spooned over.

TO MICROWAVE

Complete step 1. Put the lamb in a shallow dish and spoon over the garlic mixture. Cook, uncovered, on HIGH for 3 minutes. Cover and cook on MEDIUM for 10–15 minutes, rearranging twice, until cooked to your liking. Transfer the lamb to a warmed serving dish. Stir the remaining soured cream, the wine and redcurrant jelly into the dish. Cook on HIGH for 1–2 minutes, stirring occasionally, until hot. Complete step 4.

HONEYED LAMB NOISETTES

SERVES 6

2 large lemons	2 garlic cloves, crushed
twelve 75–100 g (3–4 oz) lean lamb noisettes	1 cm (½ inch) piece of fresh root ginger, grated (optional)
30 ml (2 tbsp) chopped fresh thyme or 5 ml (1 tsp) dried	120 ml (8 tbsp) clear honey
30 ml (2 tbsp) chopped fresh rosemary or 10 ml (2 tsp) dried	60 ml (4 tbsp) vegetable oil
	salt and pepper
1 bay leaf	bay leaves and thyme and rosemary sprigs, to garnish

1 Pare the rind off one lemon and cut into fine strips. Cover and set aside.

2 Place the lamb in a shallow, non-metallic dish. Sprinkle over the herbs and bay leaf.

3 Whisk together the grated rind of the remaining whole lemon, 90 ml (6 tbsp) lemon juice, the crushed garlic, ginger (if using), the honey and oil. Season to taste. Pour over the lamb, cover and leave to marinate in the refrigerator overnight.

4 Drain the marinade from the lamb and strain into a small saucepan. Place the meat on a rack over the grill pan. Cook under a preheated hot grill for 7 minutes on each side. Transfer to an ovenproof serving dish, cover lightly with foil and keep warm.

5 Carefully pour the grill pan juices into the strained marinade. Stir in the strips of lemon rind. Bring to the boil and simmer for 2–3 minutes or until syrupy, stirring occasionally. Adjust the seasoning and spoon over the noisettes. Garnish with bay leaves and sprigs of fresh thyme and rosemary.

LAMB NOISETTES WITH RED WINE SAUCE

SERVES 6

12 lamb noisettes	225 g (8 oz) button mushrooms
flour, for coating	300 ml (½ pint) red wine
25 g (1 oz) butter	150 ml (¼ pint) chicken stock
60 ml (4 tbsp) vegetable oil	15 ml (1 tbsp) tomato purée
2 large onions, sliced	2 bay leaves
1 garlic clove, finely chopped	salt and pepper

1 Lightly coat the lamb noisettes with flour. Heat the butter and oil in a large flameproof casserole. Add the noisettes, a few at a time, and cook over a high heat until browned on both sides. Remove from the casserole with a slotted spoon and set aside.

2 Add the onion and garlic to the casserole and fry for about 5 minutes or until golden. Add the mushrooms and fry for a further 2–3 minutes. Stir in the red wine, stock, tomato purée and bay leaves. Season to taste.

3 Return the noisettes to the casserole and bring to the boil, then cover and simmer gently for about 40 minutes or until tender, turning the meat once during this time.

4 Lift the noisettes out of the sauce and remove the string. Place the noisettes on a warmed serving dish and keep warm. Boil the remaining sauce rapidly for 5–10 minutes to reduce. Taste and adjust the seasoning, remove the bay leaves, then pour over the noisettes. Serve immediately.

MINTED LAMB BURGERS WITH CUCUMBER

SERVES 4

450 g (1 lb) lean minced lamb	1 egg, beaten
1 small onion, finely chopped	salt and pepper
100 g (4 oz) fresh breadcrumbs	30 ml (2 tbsp) plain flour
finely grated rind of ½ lemon	½ cucumber, cut into 5 cm (2 inch) long wedges
45 ml (3 tbsp) chopped mint	6 spring onions, cut into 1 cm (½ inch) pieces
	200 ml (7 fl oz) lamb or chicken stock
	15 ml (1 tbsp) dry sherry

1 Mix the lamb, onion, breadcrumbs and lemon rind with 15 ml (1 tbsp) of the chopped mint and the egg. Season to taste.

2 Shape into eight burgers with floured hands, then completely coat in the flour.

3 Dry-fry the burgers in a large heavy-based non-stick frying pan for about 6 minutes or until lightly browned, turning once. Add the cucumber and spring onions.

4 Pour in the stock and sherry, then add the remaining mint and season to taste. Bring to the boil, cover and simmer gently for about 20 minutes or until the meat is tender. Skim off any excess fat and taste and adjust the seasoning before serving.

EASTERN LAMB KEBABS

SERVES 4–6

CROWN ROAST

SERVES 6

450 g (1 lb) lean minced lamb	5 ml (1 tsp) ground fenugreek
1 large onion, grated	10 ml (2 tsp) ground turmeric
15 ml (1 tbsp) chopped fresh dill or 5 ml (1 tsp) dried	salt and pepper
30 ml (2 tbsp) chopped fresh coriander or 10 ml (2 tsp) dried	30 ml (2 tbsp) sultanas
	1 egg, beaten
	coriander sprigs, to garnish

1 Put the lamb and onion in a medium bowl. Add the remaining ingredients, except the coriander sprigs, and mix well, using your fingers.
2 Divide the mixture into 30 walnut-size pieces. Using dampened hands, form into even round shapes.
3 Thread about five balls on to each of six metal skewers, leaving about 2.5 cm (1 inch) of each skewer exposed at both sides. Place the kebabs on a grill rack as you prepare them.
4 Cook the kebabs under a preheated grill for 5–8 minutes. Turn them over and continue to cook for a further 5–8 minutes or until the meat is cooked. Garnish with coriander sprigs.

--- **TO MICROWAVE** ---

Complete steps 1 and 2. Thread the balls on to wooden skewers and arrange on a microwave roasting rack. Microwave on HIGH for 12-15 minutes, re-arranging occasionally. Stand for 2 minutes. Garnish with coriander sprigs.

2 best end necks of lamb, each with 6 cutlets, chined	juice and grated rind of ½ lemon
15 g (½ oz) butter	1 egg, beaten
1 medium onion, chopped	salt and pepper
3 celery sticks, chopped	30 ml (2 tbsp) plain flour
2 eating apples, chopped	450 ml (¾ pint) lamb or beef stock
100 g (4 oz) fresh breadcrumbs	mint sprigs, to garnish
30 ml (2 tbsp) chopped mint	

1 Trim each cutlet bone to a depth of 2.5 cm (1 inch).
2 Bend the joints around, fat side inwards, and sew together using strong cotton or fine string to form a crown. Cover the exposed bones with foil.
3 Melt the butter in a saucepan and cook the onion, celery and apples until brown. Stir in the breadcrumbs, mint, lemon juice and rind and egg. Season to taste and cool, then fill the centre of the joint with the stuffing and weigh. Roast in a preheated oven at 180°C (350°F) mark 4 for 25 minutes per 450 g (1 lb) plus 25 minutes.
4 Transfer the roast to a warmed serving dish and keep warm. Drain off all but 30 ml (2 tbsp) of the fat in the roasting tin, then add the flour and blend well. Cook for 2–3 minutes, stirring continuously. Remove from the heat and gradually add the stock. Boil for 2–3 minutes. Adjust the seasoning and serve with the roast. Garnish with mint.

--- **VARIATION** ---

For a 'Guard of Honour', trim the best end necks of lamb and interlace the bones, fat sides outwards, to form an arch. Stuff the cavity and tie as above.

BRAISED SHOULDER OF LAMB WITH APRICOT STUFFING

SERVES 6

25 g (1 oz) butter	2 kg (4½ lb) shoulder of lamb, boned
15 ml (1 tbsp) chopped onion	600 ml (1 pint) beef or lamb stock
60 ml (4 tbsp) fine fresh white breadcrumbs	225 g (8 oz) onions, quartered
15 ml (1 tbsp) chopped parsley	450 g (1 lb) carrots, diced
15–30 ml (1–2 tbsp) milk	6 celery sticks, sliced
75 g (3 oz) no-soak dried apricots, chopped	350 g (12 oz) turnips, quartered
salt and pepper	

1 Melt the butter in a saucepan, add the chopped onion and fry for about 5 minutes or until soft and transparent.

2 Remove the pan from the heat and add the breadcrumbs, parsley, milk and apricots. Season to taste.

3 Sprinkle the cut surface of the lamb with seasoning and spread the stuffing over. Roll up and tie with string. Place the joint in a greased flameproof casserole and cook in a preheated oven at 230°C (450°F) mark 8 for 15 minutes.

4 Remove the casserole from the oven and add half the stock. Reduce the oven temperature to 180°C (350°F) mark 4, re-cover and cook the meat for 45 minutes.

5 Arrange the onions, carrots, celery and turnips round the joint and add the remaining stock. Re-cover and cook for a further 1¼ hours.

6 Remove the casserole from the oven and lift the meat and vegetables on to a warmed serving dish. Skim the fat off the stock in the casserole, then boil fast for 3–5 minutes to reduce by half. Serve with the lamb.

ROLLED STUFFED BREASTS OF LAMB

SERVES 4

25 g (1 oz) butter or margarine	15 ml (1 tbsp) lemon juice
1 medium onion, chopped	pinch of grated nutmeg
25 g (1 oz) streaky bacon, chopped	1 egg, beaten
226 g (8 oz) packet frozen leaf spinach, thawed	salt and pepper
75 g (3 oz) fresh breadcrumbs	2 large breasts of lamb, boned and trimmed (total weight about 1.1 kg/ 2½ lb)
45 ml (3 tbsp) chopped parsley	45 ml (3 tbsp) vegetable oil
finely grated rind of ½ lemon	watercress, to garnish

1 Melt the butter or margarine in a saucepan, add the onion and bacon and fry for about 5 minutes or until lightly browned.

2 Drain the spinach and chop roughly. Place in a bowl with the onion and bacon, breadcrumbs, parsley, lemon rind and juice, nutmeg and egg. Mix together well and season to taste.

3 Lay the breasts of lamb, fat side down, on a work surface and spread the stuffing evenly over them with a palette knife.

4 Roll up the lamb breasts loosely and tie in several places with strong thread or fine string to hold their shape.

5 Weigh each joint and calculate the cooking time, allowing 25 minutes per 450 g (1 lb) plus 25 minutes for each joint. Heat the oil in a roasting tin and place the joints in the tin. Roast in a preheated oven at 180°C (350°F) mark 4 for the calculated cooking time, basting occasionally. Serve hot, garnished with watercress.

LAMB IN TOMATO SAUCE WITH HERB BREAD

SERVES 4

30 ml (2 tbsp) vegetable oil	60 ml (4 tbsp) red wine (optional)
1 kg (2¼ lb) boned lean shoulder of lamb, cubed	salt and pepper
1 medium onion, sliced	lamb or beef stock, if necessary
20 ml (4 tsp) plain flour	40 g (1½ oz) butter
397 g (14 oz) and 227 g (8 oz) cans tomatoes	15 ml (1 tbsp) snipped chives
30 ml (2 tbsp) tomato purée	eight 1 cm (½ inch) slices of French bread
pinch of granulated sugar	
2.5 ml (½ tsp) dried rosemary	

1 Heat the oil in a flameproof casserole, add the lamb and fry over a high heat until browned on all sides. Remove from the casserole with a slotted spoon and set aside.

2 Add the onion to the pan and fry for 5 minutes or until soft. Stir in the flour and cook for 1 minute. Add the tomatoes with their juice, the tomato purée, sugar, rosemary and wine, if using. Bring to the boil, stirring.

3 Return the meat to the pan and add salt and pepper to taste. Add a little stock, if necessary, to cover the meat. Cover the casserole and cook in the oven at 170°C (325°F) mark 3 for about 1¼ hours.

4 Meanwhile, make the herb butter. Beat the butter until soft, then beat in the chives and salt and pepper to taste.

5 Spread the butter on to the slices of French bread. Uncover the casserole and place the bread, butter side up, on top. Cook for a further hour, or until the meat is tender. Serve hot.

PARSON'S 'VENISON'

SERVES 4–6

	FOR THE MARINADE
25 g (1 oz) dripping or butter	200 ml (7 fl oz) red wine
1 small onion, finely chopped	75 ml (3 fl oz) tawny port
100 g (4 oz) mushrooms, chopped	6 juniper berries, crushed
100 g (4 oz) ham, chopped	1.25 ml (¼ tsp) ground allspice
30 ml (2 tbsp) snipped chives	30 ml (2 tbsp) vegetable oil
salt and black pepper	45 ml (3 tbsp) red wine vinegar
1.8–2 kg (4–4½ lb) leg of lamb, skinned and boned	1 bay leaf
watercress sprigs, to garnish	1.25 ml (¼ tsp) grated nutmeg

1 Melt half the dripping in a saucepan and cook the onion and mushrooms for 5 minutes or until soft, stirring frequently. Stir in the ham and chives, season and cool.

2 Season the lamb inside and out with black pepper, then spread the onion mixture over the inside. Roll up tightly and tie securely. Place in an ovenproof casserole.

3 Mix the marinade ingredients, pour over the lamb, cover and leave in a cool place for 24 hours, turning occasionally. Remove the meat from the marinade, drain and dry.

4 Melt the remaining dripping in a frying pan. Add the meat and cook until browned. Transfer to a casserole.

5 Pour the marinade into the frying pan, bring to the boil, then pour over the meat. Cover, then cook at 180°C (350°F) mark 4 for 1¾–2 hours, basting occasionally.

6 Transfer the meat to a warmed plate and keep warm. Skim the fat from the surface of the liquid, then boil the liquid rapidly until reduced and slightly thickened. Season to taste. Garnish the meat and serve with the gravy.

LAMB WITH CHERRIES

SERVES 6

225 g (8 oz) streaky bacon rashers, chopped	1 garlic clove, sliced
15 g (½ oz) butter	600 ml (1 pint) dry red wine
1.4 kg (3 lb) boneless leg or shoulder of lamb, cut into 4 cm (1½ inch) cubes	bouquet garni
	pinch of grated nutmeg
1 medium onion, sliced	salt and pepper
1 medium carrot, sliced	450 g (1 lb) fresh red cherries, stoned
1 celery stick, sliced	

1 In a large frying pan, fry the bacon in its own fat until browned. Add the butter to the pan and fry the lamb, a little at a time, until browned. Remove from the pan with the bacon and put in an ovenproof casserole.

2 Add the onion, carrot, celery and garlic to the fat remaining in the pan and fry for about 5 minutes or until lightly browned. Add the vegetables to the casserole.

3 Pour over the wine and add the bouquet garni and nutmeg. Season to taste, cover and cook in a preheated oven at 150°C (300°F) mark 3 for about 2½ hours or until tender.

4 Thirty minutes before the end of the cooking time, stir the cherries into the casserole and continue to cook until the meat is tender and the cherries soft. Serve hot.

--- COOK'S TIP ---

Look for red-skinned sour cherries for this dish. Dark-skinned Morellos are also a good choice.

ORIENTAL LAMB

SERVES 4

1.4 kg (3 lb) lean shoulder of lamb, boned	5 ml (1 tsp) ground ginger
30 ml (2 tbsp) vegetable oil	300 ml (½ pint) chicken stock
25 g (1 oz) butter or margarine	15 ml (1 tbsp) Worcestershire sauce
450 g (1 lb) small new potatoes, scrubbed or scraped	30 ml (2 tbsp) soy sauce
	salt and pepper
225 g (8 oz) small pickling onions, skinned	2 caps canned pimiento, diced
15 ml (1 tbsp) plain flour	

1 Cut the lamb into 2.5 cm (1 inch) pieces about 5 mm (¼ inch) thick, discarding any excess fat.

2 Heat the oil and butter or margarine in a large sauté pan and add the meat, a few pieces at time. Fry until browned on all sides, turning frequently. Remove from the pan with a slotted spoon.

3 Add the potatoes and onions to the fat remaining in the pan and fry until lightly browned, turning frequently.

4 Return the meat to the pan, sprinkle in the flour and ginger and stir well. Cook gently, stirring, for 2 minutes.

5 Add the stock, Worcestershire sauce and soy sauce, and season to taste. Bring to the boil, stirring, then cover and simmer for 30 minutes or until the meat is tender.

6 Add the pimientos and stir over a low heat to heat through. Taste and adjust the seasoning, then transfer the lamb to a warmed serving dish. Serve hot.

BROWN RAGOUT OF LAMB

SERVES 6

75 g (3 oz) butter, diced	salt and pepper
900 g (2 lb) boneless leg of lamb, cut into 2.5 cm (1 inch) pieces	3 carrots, cut into pieces
	12 small onions, skinned
750 ml (1¼ pints) brown stock, preferably veal	100 g (4 oz) button mushrooms
4 cloves	squeeze of lemon juice
1 onion	75 g (3 oz) shelled broad beans, cooked
3 parsley sprigs	FOR THE GARNISH
2 thyme sprigs	flesh of 2 large firm tomatoes, cut into strips
2 bay leaves	30 ml (2 tbsp) finely chopped parsley
1 rosemary sprig	

1 Melt half the butter in a frying pan and cook the lamb until brown. Transfer to a flameproof casserole.

2 Put the stock in a saucepan. Push the cloves into the unskinned onion and add to the stock with the herbs. Season and bring to the boil. Pour over the lamb, cover and cook at 180°C (350°F) mark 4 for 1 hour.

3 Add another 15 g (½ oz) butter to the frying pan and melt. Fry the carrots and small onions until browned. Drain, then stir into the casserole and cook for a further 30 minutes. Cook the mushrooms in the remaining butter with the lemon juice. Drain on kitchen paper.

4 Remove the onion and cloves from the casserole, then stir in the mushrooms and cook, uncovered, for 10 minutes. Lift the meat and vegetables from the dish and keep warm. Boil the liquid until reduced. Arrange the meat on a plate with all the vegetables. Garnish and serve.

LAMB AND ORANGE CASSEROLE WITH CHOUX DUMPLINGS

SERVES 4

45 ml (3 tbsp) vegetable oil	150 ml (¼ pint) chicken stock
900 g (2 lb) lean boneless leg of lamb, cubed	2 bay leaves
1 medium onion, chopped	salt and pepper
2 turnips, roughly chopped	50 g (2 oz) butter
3 carrots, roughly chopped	2 eggs, beaten
75 g (3 oz) plain flour	finely grated rind of 2 oranges
15 ml (1 tbsp) tomato purée	15 ml (1 tbsp) chopped parsley
300 ml (½ pint) unsweetened orange juice	

1 Heat the oil in a flameproof casserole and fry the lamb until brown. Remove and set aside. Fry the onion for 5 minutes. Add the turnips and carrots and fry for 5 minutes.

2 Stir in 15 g (½ oz) of the flour, then add the tomato purée. Add the orange juice and stock and boil, stirring.

3 Return the meat, add the bay leaves, season and stir well. Cover and cook at 180°C (350°F) mark 4 for 1½ hours.

4 To make the dumplings, sift together the remaining flour and a pinch of salt. Put the butter in a medium saucepan, add 150 ml (¼ pint) water and heat gently until the butter has melted. Bring to a rolling boil and tip in the flour and salt. Immediately take the pan off the heat and beat vigorously until the mixture forms a ball. Turn into a bowl and cool slightly, then beat in the eggs, a little at a time. The paste should be quite stiff.

5 Beat the orange rind and parsley into the choux paste. Remove the bay leaves from the casserole, then pipe or spoon eight choux balls on top. Bake, uncovered, at 200°C (400°F) mark 6 for 1 hour.

LANCASHIRE HOT POT

SERVES 4

8 middle neck lamb chops	5 ml (1 tsp) dried thyme
2 lamb's kidneys, halved and cored	salt and pepper
8 shelled oysters (optional)	450 g (1 lb) potatoes, peeled and thinly sliced
2 medium onions, sliced	450 ml (¾ pint) lamb or beef stock
100 g (4 oz) mushrooms, sliced	25 g (1 oz) lard or dripping

1 Remove any excess fat from the lamb. Select a large, deep casserole. If it is not deep enough to hold the meat, chop the ends off the bones.

2 Cut each kidney half into three or four pieces.

3 Layer the meat in the casserole with the oysters (if using), the kidneys, onions and mushrooms. Sprinkle each layer with thyme and seasoning to taste. If the casserole has a narrow top, add some of the potatoes at this stage. Pour in the stock.

4 Arrange a layer of overlapping potato slices on top. Melt the lard or dripping and brush over the potatoes. Cover and cook in a preheated oven at 170°C (325°F) mark 3 for 2 hours or until both the meat and the potatoes are tender when tested with a skewer.

5 Remove the lid carefully, increase the oven temperature to 220°C (425°F) mark 7 and continue cooking for about 20 minutes or until the potatoes are golden brown and crisp.

LAMB AND MAÎTRE D'HÔTEL BUTTER

SERVES 4

4 large lamb loin chops	salt and pepper
50 g (2 oz) butter	1 egg, beaten
50 g (2 oz) button mushrooms, finely chopped	15 ml (1 tbsp) vegetable oil
50 g (2 oz) ham, finely chopped	FOR THE BUTTER
	100 g (4 oz) butter, softened
grated rind of 1 small lemon	30 ml (2 tbsp) finely chopped parsley
25 g (1 oz) fresh breadcrumbs	squeeze of lemon juice
	salt and cayenne

1 To make the maître d'hôtel butter, beat the butter until very soft, then add the parsley, lemon juice and salt and cayenne to taste. Shape into a roll, wrap in greaseproof paper and chill in the refrigerator until required.

2 Using a sharp knife, slit the lean 'eye' of each chop horizontally through the fat edge.

3 Melt 25 g (1 oz) of the butter in a small saucepan, add the mushrooms and fry lightly until soft. Add the ham, lemon rind and breadcrumbs, season to taste and bind with a little beaten egg. Allow to cool, then stuff the mixture into the incisions in the chops. Secure each chop with strong thread or fine string.

4 Heat the oil and remaining butter in a large frying pan, add the chops and fry over a high heat, until well browned on both sides. Reduce the heat and continue to cook for 20 minutes. Remove the chops from the pan and remove the string.

5 Cut the maître d'hôtel butter into pats and place several on each of the chops to serve.

BLANQUETTE D'AGNEAU

SERVES 4

700 g (1½ lb) boneless lean shoulder of lamb, diced	300 ml (½ pint) stock or water
100 g (4 oz) carrots, sliced	25 g (1 oz) butter, softened
1 onion, sliced	45 ml (3 tbsp) plain flour
2 celery sticks, sliced	1 egg yolk
1 small bay leaf	150 ml (5 fl oz) single cream
5 ml (1 tsp) dried thyme	
salt and pepper	chopped parsley, to garnish

1 Put the meat, carrots, onion, celery, bay leaf and thyme in a large saucepan. Season to taste. Cover with stock or water, cover and simmer for 1½ hours or until the meat is tender. Remove the bay leaf.

2 Blend together the softened butter and flour and add to the stew in small knobs, stirring after each addition until the stew is thickened. Simmer for 10 minutes, adding more liquid if necessary.

3 Blend together the egg yolk and cream, add to the stew and reheat without boiling. Garnish with parsley.

VARIATION
Blanquette de Veau

This classic creamy stew can also be made with 700 g (1½ lb) pie veal. Substitute a bouquet garni for the bay leaf and thyme.

SPICED LAMB

SERVES 4

225 g (8 oz) plain flour	450 g (1 lb) onions, thinly sliced
salt and pepper	1.25 ml (¼ tsp) ground allspice
50 g (2 oz) butter	1.25 ml (¼ tsp) grated nutmeg
50 g (2 oz) lard	
700 g (1½ lb) lamb neck fillets, sliced into 12 pieces	150 ml (¼ pint) lamb or beef stock
1 large cooking apple, peeled, cored and sliced	milk, to glaze

1 Put the flour and a pinch of salt in a bowl. Rub in the butter and lard until the mixture resembles fine breadcrumbs. Add enough cold water to mix to a firm dough. Knead lightly until smooth, then chill until required.

2 Place half the lamb in the base of a 900 ml (1½ pint) pie dish. Arrange half the apple slices and half the onion slices over the top. Sprinkle over the allspice and nutmeg and season to taste. Repeat the layers, then pour over the stock.

3 Roll out the pastry to fit the dish and use to cover the pie, moistening the edges so the pastry is well sealed. Use any pastry trimmings to decorate.

4 Brush the pastry with milk and bake in a preheated oven at 200°C (400°F) mark 6 for 20 minutes. Reduce the temperature to 180°C (350°F) mark 4 and cook for a further 1¼ hours. Cover the pastry with greaseproof paper if it shows signs of becoming too brown. Serve hot.

CHILLI LAMB AND COCONUT CURRY

SERVES 4–6

50 g (2 oz) desiccated coconut	2.5 ml (½ tsp) chilli powder
200 ml (7 fl oz) milk	5 ml (1 tsp) ground cinnamon
60 ml (4 tbsp) vegetable oil	60 ml (4 tbsp) plain flour
1.4 kg (3 lb) boneless shoulder of lamb, cut into 2.5 cm (1 inch) cubes	400 ml (¾ pint) chicken stock
4 celery sticks, cut into 5 cm (2 inch) pieces	salt and pepper
1 onion, sliced	chopped parsley, to garnish
225 g (8 oz) cooking apples, peeled, cored and sliced	

1 Put the coconut in a saucepan with the milk and 200 ml (7 fl oz) water. Bring to the boil, then remove from the heat and leave to infuse for 30 minutes. Strain into a jug, pressing the coconut to extract all the juice.

2 Heat the oil in a flameproof casserole, add the lamb and cook until browned. Remove the meat with a slotted spoon.

3 Add the celery, onion and apple to the oil in the pan and cook for about 10 minutes or until browned.

4 Stir in the spices and flour, then gradually stir in the stock and coconut milk. Season to taste and bring to the boil.

5 Return the meat to the casserole, cover and cook in a preheated oven at 180°C (350°F) mark 4 for about 1¼ hours. Garnish with parsley before serving.

LAMB AND AUBERGINE MOUSSAKA

SERVES 4

900 g (2 lb) aubergines, sliced	2.5 ml (½ tsp) dried oregano
salt and pepper	2.5 ml (½ tsp) dried basil
vegetable oil, for frying	30 ml (2 tbsp) flour
350 g (12 oz) lean minced lamb	75 g (3 oz) fresh breadcrumbs
2 medium onions, chopped	15 g (½ oz) butter
45 ml (3 tbsp) tomato purée	300 ml (½ pint) milk
150 ml (¼ pint) dry white wine	75 g (3 oz) Cheddar cheese, grated
227 g (8 oz) can tomatoes	1 egg yolk

1 Put the aubergine slices in a colander, sprinkling each layer generously with salt. Leave to drain for 30 minutes.

2 Heat 15 ml (1 tbsp) oil in a saucepan, add the lamb and cook until well browned. Stir in the onion, tomato purée, wine, tomatoes with their juice, herbs and 15 ml (1 tbsp) flour. Boil, cover and simmer for 30 minutes. Season.

3 Rinse the aubergine slices and pat dry on absorbent kitchen paper. Heat some oil in a large frying pan and fry the aubergine slices, in batches, until browned on both sides. Drain well. Layer the aubergines in a shallow ovenproof dish with the lamb and 50 g (2 oz) breadcrumbs.

4 To make the sauce, melt the butter in a saucepan, stir in the remaining flour and cook for 1 minute, stirring. Remove from the heat and gradually stir in the milk. Bring to the boil and cook, stirring, until thick. Stir in 50 g (2 oz) of the cheese and the egg yolk.

5 Spoon the sauce over the moussaka, then sprinkle with the remaining cheese and breadcrumbs. Bake at 180°C (350°F) mark 4 for 45 minutes or until golden.

LAMB AND WATERCRESS BAKE

SERVES 4–6

450 g (1 lb) lean minced lamb	50 ml (2 fl oz) dry white wine
2 large onions, finely chopped	salt and pepper
2 bunches of watercress, finely chopped	25 g (1 oz) butter
	568 ml (1 pint) milk
10 ml (2 tsp) dried oregano	175 g (6 oz) Lancashire cheese, crumbled
105 ml (7 tbsp) plain flour	225 g (8 oz) oven-ready lasagne verdi
300 ml (½ pint) lamb or chicken stock	

1 Put the lamb in a large, preferably non-stick saucepan and fry in its own fat until well browned, stirring constantly. Pour off excess fat. Add the onion and cook for 5 minutes, stirring occasionally. Add the watercress, oregano and 30 ml (2 tbsp) of the flour. Cook for 1–2 minutes, then gradually stir in the stock and wine. Season to taste. Bring to the boil, then simmer gently, uncovered, for 45 minutes, stirring occasionally.

2 Put the butter, remaining flour and milk in a saucepan. Heat, whisking continuously, until the sauce thickens, boils and is smooth. Simmer for 1–2 minutes. Remove the pan from the heat and add 100 g (4 oz) of the cheese, stirring until melted. Season to taste.

3 Layer the mince mixture with the uncooked lasagne in a fairly deep ovenproof serving dish. Spoon over the cheese sauce and sprinkle with the remaining cheese.

4 Bake in a preheated oven at 190°C (375°F) mark 5 for about 40 minutes in a preheated oven or until browned. Serve hot straight from the dish.

SPICED LENTIL BAKE

SERVES 4

45 ml (3 tbsp) vegetable oil	75 g (3 oz) red lentils
8 middle neck lamb chops (total weight about 1.1 kg/ 2½ lb)	salt and pepper
	450 g (1 lb) potatoes, peeled and thinly sliced
2 medium onions, thinly sliced	450 g (1 lb) swede, thinly sliced
15 ml (1 tbsp) ground turmeric	300 ml (½ pint) lamb or chicken stock
5 ml (1 tsp) paprika	
5 ml (1 tsp) ground cinnamon	

1 Heat the oil in a large sauté or frying pan, add the chops and fry until well browned on both sides. Remove from the pan with a slotted spoon.

2 Add the onions to the pan with the turmeric, paprika, cinnamon and lentils. Fry for 2–3 minutes, then add plenty of salt and pepper and spoon into a shallow 2 litre (3½ pint) ovenproof dish.

3 Place the chops on top of the onion and lentil mixture. Arrange the vegetable slices on top of the chops, then season to taste and pour over the stock.

4 Cover the dish tightly and cook in a preheated oven at 180°C (350°F) mark 4 for about 1½ hours, or until the chops are tender. Uncover and cook for a further 30 minutes, or until lightly browned on top. Serve hot.

––––––––––– COOK'S TIP –––––––––––

There are many different types of lentil available. The red lentils used in this recipe are the most common kind, sometimes also described as 'split red lentils' or even 'Egyptian lentils'. They do not need soaking and are quick-cooking, but they tend to lose their shape.

LAMB CRUMBLE

SERVES 4

350 g (12 oz) leftover roast lamb	salt and pepper
1 medium onion	50 g (2 oz) butter
115 g (4½ oz) flour	50 g (2 oz) Cheshire or Cheddar cheese, grated
15 ml (1 tbsp) tomato purée	2.5 ml (½ tsp) dried mixed herbs
300 ml (½ pint) beef stock	

1 Mince together the meat and onion. Mix in 15 g (½ oz) flour, the tomato purée and the stock. Season to taste. Turn into a shallow ovenproof dish.

2 Put the remaining flour in a bowl and rub in the butter until the mixture resembles fine breadcrumbs. Stir in the grated cheese, herbs and seasoning. Spoon the crumble over the meat.

3 Bake in a preheated oven at 190°C (375°F) mark 5 for 45 minutes–1 hour. Serve immediately.

VARIATION
Beef Crumble

Substitute 350 g (12 oz) leftover roast beef for the lamb.

LAMB KEBABS IN SPICY YOGURT DRESSING

SERVES 4

1 large corn-on-the-cob	15 ml (1 tbsp) coriander seeds
salt and pepper	700 g (1½ lb) boned leg of lamb, cut into 2.5 cm (1 inch) cubes
8 shallots	
150 ml (5 fl oz) natural yogurt	
1 garlic clove, crushed	225 g (8 oz) courgettes, cut into 0.5 cm (¼ inch) slices
2 bay leaves, crumbled	4 tomatoes, halved
15 ml (1 tbsp) lemon juice	lemon wedges, to garnish
5 ml (1 tsp) ground allspice	

1 Blanch the corn in boiling salted water for 1 minute, drain well, then cut into eight pieces and set aside. Blanch the shallots in boiling salted water for 1 minute, skin and set aside.

2 To make the marinade, pour the yogurt into a shallow dish and stir in the garlic, bay leaves, lemon juice, allspice, coriander seeds and salt and pepper to taste.

3 Thread the lamb cubes on to eight skewers with the courgettes, tomatoes, corn and shallots. Place in the dish, spoon over the marinade, cover and leave for 2–3 hours, turning occasionally to ensure even coating.

4 Cook the kebabs under a preheated grill for 15–20 minutes, turning and brushing with the marinade occasionally. To serve, spoon the remaining marinade over the kebabs and garnish with lemon wedges.

ROAST PORK WITH APPLES

SERVES 6–8

1.6 kg (3½ lb) loin of pork	150 ml (¼ pint) dry white wine (optional)
40 g (1½ oz) butter	150 ml (¼ pint) chicken stock
coarse salt	
fresh rosemary sprig	fresh watercress sprigs, to garnish
6 large Cox's apples, cored	
salt and pepper	

1 Score the pork rind all over with a sharp knife. Rub with the butter, then sprinkle with coarse salt.

2 Place the rosemary on a rack in a roasting tin, put the pork on top and roast in a preheated oven at 180°C (350°F) mark 4 for 2 hours.

3 Season the apples to taste inside and make a shallow cut through the skin around the apples about one third of the way down. Place in a tin or ovenproof dish and baste with some of the fat from the pork. Cook on a lower shelf for the last 30 minutes of the meat roasting time.

4 Transfer the pork, still on the rack, to a plate and keep warm. Drain off most of the fat from the roasting tin, leaving the meat juices. Stir in the wine, if using, loosening the sediment at the bottom of the pan. Boil until almost completely evaporated. Stir in the stock and boil for 2–3 minutes. Strain into a sauceboat.

5 Put the pork on a warmed serving plate. Arrange the apples around the pork, garnish with watercress and serve accompanied by the gravy.

DANISH ROAST LOIN OF PORK

SERVES 6

1.5 kg (3–3½ lb) boned, rolled and tied loin of pork	18 no-soak prunes, stoned
salt and pepper	15 g (½ oz) plain flour
2 cooking apples, peeled, cored and cut into eighths	50 ml (2 fl oz) double cream

1 Score the rind of the pork with a very sharp knife, if the butcher has not already done so. Weigh the joint and calculate the cooking time, allowing 40 minutes per 450 g (1 lb).

2 Dry the rind thoroughly with absorbent kitchen paper, then rub with 10 ml (2 tsp) salt. Place the joint, rind side uppermost, on a rack in a roasting tin.

3 Roast the pork in a preheated oven at 220°C (425°F) mark 7 for 40 minutes, then remove from the oven and pour 300 ml (½ pint) water into the roasting tin, underneath the rack. Return the pork to the oven, lower the temperature to 180°C (350°F) mark 4, and roast for the remaining cooking time, adding the apples and prunes to the water for the last 45 minutes. Do not baste.

4 Transfer the pork to a warmed carving dish and leave to settle for about 15 minutes before carving. Remove the fruit from the water with a slotted spoon and keep hot.

5 Make a gravy from the pan juices. In a measuring jug, mix the flour to a paste with a little cold water. Stir in more cold water up to the 300 ml (½ pint) mark.

6 Remove the rack from the roasting tin and transfer the tin to the hob. Stir the flour mixture into the liquid in the tin, a little at a time, then bring to the boil. Simmer, stirring, until thickened, then stir in the cream and season to taste. Heat through, then pour into a gravyboat. Serve the pork with the fruit and the gravy.

41

POT ROAST OF PORK AND RED CABBAGE

SERVES 4

45 ml (3 tbsp) red wine vinegar	15 ml (1 tbsp) plain flour
450 g (1 lb) red cabbage	salt and pepper
225 g (8 oz) cooking apple	700 g (1½ lb) boned shoulder of pork, rinded
15 ml (1 tbsp) demerara sugar	coriander sprigs, to garnish

1 Bring a large saucepan of water to the boil, to which 15 ml (1 tbsp) of the vinegar has been added.
2 Meanwhile, shred the red cabbage. When the water is boiling, add the cabbage, bring back to the boil, then drain well.
3 Peel, core and slice the apple and place with the cabbage in a casserole just wide enough to take the pork joint.
4 Add the sugar, the remaining vinegar and the flour. Season to taste and stir well together.
5 Slash the fat side of the joint several times and sprinkle with plenty of salt and pepper. Place on top of the cabbage and cover the casserole.
6 Cook in a preheated oven at 190°C (375°F) mark 5 for about 1¾ hours or until the pork is tender. Slice the pork and serve on a warmed platter surrounded by cabbage. Garnish with coriander and serve the remaining cabbage in a separate serving dish.

CHILLI PORK AND BEANS

SERVES 4–6

30 ml (2 tbsp) vegetable oil	175 g (6 oz) red kidney beans, soaked in cold water overnight
900 g (2 lb) boneless pork shoulder, cut into cubes	15 ml (1 tbsp) black treacle
1 large onion, roughly chopped	15 ml (1 tbsp) French mustard
2 celery sticks, sliced	5 ml (1 tsp) chilli powder
1–2 garlic cloves, crushed	salt and pepper

1 Heat 15 ml (1 tbsp) of the oil in a flameproof casserole, add the pork in batches and fry over a high heat until coloured on all sides. Remove with a slotted spoon and drain on absorbent kitchen paper.
2 Lower the heat, then add the remaining oil to the pan with the onion, celery and garlic. Fry gently for 10 minutes or until softened.
3 Drain the kidney beans and add to the pan with 1.1 litres (2 pints) fresh water. Bring to the boil, stirring, then boil rapidly for 10 minutes.
4 Lower the heat, return the pork to the pan and add the black treacle, mustard, chilli powder and pepper to taste. Stir well to mix.
5 Cover the casserole and cook in a preheated oven at 150°C (300°F) mark 2 for 3 hours. Stir the pork and beans occasionally during the cooking time and add more water if dry. Add 5 ml (1 tsp) salt halfway through, then taste and adjust the seasoning before serving, adding more chilli powder if a hotter flavour is preferred.

PORK IN PLUM SAUCE

SERVES 4

450 g (1 lb) plums	25 g (1 oz) butter
300 ml (½ pint) rosé wine	1 large onion, chopped
salt and pepper	175 g (6 oz) white cabbage, shredded
25 g (1 oz) plain wholemeal flour	30 ml (2 tbsp) natural yogurt
700 g (1½ lb) pork fillet (tenderloin), cubed	

1 Put the plums and wine in a saucepan and simmer for 5 minutes or until tender. Strain, reserving the juice. Remove the stones from the plums and purée half in a blender or food processor.
2 Season the flour, add the pork and toss until coated.
3 Melt the butter in a large saucepan or flameproof casserole and lightly fry the onion and cabbage for 3–4 minutes. Add the meat and fry until brown on all sides.
4 Pour in the reserved plum juice and puréed plums, then simmer, uncovered, for 10–15 minutes or until tender. Add the remaining plums and yogurt and reheat gently.

--- **TO MICROWAVE** ---

Put the plums and wine in a large bowl and cook on HIGH for 3–4 minutes. Complete the remainder of step 1 and step 2. Melt the butter in a large bowl on HIGH for 45 seconds. Add the onion and cabbage and cook on HIGH for 7 minutes, stirring occasionally. Add the pork and cook on HIGH for 3 minutes. Pour in 200 ml (7 fl oz) plum juice and the puréed plums and cook on HIGH for 3–4 minutes or until boiling, stirring occasionally. Cook on LOW for 7–8 minutes or until the pork is tender. Stir in the remaining plums sauce yogurt. Stand, covered, for 5 minutes.

PORK ESCALOPES WITH JUNIPER

SERVES 4

450 g (1 lb) pork fillet (tenderloin)	4 juniper berries, lightly crushed
salt and pepper	150 ml (¼ pint) double cream
40 g (1½ oz) plain flour	chopped fresh parsley, to garnish
25 g (1 oz) butter	
75 ml (5 tbsp) dry white wine	

1 Trim any fat from the pork fillet and cut the meat into 5 mm (¼ inch) slices. Place the slices between two sheets of dampened greaseproof paper and beat out into even thinner slices, using rolling pin or meat mallet.
2 Season the flour, then dip each pork escalope in the flour, turning to coat and shaking off any excess.
3 Melt the butter in a large frying pan and fry the escalopes over a high heat for 2 minutes on each side. Remove and keep warm while making the sauce.
4 Add the wine and juniper berries to the pan and boil rapidly, scraping the bottom of the pan to loosen any sediment, until reduced by half. Pour in the cream, season to taste and bring to the boil. Boil rapidly for 1 minute, stirring. Pour over the escalopes and serve immediately, garnished with chopped parsley.

--- **COOK'S TIP** ---

Juniper berries are small purple-black berries with an aromatic scent and pine-like tang. They should be crushed before being added to a dish to release maximum flavour. They are now readily available in supermarkets.

PORK STEAKS WITH PEPPERS

SERVES 4

15 ml (1 tbsp) vegetable oil	1 red pepper, thinly sliced
15 g (½ oz) butter	1 green pepper, thinly sliced
1 medium onion, chopped	45 ml (3 tbsp) dry sherry
2.5 cm (1 inch) piece of fresh root ginger, finely grated	30 ml (2 tbsp) soy sauce
1 garlic clove, crushed	150 ml (¼ pint) unsweetened pineapple juice
four 150 g (5 oz) boneless pork loin steaks	salt and pepper

1 Heat the oil and butter in a large frying pan, add the onion, ginger and garlic and fry gently for 5 minutes or until soft. Push to one side of the pan.

2 Add the steaks to the pan and cook until brown on both sides, then add the remaining ingredients and mix thoroughly together.

3 Cover tightly and simmer gently for 8–10 minutes or until the steaks are tender and the peppers are soft. Transfer the steaks and peppers to warmed serving plates. Bring the remaining liquid in the pan to the boil and boil for 2–3 minutes or until reduced slightly. Spoon over the steaks and serve immediately.

FRUITY STUFFED PORK CHOPS

SERVES 4

4 thick pork loin chops	juice and finely grated rind of 1 large orange
60 ml (4 tbsp) vegetable oil	50 g (2 oz) no-soak prunes
1 small onion, finely chopped	50 g (2 oz) no-soak dried apricots
2 celery sticks, finely chopped	50 g (2 oz) blanched almonds
25 g (1 oz) Italian risotto rice	5 ml (1 tsp) ground cinnamon
450 ml (¾ pint) chicken stock	salt and pepper

1 Using a sharp knife, make a horizontal cut in each pork chop, working from the outside edge to the bone.

2 To make the stuffing, heat 30 ml (2 tbsp) of the oil in a heavy-based saucepan, add the onion and celery and fry gently for 5 minutes or until soft and lightly coloured.

3 Add the rice and stir well, then add 150 ml (¼ pint) of the stock and half of the orange juice. Bring to the boil, stirring all the time. Lower the heat and simmer for 15–20 minutes, stirring frequently and adding more stock if necessary. When cooked, turn into a bowl and cool.

4 Meanwhile, stone the prunes and chop finely with the apricots and almonds. Add to the rice mixture with the cinnamon. Season to taste. Spoon the stuffing into the cavities in the chops, then secure the open edges with wooden cocktail sticks. Reserve any remaining stuffing.

5 Heat the remaining oil in a flameproof casserole, add the chops and fry until browned on both sides. Pour in the remaining stock and orange juice, add any reserved stuffing, season and bring to the boil. Cover and simmer for 40 minutes or until the chops are tender, basting frequently.

6 Transfer the chops to a warmed serving dish, pour over the pan juices and sprinkle with the grated orange rind.

CRUMB-TOPPED PORK CHOPS
SERVES 4

4 lean pork loin chops	pinch of dried thyme
50 g (2 oz) fresh white breadcrumbs	finely grated rind of 1 lemon
15 ml (1 tbsp) chopped fresh parsley or 5 ml (1 tsp) dried	2.5 ml (½ tsp) coriander seeds, crushed
5 ml (1 tsp) chopped fresh mint or 2.5 ml (½ tsp) dried	1 egg, beaten
	salt and pepper

1 Cut the rind off the chops and put them in one layer in a baking tin.
2 Mix the remaining ingredients together and season to taste. Spread this mixture evenly over the chops with a palette knife.
3 Bake in a preheated oven at 200°C (400°F) mark 6 for 45–50 minutes or until golden. Serve hot.

────────── **VARIATION** ──────────
Crumb-topped Lamb Chops
Substitute four lamb chump chops for the pork and use rosemary instead of thyme in the crumb topping. Omit the coriander, if preferred.

PARCELLED PORK
SERVES 4

4 medium pork chops	90 ml (6 tbsp) dry cider
25 g (1 oz) butter	30 ml (2 tbsp) lemon juice
1 medium onion, finely chopped	150 ml (5 fl oz) soured cream
225 g (8 oz) mushrooms, sliced	salt and pepper

1 Trim the chops of any rind and excess fat. Melt the butter in a large frying pan, add the chops and cook until well browned. Remove the chops from the pan and place each one on a piece of foil about 20 cm (8 inches) square.
2 Add the onion and mushrooms to the butter remaining in the pan and cook for 5 minutes.
3 Stir in the cider and lemon juice and bring to the boil. Boil the liquid over a high heat until reduced by half, then remove from the heat and stir in the soured cream. Season well.
4 Place a quarter of the mushroom mixture on top of each chop, then shape the foil into neat parcels and seal well.
5 Place the parcels in a small ovenproof dish and bake in a preheated oven at 180°C (350°F) mark 4 for about 50 minutes or until the chops are tender.
6 To serve, place each parcel on a warmed plate and open carefully so that no juices escape.

PORK FILLET WITH WHITE WINE AND MUSHROOMS

SERVES 6

1 kg (2¼ lb) pork fillet (tenderloin)	150 ml (¼ pint) beef stock
vegetable oil, for frying	150 ml (¼ pint) dry white wine
65 g (2½ oz) butter or margarine	salt and pepper
2 medium onions, chopped	twelve 1 cm (½ inch) slices of French bread
225 g (8 oz) button mushrooms	chopped fresh parsley, to garnish
45 ml (3 tbsp) plain flour	

1 Cut the pork fillet into slices, place between two sheets of dampened greaseproof paper and beat out with a rolling pin or meat mallet. Heat 30 ml (2 tbsp) of the oil in a frying pan, add the pork and cook over a high heat until browned. Remove from the pan and set aside.

2 Melt 50 g (2 oz) of the butter or margarine in the frying pan, add the onions and fry for 5 minutes. Add the mushrooms to the pan, increase the heat and fry for 1–2 minutes, tossing constantly.

3 Blend the flour into the juices in the pan, with the remaining butter or margarine. Cook, stirring, for 1–2 minutes, then gradually blend in the stock and wine. Season to taste and simmer for 2–3 minutes.

4 Return the meat to the pan, cover and cook for 20–25 minutes or until the pork is tender.

5 Meanwhile, heat some oil in a frying pan, add the French bread slices and fry until golden brown on both sides. Drain well on absorbent kitchen paper.

6 Serve the pork hot with the French bread and sprinkled liberally with chopped parsley.

PORK WITH CIDER AND CORIANDER

SERVES 4

450 g (1 lb) pork fillet (tenderloin)	15 ml (1 tbsp) ground coriander
30 ml (2 tbsp) oil	15 ml (1 tbsp) plain flour
50 g (2 oz) butter	150 ml (¼ pint) dry cider
1 green pepper, cut into rings	150 ml (¼ pint) chicken or vegetable stock
225 g (8 oz) celery, sliced	salt and pepper
100 g (4 oz) onion, chopped	

1 Trim excess fat from the pork fillet and slice into 0.5 cm (¼ inch) thick pieces. Place between two sheets of dampened greaseproof paper and beat out until thin with a rolling pin or meat mallet.

2 Heat the oil with half the butter in a large frying pan. Add the green pepper and celery and fry gently for 2–3 minutes. Lift out with a slotted spoon and keep warm on a serving plate.

3 Add the remaining butter to the pan, increase the heat to high, then add the pork, a few pieces at a time. Cook the pork until browned on all sides, then remove from the pan.

4 Add the onion to the fat remaining in the pan and fry until golden brown. Stir in the coriander and flour and cook for 1 minute. Gradually add the cider and stock and bring quickly to the boil, stirring constantly. Return the pork to the pan, season to taste and simmer for about 5 minutes. Serve hot, with the green pepper and celery.

SWEET AND SOUR PORK

SERVES 2–3

	FOR THE SAUCE
350 g (12 oz) lean boneless pork	15 ml (1 tbsp) cornflour
15 g (½ oz) plain flour	10 ml (2 tsp) soy sauce
198 g (7 oz) can pineapple pieces	45 ml (3 tbsp) vinegar
15 ml (1 tbsp) vegetable oil	30 ml (2 tbsp) sugar
1 dessert apple, cored and sliced	150 ml (¼ pint) chicken stock
1 green pepper, chopped	

1 Cut the pork into 2.5 cm (1 inch) cubes, add to the flour and toss until coated.

2 Drain the pineapple, reserving 60 ml (4 tbsp) juice.

3 Heat the oil in a pan, add the pork and fry until lightly browned. Lower the heat and add the apple, pepper and pineapple pieces.

4 To make the sauce, put all the ingredients in a small basin and mix thoroughly, adding the reserved pineapple juice.

5 Add the sauce to the pork, bring to the boil, cover and simmer for 25–35 minutes or until the pork is tender. Serve immediately.

BARBECUED SPARE RIBS

SERVES 4–6

30 ml (2 tbsp) vegetable oil	2.5 ml (½ tsp) black pepper
1 large onion, finely chopped	2.5 ml (½ tsp) dried sage or rosemary
1 garlic clove, crushed	10 ml (2 tsp) mustard powder
150 ml (¼ pint) tomato purée	60 ml (4 tbsp) light soft brown sugar
45 ml (3 tbsp) lemon juice	100 ml (4 floz) beef stock
60 ml (4 tbsp) Worcestershire sauce	1.4 kg (3 lb) pork spare ribs, cut into serving pieces
2.5 ml (½ tsp) salt	

1 Heat the oil in a large saucepan, add the onion and garlic and cook for 5–10 minutes or until transparent.

2 Add the tomato purée, lemon juice, Worcestershire sauce, salt, pepper, sage or rosemary, mustard and sugar. Pour in the stock and simmer for 10 minutes, stirring.

3 Put the spare ribs on a rack in a roasting tin and pour the sauce over them. Roast in a preheated oven at 200°C (400°F) mark 6 for 1 hour or until crisp, basting every 15 minutes with sauce from the bottom of the pan.

——— TO MICROWAVE ———
Honeyed Spare Ribs

For an alternative sauce, mix together 100 g (4 oz) clear honey, 60 ml (4 tbsp) dark brown soft sugar, 60 ml (4 tbsp) tomato ketchup, 30 ml (2 tbsp) Worcestershire sauce, 30 ml (2 tbsp) prepared English mustard and 30 ml (2 tbsp) red wine vinegar. Roast the ribs for 30 minutes, then pour over the sauce and continue roasting until the ribs are tender and the sauce syrupy.

GOURMET PORK ROLLS

SERVES 4

350 g (12 oz) pork fillet (tenderloin)	4 slices Gruyère cheese
4 thin slices of lean cooked ham	salt and pepper
1 garlic clove, crushed	45 ml (3 tbsp) plain flour
30 ml (2 tbsp) pine nuts	15 ml (1 tbsp) vegetable oil
100 g (4 oz) fresh wholemeal breadcrumbs	200 ml (7 fl oz) dry white wine
50 g (2 oz) no-soak dried apricots, chopped	200 ml (7 fl oz) unsweetened apple juice
45 ml (3 tbsp) chopped fresh parsley or 15 ml (1 tbsp) dried	15 g (½ oz) butter
	apple slices and parsley sprigs, to garnish

1 Cut the pork into four equal pieces. Place between two sheets of dampened greaseproof paper and beat with a rolling pin or meat mallet to flatten to about 0.5 cm (¼ inch) thick. Lay a slice of ham on each escalope.

2 Mix the garlic, pine nuts, breadcrumbs, apricots and 30 ml (2 tbsp) fresh parsley or 10 ml (2 tsp) dried. Spread over each escalope and lay a slice of Gruyère cheese on top.

3 Roll up each escalope and secure with a wooden cocktail stick. Season 30 ml (2 tbsp) of the flour and use to dust the pork rolls. Heat the oil in a frying pan and cook the rolls for 5–7 minutes, turning frequently.

4 Pour in the wine and apple juice. Bring to the boil and simmer for 20–25 minutes or until the meat is tender.

5 Using a slotted spoon, transfer the rolls to a warmed dish. Remove the cocktail sticks and keep the rolls warm.

6 Increase the heat and reduce the liquor in the pan to about 150 ml (¼ pint). Mix the butter with the remaining flour and gradually whisk in until thickened. Stir in the remaining parsley, pour over the sauce and garnish.

STUFFED CABBAGE PARCELS

SERVES 4

350 g (12 oz) lean minced pork	16 large Savoy cabbage leaves
1 medium onion, finely chopped	40 g (1½ oz) butter
227 g (8 oz) can tomatoes	40 g (1½ oz) plain flour
salt and pepper	450 ml (¾ pint) milk
282 g (10 oz) can red kidney beans, drained and rinsed	50 g (2 oz) mature Cheddar cheese, grated
	pinch of cayenne

1 Put the pork in a saucepan and cook in its own fat until beginning to brown, stirring from time to time. Drain off excess fat.

2 Add the onion and fry until softened and lightly coloured. Add the tomatoes with their juice and bring to the boil, stirring. Season to taste, then simmer over a moderate heat for 20 minutes or until the pork is cooked and the sauce thick and well reduced, stirring occasionally. Stir in the kidney beans and remove the pan from the heat.

3 Blanch the cabbage for 3 minutes, in batches of four leaves at a time, in a large pan of boiling salted water. Drain the leaves, rinse and pat dry, then cut out and discard the thick central stalks.

4 Put 15–25 ml (1–1½ tbsp) filling mixture at the stalk end of each cabbage leaf. Fold the two sides inwards to cover the filling, then roll into neat parcels. Arrange, seam sides down, in a single layer in a well-buttered heatproof serving dish.

5 Heat the butter, flour and milk, whisking continuously, until the sauce thickens, boils and is smooth. Simmer for 1–2 minutes, then season. Pour over the cabbage parcels.

6 Sprinkle the parcels with cheese and cayenne and place under a preheated grill until golden brown and bubbling.

CANADIAN PORK AND VEAL PIE

SERVES 6

BAKED HAM

SERVES 8–10

50 g (2 oz) butter	about 25 g (1 oz) fresh breadcrumbs
2 large onions, finely chopped	60–90 ml (4–6 tbsp) chopped fresh parsley and thyme, mixed
450 g (1 lb) lean boneless pork	150 g (5 oz) frozen shortcrust pastry, thawed
450 g (1 lb) pie or stewing veal	225 g (8 oz) frozen puff pastry, thawed
150 ml (¼ pint) dry white wine or chicken stock	beaten egg, to glaze
5 ml (1 tsp) ground allspice	
salt and pepper	

1 Melt the butter in a large frying pan and fry the onions very gently for 10–15 minutes or until soft.
2 Meanwhile, cut the pork and veal into fine dice. Add to the onions and fry for 10 minutes.
3 Stir in the wine or stock, then add the allspice. Season, cover and cook for 30 minutes, stirring occasionally.
4 Remove the meat and onions from the cooking liquid and set aside. Boil the liquid in the pan to reduce slightly, then pour over the meat. Add enough breadcrumbs to absorb the liquid, then stir in the herbs. Leave to cool.
5 Meanwhile, roll out the shortcrust pastry on a floured surface and use to line a 23 cm (9 inch) pie plate. Pile the cooled meat mixture on top, doming it in the centre.
6 Roll out the puff pastry to a circle slightly larger than the first. Moisten the rim of shortcrust pastry with water, then place the puff pastry lid on top. Press to seal.
7 Decorate the top of the pie with pastry trimmings and make a hole in the centre. Brush with egg.
8 Bake in a preheated oven at 200°C (400°F) mark 6 for 30 minutes or until the pastry is golden brown. Serve hot.

1.8 kg (4 lb) middle gammon joint	1 bay leaf
2 medium onions, quartered	5 black peppercorns
2 medium carrots, thickly sliced	cloves
	demerara sugar, to glaze

1 Weigh the gammon and calculate the cooking time, allowing 20 minutes per 450 g (1 lb) plus 20 minutes. Place the gammon in a large saucepan and cover with cold water. Bring slowly to the boil, then drain.
2 Return the gammon to the saucepan. Add the vegetables, bay leaf and peppercorns, cover with cold water and bring slowly to the boil. Skim the surface with a slotted spoon. Cover and boil for half the calculated cooking time.
3 Drain the gammon and wrap in foil. Place in a roasting tin and bake in a preheated oven at 180°C (350°F) mark 4 until 30 minutes before the cooking time is completed.
4 Remove the foil and rind from the gammon. Score the fat in diamonds and stud with cloves. Sprinkle the surface with demerara sugar and pat in.
5 Bake at 220°C (425°F) mark 7 for 30 minutes or until crisp and golden. Serve hot or cold.

COOK'S TIP

Ham generally refers to the leg of a pig that is cured separately and sold cooked. However, this recipe uses a gammon joint, which is cured as part of the whole side of the pig and sold uncooked.

GLAZED GAMMON STEAKS

SERVES 4

15 ml (1 tbsp) soy sauce	garlic salt
2.5 ml (½ tsp) mustard powder	black pepper
15 ml (1 tbsp) golden syrup	15 ml (1 tbsp) cornflour
1.25 ml (¼ tsp) ground ginger	15 ml (1 tbsp) lemon juice
90 ml (6 tbsp) orange juice	8 bacon chops or 4 gammon steaks

1 In a small saucepan, combine the first five ingredients and add garlic salt and pepper to taste.

2 Blend the cornflour with the lemon juice, stir in a little of the mixture from the pan and then return it all to the pan. Bring to the boil, stirring all the time, until the mixture has thickened to a glaze. Remove from the heat.

3 Cut most of the fat from the bacon chops or gammon steaks and then brush half of the glaze on one side.

4 Cook under a preheated moderate grill for 15 minutes or until the meat is cooked right through, brown and bubbling. Turn several times and brush with the remaining glaze during cooking. Serve hot.

BACON CHOPS IN CIDER

SERVES 4

four 175 g (6 oz) bacon chops	15 g (½ oz) butter
15 ml (1 tbsp) prepared English mustard	25 ml (1½ tbsp) plain flour
25 g (1 oz) demerara sugar	salt and pepper
300 ml (½ pint) dry cider	chopped fresh parsley, to garnish

1 Put the chops side by side in a large ovenproof dish. Mix the mustard and sugar with enough cider to make a smooth paste. Spread over the chops and leave for 30 minutes.

2 Bake the chops in a preheated oven at 200°C (400°F) mark 6 for 15 minutes.

3 Meanwhile, put the butter, flour and remaining cider in a saucepan. Heat, whisking continuously, until the sauce thickens, boils and is smooth. Simmer for 1–2 minutes. Season to taste.

4 Pour the sauce over the chops. Bake for a further 15 minutes or until cooked. Serve garnished with parsley.

― **COOK'S TIP** ―

For a stronger cider flavour, use one third to one half more cider than the recipe states and reduce it by boiling to concentrate the flavour before using.

BACON AND LIVER ROULADES

SERVES 3–4

BACON CHOPS WITH GOOSEBERRY SAUCE

SERVES 4

4 rashers streaky bacon (about 100 g/4 oz total weight)	30 ml (2 tbsp) brandy
225 g (8 oz) lamb's liver	15 ml (1 tbsp) chopped fresh marjoram or oregano or 5 ml (1 tsp) dried
60 ml (4 tbsp) orange juice	salt and pepper

1 Cut the rind off each rasher and stretch the rashers with a blunt-edged knife. Cut each rasher across into three pieces.
2 Divide the liver into 12 even-sized pieces, removing any skin and ducts.
3 Roll a piece of bacon around each piece of liver and secure with a cocktail stick. Place in the base of a foil-lined grill pan.
4 Mix the orange juice, brandy, herbs and seasoning together and spoon over the bacon rolls. Leave to marinate in a cool place for at least 1 hour.
5 Cook under a moderate grill for 12–15 minutes, turning and basting occasionally. Remove the cocktail sticks before serving, replacing them with fresh ones if liked. Serve hot.

15 ml (1 tbsp) dark soft brown sugar	15 g (½ oz) butter
5 ml (1 tsp) mustard powder	1 large onion, chopped
pepper	150 ml (¼ pint) vegetable stock
four 175 g (6 oz) bacon chops	100 g (4 oz) gooseberries, topped and tailed

1 Mix together the brown sugar, mustard and pepper to taste and rub into both sides of the bacon chops.
2 Melt the butter in a large frying pan or flameproof casserole, add the onion and cook for 2 minutes, then add the bacon chops, half the stock and the gooseberries. Simmer gently for 15 minutes
3 Remove the chops from the pan. Purée the onions and gooseberries in a blender or food processor until smooth.
4 Return the chops and purée to the pan with the remaining stock. Simmer gently for 10 minutes or until the chops are cooked through and tender. Serve at once.

SAUSAGE YORKSHIRES WITH ONION SAUCE

SERVES 4

350 g (12 oz) pork sausagemeat	2 eggs
175 g (6 oz) cooking apple, peeled and cored	568 ml (1 pint) milk
	lard
5 ml (1 tsp) chopped parsley	175 g (6 oz) onions, sliced
salt and pepper	15 g (½ oz) butter
100 g (4 oz) plus 15 ml (1 tbsp) flour	

1 Place the sausagemeat in a bowl and grate in the apple. Stir in the parsley and season to taste. Work the ingredients together and form into 16 small balls.
2 Make a batter from the 100 g (4 oz) flour, the eggs, and 300 ml (½ pint) milk.
3 Put a little lard in the base of each of four 300 ml (½ pint) individual ramekin dishes and heat in a preheated oven at 220°C (425°F) mark 7 until sizzling hot. Divide the sausage balls between the dishes and cook in the oven for 10 minutes.
4 Pour the batter over the sausage balls and return to the oven for 35–40 minutes or until risen and golden.
5 Meanwhile, put the onion in a saucepan with the remaining milk, bring to the boil and cook until the onion is soft. To make the sauce, melt the butter in a pan, stir in the 15 ml (1 tbsp) flour and cook gently for 1 minute, stirring. Remove the pan from the heat and gradually stir in the onions and milk. Bring to the boil and continue to cook, stirring, until the sauce thickens, then season to taste.
6 When the popovers are baked, turn them out on to warmed serving plates and pour a little onion sauce into the centre of each. Serve immediately.

BACON AND APPLE PIE

SERVES 4

250 g (9 oz) plain flour	225 g (8 oz) cooking apples, peeled, cored and roughly chopped
salt and pepper	
100 g (4 oz) butter, diced	15 ml (1 tbsp) chopped parsley
225 g (8 oz) back bacon, roughly chopped	
	150 ml (¼ pint) medium-dry cider
1 medium onion, roughly chopped	1 egg, beaten, to glaze

1 To make the pastry, sift 225 g (8 oz) of the flour and a pinch of salt into a bowl. Rub in the butter until the mixture resembles breadcrumbs. Add just enough water to mix to a firm dough.
2 Gather the dough into a ball and knead lightly. Wrap the dough in foil and chill in the refrigerator for 30 minutes.
3 Meanwhile, combine the bacon, onion and apples in a 600 ml (1 pint) pie dish. Add the parsley and season to taste.
4 Blend the remaining flour with the cider, a little at a time, then pour into the pie dish.
5 Roll out the pastry on a lightly floured surface to 5 cm (2 inches) wider than the dish. Cut a 2.5 cm (1 inch) strip from the outer edge and use to line the dampened rim of the pie dish.
6 Moisten the strip of pastry, then place the lid on top and press to seal. Knock up and flute the edge.
7 Make a diagonal cross in the centre almost to the edges of the dish, then fold the pastry back to reveal the filling.
8 Brush the pastry with the egg. Bake in a preheated oven at 190°C (375°F) mark 5 for about 45 minutes or until the pastry is golden and the filling is cooked through. Serve the pie hot or cold.

BACON IN CIDER WITH SAGE AND ONION DUMPLINGS

SERVES 6

1.1 kg (2½ lb) smoked collar of bacon	50 g (2 oz) shredded suet
4 cloves	5 ml (1 tsp) rubbed sage
300 ml (½ pint) dry cider	25 g (1 oz) butter or margarine
1 bay leaf	2 medium onions, skinned
100 g (4 oz) fresh white breadcrumbs	salt and pepper
175 g (6 oz) self raising flour	parsley sprigs, to garnish

1 Place the bacon in a saucepan and cover with cold water. Bring slowly to the boil. Drain off the water. Pat the bacon dry.

2 Slice or peel off the bacon rind. Stud the fat with cloves.

3 Put the bacon in a shallow casserole with the cider and bay leaf. Cover tightly and cook in a preheated oven at 180°C (350°F) mark 4 for 2¼ hours.

4 Meanwhile, mix the breadcrumbs, flour, suet and sage together in a bowl. Rub in the butter. Coarsely grate in the onions. Bind to a soft dough with water, then add a little salt and pepper.

5 Shape the dough into 12 dumplings. Forty-five minutes before the end of the cooking time, add the dumplings to the juices surrounding the bacon. Cover again and finish cooking. Serve the bacon sliced, with a little of the cooking liquid spooned over, surrounded by the dumplings. Garnish with parsley sprigs.

LIKKY PIE

SERVES 4

225 g (8 oz) leeks, sliced	75 ml (3 fl oz) single cream
salt and pepper	2 eggs, lightly beaten
450 g (1 lb) lean boneless pork, cut into 2.5 cm (1 inch) cubes	212 g (7½ oz) packet frozen puff pastry, thawed
150 ml (¼ pint) milk	

1 Parboil the leeks in salted water for about 5 minutes. Drain well. Fill a 1.1 litre (2 pint) pie dish with the leeks and pork. Season to taste and pour in the milk.

2 Cover with foil and bake in a preheated oven at 200°C (400°F) mark 6 for about 1 hour. (Don't worry if it looks curdled.)

3 Stir the cream into the eggs, then pour into the dish. Allow the pie to cool.

4 Roll out the pastry on a lightly floured surface to 5 cm (2 inches) wider than the dish. Cut a 2.5 cm (1 inch) strip from the outer edge and use to line the dampened rim of the pie dish. Dampen the pastry rim with water, cover with the pastry lid and seal the edges well, then knock up and flute. Make a hole in the centre of the pie and use pastry trimmings to decorate.

5 Bake in a preheated oven at 220°C (425°F) mark 7 for about 25–30 minutes or until risen and golden brown.

SAUSAGE AND EGG PIE

SERVES 4–6

275 g (10 oz) frozen shortcrust pastry, thawed	150 ml (¼ pint) single cream or milk
3 eggs, hard-boiled	5 ml (1 tsp) chopped fresh sage or 2.5 ml (½ tsp) dried
10 ml (2 tsp) horseradish sauce	
225 g (8 oz) pork sausagemeat	salt and pepper
2 eggs, beaten	

1 Roll out two thirds of the pastry on a lightly floured surface and use to line a 20.5 cm (8 inch) flan ring placed on a baking sheet.

2 Shell the hard-boiled eggs and halve lengthways. Mix the horseradish sauce with the sausagemeat, divide into six and mould over the white of each egg half. Place yolk sides down in the flan case.

3 Reserve 10 ml (2 tsp) of the beaten eggs for glazing, then mix the remainder with the cream or milk and sage. Season to taste and pour into the flan case.

4 Roll out the remaining pastry and use to cover the pie, sealing the edges well. Decorate with pastry trimmings.

5 Brush the pie with the remaining beaten egg and bake in a preheated oven at 170°C (325°F) mark 3 for about 1 hour. Serve hot or cold.

CHIPOLATAS AND BEANS

SERVES 4

30 ml (2 tbsp) vegetable oil	430 g (15 oz) can red kidney beans, drained and rinsed
450 g (1 lb) pork chipolata sausages	
1 large onion, sliced	150 ml (¼ pint) beef stock
4 rashers of streaky bacon, chopped	salt and pepper
	chopped fresh parsley, to garnish

1 Heat the oil in a flameproof casserole, add the sausages and fry until browned on all sides. Remove the sausages from the pan with a slotted spoon and set aside.

2 Add the onion and bacon to the pan and fry for about 5 minutes or until they begin to turn brown, stirring occasionally.

3 Cut each sausage into four and return to the pan with the kidney beans and beef stock. Season to taste, cover and cook gently for about 15 minutes or until the sausages are tender. Serve hot, garnished with parsley.

TOAD IN THE HOLE

SERVES 3–4

450 g (1 lb) pork sausages	100 g (4 oz) plain flour
25 g (1 oz) lard or dripping	pinch of salt
225 ml (8 fl oz) milk	1 egg

1 Prick the sausages all over with a fork. Put the lard or dripping in a small roasting tin and add the sausages.
2 Bake in the oven at 220°C (425°F) mark 7 for 10 minutes or until the fat is hot.
3 Meanwhile, make the batter. Mix the milk and 50 ml (2 fl oz) water together in a jug. Put the flour and salt in a bowl. Make a well in the centre and break in the egg.
4 Mix the flour and egg together gradually, then add the milk and water, a little at a time, and beat until the mixture is smooth.
5 Pour the batter into the tin. Bake for about 30 minutes or until the batter is golden brown and well risen. Do not open the oven door during baking or the batter might sink. Serve at once.

VARIATION
Kidney Toad in the Hole

Skin, core and slice three lambs' kidneys and cook with the sausages before pouring in the batter.

ITALIAN LIVER

SERVES 4

350 g (12 oz) lamb's liver	30 ml (2 tbsp) tomato purée
salt and pepper	
25 g (1 oz) plain flour	1 garlic clove, finely chopped
40 g (1½ oz) butter or margarine	1.25 ml (¼ tsp) dried mixed herbs
450 g (1 lb) onions, thinly sliced	30 ml (2 tbsp) double cream
150 ml (¼ pint) beef stock	chopped parsley
300 ml (½ pint) milk	

1 Cut the liver into small pieces. Season the flour, add the liver and toss until coated.
2 Melt the butter or margarine in a frying pan and add the liver. Fry until browned on all sides, then remove from the pan and set aside.
3 Add the onions to the butter remaining in the pan and fry slowly for about 5 minutes or until soft. Gradually stir in the stock, milk, tomato purée, garlic and herbs. Bring the sauce to the boil, stirring continuously.
4 Add the liver to the sauce. Cover the pan and cook gently for 10–15 minutes or until the liver is tender. Adjust the seasoning to taste.
5 Replace the liver and sauce on a hot serving dish. Trickle the cream over the sauce, sprinkle with chopped parsley and serve immediately.

LIVER GOUJONS WITH ORANGE SAUCE

SERVES 4

350 g (12 oz) lamb's liver, sliced	300 ml (½ pint) lamb or beef stock
75 ml (5 tbsp) plain flour	juice and finely grated rind of 1 medium orange
salt and pepper	5 ml (1 tsp) dried sage
1 egg, beaten	a few drops of gravy browning
100 g (4 oz) medium oatmeal	60 ml (4 tbsp) vegetable oil
50 g (2 oz) butter or margarine	
1 medium onion, sliced	

1 Cut the liver into 5 cm (2 inch) pencil-thin strips. Put 45 ml (3 tbsp) of the flour in a bowl, season with salt and pepper, add the liver and toss until coated.
2 Dip the liver in the beaten egg, then roll in the oatmeal to coat. Chill in the refrigerator while preparing the sauce.
3 Melt 25 g (1 oz) of the butter or margarine in a saucepan, add the onion and fry gently for about 10 minutes or until golden brown. Add the remaining flour and cook gently, stirring, for 1–2 minutes.
4 Gradually blend in the stock, orange rind and juice and sage. Season to taste. Bring to the boil, then simmer for 10–15 minutes, stirring constantly. Add the gravy browning and taste and adjust the seasoning.
5 Heat the remaining butter or margarine and the oil in a frying pan, add the liver goujons and fry gently for 1–2 minutes or until tender.
6 Arrange the goujons on a warmed serving platter and pour over a little of the sauce. Serve the remaining sauce separately in a warmed sauceboat or jug.

LIVER IN STROGANOFF SAUCE

SERVES 4

450 g (1 lb) lamb's liver, sliced	450 g (1 lb) tomatoes, skinned and quartered, or 397 g (14 oz) can tomatoes, drained
salt and pepper	10 ml (2 tsp) dried sage
30 ml (2 tbsp) plain flour	150 ml (5 fl oz) soured cream, beaten
75 g (3 oz) butter or margarine	
225 g (8 oz) onions, thinly sliced	

1 Slice the lamb's liver into thin strips. Season the flour with salt and pepper, add the liver and toss until coated.
2 Melt the butter or margarine in a frying pan, add the onions and cook for 5–10 minutes or until lightly browned. Add the tomatoes, push to the side of the pan, then add the liver and cook over a high heat for about 5 minutes.
3 Sprinkle over the sage. Reduce the heat and stir in the soured cream.
4 Combine all the ingredients in the pan, taste and adjust the seasoning. Heat gently, but do not boil, and serve hot.

LIVER SAUTÉ

SERVES 5

LAMB'S LIVER AND MUSHROOMS

SERVES 3

salt and pepper	1 onion, thinly sliced
40 g (1½ oz) plain flour	300 ml (½ pint) beef stock
350 g (12 oz) lamb's liver, thinly sliced	15 ml (1 tbsp) tomato purée
30 ml (2 tbsp) vegetable oil	75 g (3 oz) frozen peas

1 Season the flour with salt and pepper, add the liver and toss until coated. Shake off and reserve any excess flour. Heat the oil in a frying pan and lightly fry the liver for 1 minute on each side. Remove the liver from the pan with a slotted spoon and keep hot.

2 Add the onion to the oil remaining in the pan and fry for about 5 minutes or until soft. Stir in any remaining flour and cook for 1 minute, then gradually add the stock. Bring to the boil, stirring constantly, and cook for 5 minutes.

3 Stir in the tomato purée, taste and adjust the seasoning. Return the liver to the pan with the frozen peas and cook for a further 5 minutes. Serve hot.

—————————— **VARIATION** ——————————
Kidney Sauté
Substitute 350 g (12 oz) lambs' kidneys for the liver. Skin, core and slice before tossing in the seasoned flour.

15 g (½ oz) butter or margarine	150 ml (¼ pint) beef stock
1 medium onion, sliced	4 tomatoes, skinned and roughly chopped
450 g (1 lb) lamb's liver, sliced	30 ml (2 tbsp) Worcestershire sauce
15 ml (1 tbsp) plain flour	salt and pepper
100 g (4 oz) button mushrooms	150 ml (5 fl oz) soured cream

1 Melt the butter or margarine in a large frying pan and gently fry the onion for 5 minutes or until soft.

2 Cut the liver into thin strips, add to the flour and toss until coated. Add to the pan with the mushrooms. Fry for 5 minutes, stirring well, then add the stock and bring to the boil.

3 Stir in the tomatoes and Worcestershire sauce. Season to taste, then simmer for 3–4 minutes. Stir in the soured cream and reheat without boiling. Serve hot.

—————————— **TO MICROWAVE** ——————————
Cut the butter into small pieces and melt in a large bowl on HIGH for 30 seconds. Add the onion, cover and cook on HIGH for 5–7 minutes or until softened. Coat the liver in the flour and add to the bowl with the mushrooms. Cover and cook on HIGH for 2–3 minutes or until the liver just changes colour, stirring once. Add the stock, tomatoes, Worcestershire sauce and salt and pepper, re-cover and cook on HIGH for 2–3 minutes or until boiling, stirring once. Stir in the soured cream and serve immediately.

CHICKEN LIVERS IN SHERRY CREAM SAUCE

SERVES 2

salt and pepper	75 ml (3 fl oz) sherry
25 g (1 oz) plain flour	50 ml (2 fl oz) chicken stock
225 g (8 oz) chicken livers, thawed if frozen	50 g (2 oz) black or green seedless grapes, halved
25 g (1 oz) butter or margarine	150 ml (5 fl oz) soured cream

1 Season the flour with salt and pepper, add the chicken livers and toss until coated. Shake off and reserve any excess flour.
2 Melt the butter or margarine in a medium frying pan and fry the livers with any remaining flour for about 4 minutes, stirring once or twice. Gradually stir in the sherry and stock and simmer for 1–2 minutes.
3 Add the grapes and soured cream. Heat through without boiling and serve hot.

――――――――― **TO MICROWAVE** ―――――――――

Complete step 1. Melt the butter or margarine in a large shallow dish on HIGH for 45 seconds. Add the livers with any remaining flour and cook on HIGH for 2 minutes, stirring occasionally. Gradually add the sherry and stock and cook on HIGH for 3 minutes, stirring occasionally. Add the grapes and cream and cook on HIGH for 1 minute before serving hot.

――――――――― **VARIATION** ―――――――――

If grapes are not available, substitute 25 g (1 oz) sultanas for the fresh grapes.

KIDNEYS IN BATTER

SERVES 4

225 g (8 oz) plain flour	1 large onion, very finely chopped
pinch of salt	350 g (12 oz) mushrooms, finely chopped
2 eggs	
568 ml (1 pint) milk	1 garlic clove, crushed
75 g (3 oz) butter or margarine	2 glasses of dry sherry
	150 ml (5 fl oz) double cream
8 lambs' kidneys, skinned, cored and chopped	salt and pepper

1 Sift the flour and salt into a bowl. Make a well in the centre, add the eggs and gradually blend in the flour. Gradually add the milk and whisk until smooth.
2 Melt 50 g (2 oz) of the butter or margarine in a frying pan; add the kidneys and onion and sauté for about 5 minutes or until the onion is transparent. Add the mushrooms, garlic and sherry. Cook gently for a few minutes, then add the cream.
3 Simmer gently until the sauce is reduced and thick, then season to taste.
4 Heat the remaining butter in an ovenproof dish in a preheated oven at 200°C (400°F) mark 6. Add the batter and pour the kidney mixture in the centre. Bake in the oven for 35 minutes or until the batter is crisp, golden and well risen. Serve at once.

KIDNEYS À LA CRÈME

SERVES 4

25 g (1 oz) butter or margarine	30 ml (2 tbsp) plain flour
8 lambs' kidneys, skinned, cored and halved	150 ml (¼ pint) beef stock
1 small onion, chopped	150 ml (5 fl oz) double cream
1 garlic clove, crushed	salt and pepper

1 Melt the butter or margarine in a frying pan, add the kidneys, onion and garlic and cook for 3–4 minutes or until the kidneys are evenly browned.

2 Push the kidneys to one side of the pan, stir in the flour and cook for 2 minutes, gradually adding the stock and cream. Stir gently and reheat without boiling.

3 Season to taste and serve immediately.

CREAMED KIDNEYS IN WINE

SERVES 4

25 g (1 oz) butter or margarine	25 g (1 oz) plain flour
12 lambs' kidneys, skinned, halved and cored	300 ml (½ pint) dry red wine
225 g (8 oz) mushrooms, sliced	5 ml (1 tsp) mustard powder
3 celery sticks, diced	salt and pepper
1 medium onion, finely chopped	150 ml (5 fl oz) double cream

1 Melt the butter or margarine in a medium saucepan. Add the kidneys, mushrooms, celery and onion and fry gently for 10 minutes or until tender.

2 Stir in the flour and cook for 1–2 minutes. Gradually stir in the wine and mustard, then season to taste. Cook for a further 5 minutes. Stir in the cream and reheat gently without boiling.

———————— TO MICROWAVE ————————

Melt the butter in a large bowl on HIGH for 45 seconds. Add the kidneys, mushrooms, celery and onion. Cook, covered, on HIGH for 10 minutes. Stir in the flour and cook on HIGH for 1 minute. Gradually stir in the wine, mustard and salt and pepper. Cook on HIGH for 3 minutes or until boiling and thickened, stirring occasionally. Stir in the cream and cook on HIGH for 30 seconds.

KIDNEY AND MUSHROOM SAUTÉ

SERVES 3–4

450 g (1 lb) lambs' kidneys, skinned, halved and cored	10 ml (2 tsp) whole grain mustard
15 ml (1 tbsp) vegetable oil	1 garlic clove, crushed
25 g (1 oz) butter	salt and pepper
225 g (8 oz) large flat mushrooms, sliced	chopped parsley, to garnish
30 ml (2 tbsp) single cream	

1 Cut the kidney halves in half again.
2 Heat the oil and butter in a large frying pan, add the kidney pieces and fry quickly until browned on all sides, turning frequently.
3 Stir in the mushrooms and cook for 1 minute, shaking the pan from time to time. Lower the heat and add the cream, mustard and garlic. Season to taste and heat through gently. Serve immediately, garnished with parsley.

CREAMED SWEETBREADS

SERVES 4

450 g (1 lb) lambs' sweetbreads, thawed if frozen	40 g (1½ oz) butter or margarine
1 small onion, chopped	60 ml (4 tbsp) plain flour
1 medium carrot, chopped	300 ml (½ pint) milk
a few fresh parsley stalks	a squeeze of lemon juice
1 bay leaf	chopped parsley, to garnish
salt and pepper	

1 Rinse and soak the sweetbreads in cold water for 2 hours. Drain and remove any fat.
2 Put the sweetbreads, vegetables and herbs in a saucepan with water to cover, season to taste, then simmer gently for about 15 minutes or until the sweetbreads are tender. Drain, reserving 300 ml (½ pint) of the cooking liquid, and keep hot.
3 Put the butter or margarine, flour, milk and reserved stock in a saucepan. Heat, whisking continuously, until the sauce thickens, boils and is smooth. Simmer for 1–2 minutes. Season to taste and add the lemon juice.
4 Add the sweetbreads to the sauce and simmer gently for 5–10 minutes. Garnish with parsley and serve at once.

COOK'S TIP

Sweetbreads, although considered a great delicacy, are not always readily available, so you may have to order them from your butcher. Soaking sweetbreads before use helps to keep them white.

CALF'S LIVER WITH GREEN GRAPES AND MADEIRA

SERVES 4

50 g (2 oz) butter	24 large green grapes, peeled, halved and seeded
50 g (2 oz) onion or shallot skinned and finely chopped	4 slices of calf's liver – each weighing about 75–100 g (3–4 oz), trimmed
175 ml (6 fl oz) chicken stock	
100 ml (4 fl oz) Madeira	4 sage leaves, thinly sliced
salt and freshly ground pepper	4 sage sprigs for garnish

1 Melt half the butter in a frying pan and fry the onion until golden. Add the stock and Madeira, season and bring to the boil. Boil rapidly for 4–5 minutes or until reduced and of a slightly syrupy consistency. Add the grape halves and warm through gently. Taste and adjust the seasoning.

2 Melt the remaining butter in a large frying pan. Season the liver, and fry with the sliced sage leaves for 3–5 minutes, turning once.

3 Remove the liver from the pan and serve at once with the Madeira sauce. Garnish with sprigs of fresh sage.

SWEETBREADS WITH MUSHROOMS AND WHITE WINE

SERVES 4

1½ pounds lambs' sweetbreads, thawed if frozen	2 tablespoons butter
	1 tablespoon olive oil
salt and pepper	½ pound button mushrooms, halved or sliced if large
1 onion, chopped	
1 carrot, sliced	⅔ cup heavy cream
1 celery stalk, sliced	4 teaspoons chopped fresh basil or 1 teaspoon dried
1 bouquet garni	
1¼ cups dry white wine	basil sprigs, for garnish

1 Soak the sweetbreads in salted water for about 4 hours to remove traces of blood. Change the water frequently until the sweetbreads turn white. Drain and rinse.

2 Plunge the sweetbreads into a pan of boiling salted water and blanch for 2–3 minutes. Drain and cool.

3 Peel off the skin from the sweetbreads, then cut away all gristle and stringy tissue. Slice thinly and put in a saucepan with the onion, carrot, celery and bouquet garni. Pour in the wine and season.

4 Bring to a boil, then lower the heat, cover and simmer for 10 minutes or until the sweetbreads feel tender. Remove the sweetbreads from the pan, discard the vegetables and bouquet garni, then boil the liquid to reduce to ⅔ cup.

5 Heat the butter and oil in a heavy-based skillet and sauté the mushrooms for 2 minutes.

6 Add the sweetbreads to the pan and toss to mix with the mushrooms. Pour in the cooking liquid and bring to a boil, stirring. Lower the heat and slowly stir in the cream. Heat through gently, then stir in the basil and season. Transfer to a warmed serving dish, garnish and serve.

BRAISED OXTAIL

SERVES 4

salt and pepper	15 ml (1 tbsp) tomato purée
30 ml (2 tbsp) plain flour	finely grated rind of ½ lemon
2 small oxtails (total weight about 1.4 kg/3 lb)	2 bay leaves
15 g (½ oz) butter	225 g (8 oz) carrots, thickly sliced
15 ml (1 tbsp) vegetable oil	450 g (1 lb) parsnips, cut into chunks
2 large onions, sliced	chopped parsley, to garnish
900 ml (1½ pints) beef stock	
150 ml (¼ pint) dry red wine	

1 Season the flour with salt and pepper, add the oxtail pieces and toss until coated. Shake off and reserve any excess flour. Heat the butter and oil in a large flameproof casserole, add the oxtail pieces, a few at a time and fry until browned. Remove with a slotted spoon.

2 Add the onions to the fat remaining in the casserole and fry for 5 minutes or until lightly browned. Stir in any remaining flour, the stock, red wine, tomato purée, lemon rind and bay leaves and season well. Bring to the boil and replace the meat. Cover and simmer for 3 hours, then skim well.

3 Stir the carrots and parsnips into the casserole. Re-cover the casserole and simmer for a further 30 minutes or until the meat is quite tender.

4 Skim all the fat from the surface of the casserole, remove the bay leaves, adjust the seasoning and garnish with chopped parsley.

ORANGE OXTAIL STEW

SERVES 4

2 oranges	30 ml (2 tbsp) vegetable oil
30 ml (2 tbsp) plain flour	1 onion, roughly chopped
10 ml (2 tsp) dried mixed herbs	2 celery sticks, sliced
salt and pepper	3 medium carrots, sliced
1.4 kg (3 lb) oxtail, cut into pieces	300 ml (½ pint) dry cider
	2 bay leaves

1 Cut the rind of one orange into thin matchstick strips with a cannelle knife. Blanch in boiling water for 2 minutes, then drain and reserve. Finely grate the rind of the remaining orange. Squeeze the juice from both oranges.

2 Put the flour in a large polythene bag with the herbs and salt and pepper to taste. Shake well to mix. Add the oxtail, a few pieces at a time, and shake until evenly coated.

3 Heat the oil in a large flameproof casserole, add as many pieces of oxtail as will fit on the base of the pan and fry over moderate heat until well browned. Remove with a slotted spoon and drain. Repeat with the remaining oxtail.

4 Add the onion, celery and carrots to the oil remaining in the casserole and fry gently for about 10 minutes or until softened, stirring frequently. Pour in the cider, add the grated orange rind and orange juice and bring to the boil.

5 Return the oxtail pieces to the casserole and pour in enough water to cover. Add the bay leaves, bring to the boil, then cover and cook in a preheated oven at 150°C (300°F) mark 2 for 3 hours. Cool, then chill overnight.

6 Next day, skim the fat from the casserole and remove the bay leaves. Simmer on the hob until heated through, taste and season. Garnish with the reserved orange rind.

POULTRY AND GAME

Chicken is always popular, whether cooked as a roast or as tender breast fillets in a flavoursome sauce; turkey is almost as versatile and the ideal choice for entertaining, at any time of year. Game, such as pheasant, rabbit and venison, makes a welcome change.

GOLDEN BAKED CHICKEN

SERVES 4

4 chicken portions	15 ml (1 tbsp) chopped fresh parsley and thyme or 5 ml (1 tsp) dried mixed herbs
salt and pepper	
50 g (2 oz) fresh white breadcrumbs	
1 small onion, finely chopped	50 g (2 oz) butter or margarine, melted

1 Wipe the chicken portions and season well with salt and pepper.
2 Mix the breadcrumbs with the onion and herbs.
3 Brush the chicken joints all over with the butter or margarine, add them to the herbed breadcrumbs and turn until coated. Place in a buttered ovenproof dish.
4 Bake in a preheated oven at 190°C (375°F) mark 5 for about 1 hour or until golden. Baste occasionally during cooking. Serve hot, straight from the dish.

STIR-FRIED CHICKEN WITH COURGETTES

SERVES 4

30 ml (2 tbsp) vegetable oil	1 red pepper, cut into thin strips
1 garlic clove, crushed	
450 g (1 lb) chicken breast fillets, skinned and cut into thin strips	45 ml (3 tbsp) dry sherry
	15 ml (1 tbsp) soy sauce
450 g (1 lb) courgettes, cut into thin strips	60 ml (4 tbsp) natural yogurt
	pepper

1 Heat the oil in a large frying pan or wok, add the garlic and fry for 1 minute. Add the chicken and cook for 3–4 minutes, stirring continuously.
2 Add the courgettes and pepper and continue frying for 1–2 minutes or until the chicken is cooked and the vegetables are tender but still crisp.
3 Stir in the sherry and soy sauce and cook for 1 minute or until hot. Stir in the yogurt and season to taste with pepper. Serve immediately.

CORNISH CAUDLE CHICKEN PIE

SERVES 4

50 g (2 oz) butter	150 ml (¼ pint) soured cream
1 onion, finely chopped	100 g (4 oz) puff pastry, thawed if frozen
four 100 g (4 oz) chicken legs, boned	beaten egg, to glaze
20 g (¾ oz) chopped parsley	150 ml (¼ pint) double cream
4 spring onions, chopped	1 egg, beaten
salt and pepper	
150 ml (¼ pint) milk	

1 Melt half the butter and cook the onion until soft. Transfer to a 1.1 litre (2 pint) dish.

2 Add the remaining butter to the pan, add the chicken and cook until browned. Arrange on top of the onion.

3 Stir the parsley, spring onions, salt and pepper to taste, milk and soured cream into the pan and bring to the boil. Simmer for 2–3 minutes, then pour over the chicken.

4 Cover the pie dish with foil and cook at 180°C (350°F) mark 4 for about 30 minutes. Leave to cool.

5 Roll out the pastry and use to cover the pie dish. Crimp the edges, make a small hole in the top and insert a funnel of aluminium foil.

6 Brush the top of the pie with beaten egg and bake at 220°C (425°F) mark 7 for 15–20 minutes or until brown. Reduce the temperature to 180°F (350°F) mark 4.

7 Beat the cream into the egg, then strain into a jug and pour into the pie through the foil funnel. Remove the funnel, shake the dish to distribute the cream and return the pie to the oven for about 5 minutes.

8 Leave the pie to stand in a warm place for 5–10 minutes before serving warm, or leave to cool and serve cold.

SPICED ROAST CHICKEN

SERVES 4

1.8 kg (4 lb) oven-ready chicken	5 cm (2 inch) piece of fresh root ginger, crushed
juice of 1 lemon	4 garlic cloves, crushed
10 ml (2 tsp) coriander seeds, finely crushed	5 ml (1 tsp) paprika
2.5 ml (½ tsp) chilli powder	5 ml (1 tsp) ground turmeric
300 ml (1½ pint) natural yogurt	5 ml (1 tsp) salt
60 ml (4 tbsp) chopped coriander	50 ml (2 fl oz) ghee or melted butter
60 ml (4 tbsp) chopped mint	coriander and mint sprigs and lemon wedges, to garnish

1 Prick the skin of the chicken all over with a fine skewer. Mix together the lemon juice, coriander seeds and chilli powder and brush over the chicken. Leave for 30 minutes.

2 Meanwhile, mix together the remaining ingredients, except the ghee or butter and the garnish.

3 Stand the chicken, breast side up, in a roasting tin. Brush with one quarter of the yogurt mixture. Roast in a preheated oven at 200°C (400°F) mark 6 for about 30 minutes or until the yogurt dries.

4 Turn the chicken over on its side and brush with another quarter of the yogurt mixture. Return to the oven for a further 30 minutes or until the yogurt dries again. Continue turning the chicken and brushing with yogurt twice more, until the chicken has been cooking for 2 hours.

5 Stand the chicken breast side up again, and brush with the ghee or butter. Increase the oven temperature to 200°C (425°F) mark 7 and roast the chicken for a further 15 minutes or until the juices run clear. Transfer to a warmed dish, garnish and serve.

STOVED CHICKEN

SERVES 4

25 g (1 oz) butter	2 large onions, sliced
15 ml (1 tbsp) vegetable oil	salt and pepper
4 chicken quarters, halved	10 ml (2 tsp) chopped fresh thyme or 2.5 ml (½ tsp) dried
100 g (4 oz) lean back bacon, chopped	600 ml (1 pint) chicken stock
1.1 kg (2½ lb) floury potatoes, such as King Edwards, peeled and cut into 0.5 cm (¼ inch) slices	snipped chives, to garnish

1 Heat half the butter and the oil in a large frying pan and fry the chicken and bacon for 5 minutes or until lightly browned.

2 Place a thick layer of potato slices in the base of a large ovenproof casserole and cover with a layer of onion slices. Season well, add the thyme and dot with half the remaining butter.

3 Add the chicken and bacon, season to taste and dot with the remaining butter. Cover with the remaining onions and finally another layer of potatoes. Season and dot with butter. Pour over the stock.

4 Cover the casserole and bake in a preheated oven at 150°C (300°F) mark 2 for about 2 hours or until the chicken is tender and the potatoes are cooked, adding a little more hot stock if necessary.

5 Just before serving, sprinkle with snipped chives.

CHICKEN THIGHS WITH SPICY TOMATO SAUCE

SERVES 4

15 g (½ oz) butter	8 chicken thighs
15 ml (1 tbsp) vegetable oil	397 g (14 oz) can tomatoes
1 medium onion, chopped	15 ml (1 tbsp) tomato purée
1 garlic clove, crushed	salt and pepper
5 ml (1 tsp) ground cumin	30 ml (2 tbsp) chopped fresh parsley
5 ml (1 tsp) ground coriander	
large pinch of chilli powder	

1 Heat the butter and oil in a large frying pan, add the onion and garlic, cover and cook for 4–5 minutes or until the onion is softened. Add the cumin, coriander and chilli powder and cook for 1 minute, stirring continuously.

2 Push the onions to one side of the pan, then add the chicken and brown on both sides. Stir in the tomatoes and the tomato purée and season to taste.

3 Bring to the boil, stirring continuously. Cover and simmer gently for about 30 minutes or until the chicken is tender. Stir in the parsley and serve immediately.

─── TO MICROWAVE ───

Put all the ingredients, except the butter, oil, chicken and parsley, in a large bowl. Cover and cook on HIGH for 10 minutes. Meanwhile, melt the butter and oil in a frying pan and brown the chicken on both sides. Add the chicken to the sauce, re-cover and cook on HIGH for 15 minutes or until the chicken is tender, stirring occasionally. Stir in the parsley and serve immediately.

SHREDDED CHICKEN WITH MUSHROOMS AND WALNUTS

SERVES 4

GINGERED JAPANESE CHICKEN

SERVES 4

four 100 g (4 oz) chicken breast fillets, skinned and cut into thin strips	45 ml (3 tbsp) vegetable oil
	100 g (4 oz) mushrooms, halved
5 cm (2 inch) piece of fresh root ginger, thinly sliced	¼ cucumber, cut into chunks
45 ml (3 tbsp) soy sauce	75 g (3 oz) walnut pieces, roughly chopped
60 ml (4 tbsp) dry sherry	
5 ml (1 tsp) five-spice powder	pepper

1 Put the chicken in a bowl with the ginger, soy sauce, sherry and five-spice powder. Stir well to mix, then cover and leave to marinate for at least 1 hour.
2 Remove the chicken from the marinade with a slotted spoon, reserving the marinade.
3 Heat the oil in a large frying pan or wok. Add the chicken and cook for 3–4 minutes, stirring continuously.
4 Add the mushrooms, cucumber and walnuts and continue to cook for 1–2 minutes or until the chicken is cooked and the vegetables are tender but still crisp.
5 Stir in the reserved marinade and cook for 1 minute or until hot. Season to taste with pepper. Serve immediately.

——— TO MICROWAVE ———
Complete steps 1 and 2. Put the chicken, oil, mushrooms, cucumber and walnuts in a large bowl. Cook on HIGH for 5–6 minutes, stirring frequently. Stir in the reserved marinade and cook on HIGH for 1 minute or until hot. Season to taste with pepper. Serve immediately.

1.4 kg (3 lb) oven-ready chicken	1 red pepper, sliced
15 ml (1 tbsp) plain flour	150 ml (¼ pint) chicken stock
15 ml (1 tbsp) ground ginger	45 ml (3 tbsp) soy sauce
60 ml (4 tbsp) vegetable oil	45 ml (3 tbsp) medium dry sherry
1 onion, sliced	salt and pepper
283 g (10 oz) can bamboo shoots, drained	100 g (4 oz) mushrooms, sliced

1 Cut all the flesh off the chicken and slice into chunky 'fingers', discarding the skin.
2 Mix the flour and ginger together in a polythene bag, add the chicken and toss to coat.
3 Heat the oil in a very large sauté or deep frying pan and fry the chicken and sliced onion together for 10–15 minutes or until golden.
4 Cut the canned bamboo shoots into 1 cm (½ inch) strips. Add to the pan, together with the sliced pepper, then stir in the stock, soy sauce and sherry. Season to taste. Bring to the boil, cover and simmer for 15 minutes.
5 Add the sliced mushrooms, cover again and cook for a further 5–10 minutes or until the chicken is tender.

——— COOK'S TIP ———
Bamboo shoots are used extensively in oriental cooking, although the Chinese and Japanese use fresh shoots rather than the canned version specified above. Canned bamboo shoots are available from specialist oriental food stores, large supermarkets and delicatessens. Look for those canned in water rather than vinegar as they have a milder flavour.

CHICKEN JULIENNE

SERVES 4

175 g (6 oz) long grain rice	100 g (4 oz) green beans, cooked
40 g (1½ oz) butter or margarine	pinch of dried thyme
40 g (1½ oz) plain flour	salt and pepper
300 ml (½ pint) chicken stock	15 ml (1 tbsp) chopped parsley
300 ml (½ pint) milk	100 g (4 oz) carrot, cut into julienne strips, blanched and drained
350 g (12 oz) cooked chicken, cut into long narrow strips	25 g (1 oz) flaked almonds, toasted
30 ml (2 tbsp) lemon juice	

1 Cook the rice in boiling salted water for about 10 minutes or until tender but not soft. Drain, set aside and keep hot.

2 Melt the butter or margarine in a pan, stir in the flour and cook gently for 1 minute, stirring. Remove from the heat and gradually stir in the stock and milk. Bring to the boil and continue to cook, stirring, until the sauce thickens.

3 Gently stir in the chicken, lemon juice, green beans and thyme. Season to taste and cook for 5–10 minutes or until heated through.

4 Add the parsley to the cooked rice and toss lightly. Make a border of rice on a serving dish and spoon the chicken into the centre. Sprinkle with carrots and almonds.

─────── **VARIATION** ───────
Turkey Julienne

This is a good recipe for using up leftover cooked turkey. Substitute the same amount of turkey for the chicken in the above recipe.

CHICKEN VÉRONIQUE

SERVES 4

50 g (2 oz) butter	300 ml (½ pint) chicken stock
15 ml (1 tbsp) chopped fresh tarragon or 10 ml (2 tsp) dried	150 ml (¼ pint) dry white wine
finely grated rind of 1 lemon	150 ml (5 fl oz) double cream
1 garlic clove, crushed	175 g (6 oz) green grapes, halved and seeded
salt and pepper	
1.4 kg (3 lb) oven-ready chicken	

1 Beat the butter in a bowl until soft, then mix in the tarragon, lemon rind and garlic. Season to taste. Put half the mixture in the cavity of the bird.

2 Truss the chicken. Spread the remaining butter mixture over the outside of the bird, then stand the bird on a rack in a roasting tin. Pour the chicken stock under the rack.

3 Roast the chicken in a preheated oven at 200°C (400°F) mark 6 for about 1¼ hours or until the juices run clear when the thickest part of a thigh is pierced with a skewer. Turn the bird and baste every 15 minutes.

4 Carve the chicken into neat portions, then arrange on a warmed serving platter, cover and keep warm.

5 To make the sauce, blot off any excess fat from the roasting tin with absorbent kitchen paper, then place the tin on the hob. Pour in the wine, then boil to reduce to about half, stirring to dislodge sediment.

6 Stir in the cream and continue simmering and stirring until thick, smooth and glossy. Add the grapes and heat through, then taste and adjust the seasoning.

7 Pour a little of the sauce over the chicken. Serve immediately, with the remaining sauce and grapes served in a warmed sauceboat.

CHICKEN WITH LEMON AND ALMONDS

SERVES 4

1.4 kg (3 lb) oven-ready chicken	450 ml (¾ pint) chicken stock
50 g (2 oz) blanched almonds	100 g (4 oz) button mushrooms, sliced
1 lemon, thinly sliced	15 ml (1 tbsp) cornflour
1 garlic clove	60 ml (4 tbsp) single cream
25 g (1 oz) butter, softened	watercress, to garnish
salt and pepper	

1 Wipe the chicken and loosen the skin all over the breast with your fingertips. Slip the almonds under the skin.
2 Stuff the lemon into the chicken cavity with the garlic. Truss or tie the bird securely.
3 Place the chicken in a roasting tin and spread the butter all over its surface. Season to taste. Pour the stock around the bird and roast in a preheated oven at 200°C (400°F) mark 6 for 1 hour, basting frequently.
4 Add the mushrooms to the roasting tin. Lay a piece of foil over the bird and continue cooking for a further 20 minutes or until the bird is tender.
5 Drain the bird and discard the lemon and garlic. Joint the chicken neatly so that each person has a breast and leg or thigh portion.
6 Blend the cornflour to a smooth paste with a little water and pour into the pan juices. Heat, stirring, until thickened. Add the cream and heat through without re-boiling. Adjust the seasoning and spoon over the bird just before serving. Garnish with watercress.

CHICKEN WITH APRICOTS AND BRANDY

SERVES 4–6

4 or 6 chicken breast fillets, with skin on	300 ml (½ pint) chicken stock
45 ml (3 tbsp) plain flour, plus extra for dusting	salt and pepper
	3 juniper berries (optional)
100 g (4 oz) butter	100 g (4 oz) no-soak dried apricots
60 ml (4 tbsp) dry white wine	1 bay leaf
15–30 ml (1–2 tbsp) brandy	4–6 thick round slices of bread
100 g (4 oz) bacon, chopped	150 ml (¼ pint) single cream
100 g (4 oz) mushrooms, sliced	fresh parsley, to garnish
100 g (4 oz) onion, chopped	

1 Dust the chicken with flour. Melt 40 g (1½ oz) butter in a frying pan, add the chicken and cook gently until browned. Transfer to a casserole. Add the wine and brandy to the pan, boil, then pour over the chicken.
2 Melt a further 40 g (1½ oz) butter in the pan and fry the bacon, mushrooms and onion for 5–10 minutes. Blend in 45 ml (3 tbsp) flour, then gradually stir in the stock. Season and add the juniper berries, apricots and bay leaf.
3 Pour the sauce over the chicken, cover and cook at 170°C (325°F) mark 3 for about 1½ hours or until tender.
4 Melt the remaining butter in the pan and fry the bread until crisp. Drain and keep hot.
5 When the chicken is cooked, remove from the casserole and keep hot. Remove the bay leaf, then purée the sauce. Add the cream, adjust the seasoning and reheat.
6 Arrange a chicken breast on each croûton and place on a warmed serving platter. Spoon over some sauce and garnish.

CHICKEN WITH MUSHROOMS AND BACON

SERVES 4

30 ml (2 tbsp) vegetable oil	300 ml (½ pint) chicken stock
100 g (4 oz) streaky bacon, chopped	400 g (14 oz) can chopped tomatoes
1 medium onion, chopped	1 bay leaf
1 garlic clove, crushed	salt and pepper
175 g (6 oz) button mushrooms, sliced	30 ml (2 tbsp) chopped parsley, to garnish
4 chicken quarters, skinned	

1 Heat the oil in a large saucepan, add the bacon and fry for 5 minutes or until crisp.

2 Add the onion, garlic and mushrooms to the pan and fry gently for 3–5 minutes or until the onion has softened. Add the chicken and fry for 8–10 minutes or until evenly browned, turning once.

3 Pour over the stock. Add the tomatoes with their juice and the bay leaf. Season to taste. Gradually bring to the boil, stirring occasionally. Simmer for 35–40 minutes or until tender.

4 Remove the bay leaf, transfer to a warmed serving dish and sprinkle with the chopped parsley.

TO MICROWAVE

Place the oil, bacon, onion and garlic in a large bowl, cover and microwave on HIGH for 5 minutes or until softened, stirring occasionally. Add the mushrooms, chicken, tomatoes, bay leaf and 300 ml (½ pint) boiling stock. Cover and microwave on HIGH for 20–25 minutes or until the chicken is tender and the juices run clear. Turn and rearrange the chicken portions twice during cooking. Complete step 4.

LEMON AND TURMERIC CHICKEN

SERVES 4

4 chicken breast fillets, skinned	300 ml (½ pint) milk
pared rind and juice of 1½ lemons	40 g (1½ oz) plain flour
1 onion, chopped	5 ml (1 tsp) ground turmeric, or to taste
2.5 ml (½ tsp) dried thyme	salt and pepper
150 ml (¼ pint) chicken stock	lemon slices and fresh parsley, to garnish

1 Place the chicken breasts in a roasting tin. Sprinkle with a few curls of lemon rind, the onion and thyme. Add the lemon juice to the stock and pour around the chicken. Cover with foil and bake in a preheated oven at 190°C (375°F) mark 5 for about 45 minutes or until tender.

2 Remove the chicken from the tin and keep warm. Strain the stock into a measuring jug and add the milk. Blend the flour and turmeric with a little of the milk and stock mixture in a saucepan, then gradually add all the liquid. Bring slowly to the boil, stirring constantly, until the sauce thickens. Season to taste.

3 Place the chicken on a warmed serving dish and pour over the sauce. Garnish with lemon slices and parsley.

CHICKEN WITH TARRAGON SAUCE

SERVES 6

75 g (3 oz) butter or margarine	5 ml (1 tsp) chopped fresh tarragon or 2.5 ml (½ tsp) dried
6 chicken breast fillets, skinned	45 ml (3 tbsp) grated Parmesan cheese
25 g (1 oz) plain flour	salt and pepper
450 ml (¾ pint) chicken stock	150 ml (5 fl oz) single cream
30 ml (2 tbsp) tarragon vinegar	tarragon sprigs, to garnish
10 ml (2 tsp) French mustard	

1 Melt 50 g (2 oz) butter or margarine in a frying pan, add the chicken, cover and cook gently for about 20 minutes or until tender, turning once. Drain.

2 Meanwhile, melt the remaining butter or margarine in a saucepan, stir in the flour and gradually add the stock and vinegar. Stir in the mustard, tarragon and cheese, then bring to the boil. Season to taste and simmer for 3 minutes.

3 Remove from the heat and add the cream. Heat gently without boiling. To serve, place the chicken on a warmed serving dish, spoon over the sauce and garnish.

CHICKEN WITH SAFFRON

SERVES 6

salt and pepper	30 ml (2 tbsp) dry white wine
30 ml (2 tbsp) plain flour	large pinch of saffron strands
six 175 g (6 oz) chicken breast fillets, skinned	2 egg yolks
40 g (1½ oz) butter	60 ml (4 tbsp) single cream
200 ml (7 fl oz) chicken stock	vegetable julienne, to garnish

1 Season the flour, add the chicken and turn until coated. Shake off and reserve any excess flour.

2 Melt the butter in a medium flameproof casserole, add the chicken pieces, half at a time, and fry for 5–10 minutes or until golden brown.

3 Return all the chicken pieces to the pan with any remaining flour and pour in the chicken stock and white wine.

4 Sprinkle in the saffron, pushing it down under the liquid. Bring to the boil, cover tightly and cook in a preheated oven at 180°C (350°F) mark 4 for about 50 minutes or until cooked

5 Lift the chicken out of the juices and place in a warmed serving dish. Cover and keep warm.

6 Strain the cooking juices into a small saucepan. Mix the egg yolks and cream together and stir into the cooking juices until evenly mixed.

7 Cook gently, stirring all the time, until the juices thicken slightly. Do not boil. To serve, adjust the seasoning of the sauce, spoon over the chicken and garnish with vegetable julienne. Serve immediately.

SPICED CHICKEN

SERVES 4

40 g (1½ oz) plain wholemeal flour	450 ml (¾ pint) milk
5 ml (1 tsp) curry powder	60 ml (4 tbsp) apple chutney
2.5 ml (½ tsp) cayenne	100 g (4 oz) sultanas
350 g (12 oz) boneless chicken, skinned and diced	150 ml (5 fl oz) soured cream
40 g (1½ oz) butter	2.5 ml (½ tsp) paprika
1 medium onion, chopped	

1 Mix the flour, curry powder and cayenne, add the chicken and toss until coated. Reserve any excess flour.
2 Melt the butter in a large saucepan, add the chicken and onion and fry for 5–6 minutes or until the chicken is brown and the onion is lightly coloured.
3 Stir in the remaining flour, then gradually blend in the milk. Heat gently, stirring continuously, until the sauce thickens, boils and is smooth.
4 Add the chutney and sultanas and simmer gently for 30–35 minutes or until the chicken is tender.
5 Remove the pan from the heat and drizzle with the cream. Sprinkle with the paprika and serve at once

─── TO MICROWAVE ───

Complete step 1. Cube the butter and melt in a large bowl on HIGH for 1 minute. Add the onion and cook on HIGH for 5 minutes. Add the chicken and cook on HIGH for 3–4 minutes, stirring occasionally. Stir in the flour. Gradually blend in the milk and cook on HIGH for 7–8 minutes, whisking frequently, until boiling and thickened. Add the chutney and sultanas and cook on MEDIUM for 12–15 minutes or until the chicken is tender. Drizzle with the cream. Serve at once.

CHICKEN AND REDCURRANT CURRY

SERVES 4

4 chicken leg joints	5 ml (1 tsp) chilli powder
350 g (12 oz) onions, roughly chopped	2.5 ml (½ tsp) ground turmeric
2.5 cm (1 inch) piece of fresh root ginger, finely chopped	30 ml (2 tbsp) lemon juice
2 garlic cloves, crushed	100 g (4 oz) redcurrant jelly
30 ml (2 tbsp) vegetable oil	200 ml (7 fl oz) chicken stock
10 ml (2 tsp) ground cumin	salt and pepper
10 ml (2 tsp) ground coriander	2 bay leaves
	coriander sprigs, to garnish

1 Cut the chicken legs into thighs and drumsticks. Remove skin and fat.
2 Put the onions, ginger and garlic in a blender or food processor and process until fairly smooth.
3 Heat the oil in a large heavy-based pan, add the onion paste and fry gently until golden. Add the chicken joints and fry until golden on all sides.
4 Add the cumin, coriander, chilli, turmeric and lemon juice. Cook for 5 minutes or until the chicken pieces are evenly coated with spices, then stir in the redcurrant jelly and stock. Season to taste, bring to the boil, add the bay leaves, cover and simmer for 45–50 minutes or until the chicken is tender.
5 Taste and adjust the seasoning, remove the bay leaves and garnish with coriander just before serving.

HONEY BARBECUED CHICKEN

SERVES 4

50 g (2 oz) butter	15 ml (1 tbsp) honey
100 g (4 oz) onions, finely chopped	salt and pepper
1 garlic clove, finely chopped (optional)	100 g (4 oz) long grain rice
	4 chicken drumsticks
397 g (14 oz) can tomatoes	grilled mushrooms and tomatoes and parsley sprigs, to garnish
30 ml (2 tbsp) Worcestershire sauce	

1 To make the barbecue sauce, combine the butter, onions, garlic (if using), tomatoes with their juice, Worcestershire sauce and honey in a saucepan. Season to taste and cook gently for 30 minutes.

2 Meanwhile, cook the rice in boiling salted water for about 10 minutes or until tender but not soft. Drain, set aside and keep hot.

3 Place the chicken drumsticks in the grill pan and brush liberally with the barbecue sauce. Cook under a preheated grill for 10 minutes on each side, brushing frequently with more sauce.

4 Serve on a bed of rice garnished with grilled mushrooms and tomatoes and sprigs of parsley. Serve the remaining sauce separately.

CHEESE AND ANCHOVY GRILLED CHICKEN BREASTS

SERVES 6

50 g (2 oz) can anchovy fillets in oil	6 chicken breast fillets, with skin on
30 ml (2 tbsp) finely chopped onion	vegetable oil, for brushing
5 ml (1 tsp) lemon juice	225 g (8 oz) Mozzarella cheese, sliced

1 Drain 15 ml (1 tbsp) of the oil from the anchovy can into a small saucepan. Chop the anchovies finely.

2 Heat the anchovy oil, add the anchovies and onion and cook for about 5 minutes or until a paste forms. Stir in the lemon juice, then remove from the heat and leave to cool.

3 Lift the skin from each chicken breast and rub 5 ml (1 tsp) of the anchovy mixture on the flesh underneath the skin.

4 Put the chicken pieces, skin side down, on to a rack placed over a grill pan. Cook under a preheated moderate grill for 35–40 minutes or until tender, turning once. Brush with oil occasionally during cooking, to moisten.

5 Cover the chicken breasts with slices of cheese and grill for a further 5 minutes, or until the cheese bubbles.

— **COOK'S TIP** —

If you find anchovies rather salty, soak them in milk for about 30 minutes, then drain before use.

CHICKEN SUPREMES IN WINE AND CREAM

SERVES 6

45 ml (3 tbsp) red wine vinegar	15 ml (1 tbsp) tomato purée
50 g (2 oz) unsalted butter	1 large garlic clove, crushed
six 175 g (6 oz) French-style chicken supremes (with the wing bone attached), wiped and trimmed of excess skin	150 ml (¼ pint) dry white wine
	300 ml (½ pint) chicken stock
	salt and pepper
1 small onion, roughly chopped	150 ml (5 fl oz) double cream
225 g (8 oz) tomatoes, skinned and roughly chopped	chopped parsley, to garnish

1 Place the vinegar in a small saucepan and boil to reduce by half. Heat the butter in a large sauté or deep frying pan. Add the chicken pieces and cook until browned well on all sides. Remove from the pan with a slotted spoon.

2 Add the onion, tomatoes, tomato purée and garlic to the butter remaining in the pan, cover and cook gently for about 5 minutes.

3 Add the wine and cook, uncovered, over a high heat for 5–10 minutes or until the wine reduces by half. Add the vinegar and stock, season to taste and bring to the boil.

4 Replace the chicken, covering it with the sauce. Simmer gently, covered, for about 25 minutes or until the chicken is quite tender. Lift the chicken out of the pan with a slotted spoon and keep warm.

5 Boil the sauce until it is reduced by half, then stir in the cream. Continue reducing the sauce until a thin pouring consistency is obtained.

6 Adjust the seasoning, pass the sauce through a sieve and spoon over the chicken just before serving. Garnish with chopped parsley.

CHICKEN KIEV

SERVES 4

100 g (4 oz) butter, softened	4 large chicken breast fillets, skinned
finely grated rind of ½ lemon	25 g (1 oz) plain flour
15 ml (1 tbsp) lemon juice	1 egg, beaten
15 ml (1 tbsp) chopped parsley	100 g (4 oz) fresh white breadcrumbs
1 garlic clove, crushed	vegetable oil, for deep-frying
salt and pepper	

1 Beat the butter until soft, then work in the lemon rind and juice, the parsley, garlic and salt and pepper to taste.

2 Place the butter on a sheet of non-stick or waxed paper and form into a roll. Refrigerate until firm.

3 Meanwhile, place the chicken breasts on a wooden board and pound them to an even thickness with a meat mallet or rolling pin.

4 Cut the butter into four pieces and place one piece on each of the flattened chicken breasts. Roll up the chicken, folding the ends in to enclose the butter completely. Secure with wooden cocktail sticks.

5 Season the flour with salt and pepper, add the chicken and turn until coated. Dip in beaten egg, then in breadcrumbs. Pat the crumbs firmly so that the chicken is well coated. Chill for at least 1 hour or until required.

6 Heat the oil to 170°C (325°F). Place two chicken portions in a frying basket and carefully lower into the oil. Deep-fry for about 15 minutes, then drain on absorbent kitchen paper while frying the rest. Serve immediately.

CHICKEN AND BROCCOLI PIE

SERVES 4–6

25 g (1 oz) butter	450 g (1 lb) boneless cooked chicken, cut into strips
2 carrots, diced	
8 button onions, skinned	175 g (6 oz) broccoli, blanched
100 g (4 oz) button mushrooms	grated rind of ½ lemon
25 g (1 oz) plain wholemeal flour	30 ml (2 tbsp) single cream
	salt and pepper
450 ml (¾ pint) milk, plus extra to glaze	225 g (8 oz) frozen puff pastry, thawed

1 Melt the butter in a large saucepan, add the carrots, onions and mushrooms and fry lightly for 8 minutes, stirring occasionally.

2 Stir in the flour and cook for 1–2 minutes. Gradually add the milk, stirring continuously, until the sauce thickens, boils and is smooth. Simmer for 3–4 minutes.

3 Add the chicken, broccoli, lemon rind and cream to the sauce. Season to taste and pour into a 1.1 litre (2 pint) pie dish.

4 Roll out the pastry on a lightly floured surface large enough to fit the dish. Cover the pie with the pastry and moisten the edges so the pastry is well sealed. Use any pastry trimmings to decorate. Brush with milk to glaze.

5 Bake in a preheated oven at 200°C (400°F) mark 6 for 25 minutes or until the pastry is golden brown.

CHICKEN POT PIES

SERVES 4

1 lemon	175 g (6 oz) button onions, skinned
1.1 kg (2½ lb) oven-ready chicken, with separate giblets	
	175 g (6 oz) button mushrooms, halved or sliced if large
a few sprigs of fresh tarragon	
1 bay leaf	45 ml (3 tbsp) plain flour
salt and pepper	60 ml (4 tbsp) double cream
2 leeks, sliced	368 g (13 oz) packet frozen puff pastry, thawed
2 large carrots, thinly sliced	
40 g (1½ oz) butter	a little beaten egg, to glaze

1 Prick the lemon all over with a skewer, then place inside the chicken. Put the chicken in a saucepan with the tarragon, bay leaf and seasoning. Add the giblets (except the liver), then pour in water to cover and bring to the boil. Simmer for 1¼ hours or until tender.

2 Thirty minutes before the end of cooking, add the leeks and carrots. Remove from the heat and leave to cool.

3 Remove the chicken from the cooking liquid. Cut the flesh from the bird, dice and set aside.

4 Melt the butter and lightly brown the onions.

5 Strain the chicken cooking liquid and reserve 300 ml (½ pint). Add the mushrooms, leeks and carrots to the onions. Fry gently for 1–2 minutes, then add the chicken.

6 Mix the flour to a paste with the cream. Gradually blend in the reserved cooking liquid, then add to the chicken. Season. Simmer, stirring, for 2–3 minutes, then turn into four 300 ml (½ pint) pie dishes.

7 Use the pastry to cover the pies. Brush with beaten egg. Bake at 200°C (400°F) mark 6 for 25 minutes or until the pastry is golden brown.

CORONATION CHICKEN

SERVES 8

2.3 kg (5 lb) chicken, cooked	juice of ½ lemon
25 g (1 oz) butter	4 canned apricots, drained and finely chopped
1 small onion, finely chopped	300 ml (½ pint) mayonnaise
15 ml (1 tbsp) curry paste	150 ml (5 fl oz) whipping cream
15 ml (1 tbsp) tomato purée	salt and pepper
100 ml (4 fl oz) red wine	sliced cucumber, to garnish
1 bay leaf	

1 Remove all the flesh from the chicken and dice. Discard all skin and bones.
2 Heat the butter in a small saucepan, add the onion and cook for 3 minutes or until softened. Add the curry paste, tomato purée, wine, bay leaf and lemon juice. Simmer, uncovered, for about 10 minutes or until well reduced. Strain and cool.
3 Sieve the chopped apricots to produce a purée. Beat the cooked sauce into the mayonnaise with the apricot purée.
4 Whip the cream until softly stiff and fold into the mixture. Season to taste, adding a little more lemon juice if necessary.
5 Toss the chicken pieces into the sauce and garnish with sliced cucumber.

DEVILLED POUSSINS

SERVES 6

15 ml (1 tbsp) mustard powder	15 ml (1 tbsp) lemon juice
15 ml (1 tbsp) paprika	75 g (3 oz) butter, melted
20 ml (4 tsp) ground turmeric	three 700 g (1½ lb) poussins
20 ml (4 tsp) ground cumin	15 ml (1 tbsp) poppy seeds
60 ml (4 tbsp) tomato ketchup	

1 Measure the mustard powder, paprika, turmeric and cumin into a small bowl. Add the tomato ketchup and lemon juice and beat well to form a thick, smooth paste. Slowly pour in the melted butter, stirring all the time.
2 Place the poussins on a chopping board, breast side down. With a small sharp knife, cut right along the backbone of each bird through skin and flesh.
3 With scissors, cut through the backbone to open the birds up. Turn the birds over, breast side up.
4 Continue cutting along the breast bone, splitting the birds into two equal halves.
5 Lie the birds, skin side uppermost, on a large edged baking sheet. Spread the spice paste evenly over the surface of the birds and sprinkle with the poppy seeds. Cover loosely with cling film and leave in a cool place for at least 1–2 hours.
6 Cook the poussins (uncovered on the baking sheet) in a preheated oven at 220°C (425°F) mark 7 for 15 minutes.
7 Remove the poussins from the oven and place under a preheated hot grill until the skin is well browned and crisp.
8 Return to the oven, reduce the temperature to 180°C (350°F) mark 4 and cook for a further 20 minutes or until the poussins are tender. Serve immediately.

BONED STUFFED POUSSINS

SERVES 6

ROAST TURKEY

SERVES 6–12

three 700 g (1½ lb) double poussins, boned (bones reserved)	175 g (6 oz) fresh white breadcrumbs
2 large onions, skinned	juice and grated rind of 1 lemon
1 carrot	2 eggs, size 6, beaten
1 bay leaf	pepper
6 black peppercorns	150 ml (¼ pint) dry white wine
salt	15 ml (1 tbsp) cornflour
100 g (4 oz) butter	a dash of gravy browning
175 g (6 oz) chopped nuts	
two 227 g (8 oz) packets frozen chopped spinach, thawed	

1 To make the stock, place the bones, one onion, quartered, the carrot, bay leaf, peppercorns and a little salt in a pan. Add 1 litre (1¾ pints) water and simmer, uncovered, for 30 minutes. Strain and reserve 600 ml (1 pint).
2 Chop the remaining onion. Heat 50 g (2 oz) butter, fry the onion and nuts for 2–3 minutes, then add the spinach. Cool slightly, then add the breadcrumbs, lemon juice and rind, egg to bind and seasoning.
3 Lay the birds flesh side up and divide the stuffing between them. Fold the skin over and sew up. Push a skewer through the leg and wing joints and tie the knuckle ends together. Place in a roasting tin and spread over the remaining butter. Pour over half the stock and the wine. Roast at 200°C (400°F) mark 6 for 1 hour.
4 Remove the skewers and string and cut each bird in half lengthways. Place on a serving dish. Mix the cornflour with a little water and add to the tin with the stock. Cook for 2 minutes, season, brown and serve.

2.7–3.5 kg (6–8 lb) oven-ready turkey, thawed if frozen	FOR THE HERB STUFFING
	3 large onions, skinned and chopped
1 onion, skinned	75 g (3 oz) butter
1 lemon wedge	175 g (6 oz) fresh breadcrumbs
butter	45 ml (3 tbsp) chopped fresh parsley
salt and pepper	salt and pepper
lemon juice	

1 Wash the turkey inside and out, and dry thoroughly.
2 To make the stuffing, fry the onion in the butter until softened, then stir in the remaining ingredients and mix well. Use to stuff the neck end only of the turkey. Fold the neck skin over and truss to secure.
3 Place the bird in a large roasting tin and place the onion, lemon wedge and a knob of butter inside the body. Spread butter over the turkey skin and season well with salt, pepper and a squeeze of lemon juice. Roast in the oven at 180°C (350°F) mark 4 for 2–3 hours. To test if the turkey is cooked, pierce the deepest part of the thigh with a skewer. If the juices that run out are colourless, the bird is cooked; if pink-tinged cook a little longer.
4 Transfer the turkey to a warmed serving platter and leave to rest before carving. Serve with gravy and bread sauce. Small sausages, rolls of bacon and watercress may be used to garnish the turkey. Cranberry sauce is also a traditional accompaniment.

ROAST TURKEY WITH LEMON STUFFING

3.6–5 kg (8–11¼ lb) SERVES 10–15; 5–6.8 kg (11¼–15 lb) SERVES 15–20; 6.8–9 kg (15–20¼ lb) SERVES 20–30

25 g (1 oz) butter	finely grated rind of 2 lemons
2 medium onions, finely chopped	salt and pepper
2 celery sticks, finely chopped	1 egg, beaten
225 g (8 oz) fresh wholemeal breadcrumbs	1 oven-ready turkey, thawed if frozen
60 ml (4 tbsp) chopped parsley	streaky bacon rashers

1 To make the stuffing, melt the butter in a large saucepan, add the onions and celery, cover and cook gently for about 10 minutes or until very soft, stirring occasionally.
2 Remove from the heat and add the breadcrumbs, parsley and lemon rind. Season to taste and stir in the egg.
3 Wash the inside of the bird and stuff at the neck end only before folding the neck skin over. Make the turkey plump and as even in shape as possible, then truss it with the wings folded under the body and the legs tied together.
4 Weigh the turkey and calculate the cooking time, allowing 20 minutes per 450 g (1 lb) plus 20 minutes.
5 Place the turkey in a roasting tin, then sprinkle with salt and pepper.
6 Place the streaky bacon rashers over the breast to prevent it from becoming dry. Roast in a preheated oven at 180°C (350°F) mark 4, basting occasionally. Put a piece of foil over the bird if it shows signs of becoming too brown.
7 Leave the turkey to rest for 10 minutes, then carve. Serve with the traditional accompaniments of thin gravy, bread sauce, small sausages and bacon rolls.

TURKEY BREAST WITH ASPARAGUS

SERVES 4

225 g (8 oz) thin asparagus stalks	300 ml (½ pint) chicken stock
two 225 g (8 oz) turkey breast fillets, skinned and halved	5 ml (1 tsp) chopped fresh sage or 2.5 ml (½ tsp) dried
30 ml (2 tbsp) plain flour	60 ml (4 tbsp) dry white wine
salt and pepper	150 ml (5 fl oz) soured cream
15 g (½ oz) butter	
15 ml (1 tbsp) vegetable oil	

1 Cut off the ends of the asparagus if they are tough and woody. Trim them all to the same length, cut off the tips and cut the stalks into three pieces.
2 Put the turkey pieces on a wooden board and beat out slightly with a rolling pin or meat mallet. Season the flour with salt and pepper, add the turkey pieces and turn until coated. Shake off any excess flour. Heat the butter and oil in a large frying pan, add the turkey and fry until lightly browned on both sides. Add the chicken stock, asparagus stalks, reserving the tips, the sage and wine, cover and cook gently for 15–20 minutes or until tender.
3 Five minutes before the end of the cooking time, add the reserved asparagus tips and the cream. Season to taste.

TURKEY ESCALOPES WITH DAMSONS

SERVES 4

two 225 g (8 oz) turkey breast fillets, skinned and cut widthways into 5 cm (2 inch) slices	5 ml (1 tsp) chopped fresh thyme or 1.25 ml (¼ tsp) dried
75 ml (3 fl oz) unsweetened apple juice	15 g (½ oz) butter
45 ml (3 tbsp) soy sauce	15 ml (1 tbsp) vegetable oil
45 ml (3 tbsp) dry sherry	225 g (8 oz) damsons, halved and stoned
1 small garlic clove, crushed	pepper

1 Place the turkey slices between two sheets of dampened greaseproof paper and beat out with a rolling pin or meat mallet until about 2.5 cm (1 inch) thick.

2 Place the turkey slices in a large shallow dish and pour over the apple juice, soy sauce, sherry, garlic and thyme. Cover and leave in the refrigerator to marinate for 3–4 hours or overnight.

3 Remove the turkey from the marinade, reserving the marinade. Heat the butter and oil in a frying pan, add the turkey and fry quickly until browned on both sides. Add the damsons, reserved marinade and pepper to taste.

4 Cover and simmer gently for 10–15 minutes or until tender, stirring occasionally.

─────── VARIATION ───────
Turkey Escalopes with Plums
Substitute plums for damsons in the above recipe if damsons are not available.

TURKEY ESCALOPES WITH HAZELNUT CREAM SAUCE

SERVES 4

450 g (1 lb) turkey breast fillets, thinly sliced	25 g (1 oz) hazelnuts, finely chopped
50 g (2 oz) butter	salt and pepper
60 ml (4 tbsp) sweet sherry	paprika, to garnish
60 ml (4 tbsp) double cream	

1 Place the turkey slices between two sheets of dampened greaseproof paper and beat out with a rolling pin or meat mallet into small escalopes.

2 Melt the butter in a frying pan and cook the escalopes quickly for 4–5 minutes, turning once. Remove from the pan and keep warm.

3 Reduce the heat and stir the sherry, cream and hazelnuts into the pan. Season to taste and cook, stirring, for 1 minute. Pour over the escalopes and serve immediately with a light dusting of paprika.

TURKEY ESCALOPES WITH CRANBERRY AND COCONUT

SERVES 4

450 g (1 lb) turkey breast fillets, skinned	1 egg, beaten
salt and pepper	15 g (½ oz) desiccated coconut
20 ml (4 tsp) Dijon mustard	40 g (1½ oz) fresh breadcrumbs
60 ml (4 tbsp) cranberry sauce	50 g (2 oz) butter or margarine
15 g (½ oz) plain flour	

1 Thinly slice the turkey breasts to give four portions.

2 Place the turkey pieces between two sheets of dampened greaseproof paper and beat out with a rolling pin or meat mallet to make thin escalopes. Season to taste, then spread each portion with mustard and cranberry sauce.

3 Roll up the escalopes, starting from the thin end, and secure with a cocktail stick. Dust each portion with flour, then brush with egg. Combine the coconut and breadcrumbs, then coat the turkey escalopes with the mixture.

4 Melt the butter or margarine in a frying pan, add the turkey portions, and fry until brown on both sides. Transfer to a baking tin just large enough to take the turkey in a single layer and baste with more fat. Bake in a preheated oven at 180°C (350°F) mark 4 for about 40 minutes or until the turkey is tender.

COOK'S TIP

Cranberry sauce is traditionally associated with turkey. Cultivated mainly in America, the fresh fruit have a limited season, but they can also be bought frozen or canned throughout the year. The sauce is available bottled, from supermarkets.

TURKEY SAUTÉ WITH LEMON AND WALNUTS

SERVES 4

450 g (1 lb) turkey breast fillets, skinned	60 ml (4 tbsp) chicken stock
30 ml (2 tbsp) cornflour	30 ml (2 tbsp) lemon juice
30 ml (2 tbsp) vegetable oil	45 ml (3 tbsp) lemon marmalade
1 green pepper, thinly sliced	5 ml (1 tsp) white wine vinegar
40 g (1½ oz) walnut halves or pieces	1.25 ml (¼ tsp) soy sauce
25 g (1 oz) butter or margarine	salt and pepper

1 Cut the turkey flesh into 5 cm (2 inch) pencil thin strips. Add to the cornflour and toss until coated.

2 Heat the oil in a large sauté or deep frying pan, add the pepper strips and walnuts and fry for 2–3 minutes. Remove from the pan with slotted spoon.

3 Add the butter or margarine to the oil remaining in the pan and fry the turkey strips for 10 minutes or until golden. Add the stock and lemon juice, stirring well to scrape up any sediment at the bottom of the pan. Add the lemon marmalade, vinegar and soy sauce. Season to taste.

4 Return the walnuts and green pepper to the pan. Cook gently for a further 5 minutes or until the turkey is tender. Taste and adjust the seasoning and serve immediately.

VARIATION

Turkey Sauté with Orange and Walnuts
Substitute 30 ml (2 tbsp) orange juice and 45 ml (3 tbsp) orange marmalade for the lemon juice and marmalade in the above recipe. Garnish with thin slices or wedges of orange.

CASSEROLED TURKEY IN RED WINE

SERVES 4

25 g (1 oz) butter	1 bay leaf
30 ml (2 tbsp) vegetable oil	150 ml (¼ pint) red wine
450–700 g (1–1½ lb) turkey casserole meat	salt and pepper
100 g (4 oz) lean streaky bacon, diced	12 small onions or shallots, skinned
30 ml (2 tbsp) plain flour	chopped fresh parsley and pastry crescents or croûtons, to garnish
good pinch of dried thyme	

1 Heat half the butter with half the oil in a large frying pan. When foaming, add the turkey meat and fry until well browned. Remove with a slotted spoon and place in a casserole.

2 Add the bacon to the fat remaining in the frying pan and fry until beginning to brown. Remove the bacon with a slotted spoon and add to the turkey.

3 Stir the flour, thyme and bay leaf into the fat in the frying pan and cook gently for a few minutes. Slowly stir in the red wine and 300 ml (½ pint) water. Season to taste. Bring to the boil, stirring, then pour over the turkey.

4 Cover the casserole tightly and cook in a preheated oven at 150°C (300°F) mark 2 for about 2 hours.

5 Thirty minutes before the end of the cooking time, melt the remaining butter and oil in a frying pan. Add the onions or shallots and cook slowly until golden brown and tender. Add the onions to the casserole, re-cover and cook for a further 20 minutes. Garnish with parsley and pastry crescents or croûtons and serve hot.

TURKEY IN SPICED YOGURT

SERVES 6

about 1.1 kg (2½ lb) turkey leg meat on the bone	30 ml (2 tbsp) lemon juice
7.5 ml (1½ tsp) ground cumin	45 ml (3 tbsp) vegetable oil
7.5 ml (1½ tsp) ground coriander	225 g (8 oz) onion, sliced
2.5 ml (½ tsp) ground turmeric	45 ml (3 tbsp) desiccated coconut
2.5 ml (½ tsp) ground ginger	30 ml (2 tbsp) plain flour
salt and pepper	150 ml (¼ pint) chicken stock
300 ml (10 fl oz) natural yogurt	chopped parsley, to garnish

1 Cut the turkey meat off the bone into large fork-sized pieces, discarding the skin. There should be about 900 g (2 lb) meat.

2 In a large bowl, mix the spices with the seasoning, yogurt and lemon juice. Stir well until evenly blended

3 Fold the turkey meat into the yogurt mixture, turning until coated. Cover tightly with cling film and refrigerate for several hours.

4 Heat the oil in a medium flameproof casserole, add the onion and fry for 5–10 minutes or until lightly browned. Add the coconut and flour and fry gently, stirring, for about 1 minute.

5 Remove from the heat and stir in the turkey with its marinade and the stock. Return to the heat and bring slowly to the boil, stirring all the time. Cover tightly and cook in a preheated oven at 170°C (325°F) mark 3 for 1–1¼ hours or until the turkey is tender.

6 Adjust the seasoning and serve garnished with parsley.

QUICK TURKEY CURRY

SERVES 4–6

30 ml (2 tbsp) vegetable oil	2.5 ml (½ tsp) chilli powder
3 bay leaves	salt and pepper
2 cardamom pods, crushed	50 g (2 oz) unsalted cashew nuts
1 cinnamon stick, broken into short lengths	700 g (1½ lb) turkey breast fillets, skinned and cut into bite-sized pieces
1 medium onion, thinly sliced	
1 green pepper, chopped (optional)	2 medium potatoes, blanched, peeled and cut into chunks
10 ml (2 tsp) paprika	
7.5 ml (1½ tsp) garam masala	4 tomatoes, skinned and chopped
2.5 ml (½ tsp) ground turmeric	bay leaves, to garnish

1 Heat the oil in a flameproof casserole, add the bay leaves, cardamom and cinnamon and fry over a moderate heat for 1–2 minutes. Add the onion and green pepper (if using), with the spices and salt and pepper to taste. Pour in enough water to moisten, then stir to mix for 1 minute.

2 Add the cashews and turkey, cover and simmer for 20 minutes. Turn the turkey occasionally during this time to ensure even cooking.

3 Add the potatoes and tomatoes and continue cooking for a further 20 minutes or until the turkey and potatoes are tender. Taste and adjust the seasoning before serving. Garnish with bay leaves.

TURKEY TETRAZZINI

SERVES 6

225 g (8 oz) spaghetti	1.25 ml (¼ tsp) grated nutmeg
75 g (3 oz) butter or margarine	salt and pepper
45 ml (3 tbsp) plain flour	100 g (4 oz) button mushrooms, sliced
300 ml (½ pint) hot turkey or chicken stock	350–450 g (12–16 oz) cooked turkey, sliced or cut into bite-sized pieces
100 ml (4 fl oz) double cream	
45 ml (3 tbsp) dry sherry	30 ml (2 tbsp) grated Parmesan cheese

1 Cook the spaghetti in boiling salted water for about 11 minutes or until just tender.

2 Meanwhile, make the sauce. Melt half the butter or margarine in a heavy-based saucepan, sprinkle in the flour and stir over gentle heat for 1–2 minutes. Gradually stir in the hot stock, then bring to the boil. Simmer, stirring all the time, until thick and smooth.

3 Remove the sauce from the heat and leave to cool for about 5 minutes, then stir in the cream, sherry and nutmeg. Season to taste.

4 Melt the remaining butter or margarine in a separate pan. Add the mushrooms and fry gently until soft.

5 Drain the spaghetti and arrange half of it in the base of a greased baking dish.

6 Arrange the turkey and mushrooms over the top. Cover with the remaining spaghetti, then coat with the sauce.

7 Sprinkle with the Parmesan and bake in a preheated oven at 190°C (375°F) mark 5 for 30 minutes or until golden and bubbling.

STUFFED TURKEY LEGS

SERVES 6

2 turkey legs (drumsticks) (at least 900 g/2 lb total weight)	25 g (1 oz) plain flour
	1 egg white, beaten
225 g (8 oz) pork sausagemeat	175 g (6 oz) fresh white breadcrumbs
15 ml (1 tbsp) chopped fresh tarragon or 2.5 ml (½ tsp) dried	100 g (4 oz) butter or margarine, softened
10 ml (2 tsp) chopped parsley	15 ml (1 tbsp) French mustard
salt and pepper	watercress, to garnish
50 g (2 oz) button mushrooms, sliced	

1 Skin the turkey legs, slit the flesh and carefully ease out the bone and large sinews.
2 Mix the sausagemeat and herbs, season to taste and spread one quarter of the mixture over each boned leg. Cover with a layer of sliced mushrooms, then top with more sausagemeat stuffing.
3 Reshape the stuffed turkey legs, then sew them up neatly, using fine string.
4 Dip the legs in flour, brush with beaten egg white and place, seam side down, in a greased roasting tin.
5 Beat together the breadcrumbs, butter or margarine and mustard. Spread over the tops and sides only of the legs.
6 Bake in a preheated oven at 190°C (375°F) mark 5 for about 1 hour 40 minutes or until the turkey is tender with a crisp, golden crust. Remove the string, slice, and serve garnished with watercress.

TURKEY BALLS WITH CRANBERRY AND ORANGE SAUCE

SERVES 4

15 g (½ oz) butter	FOR THE SAUCE
1 onion, chopped	50 g (2 oz) caster sugar
1 garlic clove, crushed	150 ml (¼ pint) fresh orange juice
30 ml (2 tbsp) chopped fresh thyme or 10 ml (2 tsp) dried	175 g (6 oz) fresh cranberries
350 g (12 oz) lean minced turkey	5 ml (1 tsp) grated orange rind
75 g (3 oz) fresh breadcrumbs	

1 Melt the butter in a small saucepan. Add the onion, garlic and thyme and sauté for 3–5 minutes, then leave to cool.
2 Place the turkey and breadcrumbs in a medium bowl, add the onion mixture and mix thoroughly.
3 Divide the mixture into walnut-sized balls and place on a lightly greased baking sheet. Bake in a preheated oven at 200°C (400°F) mark 6 for 30–40 minutes or until cooked through.
4 Meanwhile, to make the sauce, place the sugar and fresh orange juice in a medium saucepan and heat gently, stirring, until the sugar has dissolved. Add the cranberries and grated orange rind and bring to the boil. Cover and simmer for 5–10 minutes or until the cranberries have softened. Serve with the turkey balls.

TURKEY AND BACON KEBABS

SERVES 4

MARINATED TURKEY WITH ASPARAGUS

SERVES 4–6

30 ml (2 tbsp) cranberry sauce	salt and pepper
90 ml (6 tbsp) vegetable oil	700 g (1½ lb) boneless turkey escalopes
45 ml (3 tbsp) fresh orange juice	1 small onion
1 garlic clove, crushed	6 streaky bacon rashers, halved
2.5 ml (½ tsp) ground allspice	1 large red pepper, cut into chunks

1 Put the cranberry sauce, oil and orange juice in a shallow dish with the garlic, allspice and seasoning to taste. Whisk with a fork until well combined.
2 Cut the turkey into bite-sized pieces and place in the dish. Stir to coat in the oil and orange juice mixture, then cover and leave to marinate for at least 4 hours, stirring occasionally.
3 Cut the onion into squares or even-sized chunks. Form the bacon rashers into small rolls. Drain the turkey from the marinade, reserving the marinade.
4 Thread the turkey, onion and red pepper on to oiled skewers with the bacon, dividing the ingredients as evenly as possible.
5 Cook under a preheated moderate grill for about 20 minutes, turning the skewers frequently and basting with the remaining marinade. Serve hot.

COOK'S TIP

Don't be tempted to reduce the marinating time suggested above as the longer the turkey is marinated the more tender and succulent it will be. If marinating in the refrigerator overnight, allow the turkey to come to room temperature before grilling.

900 g (2 lb) turkey breast fillets	20 ml (4 tsp) ground ginger
900 ml (1½ pints) chicken stock	450 ml (¾ pint) French dressing
salt and pepper	450 g (1 lb) fresh asparagus, scraped and trimmed
30 ml (2 tbsp) chopped parsley	5 ml (1 tsp) salt
50 g (2 oz) walnuts, chopped	celery leaves, to garnish
1 garlic clove, crushed	

1 Put the turkey fillets in a large saucepan and add enough chicken stock to cover. Season to taste. Poach for about 20 minutes or until tender. Leave to cool in the liquid.
2 Meanwhile, to make the marinade, stir the parsley, walnuts, garlic and ginger into the French dressing.
3 Tie the asparagus stalks into two neat bundles. Wedge upright in a large deep saucepan and cover the tips with foil.
4 Pour in enough boiling water to come three-quarters of the way up the asparagus stalks. Add salt, return to the boil and simmer gently for about 10 minutes.
5 Lift the bundles carefully out of the water, place in a dish and remove the string. Whilst still hot, pour over half the dressing. Leave the asparagus to cool.
6 Cut the turkey into 0.5 cm (¼ inch) wide strips. Marinate in the remaining dressing for 3–4 hours.
7 To serve, arrange the turkey strips and asparagus in a serving dish and garnish with celery leaves. Serve chilled.

DUCKLING WITH GREEN PEAS

SERVES 4

ROAST DUCK WITH APPLE STUFFING

SERVES 4

2 kg (4½ lb) oven-ready duckling	450 g (1 lb) fresh or frozen peas
salt and pepper	few sprigs of fresh herbs, such as savory, thyme or mint
16 pickling or small onions, chopped	
50 g (2 oz) smoked streaky bacon, diced	60 ml (4 tbsp) chicken stock

1 Weigh the duckling, prick the skin all over with a sharp skewer or fork and rub with salt. Place the duckling on a wire rack or trivet in a roasting tin and roast in a preheated oven at 180°C (350°F) mark 4 for 30–35 minutes per 450 g (1 lb).
2 Thirty minutes before the end of the cooking time, drain off the fat from the roasting tin, transferring 30 ml (2 tbsp) of it to a saucepan, and discarding the remainder. Add the onions to the pan and cook, turning frequently, until lightly browned. Add the bacon and cook for 2 minutes or until the fat starts to run.
3 If using fresh peas, blanch them for 3 minutes in boiling water, then refresh and drain well. Do not blanch frozen peas. Mix the peas with the onions, bacon and herbs and season to taste with pepper.
4 Stir the stock into the sediment in the roasting tin, then stir in the pea mixture. Return the duckling to the roasting tin, still on the rack, and continue cooking for the remaining 30 minutes. Serve the duckling on a larger platter surrounded by the vegetables and cooking juice.

15 g (½ oz) butter	salt and pepper
1 celery stick, finely chopped	1 egg, beaten
2 small onions, chopped	1.8 kg (4 lb) oven-ready duck (with separate giblets)
100 g (4 oz) fresh white breadcrumbs	1 bay leaf
1 small eating apple, peeled, cored and grated	15 ml (1 tbsp) plain flour
15 ml (1 tbsp) chopped fresh sage or 5 ml (1 tsp) dried	watercress, to garnish

1 Melt the butter in a saucepan, add the celery and half the chopped onions and fry gently for about 5 minutes.
2 Mix the breadcrumbs, apple, sage, celery and onion. Season, then bind with egg. Cool for 15 minutes.
3 Stuff the neck cavity of the duck with the apple stuffing, then sew or truss the duck to keep in the stuffing.
4 Weigh the stuffed duck and calculate the cooking time, allowing 30–35 minutes per 450 g (1 lb). Put the duck on a wire rack in a roasting tin. Prick the skin of the duck all over and sprinkle with salt and pepper. Roast at 180°C (350°F) mark 4 for the calculated time.
5 To make the gravy, put the giblets in a saucepan with the remaining onion, 600 ml (1 pint) water, the bay leaf and seasoning. Simmer for 1 hour, then strain.
6 When the duck is cooked, remove from the tin and keep warm. Pour off any excess fat from the tin, leaving about 30 ml (2 tbsp). Transfer to the hob and blend in the flour. Cook until browned, stirring continuously. Stir in the stock and boil, stirring. Taste and season.
7 To serve, joint the duck into four portions and arrange on a warmed dish. Pour gravy round, garnish and serve.

DUCKLING ROULADES WITH PEACHES

SERVES 6

six 350 g (12 oz) duckling wing portions, skinned	25 g (1 oz) chopped hazelnuts
slices of onion and carrot	2 firm, ripe peaches, skinned and chopped
1 bay leaf	30 ml (2 tbsp) brandy
salt and pepper	50 g (2 oz) fresh wholemeal breadcrumbs
65 g (2½ oz) butter	
1 small onion, finely chopped	30 ml (2 tbsp) plain flour

1 Carefully fillet the duckling flesh in one piece away from the breastbone. Place the breast meat between two sheets of dampened greaseproof paper and beat out thinly. Cut any meat off the wings, chop finely and set aside.

2 To make the stock, place the wing bones in a saucepan together with the slices of onion and carrot, the bay leaf and seasoning. Just cover with water and bring to the boil. Simmer, uncovered, for 30–40 minutes or until about 300 ml (½ pint) stock remains. Strain the stock.

3 To make the stuffing, melt 25 g (1 oz) butter in a frying pan and fry the onion, chopped duckling flesh and hazelnuts for 3–4 minutes, turning frequently. Stir in the peaches and fry until soft. Remove from the heat, stir in the brandy, breadcrumbs and seasoning, and cool.

4 Divide the stuffing between the duckling fillets and roll up tightly. Secure with wooden cocktail sticks, then sprinkle with flour.

5 Melt the remaining butter in a large flameproof casserole and cook the duckling rolls until lightly browned. Sprinkle in any remaining flour, then pour in 300 ml (½ pint) stock. Season to taste. Bring to the boil, cover and bake in the oven at 180°C (350°F) mark 4 for 40 minutes. Adjust the seasoning and skim before serving.

DUCKLING WITH BRANDY AND GREEN PEPPERCORN SAUCE

SERVES 6

6 duckling portions	30 ml (2 tbsp) plain flour
salt and pepper	300 ml (½ pint) chicken stock
3 large oranges	
45 ml (3 tbsp) vegetable oil	30 ml (2 tbsp) brandy
1 onion, chopped	a dash of gravy browning
30 ml (2 tbsp) green peppercorns, lightly crushed	

1 Wipe the duckling portions all over and pat dry with absorbent kitchen paper. Place on a rack in a roasting tin.

2 Prick the skin well with a fork and sprinkle with salt. Roast in a preheated oven at 180°C (350°F) mark 4 for about 1 hour or until the juices run clear, basting occasionally.

3 Meanwhile, to make the sauce, remove the rind from one orange and cut it into fine shreds. Blanch in boiling water for 1 minute, then drain. Squeeze the juice from the orange and reserve. Thinly slice the remaining oranges.

4 Heat the oil in a medium saucepan, add the chopped onion and fry gently until golden.

5 Stir in the lightly crushed peppercorns and flour and cook gently, stirring, for 1–2 minutes. Blend in the stock with the orange juice. Season to taste and bring to the boil, stirring all the time, then simmer for about 4 minutes.

6 Warm the brandy slightly in a small saucepan, ignite and, when the flames die down, add to the sauce with a dash of gravy browning and a few orange shreds. Adjust the seasoning.

7 Heat the sauce to boiling point and pour into a warmed sauceboat. Garnish the duck portions with orange slices and the remaining orange shreds.

DUCK WITH CUMBERLAND SAUCE

SERVES 4

4 duckling portions	60 ml (4 tbsp) redcurrant jelly
salt and pepper	10 ml (2 tsp) cornflour
finely shredded rind and juice of 1 large orange	60 ml (4 tbsp) port
finely shredded rind and juice of 1 lemon	30 ml (2 tbsp) brandy
	lemon balm sprigs, to garnish

1   Prick the duckling portions all over with a sharp skewer or fork, then sprinkle with salt and pepper.

2   Place the duckling portions on a wire rack in a roasting tin and roast in a preheated oven at 190°C (375°F) mark 5 for 45–60 minutes or until the skin is crisp and the juices run clear when the thickest parts of the duckling portions are pricked with a skewer.

3   Meanwhile, to make the sauce, put the orange and lemon juices in a small saucepan, add the shreds of orange and lemon rind, cover and simmer gently for 5 minutes.

4   Add the redcurrant jelly to the citrus juices and let it melt slowly over a gentle heat. Mix the cornflour with the port, then stir into the sauce and bring to the boil, stirring, until the sauce thickens.

5   When the duckling portions are cooked, put them on a warmed serving dish and keep hot while you finish the sauce. Pour off the fat from the roasting tin, leaving the cooking juices behind. Add the brandy and stir over a gentle heat, scraping up the sediment from the bottom of the tin.

6   Add the sauce to the brandy, stir well and serve with the duckling. Garnish with lemon balm.

DUCK JULIENNE EN CROÛTE

SERVES 4

25 g (1 oz) butter	175 g (6 oz) carrots, peeled
2 garlic cloves, crushed	2 courgettes
30 ml (2 tbsp) chopped fresh parsley or 10 ml (2 tsp) dried	450 g (1 lb) frozen puff pastry, thawed
four 200 g (7 oz) duck breasts, boned and skinned	salt and pepper
	1 egg, beaten

1   Melt the butter in a large frying pan, add the garlic and parsley and fry for 2 minutes. Add the duck breasts and fry until browned. Drain and cool.

2   Cut the carrots and courgettes into thin 5 cm (2 inch) strips. Blanch in boiling water for 1–2 minutes, then drain and rinse under cold running water.

3   Roll out one third of the pastry to a 40.5 x 15 cm (16 x 6 inch) rectangle. Divide into four 10 x 15 cm (4 x 6 inch) bases and place on a lightly greased baking sheet. Roll the remaining two thirds to a 51 x 15 cm (20 x 6 inch) rectangle. Divide into four 12.5 x 15 cm (5 x 6 inch) lids.

4   Divide the vegetables between the bases, leaving 0.5 cm (¼ inch) border. Place the duck breasts on the vegetables and season well. Brush the border with egg. Add the lids and seal.

5   Brush with beaten egg and bake in a preheated oven at 200°C (400°F) mark 6 for 45–55 minutes.

─── **TO MICROWAVE** ───

Complete step 1. Cut the carrots and courgettes into thin 5 cm (2 inch) strips. Place in a medium bowl and cover with boiling water. Cook on HIGH for 1–1½ minutes, drain and rinse under cold running water. Complete steps 3–5.

DUCK WITH MANGO

SERVES 4

1 ripe, but still firm mango	2.5 ml (½ tsp) ground allspice
four 275 g (10 oz) duck portions	45 ml (3 tbsp) plum jam
60 ml (4 tbsp) peanut oil	20 ml (4 tsp) wine vinegar
	salt and pepper

1 Skin and thickly slice the mango on either side of the large central stone.

2 Remove any excess fat from the duck portions. Divide each portion into three and place in a saucepan. Cover with cold water and bring to the boil. Lower the heat and simmer gently for 15–20 minutes. Drain well and pat dry with absorbent kitchen paper. Trim the bones.

3 Heat the oil in a wok or large frying pan until hot and smoking. Add the duck pieces and allspice and cook until well browned on all sides.

4 Stir in the jam and vinegar. Cook for a further 2–3 minutes, stirring constantly, until well glazed. Stir in the mango slices and season to taste. Heat through, then turn into a warmed serving dish and serve immediately.

-------------- VARIATION --------------
Tropical Duck
Other tropical fruits could be used instead of the mango in the above recipe. Try guava, papaya or lychees.

SWEET AND SOUR DUCK JOINTS

SERVES 4

4 duck portions	30 ml (2 tbsp) dry sherry
salt and pepper	juice of 1 orange
60 ml (4 tbsp) soy sauce	2.5 ml (½ tsp) ground ginger
45 ml (3 tbsp) soft brown sugar	a few orange slices and watercress sprigs, to garnish
45 ml (3 tbsp) honey	
45 ml (3 tbsp) wine or cider vinegar	

1 Prick the duck portions all over with a fork, then sprinkle the skin liberally with salt and pepper.

2 Place on a rack in a roasting tin and roast in a preheated oven at 190°C (375°F) mark 5 for 45–60 minutes or until the skin is crisp and the juices run clear when the thickest part of each joint is pierced with a skewer.

3 Meanwhile, to make the sauce, mix together all the remaining ingredients in a saucepan, add 150 ml (¼ pint) water and bring to the boil. Simmer, stirring constantly, for about 5 minutes to allow the flavours to blend and the sauce to thicken slightly. Add salt and pepper to taste.

4 Trim the duck joints neatly by cutting off any knuckles or wing joints. Arrange the duck on a warmed serving platter and coat with some of the sauce. Garnish with orange and watercress.

RABBIT CASSEROLE WITH SAGE DUMPLINGS

SERVES 4

100 g (4 oz) bacon	600 ml (1 pint) chicken stock
4 rabbit portions	salt and pepper
4 celery sticks, chopped	75 g (3 oz) self-raising flour
2 leeks, sliced	40 g (1½ oz) shredded beef suet
1 bay leaf	
225 g (8 oz) carrots, sliced	5 ml (1 tsp) chopped fresh sage or 2.5 ml (½ tsp) dried
30 ml (2 tbsp) plain flour	

1 Using a sharp pair of kitchen scissors, snip the bacon into a flameproof casserole. Fry for 5 minutes or until the fat runs. Add the rabbit and fry gently, then add the celery, leeks, bay leaf and carrots.

2 Sprinkle over the plain flour and stir well, then gradually add the stock and bring to the boil, stirring. Season to taste.

3 Cover the casserole and cook in a preheated oven at 170°C (325°F) mark 3 for about 1½ hours or until the rabbit is tender.

4 To make the dumplings, combine the self-raising flour, shredded suet, sage and salt and pepper in a bowl. Stir in just enough water to mix to a soft dough.

5 Divide the dough into four portions, then shape evenly into balls and place on top of casserole. Re-cover and cook for 20–25 minutes or until the dumplings are well risen and cooked through.

RABBIT CASSEROLE WITH CIDER AND MUSTARD

SERVES 4

50 g (2oz) butter or margarine	25 g (1 oz) plain flour
100 g (4 oz) streaky bacon, diced	1 rabbit, jointed
12–18 small button onions, skinned	10 ml (2 tsp) French mustard
salt and pepper	300 ml (½ pint) dry cider
	450 ml (¾ pint) chicken stock

1 Melt the butter or margarine in a frying pan, add the bacon and onions and fry for 5 minutes or until lightly browned. Remove to a casserole with a slotted spoon.

2 Season the flour with salt and pepper, add the rabbit portions and turn until coated. Shake off and reserve any excess flour. Add the rabbit to the fat remaining in the pan and fry for about 8 minutes or until golden brown. Arrange in the casserole.

3 Stir the remaining flour and the French mustard into the pan. Gradually add the cider and stock, season to taste, then bring to the boil and pour over the rabbit.

4 Cover and cook in a preheated oven at 170°C (325°F) mark 3 for about 2 hours or until the rabbit is tender. Adjust the seasoning before serving.

COOK'S TIP

Small button onions can be very fiddly to skin. Soak them in boiling water for 1–2 minutes first, then the skins should slip off easily. Leave the root ends intact so the onions stay whole during cooking.

GAME PIE

SERVES 4–6

450 g (1 lb) boned game (pigeon, venison, partridge, hare or pheasant)	45 ml (3 tbsp) vegetable oil
30 ml (2 tbsp) plain flour	300 ml (½ pint) red wine
10 ml (2 tsp) dried thyme	6 juniper berries, lightly crushed
2.5 ml (½ tsp) ground cinnamon	350 g (12 oz) pork sausagemeat
salt and pepper	225 g (8 oz) packet frozen puff pastry, thawed
	1 egg, beaten, to glaze

1 Cut the meat into even-sized cubes. Mix the flour with the thyme, cinnamon and seasoning, add the meat and toss until coated.

2 Heat the oil in a flameproof casserole, add the meat and fry over a moderate heat for 5 minutes or until browned on all sides. Pour in the wine, add the juniper berries, then cover and simmer gently for 1–1½ hours or until tender. Leave until cold, preferably overnight.

3 Put half the sausagemeat in the bottom of an ovenproof pie dish. Put the game mixture on top, then cover with the remaining sausagemeat and level the surface.

4 Roll out the pastry on a lightly floured surface to 5 cm, (2 inches) wider than the pie dish. Cut a 2.5 cm (1 inch) strip from the outer edge and use to line the dampened rim of the dish.

5 Moisten the strip of dough, then place the pastry lid on top and press to seal. Knock up and flute the edge. Use pastry trimmings to decorate.

6 Brush the pastry with beaten egg, then bake in a preheated oven at 200°C (400°F) mark 6 for 30 minutes or until the pastry is golden brown and crisp. Leave to stand for 15 minutes before serving, or serve cold.

ROAST PHEASANT WITH HERBY FORCEMEAT BALLS

SERVES 4

2 young oven-ready pheasants	finely grated rind of ½ lemon
150 g (5 oz) butter	25 g (1 oz) shredded beef suet
10 ml (2 tsp) dried thyme	15 ml (1 tbsp) chopped fresh parsley
salt and pepper	15 ml (1 tbsp) chopped fresh lemon thyme or 10 ml (2 tsp) dried
4 rashers of smoked streaky bacon	
450 ml (¾ pint) giblet or chicken stock	15 ml (1 tbsp) chopped sage
225 g (8 oz) pork sausagemeat	1 onion, finely chopped
50 g (2 oz) fresh white breadcrumbs	1 egg, beaten

1 Wash the insides of the pheasants, then dry. Put 15 g (½ oz) butter and 5 ml (1 tsp) thyme inside each bird. Season the birds inside, then truss.

2 Spread the breast of each bird with 25 g (1 oz) softened butter and sprinkle with salt and pepper. Use two bacon rashers to cover each pheasant breast. Stand the pheasants on a rack in a roasting tin, then pour in the stock. Roast at 200°C (400°F) mark 6 for 25 minutes.

3 Mix the sausagemeat, breadcrumbs, lemon rind, suet and herbs together.

4 Melt 50 g (2 oz) butter in a small pan, add the onion and fry gently for 5 minutes or until soft. Mix into the sausagemeat, season, then bind with beaten egg. Form into small balls.

5 Remove the bacon rashers, roll them up and pierce them on to small metal skewers. Arrange on the rack around the pheasants, together with the forcemeat balls.

6 Return to the oven and roast for a further 20 minutes or until the pheasants are tender. Serve hot.

PHEASANT BREASTS WITH VERMOUTH

SERVES 4

1 brace of pheasants	150 ml (¼ pint) chicken stock
salt and pepper	30 ml (2 tbsp) chopped fresh sage or 5 ml (1 tsp) dried
30 ml (2 tbsp) plain flour	
30 ml (2 tbsp) vegetable oil	
50 g (2 oz) onion, finely chopped	30 ml (2 tbsp) single cream
	175 g (6 oz) green grapes, halved and seeded, if necessary
150 ml (¼ pint) dry vermouth	
	sage leaves, to garnish

1 Using a sharp knife, cut all the breast flesh off the bone of each pheasant, keeping each fillet in one piece. You will have four breast fillets, two from each bird. (Use the legs and carcass for a casserole.) Ease off the skin of the fillets, and trim away any fat.

2 Season the flour with salt and pepper, add the breast fillets and turn until coated. Shake off and reserve any excess flour. Heat the oil in a medium sauté pan, add the pheasant and fry until well browned. Remove from the pan with a slotted spoon.

3 Add the onion and any remaining flour to the fat remaining in the pan and cook, stirring, for 1–2 minutes. Blend in the vermouth, stock, sage and seasoning. Bring to the boil, stirring, then return the pheasant to the pan.

4 Cover tightly and simmer for about 30 minutes, turning once. Lift the pheasant out of the juices and place on a warmed serving dish. Cover and keep warm.

5 Stir the cream and grapes into the juices and simmer for 1 minute. Adjust the seasoning. Spoon over the pheasant and garnish with sage leaves.

PHEASANT WITH CHESTNUTS

SERVES 4

25 g (1 oz) butter	450 ml (¾ pint) chicken stock
15 ml (1 tbsp) vegetable oil	150 ml (¼ pint) dry red wine
2 oven-ready pheasants, jointed	
	salt and pepper
2 medium onions, sliced	juice and grated rind of ½ orange
225 g (8 oz) peeled chestnuts	
	10 ml (2 tsp) redcurrant jelly
45 ml (3 tbsp) plain wholemeal flour	
	bouquet garni

1 Heat the butter and oil in a large frying pan, add the pheasant joints and fry for about 5 minutes or until browned. Remove from the pan and put into an ovenproof casserole.

2 Add the onions and chestnuts to the oil and butter remaining in the pan and fry for a few minutes or until brown, then add to the pheasant.

3 Stir the flour into the fat remaining in the pan and cook, stirring, for 2–3 minutes. Remove from the heat and gradually stir in the stock and wine. Bring to the boil, stirring continuously, until thickened and smooth. Season to taste and pour over the pheasant in the casserole. Add the orange juice and rind, redcurrant jelly and bouquet garni.

4 Cover the casserole and cook in a preheated oven at 180°C (350°F) mark 4 for about 1 hour or until the pheasant is tender. Remove the bouquet garni.

PHEASANT AU PORTO

SERVES 6

30 ml (2 tbsp) vegetable oil	50 g (2 oz) sultanas
3 young oven-ready pheasants	salt and pepper
300 ml (½ pint) chicken stock	20 ml (4 tsp) cornflour
120 ml (8 tbsp) port	25 g (1 oz) flaked almonds, toasted, to garnish
juice and finely grated rind of 2 oranges	

1 Heat the oil in a large flameproof casserole. When hot, add the pheasants and cook, turning, until brown all over.
2 Pour the stock and port over the birds. Add the orange juice and rind with the sultanas and season well. Bring to the boil. Cover tightly and cook in a preheated oven at 170°C (325°F) mark 3 for 1–1½ hours.
3 Remove the pheasants from the casserole, then joint each into two or three pieces, depending on size, and arrange on a warmed serving dish. Keep warm.
4 Mix the cornflour to a smooth paste with a little water, stir into the juices in the casserole and bring to the boil, stirring. Adjust the seasoning and spoon over the pheasant. Garnish with toasted flaked almonds.

ROAST GOOSE WITH APPLES AND PRUNES

SERVES 8

4–5 kg (9–11 lb) oven-ready goose, with separate giblets	15 ml (1 tbsp) chopped fresh sage or 5 ml (1 tsp) dried
salt and pepper	100 g (4 oz) fresh wholemeal breadcrumbs
15 g (½ oz) butter	6 Cox's Orange Pippin apples
1 large onion, chopped	
450 g (1 lb) no-soak prunes	300 ml (½ pint) dry white wine
60 ml (4 tbsp) port	

1 Prick the skin of the goose all over with a sharp skewer. Pull the inside fat out and reserve. Rub salt over the skin.
2 To make the stuffing, melt the butter in a large frying pan, add the onion and cook for 5–6 minutes or until softened. Separate the goose liver from the giblets and chop, then add to the onion and cook for 2–3 minutes.
3 Remove the stones from half of the prunes and discard. Chop the prunes roughly and stir into the onion with the port. Cover and simmer gently for 5 minutes. Add the sage and breadcrumbs and mix thoroughly together. Season.
4 Spoon the stuffing into the neck end of the goose, then truss with strong cotton or fine string. Weigh the bird.
5 Put the goose on a wire rack in a roasting tin. Cover the breast with the reserved fat and then with foil. Roast in a preheated oven at 200°C (400°F) mark 6 for 15 minutes per 450 g (1 lb) plus 15 minutes, basting frequently.
6 Thirty minutes before the end of the cooking time, drain the fat from the roasting tin and discard. Core the apples and cut into eighths, then add to the tin with the remaining prunes and wine. Remove the foil and goose fat and cook, uncovered, for the last 30 minutes.
7 Serve with the cooking juices and fruit.

CASSEROLED PIGEONS WITH CIDER AND APPLE

SERVES 4

3 medium carrots	sprig of thyme
3 celery sticks	1 bay leaf
4 small eating apples	pinch of cayenne
salt and pepper	pinch of grated nutmeg
4 oven-ready pigeons	20 ml (4 tsp) redcurrant jelly
45 ml (3 tbsp) vegetable oil	Worcestershire sauce (optional)
40 g (1½ oz) butter	
1 medium onion, chopped	watercress sprigs, to garnish
450 ml (¾ pint) dry cider	
150 ml (¼ pint) chicken stock	

1 Roughly chop one carrot and one celery stick. Peel, core and chop two apples. Season the pigeons and brown in 30 ml (2 tbsp) oil and 25 g (1 oz) butter.

2 Fry the chopped onion, carrot, celery and apples. Transfer to a casserole and add the pigeons. Pour the cider and stock into a pan and bring to the boil. Add to the casserole with the herbs and spices. Cover and cook at 150°C (300°F) mark 2 for 1½–2 hours or until tender.

3 Meanwhile, cut the remaining apples in half crossways and scoop out the centres. Place a little redcurrant jelly in the centre of each and place on a greased baking tray. Bake the apples for about 20 minutes or until tender.

4 Cut the remaining carrots and celery into julienne strips and fry in the remaining oil and butter until soft.

5 When the pigeons are cooked, remove them from the casserole and keep warm. Strain the juices into a saucepan and cook until syrupy. Season to taste and add a dash of Worcestershire sauce if the sauce is too sweet.

6 Serve the pigeons on a pool of the sauce and garnish.

VENISON ESCALOPES WITH RED WINE

SERVES 6

six 175 g (6 oz) escalopes of venison cut from the haunch (leg)	300 ml (½ pint) dry red wine
1 small onion, finely chopped	15 g (½ oz) butter
1 bay leaf	15 ml (1 tbsp) vegetable oil
2 parsley sprigs	30 ml (2 tbsp) redcurrant jelly
8 juniper berries	salt and pepper

1 Put the escalopes in a large shallow dish and sprinkle with the onion, bay leaf, parsley and juniper berries. Pour on the wine, cover and marinate in the refrigerator for 3–4 hours or overnight, turning the escalopes occasionally.

2 Remove the escalopes from the marinade, reserving the marinade. Heat the butter and oil in a large frying pan, add the escalopes and fry for 3–4 minutes on each side. Transfer to a warmed serving dish and keep warm while making the sauce.

3 Strain the reserved marinade into the frying pan and stir to loosen any sediment. Increase the heat and boil rapidly for 3–4 minutes or until reduced. Stir in the redcurrant jelly and season to taste. Cook for 1–2 minutes, stirring, then pour over the escalopes. Serve immediately.

--- COOK'S TIP ---

You can buy venison from any butcher with a game licence. Young venison is usually tender enough not to need hanging, but older, tougher animals will benefit from it. Your butcher can advise on this.

FISH AND SHELLFISH

Fish is both nutritious and flavoursome and can be cooked in a wonderful variety of ways. Shellfish always adds a touch of luxury, whether cooked on its own or used to add variety to a Gratin of Seafood or a champagne sauce to serve with pasta.

COD WITH CORIANDER IN CREAM

SERVES 4

450 g (1 lb) thick-cut cod fillet	15–30 ml (1–2 tbsp) lemon juice
30 ml (2 tbsp) plain flour	15 ml (1 tbsp) capers
10 ml (2 tsp) ground coriander	1 egg yolk
salt and pepper	90 ml (6 tbsp) single cream
50 g (2 oz) butter	

1 Skin the fish and divide into four portions. Mix the flour, coriander and seasoning and use to coat the fish.
2 Heat the butter in a medium sauté pan, add the fish pieces and sauté gently until golden, turning only once.
3 Add 15 ml (1 tbsp) lemon juice to the pan with the capers, cover tightly and continue cooking for a further 4–5 minutes. Place the fish on a warmed serving dish.
4 Mix the egg yolk and cream together, stir into the pan juices and heat gently, without boiling, until the sauce thickens. Adjust the seasoning and spoon over the fish.

TANDOORI COD

SERVES 4

four 200 g (7 oz) cod fillets	15 ml (1 tbsp) chopped fresh coriander or 5 ml (1 tsp) ground coriander
60 ml (4 tbsp) natural yogurt	
30 ml (2 tbsp) lemon juice	15 ml (1 tbsp) vegetable oil
15 ml (1 tbsp) tandoori paste	coriander sprigs, to garnish

1 Place the fish fillets in a shallow dish. Mix all the remaining ingredients, except the garnish.
2 Spread the yogurt mixture evenly over the fish, turning the fillets to ensure they are evenly coated. Cover and refrigerate for 8 hours or overnight.
3 Cover the grill pan with foil and add the fillets, leaving any excess marinade in the dish.
4 Cook the fillets under a preheated grill for 5–7 minutes, basting them with the remaining marinade. Turn over and grill for a further 5 minutes or until the fish is firm and flakes easily, basting frequently. Transfer the fillets to a warmed serving dish and garnish with coriander sprigs.

COD IN CREAM AND CELERY SAUCE

SERVES 4

4 cod steaks or cutlets	75 ml (2½ fl oz) double cream
15 ml (1 tbsp) lemon juice	2.5 ml (½ tsp) dried thyme
salt and pepper	50 g (2 oz) Lancashire cheese, crumbled
25 g (1 oz) butter	
3 celery sticks, chopped	2 tomatoes, sliced
25 g (1 oz) plain flour	parsley, to garnish
225 ml (8 fl oz) milk	

1 Sprinkle the fish with lemon juice and season to taste. Cook under a preheated grill or bake in a preheated oven at 200°C (400°F) mark 6 for 20 minutes. Place in a warmed, shallow, heatproof serving dish and keep warm.

2 Melt the butter in a saucepan, add the celery and fry for about 10 minutes or until tender. Stir in the flour and cook gently for 1 minute, stirring. Remove the pan from the heat and gradually stir in the milk and cream. Bring slowly to the boil and simmer gently, stirring constantly, until the sauce thickens.

3 Season the sauce to taste, then add the thyme and 25 g (1 oz) cheese. Pour the sauce over the fish and sprinkle with the remaining cheese.

4 Arrange the tomatoes on the dish and place under the grill to brown. Serve hot, garnished with parsley.

VARIATION

Haddock in Cream and Leek Sauce
Substitute haddock for the cod in the above recipe and use 1 large leek instead of the celery. Any other white fish would also be suitable.

HADDOCK AU GRATIN

SERVES 6

175 g (6 oz) fresh haddock fillet	50 g (2 oz) butter
175 g (6 oz) smoked haddock fillet	100 g (4 oz) button mushrooms, sliced
60 ml (4 tbsp) dry white wine	30 ml (2 tbsp) plain flour
	pepper
6 peppercorns	50 g (2 oz) Red Leicester cheese, grated
1 bay leaf	25 g (1 oz) fresh breadcrumbs
1 small onion, sliced	

1 Place the fresh and smoked fish in a saucepan with 300 ml (½ pint) water and the wine. Add the peppercorns, bay leaf and onion and bring to the boil. Cover and poach gently for about 15 minutes.

2 Strain off the liquid and reserve. Flake the fish, discarding skin and bones. Discard the flavouring ingredients.

3 Melt the butter in a saucepan, add the mushrooms and sauté for 2 minutes. Stir in the flour and cook gently for 1 minute, stirring. Remove the pan from the heat and gradually stir in the strained cooking liquid. Bring to the boil and continue to cook, stirring, until the sauce thickens. Add the fish, half the grated cheese and season to taste with pepper.

4 Spoon the mixture into six individual soufflé dishes. Top with the remaining cheese and the breadcrumbs.

5 Bake in a preheated oven at 220°C (425°F) mark 7 for about 15 minutes or until golden brown. Serve hot.

HADDOCK AND CARAWAY CHEESE SOUFFLÉ

SERVES 4

450 g (1 lb) floury potatoes	25 g (1 oz) plain flour
450 g (1 lb) fresh haddock fillets	2.5 ml (½ tsp) caraway seeds
100 g (4 oz) button mushrooms, thinly sliced	100 g (4 oz) mature Cheddar cheese, grated
300 ml (½ pint) milk	2 eggs, separated
1 bay leaf	salt and pepper
25 g (1 oz) butter	

1 Scrub the potatoes, then cook in boiling salted water for about 15 minutes or until tender. Drain and peel, then mash three-quarters of the potatoes. Grate the remaining quarter into a bowl and set aside.

2 Meanwhile, place the haddock, mushrooms, milk and bay leaf in a small saucepan. Cover and poach for 15–20 minutes or until tender. Drain, reserving the milk and mushrooms. Flake the fish, discarding the skin and bay leaf.

3 To make the sauce, melt the butter in a saucepan, stir in the flour and cook gently for 1 minute, stirring. Remove from the heat, add the caraway seeds and gradually stir in the milk. Bring to the boil, stirring, and simmer for 2–3 minutes or until thickened and smooth.

4 Stir the mashed potato into the sauce with 75 g (3 oz) cheese, the egg yolks, fish and mushrooms. Season well.

5 Stiffly whisk the egg whites and fold into the fish. Turn into a buttered 1.6 litre (2¾ pint) soufflé dish.

6 Sprinkle over the reserved grated potato and remaining grated cheese. Bake in a preheated oven at 190°C (375°F) mark 5 for about 1 hour or until just set and golden brown.

CREAMY COD BAKE

SERVES 4

	FOR THE CHEESE SAUCE
454 g (1 lb) packet frozen leaf spinach	25 g (1 oz) butter or margarine
50 g (2 oz) butter or margarine	25 g (1 oz) plain flour
4 frozen cod steaks	450 ml (¾ pint) milk
2.5 ml (½ tsp) grated nutmeg	100 g (4 oz) grated Cheddar cheese
salt and pepper	5 ml (1 tsp) mustard powder
100 g (4 oz) Cheddar cheese, grated	salt and pepper
two 25 g (0.88 oz) packets cheese and onion crisps, finely crushed	

1 To make the cheese sauce, melt the butter in a saucepan, add the flour and cook gently, stirring, for 2 minutes. Remove from the heat and blend in the milk. Bring to the boil and cook, stirring, until thick.

2 Simmer the sauce gently for 2–3 minutes, then add the cheese and stir until melted. Add the mustard and season.

3 Put the frozen spinach in a heavy-based saucepan and heat gently until thawed, adding a few spoonfuls of water if necessary to prevent the spinach sticking. Meanwhile, melt half the butter in a frying pan and fry the cod until golden.

4 Transfer the spinach to the base of an ovenproof dish and mix in the remaining butter or margarine with half the nutmeg and seasoning to taste. Arrange the steaks on top of the spinach and pour over any cooking juices.

5 Stir the remaining nutmeg into the cheese sauce, then pour the sauce evenly over the fish to cover it completely. Mix the grated cheese with the crisps and sprinkle over.

6 Bake in a preheated oven at 190°C (375°F) mark 5 for 30 minutes until golden brown and bubbling. Serve hot.

SPANISH COD WITH PEPPERS, TOMATOES AND GARLIC

SERVES 4

700 g (1½ lb) cod fillets	450 g (1 lb) tomatoes, skinned and chopped
1 litre (1¾ pints) mussels (about 450 g/1 lb)	300 ml (½ pint) white wine
30 ml (2 tbsp) vegetable oil	2.5 ml (½ tsp) Tabasco sauce
2 onions, sliced	1 bay leaf
1 red pepper, sliced	salt and pepper
1 green pepper, sliced	
1–2 garlic cloves, crushed	

1 Using a sharp knife, skin the cod and cut it into chunks.
2 Scrub the mussels, discarding any which are open. Place in a pan, cover and cook over a high heat for about 8 minutes or until the mussels have opened. Discard any that do not open.
3 Shell all but four of the mussels. Heat the oil in a frying pan and cook the onions, peppers and garlic for about 5 minutes or until starting to soften. Add the tomatoes and wine, bring to the boil and simmer for 5 minutes, then add the Tabasco.
4 Using a slotted spoon, remove the vegetables from the wine sauce and layer them with the fish chunks in a casserole. Add the bay leaf and seasoning and pour over the sauce. Push the four unshelled mussels into the top layer. Cover and cook in a preheated oven at 180°C (350°F) mark 4 for 1 hour.

COD IN A SPICY YOGURT CRUST

SERVES 4

30 ml (2 tbsp) chopped mint	10 ml (2 tsp) ground cumin
1 medium onion or 2 large spring onions, roughly chopped	10 ml (2 tsp) dried dill
	150 ml (5 fl oz) natural yogurt
2 garlic cloves, crushed	salt and pepper
5 ml (1 tsp) paprika	four 225 g (8 oz) thick cod steaks or fillets
30 ml (2 tbsp) coriander seeds	

1 First make the marinade mixture. Put the mint, onion, garlic, paprika, coriander, cumin, dill and yogurt in a blender or food processor and process until a thick paste is formed. Season the mixture to taste with salt and pepper.
2 Place the fish in a single layer in a shallow heatproof dish. Spread the paste all over the top of the fish and leave in a cool place to marinate for 2–3 hours.
3 Cook under a preheated hot grill, basting occasionally, until the fish is cooked and the yogurt mixture has formed a crust. Serve immediately.

--- **VARIATION** ---

Haddock in a Spicy Yogurt Crust
Substitute haddock for cod in the above recipe. Steaks or fillets are equally suitable.

HALIBUT CREOLE
SERVES 4

30 ml (2 tbsp) vegetable oil	1.25 ml (¼ tsp) Tabasco sauce
1 onion, chopped	30 ml (2 tbsp) chopped fresh parsley or 10 ml (2 tsp) dried
2 garlic cloves, crushed	
1 celery stick, chopped	salt and pepper
1 green pepper, chopped	butter, for greasing
397 g (14 oz) can chopped tomatoes	four 275–350 g (10–12 oz) halibut steaks
5 ml (1 tsp) brown sugar	

1   Heat the oil in a medium saucepan, add the onion and garlic and fry for 3 minutes. Add the celery and pepper and cook for 5 minutes or until softened.

2   Add the tomatoes, sugar, Tabasco and parsley and season to taste. Cook for 15–20 minutes or until the vegetables have softened and the sauce has thickened.

3   Butter a large shallow dish and lay the halibut steaks in it. Pour the creole sauce over the fish and cover with foil. Bake in a preheated oven at 200°C (400°F) mark 6 for 25–30 minutes or until the fish is firm and flakes easily.

4   Transfer the fish to a warmed serving platter and spoon the remaining sauce over the top.

TO MICROWAVE

Place the oil, onion and garlic in a medium bowl. Cover and cook on HIGH for 3 minutes. Add the celery, green pepper, tomatoes, sugar, Tabasco, parsley and seasoning. Cook, uncovered, on HIGH for 9–10 minutes. Arrange the fish in a buttered shallow dish and pour over the sauce. Cover and microwave on HIGH for 12–14 minutes or until the fish is firm and flakes easily. Complete step 4.

SOLE BONNE FEMME
SERVES 4

2 sole fillets	salt and pepper
2 shallots, or 2–3 slices of onion, finely chopped	1 bay leaf
	40 g (1½ oz) butter
100 g (4 oz) button mushrooms	30 ml (2 tbsp) plain flour
45 ml (3 tbsp) dry white wine	about 150 ml (¼ pint) milk
	45 ml (3 tbsp) single cream

1   Trim off the fins, wash and wipe the fillets and fold each into three. Put the shallots or onion in the bottom of an ovenproof dish with the stalks from the mushrooms, (finely chopped). Cover with the fish, pour round the wine and 15 ml (1 tbsp) water, season to taste and add the bay leaf.

2   Cover with foil or a lid and bake in a preheated oven at 180°C (350°F) mark 4 for about 15 minutes or until tender. Strain off the cooking liquid and keep the fish warm.

3   Melt half the butter in a frying pan, add the mushrooms and fry gently until just beginning to soften, then drain well.

4   Melt the remaining butter in a saucepan, stir in the flour and cook gently for 1 minute, stirring. Remove from the heat and gradually stir in the cooking liquid from the fish, made up to 300 ml (½ pint) with milk.

5   Bring to the boil and continue to cook, stirring, until the sauce thickens, then remove from the heat and stir in the cream. Pour the sauce over the fish and serve garnished with the mushroom caps.

SOLE 'STEWED' IN CREAM

SERVES 4

MOUSSELINES OF SOLE WITH PRAWNS

SERVES 6

4 sole fillets, skinned and cut in half lengthways	FOR THE GARNISH
25 g (1 oz) butter	lobster coral or salmon eggs (optional)
15 ml (1 tbsp) finely chopped shallots	cooked crayfish or prawns (optional)
300 ml (½ pint) fish stock	puff pastry fleurons or bread croûtes
blade of mace	parsley sprigs
225 ml (8 fl oz) double cream	lemon twists
salt and white pepper	

1 Tie each strip of sole into a loose knot in the centre.

2 Melt half the butter in a large frying pan, add the shallot, cover and cook for about 5 minutes or until softened, shaking the pan occasionally. Stir in the stock and mace and boil rapidly until reduced to 50 ml (2 fl oz). Remove the mace.

3 Stir half the cream into the shallots and bring to the boil. Lower the heat, season lightly and gently lower the fish into the pan. Spoon cream over the fish. Cover with buttered greaseproof paper and poach gently for about 3 minutes, or until the fish just flakes.

4 Carefully transfer the fish to a warmed plate using a fish slice, cover and keep warm. Boil the cooking liquid until slightly thickened. Stir in the remaining butter and adjust the seasoning, if necessary.

5 Spoon the sauce over four warmed serving plates. Arrange the fish on top and garnish attractively.

450 g (1 lb) sole fillets, skinned and chopped	3 egg yolks, beaten
50 g (2 oz) peeled prawns	75 g (3 oz) butter, softened
1 egg white	10 ml (2 tsp) lemon juice
1.25 ml (¼ tsp) salt	5 ml (1 tsp) tomato purée
1.25 ml (¼ tsp) white pepper	fresh dill sprigs and whole prawns in their shells, to garnish
450 ml (¾ pint) double cream	

1 Combine the chopped fish with the prawns and egg white and season to taste. Put the mixture in a blender or food processor with 300 ml (½ pint) cream and blend until smooth.

2 Butter six 150 ml (¼ pint) ovenproof ramekin dishes and press the mixture well down into the dishes. Cover and chill for 3 hours.

3 Place the ramekins in a roasting tin and pour in enough boiling water to come halfway up the dishes. Cook in a preheated oven at 150°C (300°F) mark 2 for 30–40 minutes. Turn out on to a wire rack to drain. Keep warm.

4 Put the egg yolks, a knob of butter and the lemon juice in the top of a double boiler or in a heatproof bowl over a pan of simmering water. Heat gently, stirring, until of a coating consistency.

5 Remove from the heat and slowly beat in the remaining butter and the tomato purée. Whip the remaining cream until softly stiff and fold into the sauce. Return to the heat to thicken without boiling.

6 Place the moulds in a warmed serving dish and coat with the sauce. Garnish with dill and whole prawns and serve hot.

MUSHROOM-STUFFED PLAICE

SERVES 4

50 g (2 oz) butter	4 large plaice fillets, skinned
1 small onion, finely chopped	25 g (1 oz) plain flour
225 g (8 oz) flat mushrooms, finely chopped	150 ml (¼ pint) milk
	a few drops of lemon juice
grated nutmeg	15 ml (1 tbsp) double cream
salt and pepper	
30 ml (2 tbsp) finely chopped parsley	chopped parsley, to garnish

1 Melt half the butter in a frying pan, add the onion and fry gently for 5–10 minutes or until soft and golden. Add the mushrooms and cook for about 20 minutes or until all the juices have evaporated.

2 Remove from the heat, season with nutmeg, salt and pepper, then transfer all but 30 ml (2 tbsp) of the mixture to a bowl and mix with 15 ml (1 tbsp) of the parsley.

3 Cut the fish fillets in half lengthways and spread an equal quantity of the mushroom mixture on the skinned side of each piece of fish. Roll up the fillets from the head to tail and place close together in a baking dish.

4 Pour in 150 ml (¼ pint) water and place a piece of buttered foil on top of the fish. Bake in a preheated oven at 180°C (350°F) mark 4 for 20–25 minutes or until tender. Strain off the cooking liquid and transfer the fish to a warmed serving dish. Keep warm.

5 Melt the remaining butter in a saucepan, stir in the flour and cook for 2 minutes, stirring continuously. Remove from the heat and gradually stir in the cooking liquid and milk. Bring to the boil, stirring all the time. Add the remaining mushroom mixture, season with salt, pepper and lemon juice and stir in the cream. Pour over the fish.

STUFFED PLAICE WITH LEMON SAUCE

SERVES 4

4 small whole plaice, cleaned	1.25 ml (¼ tsp) mustard powder
65 g (2½ oz) butter	salt and pepper
100 g (4 oz) button mushrooms, finely chopped	1 egg, beaten
	150 ml (¼ pint) dry white wine
100 g (4 oz) white breadcrumbs	25 g (1 oz) plain flour
90 ml (6 tbsp) chopped parsley	60 ml (4 tbsp) single cream
45 ml (3 tbsp) green peppercorns, crushed	lemon slices and parsley sprigs, to garnish
juice and finely grated rind of 2 lemons	

1 With the white skin uppermost, cut down the backbone of each of the four plaice. Carefully make a pocket on each side of the backbone by easing up the white flesh.

2 To make the stuffing, beat 15 g (½ oz) butter until softened, then add the mushrooms, breadcrumbs, parsley, 30 ml (2 tbsp) peppercorns, lemon rind and mustard. Season to taste. Moisten with egg and a little lemon juice.

3 Spoon the stuffing into the pockets in the fish. Place in a buttered ovenproof dish, pour in the wine, cover with foil and cook at 190°C (375°F) mark 5 for 30 minutes.

4 Remove the fish and place on a serving dish. Cover and keep warm. Strain and reserve the cooking liquid.

5 To make the sauce, melt the remaining butter in a saucepan, add the flour and cook for 1–2 minutes. Gradually stir in the fish cooking juices, 150 ml (¼ pint) water and the remaining lemon juice. Bring to the boil, stirring, then stir in the remaining peppercorns and the cream. Season.

6 Garnish the fish and serve with the sauce.

TROUT IN CREAM

SERVES 4

4 trout	150 ml (5 fl oz) single cream
juice of 1 lemon	30 ml (2 tbsp) fresh breadcrumbs
15 ml (1 tbsp) chopped chives	a little butter, melted
15 ml (1 tbsp) chopped parsley	

1 Clean the fish, leaving the heads on if wished. Wash and wipe the fish and lay them in a buttered shallow flameproof dish.

2 Sprinkle over the lemon juice, herbs and about 15 ml (1 tbsp) water. Cover with foil.

3 Cook in a preheated oven at 180°C (350°F) mark 4 for 10–15 minutes or until tender.

4 Heat the cream gently and pour over the fish. Sprinkle with breadcrumbs and melted butter and brown under a hot grill. Serve immediately.

BAKED TROUT WITH HAZELNUTS AND DILL

SERVES 4

four 275 g (10 oz) trout, cleaned	1 shallot, finely chopped
40 ml (8 tsp) lemon juice	75 g (3 oz) hazelnuts
salt and pepper	50 g (2 oz) butter
4 dill sprigs	lemon slices and dill, to garnish
100 ml (4 fl oz) dry white wine	

1 Cut the fins from the fish, then sprinkle 30 ml (6 tsp) of the lemon juice over the skin and the cavities. Season to taste inside and out and put a sprig of dill in each cavity.

2 Place the trout in a baking dish large enough to hold them tightly in one layer. Pour over the wine and add the shallot. Cover the dish with greased greaseproof paper, then bake in a preheated oven at 180°C (350°F) mark 4 for 20–25 minutes or until the flesh flakes easily.

3 Meanwhile, place the hazelnuts under a moderately hot grill for about 5 minutes or until the skins dry out and flake. Rub off the skins and chop the nuts. Melt the butter in a saucepan, add the hazelnuts and cook over a moderately high heat, stirring frequently, until golden brown. Add the remaining lemon juice and season to taste.

4 Carefully transfer the trout to four warmed serving plates. Boil the cooking juices rapidly until reduced to about 45 ml (3 tbsp). Spoon the juices, hazelnuts and butter over the fish. Garnish and serve at once.

BAKED TROUT WITH CUCUMBER SAUCE

SERVES 4

four 275 g (10 oz) trout, cleaned	300 ml (10 fl oz) soured cream
salt and pepper	5 ml (1 tsp) tarragon vinegar
300 ml (½ pint) fish or vegetable stock	5 ml (1 tsp) chopped tarragon
½ small cucumber	tarragon, to garnish

1 Arrange the trout in a single layer in a shallow ovenproof dish. Season to taste and pour over the stock.
2 Cover and bake in a preheated oven at 180°C (350°F) mark 4 for about 25 minutes or until the trout are tender.
3 Remove the fish from the cooking liquor and carefully peel off the skin, leaving the head and tail intact. Leave to cool.
4 Just before serving, make the sauce. Coarsely grate the cucumber into a bowl, then add the cream, vinegar and chopped tarragon. Season to taste.
5 Coat the trout in some of the sauce, leaving the head and tail exposed. Garnish with tarragon. Serve the remaining sauce separately in a bowl.

——————— TO MICROWAVE ———————

Cook two trout at a time. Arrange in a shallow dish, cover and cook on HIGH for 5–7 minutes or until tender. Repeat with the remaining two trout. Complete the recipe as above.

TROUT STUFFED WITH SPINACH AND WALNUTS

SERVES 4

4 small trout, cleaned, boned and heads removed	juice of 1 lemon
75 g (3 oz) butter	30 ml (2 tbsp) chopped fresh parsley or 10 ml (2 tsp) dried
1 onion, finely chopped	5 ml (1 tsp) grated nutmeg
350 g (12 oz) frozen chopped spinach, thawed	salt and pepper
50 g (2 oz) fresh breadcrumbs	parsley sprigs and lemon and lime slices, to garnish
50 g (2 oz) walnuts, chopped	

1 Butter a large, shallow ovenproof dish and lay the trout in it.
2 Melt 50 g (2 oz) of the butter in a deep frying pan, add the onion and cook for 4–5 minutes or until soft. Stir in the spinach and cook for 5 minutes, stirring frequently.
3 Add the breadcrumbs, walnuts, lemon juice, parsley and nutmeg. Stir well to combine and continue to cook over a gentle heat for 10 minutes, stirring frequently. Remove from the heat and leave to cool.
4 Spoon the stuffing into the cavity of each fish. Lay the fish on their sides and dot with the remaining butter. Season and cover with buttered foil.
5 Cook in a preheated oven at 180°C (350°F) mark 4 for 40–60 minutes or until the fish is firm and flakes easily. Skin the fish, transfer to a warmed serving dish, garnish and serve.

GREY MULLET COOKED IN LEMON AND RED WINE

SERVES 4

15 g (½ oz) butter	salt and pepper
450 g (1 lb) eating apples, peeled, cored and sliced	four 275 g (10 oz) grey mullet, cleaned
6 spring onions, sliced	2 lemons, sliced
juice and finely grated rind of 1 lemon	300 ml (½ pint) dry red wine
1–2 garlic cloves, crushed	60 ml (4 tbsp) double cream

1 To make the stuffing, melt the butter in a medium saucepan and add the apples, spring onions, lemon rind, 30 ml (2 tbsp) of the lemon juice and the garlic. Fry lightly, then season to taste.

2 Make three slashes across both sides of each grey mullet and insert the lemon slices. Sprinkle the cavity of each fish with the remaining lemon juice and fill with the stuffing. Put into a large ovenproof dish.

3 Pour over the red wine and bake in a preheated oven at 180°C (350°F) mark 4 for 20–30 minutes or until tender. Remove the fish and place on a serving dish. Keep hot.

4 Pour the cooking liquid into a small saucepan, stir in the cream and reheat gently. Pour over the fish and serve.

——— TO MICROWAVE ———

Melt the butter in a medium bowl on HIGH for 30 seconds. Add the apples, spring onions, lemon rind, 30 ml (2 tbsp) of the lemon juice and the garlic. Cook on HIGH for 8 minutes. Complete step 2. Put the fish into a shallow dish and pour over the red wine. Cook on HIGH for 10 minutes or until tender, rearranging once. Complete step 4. Stir the cream into the cooking liquid and cook on HIGH for 1 minute. Serve poured over the fish.

STEAMED MULLET WITH CHILLI SAUCE

SERVES 2

one 550 g (1¼ lb) grey mullet, cleaned	1 small red pepper, cut into matchsticks
75 ml (5 tbsp) tomato ketchup	1 small green pepper, cut into matchsticks
15 ml (1 tbsp) soy sauce	5 ml (1 tsp) cornflour
pinch of chilli powder	15 ml (1 tbsp) chopped parsley
75 ml (5 tbsp) white wine	salt and pepper

1 Place the mullet in a shallow dish.

2 Whisk together the tomato ketchup, soy sauce, chilli powder and wine. Make three deep slashes in the side of each fish. Pour over the marinade, cover and leave for 2 hours.

3 Drain off the marinade and reserve. Place the fish on a rack over a roasting tin half full of water and cover tightly with foil. Steam the fish over a medium heat for 20–25 minutes or until the fish is cooked. (When cooked, the eyes should be white.)

4 To make the chilli sauce, place the marinade and peppers in a saucepan. Mix the cornflour to a smooth paste with 15 ml (1 tbsp) water and stir into the sauce. Bring to the boil and simmer for 4–5 minutes, stirring. Stir in the parsley and season to taste.

5 Carefully lift the steamed mullet on to a warmed serving plate. Spoon over the sauce and serve.

SKATE WITH CAPERS

SERVES 4

MONKFISH WITH LIME AND PRAWNS

SERVES 4

two 550 g (1¼ lb) skate wings, halved	45 ml (3 tbsp) drained capers
salt	30 ml (2 tbsp) vinegar from the capers
50 g (2 oz) butter	

1 Put the skate in a roasting tin and cover with salted water. Bring to the boil, then simmer for 10–15 minutes or until tender.

2 Meanwhile, melt the butter in a small saucepan and cook until it turns golden brown. Add the capers and vinegar and cook until bubbling.

3 Drain the fish and place on warmed serving plates. Pour over the sauce and serve at once.

COOK'S TIP

The 'wings' are the only edible part of the skate. They may look bony but in fact the bones are soft and gelatinous, and the flesh is easily picked off them when the fish is cooked.

550 g (1¼ lb) monkfish	150 ml (¼ pint) dry white wine
salt and pepper	juice and finely grated rind of 1 lime
15 ml (1 tbsp) plain flour	
30 ml (2 tbsp) vegetable oil	pinch of sugar
1 small onion, chopped	100 g (4 oz) peeled prawns
1 garlic clove, chopped	lime slices, to garnish
225 g (8 oz) tomatoes, skinned and chopped	

1 Using a sharp knife, skin the fish, if necessary, then cut the flesh into 2.5 cm (1 inch) chunks. Season the flour with salt and pepper, add the fish and toss until coated.

2 Heat the oil in a flameproof casserole, add the onion and garlic and fry gently for 5 minutes. Add the fish and fry until golden.

3 Stir in the tomatoes, wine, lime rind and juice, sugar and seasoning. Bring to the boil.

4 Cover and cook in a preheated oven at 180°C (350°F) mark 4 for 15 minutes. Add the prawns and continue to cook for a further 15 minutes or until the monkfish is tender. Garnish with lime slices.

FRICASSÉE OF MONKFISH WITH CORIANDER

SERVES 6

700 g (1½ lb) monkfish fillets	40 g (1½ oz) butter
450 g (1 lb) halibut cutlets	45 ml (3 tbsp) plain flour
150 ml (¼ pint) dry vermouth	30 ml (2 tbsp) chopped coriander
1 small onion, sliced	60 ml (4 tbsp) single cream
salt and pepper	coriander sprigs, to garnish
100 g (4 oz) small button mushrooms	

1 Cut the monkfish and halibut into large, fork-sized pieces, discarding skin and bone.
2 Place the fish in a medium saucepan, cover with cold water and bring slowly to the boil. Strain the fish in a colander and rinse off any scum.
3 Return the fish to the clean pan and pour over the vermouth and 300 ml (½ pint) water. Add the onion, season to taste and bring to the boil. Cover the pan, reduce the heat and simmer gently for 8–10 minutes or until the fish is just tender and beginning to flake, adding the mushrooms after 6 minutes' cooking.
4 Strain off the cooking liquor and reserve.
5 Melt the butter in a separate saucepan, stir in the flour and cook for 1–2 minutes. Gradually add the cooking liquor. Bring slowly to the boil, stirring all the time, and bubble for 2 minutes or until thickened and smooth.
6 Stir in the chopped coriander, cream, mushrooms, onion and fish and adjust the seasoning. Warm through gently, being careful not to break up the fish. Serve hot, garnished with sprigs of coriander.

MONKFISH AND MUSSEL SKEWERS

SERVES 6

12 streaky bacon rashers, halved	juice and finely grated rind of 1 large lemon
900 g (2 lb) monkfish, skinned, boned and cut into 2.5 cm (1 inch) cubes	4 garlic cloves, crushed
36 frozen cooked mussels, thawed	salt and pepper
	shredded lettuce, to serve
25 g (1 oz) butter	lemon slices, to garnish
60 ml (4 tbsp) chopped parsley	

1 Roll the bacon rashers up neatly. Thread the cubed fish, mussels and bacon alternately on to 12 oiled skewers.
2 Melt the butter in a saucepan, remove from the heat, then add the parsley, lemon juice and rind and garlic. Season to taste. (Take care when adding salt as both the mussels and the bacon are naturally salty.)
3 Place the skewers on an oiled grill rack. Brush with the butter mixture, then cook under a preheated moderate grill for 15 minutes. Turn the skewers frequently during cooking and brush with the butter mixture with each turn.
4 Arrange the hot skewers on a serving platter lined with shredded lettuce. Garnish with lemon slices and serve at once with any remaining flavoured butter.

--- COOK'S TIP ---

Keep the skewers well brushed with butter while grilling to prevent the fish from drying out.

SALMON WITH HERB SAUCE

SERVES 4

900 g (2 lb) salmon, cleaned	45 ml (3 tbsp) chopped parsley
45 ml (3 tbsp) lemon juice	30 ml (2 tbsp) chopped chervil
50 g (2 oz) butter	5 ml (1 tsp) chopped dill
salt and pepper	150 ml (¼ pint) mayonnaise
1 bunch of watercress, roughly chopped	fresh herbs and lemon rind shapes, to garnish (optional)
100 g (4 oz) fresh spinach leaves, roughly chopped	

1 Place the fish in the centre of a large piece of foil. Add 30 ml (2 tbsp) of the lemon juice, then dot with 25 g (1 oz) of the butter. Season to taste.

2 Seal the foil, weight the fish and place on a baking sheet. Calculate the cooking time at 10 minutes per 450 g (1 lb). Bake in a preheated oven at 180°C (350°F) mark 4 until tender.

3 Remove the fish from the foil, reserving the cooking liquor, then carefully remove the skin while still warm. Place the fish on a serving dish and leave to cool.

4 To make the sauce, put the cooking liquor and the remaining 25 g (1 oz) butter in a saucepan and heat gently. Add the watercress, spinach, parsley, chervil and dill, then cook for 2–3 minutes or until softened.

5 Put the sauce in a blender or food processor and blend until smooth. Transfer to a bowl, add the remaining lemon juice and season to taste. Leave to cool, then fold in the mayonnaise. Turn into a small serving jug and refrigerate until required.

6 Garnish the fish decoratively with herbs and lemon rind shapes, and serve with the herb sauce.

SUMMER POACHED SALMON

SERVES 15

1.8 kg (4 lb) salmon, tail and fins trimmed and eyes removed	salt and pepper
150 ml (¼ pint) dry white wine	300 ml (½ pint) liquid aspic jelly
1 onion, sliced	whole prawns, cucumber slices, endive and chicory, to garnish
1 bay leaf	mayonnaise, to serve

1 Place the salmon in a fish kettle. Pour over the wine and enough water just to cover the fish. Add the onion and bay leaf and season to taste. Bring slowly to the boil, cover and simmer for 25 minutes.

2 Lift the salmon out of the cooking liquid and leave to cool for 2–3 hours. Ease off the skin and place the fish on a serving platter.

3 As the aspic begins to set, brush some over the fish. Leave to set in a cool place for 1–1½ hours. Coat with several layers of aspic.

4 Garnish the salmon with prawns and cucumber slices and brush more aspic on top. Arrange endive, chicory, sliced cucumber and lemon on the side of the dish and serve with mayonnaise.

—— **COOK'S TIP** ——

This is an ideal dish to serve for a summer buffet. Pay particular attention to the garnishing and allow yourself a little extra time for those important finishing touches. The result can look spectacular.

SALMON WITH FENNEL SAUCE

SERVES 4

four 175 g (6 oz) salmon steaks	2 egg yolks
2 shallots, chopped	100 g (4 oz) butter, softened
1 small fennel bulb, finely chopped	salt and pepper
1 bay leaf	lemon juice, to taste
2 parsley stalks, crushed	fennel sprigs, to garnish
150 ml (¼ pint) dry white wine	

1 Place the salmon steaks in a shallow ovenproof dish. Scatter the shallots, fennel, bay leaf and parsley over the top. Pour in the wine, cover tightly and bake in a preheated oven at 180°C (350°F) mark 4 for 15 minutes or until the fish is tender.
2 Strain off 100 ml (4 fl oz) of the cooking liquor into a saucepan. Reserve 10 ml (2 tsp) of the chopped fennel. Turn off the oven, re-cover the salmon and keep warm.
3 Boil the strained liquor until reduced to 15 ml (1 tbsp). Beat the egg yolks together in a medium heatproof bowl, then stir in the reduced liquor and work in half the butter.
4 Place the bowl over a saucepan of hot water and whisk with a balloon whisk until the butter has melted. Gradually whisk in the remaining butter, whisking well after each addition, to make a thick, fluffy sauce. Remove the bowl from the heat.
5 Add the reserved cooked fennel to the sauce and season to taste, adding a little lemon juice, if necessary.
6 Transfer the salmon to a warmed serving plate. Spoon the sauce over and garnish with fennel sprigs.

SOURED CREAM SALMON PIE

SERVES 8

450 g (1 lb) salmon	150 ml (5 fl oz) soured cream
60 ml (4 tbsp) dry white wine	30 ml (2 tbsp) chopped parsley
salt and pepper	450 g (1 lb) self-raising flour
190 g (6½ oz) butter	50 g (2 oz) lard
40 g (1½ oz) plain flour	milk, to bind
225 g (8 oz) Cheddar cheese, grated	beaten egg, to glaze
3 eggs, hard-boiled and chopped	

1 Place the salmon in a large saucepan and just cover with cold water. Add the wine, season to taste and simmer for about 20 minutes. Remove the fish from the stock and flake, discarding bones and skin. Reserve the stock.
2 Melt 40 g (1½ oz) butter in a saucepan and stir in the plain flour. Remove the pan from the heat and gradually stir in 300 ml (½ pint) reserved fish stock. Bring to the boil and continue to cook, stirring, for 2 minutes. Remove from the heat and stir in 200 g (7 oz) grated cheese, the chopped eggs, soured cream and parsley. Season and cool.
3 To make the pastry, mix the self-raising flour and remaining cheese in a bowl, add the remaining butter and the lard and rub in until the mixture resembles fine breadcrumbs. Add a little milk to bind the mixture.
4 Roll out one third of the pastry on a lightly floured surface to a 30.5 x 10 cm (12 x 4 inch) oblong and place on a baking sheet. Top with some of the sauce mixture, the salmon, then more sauce.
5 Roll out the remaining pastry and use to cover the pie, sealing the edges well. Brush with beaten egg and bake at 190°C (375°F) mark 5 for about 40 minutes. Serve warm.

FISH WELLINGTON
SERVES 6–8

INDONESIAN FISH CURRY
SERVES 4

25 g (1 oz) butter	salt and pepper
100 g (4 oz) mushrooms, chopped	368 g (13 oz) packet frozen puff pastry, thawed
50 g (2 oz) onion, finely chopped	2 large cod or haddock fillets, (about 900 g/2 lb), skinned
175 g (6 oz) smooth liver pâté or liver sausage	
60 ml (4 tbsp) double cream	beaten egg, to glaze

1 Melt the butter in a frying pan, add the mushrooms and onion and fry for about 5 minutes or until soft.
2 Mash the liver pâté or sausage in a bowl and stir in the cream, onion and mushrooms. Season to taste.
3 Roll out the pastry on a lightly floured surface to a 35 x 30.5 cm (14 x 12 inch) rectangle. Place one fish fillet in the centre of the pastry, spread the filling mixture over the fillet, then top with the other fillet. Trim the pastry, allowing a good 10 cm (4 inch) border. Reserve the trimmed pastry.
4 Brush round the edges of the pastry with beaten egg, then carefully fold it over the fish and neatly wrap it up like a parcel.
5 Place the parcelled fish on a baking sheet with the sealed edges underneath. Brush with beaten egg. Roll and cut the pastry trimmings into decorative fish shapes and place on top of the pastry parcel.
6 Bake in a preheated oven at 220°C (425°F) mark 7 for about 25 minutes or until the pastry is golden brown and the fish is cooked through.

1 small onion, chopped	salt
1 garlic clove, chopped	700 g (1½ lb) haddock fillets, skinned and cut into bite-sized pieces
2.5 cm (1 inch) piece of fresh root ginger, chopped	
5 ml (1 tsp) ground turmeric	225 g (8 oz) peeled prawns
2.5 ml (½ tsp) laos powder	300 ml (½ pint) coconut milk
1.25 ml (¼ tsp) chilli powder	juice of 1 lime
30 ml (2 tbsp) vegetable oil	shredded coconut and lime wedges, to garnish

1 Put the first seven ingredients in an electric blender or food processor with 2.5 ml (½ tsp) salt and blend to a paste.
2 Transfer the mixture to a flameproof casserole and fry gently, stirring, for 5 minutes. Add the haddock pieces and prawns and fry for a few minutes more, tossing the fish to coat with the spice mixture.
3 Pour in the coconut milk, shake the pan and turn the fish gently in the liquid. (Take care not to break up the pieces of fish.) Bring slowly to the boil, then lower the heat, cover and simmer for 10 minutes or until tender.
4 Add the lime juice, taste and adjust the seasoning, then transfer to a warmed serving dish and sprinkle with coconut. Serve hot, garnished with lime wedges.

─── **COOK'S TIP** ───
Loas powder is used extensively in the cooking of South-East Asia. It comes from a root rather like ginger and has a peppery hot taste.
 To make 300 ml (½ pint) coconut milk, break 100 g (4 oz) block creamed coconut into a jug and pour in 300 ml (½ pint) boiling water. Stir, then strain.

FISH IN SPICY SAUCE WITH TOMATOES

SERVES 4

700 g (1½ lb) white fish (cod, halibut or haddock), skinned and filleted	5 ml (1 tsp) ground turmeric
60 ml (4 tbsp) ghee or vegetable oil	1.25 ml (¼ tsp) chilli powder
7.5 ml (1½ tsp) coriander seeds	5 ml (1 tsp) salt
5 ml (1 tsp) black peppercorns	4 tomatoes, skinned and roughly chopped
1 garlic clove, crushed	2.5 ml (½ tsp) garam masala
	chopped coriander, to garnish

1 Wash the fish under cold running water and pat dry with absorbent kitchen paper. Cut into 2.5 cm (1 inch) cubes.

2 Heat the ghee or oil in a heavy-based frying pan. Add the fish, a few pieces at a time, and fry gently for 2–3 minutes. Remove the fish carefully from the pan with a slotted spoon and set aside on a plate.

3 Put the coriander seeds, peppercorns and garlic in a small electric mill or pestle and mortar and grind to a smooth paste.

4 Add the spice paste to the frying pan with the turmeric, chilli powder and salt, and fry gently for 2 minutes.

5 Stir in the tomatoes and 300 ml (½ pint) water. Bring to the boil, then lower the heat and cook over a medium heat for 5 minutes. Add the fish and simmer, shaking the pan occasionally, for a further 10 minutes or until the fish is tender. *Do not stir.* Remove from the heat.

6 Sprinkle the garam masala over the fish, cover the pan and let the fish stand for 2 minutes, then turn into a warmed serving dish. Garnish with chopped coriander and serve immediately.

ITALIAN FISH STEW

SERVES 4

a good pinch of saffron strands	450 g (1 lb) tomatoes, skinned, seeded and chopped
about 900 g (2 lb) mixed fish fillets (red mullet, bream, bass, brill, monkfish, plaice or cod)	2 canned anchovy fillets, drained
10–12 unpeeled cooked prawns	150 ml (¼ pint) dry white wine
60 ml (4 tbsp) olive oil	2 bay leaves
1 large onion, finely chopped	45 ml (3 tbsp) chopped basil
3 garlic cloves, crushed	salt and pepper
2 slices of canned pimiento, drained and sliced	10–12 mussels, in their shells
	4 slices of hot toast, to serve

1 To prepare the saffron water, soak the saffron strands in a little boiling water for 30 minutes. Meanwhile, skin the fish and cut into bite-sized pieces. Peel the prawns.

2 Heat the oil in a large heavy-based pan, add the onion, garlic and pimiento and fry for 5 minutes or until soft.

3 Add the tomatoes and anchovies and stir with a wooden spoon to break them up. Pour in the wine and 150 ml (¼ pint) water and bring to the boil, then lower the heat and add the bay leaves and half the basil. Simmer, uncovered, for 20 minutes, stirring occasionally.

4 Add the firm fish to the tomato mixture, then strain in the saffron water and season to taste. Cook for 10 minutes, then add the delicate fish and cook for a further 5 minutes.

5 Add the prawns and mussels, cover and cook for 5 minutes or until the mussels open. Discard the bay leaves and any mussels that do not open.

6 To serve, put one slice of toast in each of four individual bowls. Spoon over the stew and sprinkle with basil.

MEDITERRANEAN FISH STEW WITH AÏOLI

SERVES 4

10 garlic cloves	1 small onion, thinly sliced
1 egg yolk	1 leek, thinly sliced
300 ml (½ pint) olive oil	1–2 parsley sprigs
juice of 1 lemon	1 bay leaf
salt and pepper	1 thin strip of orange rind
900 g (2 lb) firm white fish fillets (bass, turbot, whiting, monkfish or halibut), skinned	1 small baguette (French loaf), sliced, to serve
	chopped parsley, to garnish
1.1 litres (2 pints) fish stock	

1 First make the aïoli. Roughly chop eight of the garlic cloves and put in a mortar with the egg yolk. Crush with a pestle. Add the oil a drop at a time and work until the ingredients emulsify and thicken. Continue adding the oil in a thin, stready stream, beating vigorously until the mayonnaise is very thick and smooth.

2 Beat in the lemon juice and 5 ml (1 tsp) lukewarm water. Season to taste and set aside in a cool place.

3 Cut the fish into thick chunks and place in a large saucepan. Pour in the stock, then add the next five ingredients, with the remaining garlic, halved. Season to taste, cover and simmer for 15 minutes or until tender.

4 Transfer the fish and vegetables to a warmed serving dish with a slotted spoon. Keep warm.

5 Strain the cooking liquid into a jug and blend a few spoonfuls into the aïoli. Toast the baguette and keep warm.

6 Put the aïoli in a heavy-based saucepan, then gradually whisk in the remaining cooking liquid. Heat through gently, stirring constantly. Adjust the seasoning. Pour over the fish and sprinkle with parsley. Serve with the toast.

SPECIAL PARSLEY FISH PIE

SERVES 4

450 g (1 lb) whiting fillet	2 eggs, hard-boiled and chopped
300 ml (½ pint) plus 90 ml (6 tbsp) milk	150 ml (¼ pint) single cream
1 bay leaf	30 ml (2 tbsp) chopped parsley
6 peppercorns	100 g (4 oz) peeled prawns
1 onion, sliced	900 g (2 lb) potatoes, peeled
salt and pepper	
65 g (2½ oz) butter	
45 ml (3 tbsp) plain flour	1 egg, beaten, to glaze

1 Place the whiting in a saucepan and pour over the 300 ml (½ pint) milk. Add the bay leaf, peppercorns, onion and a pinch of salt. Simmer for 10 minutes. Lift the fish from the pan, flake the flesh and remove the skin and bones. Strain the cooking liquid and reserve.

2 To make the sauce, melt 40 g (1½ oz) of the butter in the saucepan, add the flour and cook gently, stirring, for 1–2 minutes. Remove from the heat and gradually blend in the reserved cooking liquid. Bring to the boil, stirring constantly, then simmer until thickened and season.

3 Add the eggs to the sauce with the cream, fish, parsley and prawns. Taste and adjust the seasoning, then spoon the mixture into a 29.5 cm (11 inch) oval baking dish.

4 Meanwhile, boil the potatoes, drain and mash without any liquid. Heat the 90 ml (6 tbsp) milk and remaining butter and beat into the potatoes. Season to taste. Pipe or spoon over the fish mixture.

5 Bake in the oven at 200°C (400°F) mark 6 for 10–15 minutes or until the potato is set. Brush the beaten egg over the pie. Return to the oven for a further 15 minutes or until the potato is golden brown.

FISHERMAN'S HOT POT

SERVES 4

450 g (1 lb) cod fillet, skinned	1 medium onion, thinly sliced
40 g (1½ oz) plain flour	225 g (8 oz) mushrooms, sliced
700 g (1½ lb) potatoes, peeled	15 g (½ oz) butter
15–30 ml (1–2 tbsp) lemon juice	150 ml (¼ pint) milk
salt and pepper	100 g (4 oz) Cheddar cheese, grated

1 Cut the cod into 2 cm (¾ inch) squares and toss in 25 g (1 oz) flour.

2 Cook the potatoes in boiling salted water for about 15 minutes or until tender, but not soft, then slice them thinly. Arrange one third in the bottom of a buttered ovenproof casserole. Cover with half the cod, sprinkle with half the lemon juice and season well.

3 Combine the onion and mushrooms and arrange half the mixture over the fish. Cover with the remaining cod, lemon juice, one third of the potatoes and the remaining onions and mushrooms.

4 Melt the butter in a saucepan, stir in the remaining 15 g (½ oz) flour and cook gently for 1 minute, stirring. Remove the pan from the heat and gradually stir in the milk. Bring to the boil and continue to cook, stirring, until the sauce thickens, then add half the cheese and season to taste.

5 Pour the sauce over the ingredients in the casserole, put the remaining potato slices on top, and sprinkle with the remaining cheese.

6 Bake, uncovered, in a preheated oven at 200°C (400°F) mark 6 for about 40 minutes or until golden.

TOMATO FISH BAKE

SERVES 4

50 g (2 oz) fresh breadcrumbs	25 g (1 oz) butter
50 g (2 oz) Cheddar cheese, grated	50 g (2 oz) mushrooms, sliced
1 small onion, finely chopped	25 g (1 oz) plain flour
2.5 ml (½ tsp) dried mixed herbs	30 ml (2 tbsp) tomato purée
300 ml (½ pint) milk, plus 30–45 ml (2–3 tbsp)	5 ml (1 tsp) lemon juice
salt and pepper	pinch of sugar
450 g (1 lb) white fish	450 g (1 lb) potatoes, peeled
	chopped parsley or watercress, to garnish

1 To make the stuffing, mix the breadcrumbs, grated cheese, onion and herbs with the 30–45 ml (2–3 tbsp) milk. Season to taste.

2 Wash and skin the fish. Place half on the base of a buttered shallow flameproof dish. Spread the stuffing over the fish and top with the remaining fish.

3 Melt the butter in a saucepan and fry the mushrooms for about 5 minutes or until soft. Add the flour, the remaining 300 ml (½ pint) milk, the tomato purée, lemon juice, sugar and seasoning. Heat, whisking continuously, until the sauce thickens. Pour over the fish. Bake in a preheated oven at 190°C (375°F) mark 5 for 20 minutes.

4 Meanwhile, cook the potatoes in boiling salted water for about 20 minutes or until tender. Drain and mash. Remove the fish from the oven and pipe a border of mashed potato around the dish. Return to the oven or place under a preheated hot grill to brown. Garnish with chopped parsley or watercress.

HOT FISH TERRINE WITH GRUYÈRE SAUCE

SERVES 6

FISH MOUSSES WITH CORIANDER AND TOMATO SAUCE

SERVES 4

75 g (3 oz) butter	3 eggs
1 garlic clove, crushed	1 egg yolk
60 ml (4 tbsp) plain flour	salt and pepper
750 ml (1¼ pints) milk	30 ml (2 tbsp) chopped parsley
550 g (1¼ lb) hake fillets, skinned and chopped	100 g (4 oz) peeled cooked prawns, chopped
150 ml (¼ pint) double cream	100 g (4 oz) Gruyère cheese, grated
10 ml (2 tsp) anchovy essence	

1 Lightly butter and base-line a 1.6 litre (2¾ pint) shallow loaf tin or terrine.

2 Melt 40 g (1½ oz) butter and add the garlic. Stir in 45 ml (3 tbsp) flour and cook, stirring, for 1–2 minutes. Off the heat, blend in 450 ml (¾ pint) milk. Bring to the boil, stirring, then simmer for 2 minutes or until thick.

3 Turn the sauce into a blender or food processor. Add the hake, cream, anchovy essence, eggs and egg yolk and blend to a purée. Season lightly.

4 Spoon half the fish mixture into the tin. Sprinkle with parsley and half the prawns, then spoon in the rest of the fish mixture. Cover with buttered greaseproof paper. Place in a roasting tin and pour in hot water to come halfway up the sides. Cook at 150°C (300°F) mark 2 for 1¾ hours.

5 Just before the terrine is cooked, make the sauce. Melt 25 g (1 oz) butter, add the remaining flour and cook, stirring, for 1–2 minutes. Off the heat, blend in the remaining milk. Cook, stirring, for 2 minutes until thick. Stir in the cheese and remaining prawns. Season to taste.

6 Invert the terrine on to a warmed serving dish and drain off the juices. Spoon over a little sauce before serving.

225 g (8 oz) haddock or cod fillets, skinned	pinch of cayenne
	FOR THE SAUCE
100 g (4 oz) peeled prawns	25 g (1 oz) butter
1 egg	3 spring onions, chopped
150 ml (¼ pint) double cream	400 g (14 oz) can chopped tomatoes
150 ml (¼ pint) natural yogurt	15 ml (1 tbsp) tomato purée
30 ml (2 tbsp) chopped fresh coriander or 10 ml (2 tsp) ground coriander	5 ml (1 tsp) sugar
	15 ml (1 tbsp) chopped fresh coriander or 5 ml (1 tsp) ground coriander
10 ml (2 tsp) lemon juice	
salt and pepper	coriander sprigs, to garnish

1 Put the fish and prawns in a blender or food processor and blend to a purée. Blend in the egg, cream, yogurt, coriander and lemon juice and season to taste with salt, pepper and cayenne.

2 Butter four 175 ml (6 fl oz) ovenproof ramekin dishes and divide the fish mixture between them. Cover loosely with foil, place in a roasting tin and pour in enough hot water to come halfway up the sides. Cook in a preheated oven at 180°C (350°F) mark 4 for 20–30 minutes or until firm.

3 For the sauce, melt the butter in a small saucepan, add the spring onions and cook for 3 minutes. Put the tomatoes in a food processor or blender and purée until smooth. Add the tomatoes to the onions and stir in the tomato purée and sugar. Cook for 5–6 minutes. Sieve the sauce and stir in the chopped coriander. Unmould the mousses and serve with the sauce. Garnish with coriander sprigs.

FISH MEDALLIONS WITH DILL SAUCE

SERVES 4

225 g (8 oz) salmon fillets, skinned	FOR THE SAUCE
	25 g (1 oz) butter
350 g (12 oz) plaice fillets, skinned	1 small onion, very finely chopped
150 ml (¼ pint) dry white wine	15 ml (1 tbsp) plain flour
	300 ml (½ pint) single cream
30 ml (2 tbsp) lemon juice	1 bay leaf
pepper	30 ml (2 tbsp) chopped fresh dill or 10 ml (2 tsp) dried
a few dill sprigs	
	salt and pepper

1 Cut the fish fillets lengthways into 0.5 cm (¼ inch) thick strips. Using two of one colour and one of the other, lay alternate colours alongside each other and coil round to form a spiral, securing with a wooden cocktail stick. Continue to make eight medallions.
2 Place the wine and lemon juice in a frying pan. Add the medallions, season with pepper and scatter over the dill sprigs. Poach gently for 5–7 minutes or until the fish is firm and moist. Remove the dill sprigs and cocktail sticks. Transfer the medallions to a warmed serving dish and cover with foil to keep warm.
3 For the sauce, melt the butter in a saucepan and cook the onion for 2–3 minutes or until softened. Stir in the flour and cook, stirring continuously, for a further minute. Remove from the heat and gradually stir in the cream. Add the bay leaf. Heat gently, without boiling, for 3–5 minutes or until the sauce is thickened, stirring continuously. Remove the bay leaf and stir in the dill. Season to taste.
4 Serve the fish medallions with the dill sauce.

HERRINGS IN OATMEAL

SERVES 2

2 medium herrings, cleaned, heads and tails removed	15 ml (1 tbsp) vegetable oil
	15 g (½ oz) butter
salt and pepper	lemon wedges, to serve
50 g (2 oz) medium oatmeal	

1 To remove the backbone of the fish, open out on a board, cut side down, and press lightly with the fingers along the middle of the back. Turn the fish over and ease the backbone up with your fingers. Fold the fish in half. Season well and coat with the oatmeal.
2 Heat the oil and butter in a large frying pan and fry the herrings for about 5 minutes on each side. Drain well before serving hot with lemon wedges.

───────── **TO MICROWAVE** ─────────

Complete step 1. Heat a large browning dish on HIGH for 5–8 minutes or according to the manufacturer's instructions. Put the oil and butter into the browning dish, then quickly add the herrings. Cook on HIGH for 1 minute, then turn over and cook on HIGH for 1–2 minutes or until tender. Serve hot with lemon wedges.

STUFFED HERRINGS

SERVES 4

65 g (2½ oz) butter	juice and finely grated rind of 1 lemon
1 medium onion, finely chopped	45 ml (3 tbsp) chopped fresh mixed herbs (chives, parsley, rosemary, thyme)
50 g (2 oz) fresh wholemeal breadcrumbs	
50 g (2 oz) walnut pieces, roughly chopped	salt and pepper
15 ml (1 tbsp) prepared English mustard	four 275 g (10 oz) herrings, cleaned, boned and heads and tails, removed

1 Melt 15 g (½ oz) of the butter in a saucepan, add the onion and fry gently for about 5 minutes or until softened, stirring occasionally.

2 Meanwhile, mix together the breadcrumbs, walnuts, mustard, lemon rind, 15 ml (1 tbsp) lemon juice and the mixed herbs. Season to taste. Add the onion and mix together well.

3 Open the herring fillets and lay skin side down. Press the stuffing mixture evenly over each fillet. Fold the herring fillets back in half and slash the skin several times.

4 Melt the remaining butter in a large frying pan, add the fish and fry for about 10 minutes or until they are tender and browned on each side, turning the fish once.

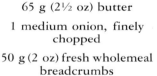

--- **VARIATION** ---

Stuffed Mackerel

Substitute four mackerel for the herrings in the above recipe if preferred.

MACKEREL PARCELS

SERVES 4

four 175 g (6 oz) fresh mackerel	30 ml (2 tbsp) chopped mint
about 25 g (1 oz) margarine	5 ml (1 tsp) sugar
½ large cucumber, sliced	salt and pepper
60 ml (4 tbsp) white wine vinegar	natural yogurt and mint leaves, to serve

1 With the back of a knife and working from the tail towards the head, scrape off the scales from the skin of the mackerel. Cut off the heads just below the gills with a sharp knife. Cut off the fins and tails with kitchen scissors.

2 Slit the underside of the fish open from head to tail end with a sharp knife or scissors. With the flat of the knife blade, scrape out the entrails of the fish, together with any membranes and blood. Wash the fish thoroughly.

3 Lay the fish flat on a board or work surface with the skin uppermost. Press firmly along the backbone with your knuckles to flatten the fish and loosen the backbone.

4 Turn the fish over and lift out the backbone. Cut each fish lengthways into two fillets. Dry thoroughly.

5 Grease eight squares of kitchen foil with a little margarine. Put a mackerel fillet in the centre of each square, skin side down.

6 Arrange cucumber slices down one half of the length of each fillet, then sprinkle with vinegar, mint and sugar. Season. Dot with the remaining margarine.

7 Fold the mackerel fillets over lengthways to enclose the cucumber filling, then wrap in the foil. Place the foil parcels in a single layer in an ovenproof dish. Cook at 200°C (400°F) mark 6 for 30 minutes or until tender.

8 To serve, unwrap the foil parcels and carefully place the mackerel fillets in a circle on a warmed platter. Spoon the yogurt in the centre and garnish with mint.

GRILLED MACKEREL WITH SAGE SAUCE

SERVES 4

4 mackerel, cleaned	75 ml (3 fl oz) dry white wine
salt and pepper	75 ml (3 fl oz) dry vermouth
150 ml (¼ pint) olive oil	
30 ml (2 tbsp) lemon juice	5 ml (1 tsp) very finely chopped sage

1 Cut the fins from the mackerel and cut three diagonal slits in the skin across both sides of each fish. Season the fish inside and out, then place in a dish large enough to hold them in a single layer.

2 Mix the oil, lemon juice and wine together and pour over the fish. Cover and leave to marinate in a cool place for 1½ hours, turning the fish occasionally.

3 Remove the mackerel from the marinade. Cook under a preheated hot grill for 5–8 minutes on each side, depending on the thickness of the fish, until the flesh flakes easily. Transfer to a warmed serving dish, cover and keep hot.

4 Carefully remove the oil from the top of the marinade and pour the marinade into a saucepan with the cooking juices from the grill pan. Add the vermouth and sage leaves and simmer for 2–3 minutes. Season to taste and pour over the mackerel.

SMOKED MACKEREL SOUFFLÉ

SERVES 4

200 ml (7 fl oz) milk	25 g (1 oz) butter
a few onion and carrot slices	salt and pepper
1 bay leaf	4 eggs, separated
6 black peppercorns	75 g (3 oz) cooked smoked mackerel, skinned, boned and finely flaked
30 ml (2 tbsp) plain flour	

1 Grease a 1.3 litre (2¼ pint) soufflé dish.

2 Put the milk in a medium saucepan with the onion and carrot slices, bay leaf and peppercorns. Bring slowly to the boil, remove from the heat, cover and leave to infuse for 30 minutes. Strain and reserve the milk.

3 Put the flour, butter and reserved milk in a medium saucepan. Heat, whisking continuously, until the sauce thickens, boils and is smooth. Simmer for 1–2 minutes. Season to taste, then leave to cool slightly.

4 Beat the egg yolks into the cooled sauce, one at a time. Sprinkle the fish over the sauce and stir in until evenly blended. Whisk all the egg whites until stiff.

5 Mix one large spoonful of egg white into the sauce to lighten its texture. Gently pour the sauce over the remaining egg whites and fold the ingredients lightly together.

6 Pour the soufflé mixture gently into the prepared dish and smooth the surface.

7 Place the soufflé on a baking sheet and bake in a preheated oven at 180°C (350°F) mark 4 for about 30 minutes or until golden brown on top, well risen and just firm to the touch. Serve immediately.

CHEESY SMOKED SALMON ROULADE

SERVES 4–6

FOR THE ROULADE	FOR THE FILLING
100 g (4 oz) butter	225 g (8 oz) smoked salmon, finely shredded
100 g (4 oz) plain flour	75 ml (5 tbsp) double cream
300 ml (½ pint) milk	
100 g (4 oz) Gruyère cheese, grated	5 ml (1 tsp) lemon juice
4 eggs, separated	15 ml (1 tbsp) chopped fresh dill or 5 ml (1 tsp) dried
30 ml (2 tbsp) freshly grated Parmesan cheese	dill sprigs and lemon slices, to garnish

1 Grease and line a 23 x 33 cm (9 x 13 inch) Swiss roll tin. Grease the paper.

2 To make the roulade, melt the butter in a saucepan, stir in the flour and cook for 1 minute. Remove from the heat and gradually stir in the milk. Gently bring to the boil, stirring continuously. Beat in the Gruyère and egg yolks.

3 Whisk the egg whites until stiff. Fold into the cheese mixture and pour into the prepared tin. Bake in a preheated oven at 190°C (375°F) mark 5 for 25–30 minutes or until firm to the touch and golden.

4 Lay a sheet of greaseproof paper on a work surface and sprinkle with the Parmesan cheese. Turn the roulade on to the paper and remove the lining paper. Cover with a damp cloth.

5 To make the filling, place the smoked salmon in a small saucepan and stir in the cream, lemon juice and chopped dill. Heat very gently for 1–2 minutes. Spread the filling over the roulade and roll up, using the greaseproof paper to assist. Serve immediately cut into slices and garnished with dill sprigs and lemon slices.

ITALIAN SQUID STEW

SERVES 4

1 kg (2¼ lb) small squid	2 garlic cloves, crushed
75 ml (5 tbsp) olive oil	juice of ½ lemon
salt and pepper	15 ml (1 tbsp) chopped parsley
75 ml (3 fl oz) dry white wine	

1 Wash the squid in plenty of cold water. Grip the head and tentacles firmly and pull them away from the body. The entrails will follow. Discard these and pull out the transparent quill.

2 With your hands, carefully peel the skin from the body and fins of the squid.

3 Cut the tentacles from the head and remove the skin. Reserve two ink sacs, being careful not to pierce them. Discard the rest of the head.

4 Cut the squid bodies into 0.5 cm (¼ inch) rings. Place in a bowl with the tentacles and spoon over 45 ml (3 tbsp) of the oil. Season well and leave for 3 hours.

5 Pour the squid and marinade into a large frying pan and cook the squid for 5 minutes, turning frequently. Add the wine and garlic and cook for a further 5 minutes. Add the ink sacs, breaking them up with a spoon.

6 Cover and cook over a low heat for about 40 minutes or until the squid is tender.

7 Add the remaining oil, the lemon juice and parsley. Stir for 3 minutes over a high heat, taste and adjust the seasoning and serve.

SCALLOPS IN CREAMY BASIL SAUCE

SERVES 4

900 g (2 lb) shelled scallops, thawed if frozen	150 ml (¼ pint) dry white wine
30 ml (2 tbsp) vegetable oil	20 ml (4 tsp) chopped basil
15 g (½ oz) butter	salt and pepper
1 small onion, finely chopped	150 ml (5 fl oz) double cream
2 garlic cloves, crushed	a few fresh basil sprigs, to garnish

1 Cut the scallops (including the coral) into fairly thick slices. Pat dry with absorbent kitchen paper and set aside.
2 Heat the oil and butter in a large frying pan, add the onion and garlic, and fry gently for 5 minutes or until soft and lightly coloured.
3 Add the scallops to the pan and toss to coat in the oil and butter. Stir in the wine and basil and season to taste.
4 Fry the scallops over a moderate heat for 10 minutes or until they are tender, turning them constantly so that they cook evenly on all sides. Do not overcook or they will become tough and rubbery.
5 Remove the scallops from the liquid with a slotted spoon and set aside on a plate. Boil the liquid until reduced by about half, then stir in the cream, a little at a time, and simmer until the sauce is thick.
6 Return the scallops to the pan and heat gently. Taste and adjust the seasoning and serve garnished with basil.

MUSSEL AND ONION STEW

SERVES 4

2 kg (4½ lb) fresh mussels, scrubbed and 'beards' removed	25 g (1 oz) plain wholemeal flour
150 ml (¼ pint) dry white wine	300 ml (½ pint) milk
25 g (1 oz) butter	30 ml (2 tbsp) chopped parsley
2 large onions, chopped	30 ml (2 tbsp) single cream

1 Discard any mussels that are cracked or do not close when tapped sharply with a knife.
2 Put the wine in a large saucepan and bring to the boil. Add the mussels, cover and cook over a high heat for 3–4 minutes or until the mussels open, shaking the pan occasionally. Discard any mussels that have not opened.
3 Drain the mussels, reserving the juice. Remove the mussels from the shells.
4 Melt the butter in a saucepan, add the onions and fry lightly for about 5 minutes or until soft but not coloured. Stir in the flour and cook for 1 minute.
5 Gradually add the milk and the mussel cooking liquid, stirring, until the sauce thickens, boils and is smooth. Simmer for 1–2 minutes.
6 Return the mussels to the pan with the parsley and cream. Reheat gently and serve at once.

MUSSELS AND CLAMS WITH TOMATOES

SERVES 2–3

900 g (2 lb) fresh mussels, scrubbed and 'beards' removed	150 ml (¼ pint) dry white wine
450 g (1 lb) small clams, such as venus clams	225 g (8 oz) ripe tomatoes, chopped
25 g (1 oz) butter	finely grated rind of 1 lemon
1–2 large garlic cloves, crushed	30 ml (2 tbsp) chopped parsley
1 small onion, finely chopped	salt and pepper

1 Discard any cracked mussels, or any that do not close when tapped sharply with a knife. Scrub the clams thoroughly and discard any that are cracked or open.
2 Melt the butter in a saucepan and cook the garlic and onion until soft. Add the wine, tomatoes, lemon rind and half the parsley. Bring to the boil.
3 Add the mussels and clams to the pan, cover and cook over a high heat for 3–4 minutes or until the mussels and clams are open, shaking the pan occasionally. Discard any mussels or clams that have not opened.
4 Season to taste. Transfer to two or three large bowls or soup plates and sprinkle with the remaining parsley.

TAGLIATELLE WITH SEAFOOD AND CHAMPAGNE SAUCE

SERVES 4

16 fresh mussels, scrubbed and 'beards' removed	225 g (8 oz) fresh tagliatelle
175 g (6 oz) fresh clams, scrubbed	75 g (3 oz) butter
150 ml (¼ pint) fish stock	salt and pepper
one 300 g (11 oz) red mullet, filleted	50 g (2 oz) leek, cut into fine julienne strips
175 g (6 oz) salmon fillets, skinned	150 ml (¼ pint) champagne or sparkling dry white wine
4 large uncooked Pacific prawns, peeled and deveined	300 ml (½ pint) double cream
4 fresh scallops, shelled	pinch of cayenne
	12 fresh basil leaves

1 Discard any open mussels or clams which do not close when tapped. Place in a pan with the stock, cover and cook until the shells open. Discard any closed shells. Leave to cool, then remove the mussels and clams from their shells. Strain the stock and reserve.
2 Cut the fish into 1 cm (½ inch) strips. Cut each prawn in half. Separate the coral from each scallop and cut the scallops in half crossways.
3 Cook the tagliatelle in boiling salted water for 2–3 minutes. Drain and toss in half the butter. Season.
4 Melt the remaining butter in a saucepan and fry the leeks, prawns and scallop coral for 30 seconds. Add the fish fillets, champagne and reserved stock and simmer for 1 minute. Remove the fish from the pan and keep warm.
5 Boil the cooking liquid rapidly until reduced by half. Add the cream and boil until thick. Season and add the cayenne. Return the fish to the sauce with the seafood and basil. Warm and serve with the tagliatelle.

BUTTER BEAN AND TUNA GRATIN

SERVES 4

225 g (8 oz) dried butter beans	450 g (1 lb) fresh or frozen broccoli
450 ml (¾ pint) milk	198 g (7 oz) can tuna, drained
a small piece of onion	salt and pepper
a small piece of carrot	40 g (1½ oz) butter
1 bay leaf	60 ml (4 tbsp) plain flour
6 peppercorns	50 g (2 oz) Cheddar cheese, grated
a blade of mace	

1 Soak the beans overnight in cold water.
2 Put the milk, vegetables, bay leaf and spices in a saucepan and bring slowly to the boil. Remove from the heat, cover and leave to infuse for 30 minutes, then strain and reserve.
3 Drain the beans and cook in a pan of gently boiling water for 1¼ hours or until tender. Drain well.
4 Meanwhile, break the broccoli into florets and cook in a little boiling salted water for about 5 minutes or until just tender. Drain and arrange in a buttered shallow ovenproof dish.
5 Flake the tuna and combine with the cooked beans. Season to taste and pile in the centre of the dish.
6 To make the sauce, melt the butter in a saucepan, stir in the flour and cook gently for 1 minute, stirring. Remove the pan from the heat and gradually stir in the strained milk. Bring to the boil and continue to cook, stirring, until the sauce thickens, then season to taste. Pour over the tuna and broccoli mixture.
7 Sprinkle with the cheese and bake in a preheated oven at 200°C (400°F) mark 6 for 15–20 minutes or until golden.

FISHERMAN'S PIE

SERVES 4

65 g (2½ oz) butter or margarine	100 g (4 oz) button mushrooms, halved
100 g (4 oz) red pepper, thinly sliced	450 ml (¾ pint) tomato juice
100 g (4 oz) green pepper, thinly sliced	550 g (1¼ lb) cod fillet, skinned
50 g (2 oz) onion, sliced	450 g (1 lb) potatoes, peeled and thinly sliced
salt and pepper	50 g (2 oz) Edam cheese, grated

1 Melt 25 g (1 oz) of the butter or margarine in a frying pan, add the peppers and onion and fry gently for 10 minutes or until soft but not coloured. Transfer to a 2.3 litre (4 pint) ovenproof dish. Season well.
2 Cook the mushrooms in the fat remaining in the frying pan, stirring frequently, for 3–4 minutes or until evenly coloured.
3 Pour the tomato juice evenly over the pepper and onion mixture in the dish.
4 Cut the fish into large cubes. Arrange the cubes on top of the tomato juice, pressing them down gently into the juice. Top with the mushrooms. Season again with salt and pepper.
5 Arrange the sliced potatoes on top of the mushrooms. Melt the remaining butter or margarine and brush over the potatoes. Bake in the oven at 190°C (375°F) mark 5 for 25 minutes.
6 Sprinkle the grated cheese over the pie, return to the oven and bake for a further 15 minutes or until melted and bubbling. Serve hot, straight from the dish.

SEAFOOD STIR-FRY

SERVES 4

2 celery sticks, trimmed	1 garlic clove, crushed
1 medium carrot	100 g (4 oz) peeled prawns
350 g (12 oz) coley, haddock or cod fillets, skinned	425 g (15 oz) can whole baby sweetcorn, drained
350 g (12 oz) Iceberg or Cos lettuce	5 ml (1 tsp) anchovy essence
about 45 ml (3 tbsp) peanut oil	salt and pepper

1 Slice the celery and carrot into thin matchsticks, 5 cm (2 inches) long. Cut the fish into 2.5 cm (1 inch) chunks.
2 Shred the lettuce finely with a sharp knife, discarding the core and any thick stalks.
3 Heat 15 ml (1 tbsp) of the oil in a wok or large frying pan until smoking. Add the lettuce and fry for about 30 seconds or until lightly cooked. Transfer to a warmed serving dish with a slotted spoon and keep warm.
4 Heat another 30 ml (2 tbsp) oil in the pan until smoking. Add the celery, carrot, white fish and garlic and stir-fry over a high heat for 2–3 minutes, adding more oil if necessary.
5 Lower the heat and add the prawns, baby sweetcorn and anchovy essence. Toss well together for 2–3 minutes to heat through and coat all the ingredients in the sauce (the fish will flake apart).
6 Season to taste, spoon on top of the lettuce and serve immediately.

CURRIED PRAWN CRÊPES

SERVES 4

100 g (4 oz) plain flour	FOR THE FILLING
salt	25 g (1 oz) butter
1 egg, beaten	15 ml (1 tbsp) curry powder
300 ml (½ pint) milk	25 g (1 oz) plain flour
vegetable oil, for frying	300 ml (½ pint) milk
100 g (4 oz) mature Cheddar cheese, grated	225 g (8 oz) peeled prawns
parsley sprigs and lemon wedges, to garnish	30 ml (2 tbsp) chopped fresh parsley or 10 ml (2 tsp) dried
	salt and pepper

1 To make the crêpes, sift the flour and salt into a bowl. Add the egg and 150 ml (¼ pint) of the milk and beat well. Gradually beat in the remaining milk.
2 Heat a small frying pan or crêpe pan and brush with oil. Add about 45 ml (3 tbsp) of the batter and swirl to coat the pan. Cook for 1–2 minutes or until the underside is golden, then flip over and cook the other side until golden. Turn on to a plate and repeat the process, making eight to ten crêpes.
3 To make the filling, melt the butter in a saucepan, stir in the curry powder and flour and cook for 1 minute. Remove from the heat and gradually stir in the milk. Return to the heat and slowly bring to the boil, stirring continuously. Add the prawns and parsley and season.
4 Divide the filling between the crêpes, placing it towards one edge. Roll up the crêpes and arrange, side by side, in an ovenproof dish. Sprinkle over the cheese.
5 Bake in a preheated oven at 180°C (350°F) mark 4 for 15–20 minutes. Garnish with parsley and lemon.

VEGETARIAN DISHES

Full of goodness and flavour, vegetarian dishes can be both satisfying and simple for family meals, yet special enough for entertaining. Carefully selected combinations of vegetables, herbs, nuts and seeds are delicious served in a wide range of wholesome dishes.

GRANDMA'S CHEESE PUDDING

SERVES 8

1.1 litres (2 pints) milk	8 eggs
100 g (4 oz) fresh breadcrumbs	5 ml (1 tsp) French mustard
450 g (1 lb) Cheddar cheese, grated	salt and pepper

1 Put the milk in a saucepan and bring to the boil. Place the breadcrumbs in a bowl and pour the hot milk over. Stir in the cheese.
2 Lightly beat the eggs with the mustard and the milk and breadcrumb mixture. Season to taste.
3 Butter a shallow 2.8 litre (5 pint) ovenproof dish and pour in the cheese pudding mixture. Bake in a preheated oven at 180°C (350°F) mark 4 for about 45 minutes or until lightly set and golden. Serve at once.

STUFFED AUBERGINES

SERVES 4

2 aubergines	1 shallot, chopped
25 g (1 oz) butter or margarine	1 onion, chopped
4 small tomatoes, skinned and chopped	50 g (2 oz) brown breadcrumbs
10 ml (2 tsp) chopped fresh marjoram or 5 ml (1 tsp) dried	salt and pepper
	50 g (2 oz) cheese, grated
	parsley sprigs, to garnish

1 Steam or boil the aubergines for 30 minutes or until tender. Cut in half lengthways, scoop out the flesh and chop finely. Reserve the shells.
2 Melt the butter in a saucepan, add the tomatoes, marjoram, shallot and onion and cook for 10 minutes. Stir in the aubergine and a few breadcrumbs, then season.
3 Stuff the aubergine shells with this mixture, then sprinkle with the remaining breadcrumbs and the grated cheese. Grill until golden brown. Garnish and serve.

CHEESE SOUFFLÉ

SERVES 4

40 g (1½ oz) butter	10 ml (2 tsp) French mustard
200 ml (7 fl oz) milk	salt and pepper
1 onion, sliced	4 eggs, separated, plus 1 egg white
1 carrot, sliced	
1 bay leaf	150 g (5 oz) Double Gloucester cheese, grated
6 peppercorns	
30 ml (2 tbsp) plain flour	

1 Grease the inside of a 1.4 litre (2½ pint) soufflé dish with 15 g (½ oz) butter.

2 Place the milk, onion, carrot, bay leaf and peppercorns in a saucepan, bring slowly to the boil, then remove from the heat. Leave to infuse for 15 minutes, then strain and reserve the milk.

3 Melt the remaining butter in a saucepan, stir in the flour and cook gently for 1 minute, stirring. Remove from the heat and gradually stir in the reserved milk. Bring to the boil and continue to cook, stirring, until the sauce thickens, then add the mustard and season to taste. Leave to cool slightly.

4 Beat the egg yolks into the sauce, one at a time. Add the cheese, reserving 15 ml (1 tbsp), and stir until well blended.

5 Whisk the egg whites until stiff. Mix in one spoonful of sauce, then pour the remaining sauce over the egg whites and fold the ingredients lightly together.

6 Turn the mixture gently into the prepared dish. Smooth the top and sprinkle over the remaining cheese. Place on a baking sheet and bake in the centre of the oven at 180°C (350°F) mark 4 for 30 minutes. Serve at once.

COURGETTE, PARMESAN AND TOMATO BAKE

SERVES 4

700 g (1½ lb) courgettes	30 ml (2 tbsp) tomato purée
salt and pepper	
about 150 ml (¼ pint) vegetable oil	15 ml (1 tbsp) chopped fresh marjoram or 5 ml (1 tsp) dried
1 medium onion, finely chopped	
	two 170 g (6 oz) packets Mozzarella cheese, thinly sliced
450 g (1 lb) tomatoes, skinned and chopped	
1 large garlic clove, crushed	75 g (3 oz) freshly grated Parmesan cheese

1 Cut the courgettes into 0.5 cm (¼ inch) thick slices. Put in a colander, sprinkling each layer generously with salt, and leave for at least 20 minutes.

2 Heat 30 ml (2 tbsp) of the oil in a saucepan, add the onion and fry for about 5 minutes or until just beginning to brown.

3 Stir in the tomatoes, garlic and tomato purée and season to taste. Simmer for about 10 minutes, stirring to break down the tomatoes. Stir in the marjoram and remove from the heat.

4 Rinse the courgettes and pat dry with absorbent kitchen paper. Heat half the remaining oil in a frying pan, add half the courgettes and fry until golden brown. Drain well on absorbent kitchen paper while frying the remaining courgettes in the remaining oil.

5 Layer the courgettes, tomato sauce and Mozzarella cheese in a shallow ovenproof dish, finishing with a layer of Mozzarella. Sprinkle with the Parmesan cheese.

6 Bake in a preheated oven at 180°C (350°F) mark 4 for about 40 minutes or until brown and bubbling. Serve hot, straight from the dish.

ITALIAN STUFFED TOMATOES

SERVES 4–6

15 ml (1 tbsp) olive oil	45 ml (3 tbsp) pine nuts
4 spring onions, finely chopped	397 g (14 oz) can flageolet beans, drained
2 garlic cloves, crushed	salt and pepper
15 ml (1 tbsp) tomato purée	4 large beefsteak tomatoes or 6 medium tomatoes
12 pimiento-stuffed green olives, sliced	basil sprigs, to garnish
30 ml (2 tbsp) chopped fresh basil or 15 ml (1 tbsp) dried	

1 Heat the oil in a large saucepan and cook the spring onions and garlic for 2–3 minutes or until soft.
2 Add the tomato purée, olives, basil and nuts and cook for 2 minutes. Stir in the beans. Season.
3 Slice the tops off the tomatoes, reserving them for the lids, and scoop out the seeds and flesh to make them hollow. Chop the flesh and add to the filling mixture. Arrange the tomato shells in a buttered ovenproof dish and divide the filling between them. Add the lids and cover with foil.
4 Bake in a preheated oven at 180°C (350°F) mark 4 for 15–20 minutes. Garnish and serve.

JERUSALEM ARTICHOKE GRATIN

SERVES 4

900 g (2 lb) Jerusalem artichokes	3 medium leeks, thickly sliced
salt and pepper	225 g (8 oz) fresh or frozen peas
75 g (3 oz) butter or margarine	150 ml (¼ pint) double cream
15 ml (1 tbsp) olive oil	75 g (3 oz) Gruyère cheese, grated
225 g (8 oz) button onions, skinned	75 g (3 oz) Cheddar cheese, grated
2 garlic cloves, crushed	50 g (2 oz) dried wholemeal breadcrumbs
150 ml (¼ pint) dry white wine or vegetable stock	
1.25 ml (¼ tsp) grated nutmeg	

1 Parboil the artichokes in salted water for 10 minutes. Remove with a slotted spoon and leave to cool.
2 Peel the artichokes and slice thickly. Set aside.
3 Heat 50 g (2 oz) butter with the oil in a saucepan, add the onions and garlic and toss until well coated.
4 Pour in the wine or stock and 150 ml (¼ pint) water and bring to the boil. Add the nutmeg, cover and simmer for 10 minutes. Add the artichokes, leeks and peas and continue simmering for 5 minutes or until tender. Transfer the vegetables to a flameproof gratin dish.
5 Boil the cooking liquid rapidly until reduced by about half, then lower the heat and stir in the cream.
6 Mix the two cheeses together. Stir half into the sauce, season and stir until melted.
7 Pour the cheese sauce over the vegetables. Mix the remaining cheese and breadcrumbs, then sprinkle on top.
8 Dot the remaining butter over the gratin, then bake at 220°C (425°F) mark 7 for 10 minutes or until golden.

CYPRUS STUFFED PEPPERS

SERVES 4

8 peppers	5 ml (1 tsp) sugar
75 ml (5 tbsp) olive oil	salt and pepper
2 onions, chopped	45 ml (3 tbsp) chopped coriander
4 garlic cloves, crushed	225 g (8 oz) Italian risotto rice
350 g (12 oz) tomatoes, skinned, seeded and chopped	2.5 ml (½ tsp) ground cinnamon
15 ml (1 tbsp) tomato purée	

1 Cut the stalk end off each pepper and reserve. Remove the cores and seeds and discard. Wash and pat dry.

2 Heat 60 ml (4 tbsp) oil in a frying pan, add the peppers and fry for 10 minutes, turning frequently. Remove from the pan with a slotted spoon and drain.

3 To make the stuffing, drain off all but 30 ml (2 tbsp) oil from the pan, then add the onions and garlic and fry very gently for about 15 minutes. Add the tomatoes and fry gently to soften, stirring constantly. Increase the heat and cook rapidly until thick and pulpy.

4 Lower the heat and add the tomato purée and sugar. Season to taste and simmer gently for 5 minutes. Remove from the heat and stir in the coriander and rice. Spoon into the peppers, dividing it equally between them.

5 Stand the peppers close together in a large heavy-based pan or flameproof casserole. Sprinkle with the cinnamon, then the remaining oil. Put the reserved 'lids' on top.

6 Pour 150 ml (¼ pint) water into the base of the pan, then bring to the boil. Lower the heat, cover with a plate which just fits inside the pan, then place weights on top.

7 Simmer gently for 1 hour, then remove from the heat and leave to cool. Chill in the refrigerator overnight, still with the weights on top. Serve the peppers chilled.

CABBAGE AND HAZELNUT ROLLS

MAKES 16

450 g (1 lb) potatoes, peeled	50 g (2 oz) hazelnuts, toasted and chopped
salt and pepper	2 eggs, beaten
900 g (2 lb) green cabbage, roughly chopped	100 g (4 oz) dry breadcrumbs
45 ml (3 tbsp) milk, if necessary	vegetable oil, for deep frying
50 g (2 oz) butter	lemon twists, to garnish
50 g (2 oz) plain flour	

1 Cook the potatoes in boiling salted water for 20 minutes or until tender. Drain and mash without adding liquid.

2 Cook the cabbage in boiling salted water for 5–10 minutes or until just tender. Drain well, then put in a blender or food processor and blend to a purée, adding the milk if necessary – you should have 450 ml (¾ pint) purée.

3 Melt the butter in a saucepan, add the flour and cook gently, stirring, for 1–2 minutes. Gradually blend in the cabbage purée, bring to the boil and simmer for 5 minutes.

4 Stir the mashed potatoes and hazelnuts into the sauce, season to taste and mix well. Transfer to a bowl, cool, cover and chill for at least 1½ hours or until firm.

5 With dampened hands, shape the mixture into 16 rolls. Place on a greased baking sheet and chill again for at least 20 minutes.

6 Coat the rolls in beaten egg, then roll in the breadcrumbs. Heat the oil to 180°C (350°F) in a deep-fat fryer. Deep-fry the rolls in batches for about 4 minutes or until crisp and golden. Remove with a slotted spoon and drain on absorbent kitchen paper while frying the remainder. Serve hot, garnished with lemon twists.

BAKED POTATOES WITH CHICK-PEAS

SERVES 4

four 275 g (10 oz) baking potatoes	2.5 ml (½ tsp) ground cumin
45 ml (3 tbsp) vegetable oil	400 g (14 oz) can chick-peas, drained
salt and pepper	60 ml (4 tbsp) chopped parsley
1 medium onion, roughly chopped	150 ml (¼ pint) natural yogurt
2.5 ml (½ tsp) ground coriander	chopped parsley, to garnish

1 Scrub the potatoes and pat dry. Brush them with 15 ml (1 tbsp) of the vegetable oil and sprinkle lightly with salt.

2 Run thin skewers through the potatoes to help conduct the heat through them. Place them directly on the oven shelves and bake in a preheated oven at 200°C (400°F) mark 6 for 1¼ hours or until tender.

3 Meanwhile, heat the remaining oil in a large saucepan, add the onion, coriander and cumin and fry for 4 minutes, stirring occasionally. Add the chick-peas and cook for a further 1–2 minutes, stirring all the time.

4 Halve the potatoes and scoop out the flesh, keeping the skin intact. Add the potato flesh to the chick-pea mixture with the parsley and yogurt. Mash until smooth, then season to taste.

5 Place the potato skins on a baking sheet and fill with the potato and chick-pea mixture. Return to the oven and bake for a further 10–15 minutes. Serve hot, sprinkled with chopped parsley.

CAULIFLOWER AND COURGETTE BAKE

SERVES 4

700 g (1½ lb) cauliflower	45 ml (3 tbsp) wholemeal flour
salt and pepper	150 ml (¼ pint) milk
50 g (2 oz) butter or margarine	3 eggs, separated
225 g (8 oz) courgettes, thinly sliced	15 ml (1 tbsp) grated Parmesan cheese

1 Divide the cauliflower into small florets, trimming off thick stalks and leaves. Cook in boiling salted water for 10–12 minutes or until tender.

2 Meanwhile, in a separate pan, melt 25 g (1 oz) of the butter or margarine, add the courgettes and cook until beginning to soften. Remove from the pan with a slotted spoon and drain on absorbent kitchen paper.

3 Melt the remaining butter or margarine in the pan, stir in the flour and cook, stirring, for 1–2 minutes. Remove from the heat and add the milk, a little at a time, whisking constantly after each addition. Return to the heat and bring to the boil, stirring. Simmer until thickened.

4 Drain the cauliflower well and place in a blender or food processor with the warm sauce, egg yolks and plenty of seasoning. Blend together until evenly mixed, then turn into a large bowl.

5 Whisk the egg whites until stiff and carefully fold into the cauliflower mixture.

6 Spoon half the mixture into a 1.6 litre (2¾ pint) soufflé dish. Arrange the courgettes on top, reserving a few for garnish, then cover with the remaining cauliflower mixture. Top with the reserved courgettes.

7 Sprinkle over the Parmesan cheese and bake in a preheated oven at 190°C (375°F) mark 5 for 35–40 minutes or until golden. Serve immediately.

LEEK AND MACARONI GRATIN

SERVES 4

100 g (4 oz) short-cut macaroni	175 g (6 oz) Double Gloucester cheese with chives, grated
50 g (2 oz) butter	salt and pepper
275 g (10 oz) leeks, roughly chopped	25 g (1 oz) breadcrumbs
25 g (1 oz) plain flour	30 ml (2 tbsp) chopped chives
568 ml (1 pint) milk	

1 Cook the macaroni in boiling salted water for 8–10 minutes or until tender, but not soft. Drain well.

2 Melt the butter in a frying pan, add the leeks and sauté for 2 minutes. Stir in the flour and cook gently for 1 minute, stirring. Remove the pan from the heat and gradually stir in the milk. Bring to the boil and continue to cook, stirring for 2 minutes. Remove from the heat and stir in the macaroni and all but 30 ml (2 tbsp) cheese. Season to taste.

3 Spoon the mixture into a buttered 1.1 litre (2 pint) shallow ovenproof dish. Mix together the breadcrumbs, chives and remaining cheese and sprinkle evenly in lines across the dish.

4 Bake in a preheated oven at 190°C (375°F) mark 5 for 30–35 minutes or until golden. Serve immediately.

PASTA AND MUSHROOMS BAKED WITH TWO CHEESES

SERVES 2–3

225 g (8 oz) ribbon noodles	60 ml (4 tbsp) double cream
25 g (1 oz) butter	salt and pepper
1 garlic clove, crushed	1 egg, lightly beaten
225 g (8 oz) mushrooms, thinly sliced	100 g (4 oz) Mozzarella cheese
50 g (2 oz) Stilton cheese	

1 Cook the noodles in boiling salted water for about 7 minutes or until just tender.

2 Meanwhile, melt the butter in a large frying pan, add the garlic and mushrooms and fry for about 5 minutes or until just softened, stirring frequently. Crumble in the Stilton cheese and cook for 1–2 minutes, stirring continuously. Stir in the cream and season to taste.

3 Drain the pasta and season with lots of pepper. Mix into the mushroom sauce. Stir in the egg and mix thoroughly.

4 Turn the mixture into a buttered ovenproof dish and grate the Mozzarella on top. Cover with foil and bake in a preheated oven at 180°C (350°F) mark 4 for 10 minutes, then remove the foil and bake at 220°C (425°F) mark 7 for a further 10–15 minutes or until brown and crusty on top.

— TO MICROWAVE —

Complete step 1. Meanwhile, put the butter, garlic and mushrooms in a large bowl, cover and cook on HIGH for 3–4 minutes or until the mushrooms are softened, stirring occasionally. Stir in the Stilton cheese and the cream and cook on HIGH for 2 minutes, stirring once. Complete step 3. Turn the mixture into a buttered flameproof dish and grate the Mozzarella on top. Cook on HIGH for 3–4 minutes or until heated through. Brown the top under a hot grill.

VEGETABLE LASAGNE

SERVES 4

SPAGHETTI WITH RATATOUILLE SAUCE

SERVES 4

225 g (8 oz) carrots, thinly sliced	1 chicken stock cube
225 g (8 oz) courgettes, thinly sliced	25 g (1 oz) butter
1 onion, thinly sliced	30 ml (2 tbsp) plain flour
100 g (4 oz) green pepper, thinly sliced	300 ml (½ pint) milk
100 g (4 oz) celery, thinly sliced	salt and pepper
	175 g (6 oz) lasagne
	175 g (6 oz) Cheddar cheese, grated

1 aubergine	3 medium courgettes, cut into thin strips
salt and pepper	350 g (12 oz) tomatoes, skinned and finely chopped
1 onion, finely chopped	10 ml (2 tsp) chopped basil
1 garlic clove, crushed	400 g (14 oz) wholewheat spaghetti
1 green pepper, cut into thin strips	freshly grated Parmesan cheese, to serve
1 red pepper, cut into thin strips	

1 Place the vegetables in a saucepan with the stock cube and pour over 150 ml (¼ pint) boiling water. Bring to the boil, cover and simmer for 10 minutes.

2 Melt the butter in a pan, stir in the flour and cook gently for 1 minute, stirring. Remove from the heat and gradually stir in the milk. Bring to the boil and continue to cook, stirring, until the sauce thickens, then season to taste. If the sauce is too thick, add a little stock from the vegetables.

3 Meanwhile, cook the lasagne in fast boiling salted water until tender, but not soft, or according to packet instructions. Drain, being careful not to break up the lasagne sheets.

4 Make alternate layers of lasagne, vegetables and cheese (use 100 g/4 oz) in a 1.7 litre (3 pint) shallow ovenproof dish, finishing with a layer of lasagne. Top with the sauce, then sprinkle over the remaining cheese.

5 Bake in a preheated oven at 190°C (375°F) mark 5 for about 30 minutes.

1 Dice the aubergine, then spread out on a plate and sprinkle with salt. Leave for 30 minutes or until the juices flow.

2 Tip the diced aubergine into a sieve and rinse under cold running water. Put into a large, heavy-based saucepan with the prepared vegetables and basil. Season to taste, cover and cook over a moderate heat for 30 minutes. Shake the pan and stir the vegetables frequently during this time, to encourage the juices to flow.

3 Meanwhile, plunge the spaghetti into a large saucepan of boiling salted water. Simmer, uncovered, for 12 minutes or according to packet instructions, until *al dente* (tender but firm to the bite).

4 Drain the spaghetti thoroughly and turn into a warmed serving dish. Taste and adjust the seasoning of the ratatouille sauce, then pour over the spaghetti. Serve immediately, with the Parmesan cheese.

FRESH TAGLIATELLE WITH LEEK AND ROQUEFORT SAUCE

SERVES 4

75 g (3 oz) butter	5 ml (1 tsp) olive oil
1 garlic clove, crushed	pepper
450 g (1 lb) leeks, sliced	150 ml (¼ pint) whipping cream
150 g (5 oz) Roquefort cheese, roughly chopped	15–30 ml (1–2 tbsp) grated Parmesan cheese
30 ml (2 tbsp) chopped fresh chervil or 10 ml (2 tsp) dried	chervil sprigs, to garnish
700 g (1½ lb) fresh tagliatelle	

1 Melt 50 g (2 oz) of the butter in a medium saucepan, add the garlic and leeks and fry for 2–3 minutes or until softened.
2 Stir in the Roquefort cheese and chervil. Cook for 2–3 minutes or until the cheese has melted, stirring constantly.
3 Meanwhile, add the tagliatelle to a large saucepan of boiling water, with the olive oil added, and cook for 3–4 minutes. Drain and return to the clean pan. Add the remaining butter, toss well and season with pepper.
4 Pour the cream into the sauce, whisking vigorously. Cook, stirring, for a few minutes or until thick.
5 Serve the tagliatelle on warmed individual serving plates with the sauce poured over. Sprinkle with Parmesan cheese and garnish with chervil sprigs.

TO MICROWAVE

Dice the butter into a medium bowl. Cover and cook on HIGH for 1 minute. Add the garlic and leeks. Cover and cook on HIGH for 2–3 minutes. Add the cheese and chervil and cook for 1–1½ minutes. Whisk in the cream and cook on HIGH for 1–1½ minutes. Complete steps 3 and 5 as above.

TAGLIATELLE WITH CHEESE AND NUT SAUCE

SERVES 4

400 g (14 oz) wholewheat or green (spinach) tagliatelle	5 ml (1 tsp) chopped fresh sage or 2.5 ml (½ tsp) dried
salt and pepper	75 ml (5 tbsp) olive oil
100 g (4 oz) Gorgonzola cheese	15 ml (1 tbsp) chopped parsley, to garnish
100 g (4 oz) walnuts, chopped	

1 Plunge the tagliatelle into a large saucepan of boiling salted water. Simmer, uncovered, for 10 minutes, or according to packet instructions, until *al dente* (tender but firm to the bite).
2 Meanwhile, crumble the cheese into a blender or food processor. Add two thirds of the walnuts and the sage and blend to combine.
3 Add the oil gradually through the funnel (as when making mayonnaise) and blend until the sauce is evenly incorporated.
4 Drain the tagliatelle well and return to the pan. Add the nut sauce and fold in gently to mix. Season to taste.
5 Transfer the pasta and sauce to a warmed serving bowl and sprinkle with the remaining walnuts. Serve immediately, garnished with chopped parsley.

RATATOUILLE PASTA BAKE

SERVES 4–6

30 ml (2 tbsp) olive oil	30 ml (2 tbsp) chopped fresh basil or 5 ml (1 tsp) dried
1 large onion, thinly sliced	pinch of sugar
1 red pepper, cut into 5 cm (2 inch) strips	salt and pepper
1 yellow pepper, cut into 5 cm (2 inch) strips	450 ml (¾ pint) vegetable stock
225 g (8 oz) courgettes, cut into 5 cm (2 inch) strips	350 g (12 oz) mixed coloured pasta twists
450 g (1 lb) ripe tomatoes, skinned and chopped	50 g (2 oz) butter
2 garlic cloves, crushed	175 g (6 oz) mature Cheddar cheese, grated
30 ml (2 tbsp) tomato purée	

1 Heat the oil in a large pan, add the onion and peppers, and cook for 5 minutes or until softened, stirring. Add the courgettes and cook for 5 minutes.
2 Stir in the tomatoes, garlic, tomato purée, basil and sugar. Season to taste and simmer for 25–30 minutes, stirring occasionally and gradually adding the stock.
3 Meanwhile, bring a large saucepan of salted water to the boil and add the pasta twists. Cook for 15–20 minutes, stirring occasionally. Drain, then return to the pan, add the butter, toss well and season to taste. Transfer to a deep flameproof dish.
4 Pour the ratatouille sauce over the pasta and sprinkle over the cheese. Grill until golden.

WHOLEWHEAT MACARONI BAKE

SERVES 4–6

175 g (6 oz) wholewheat macaroni	5 ml (1 tsp) dried oregano
salt and pepper	30 ml (2 tbsp) plain wholemeal flour
1 onion, chopped	300 ml (½ pint) milk
30 ml (2 tbsp) vegetable oil	100 g (4 oz) low-fat soft cheese
225 g (8 oz) button mushrooms	1 egg, beaten
350 g (12 oz) tomatoes, skinned and roughly chopped	5 ml (1 tsp) English mustard powder
300 ml (½ pint) vegetable stock	30 ml (2 tbsp) wholemeal breadcrumbs
15 ml (1 tbsp) tomato purée	30 ml (2 tbsp) grated Parmesan cheese
5 ml (1 tsp) dried mixed herbs	

1 Cook the macaroni in boiling salted water for 10 minutes. Drain. Fry the onion in the oil for 5 minutes.
2 Cut the small mushrooms in half and slice the larger ones. Add to the pan and toss with the onion for 1–2 minutes.
3 Add the tomatoes and stock and bring to the boil, stirring constantly. Lower the heat, add the tomato purée and herbs and season to taste. Simmer for 10 minutes.
4 Put the flour and milk in a blender and blend for 1 minute. Transfer to a pan and simmer, stirring constantly, for 5 minutes or until thick. Remove from the heat and beat in the cheese, egg and mustard. Season.
5 Mix the macaroni with the mushroom and tomato sauce, then pour into a baking dish. Pour over the cheese sauce and sprinkle with breadcrumbs and Parmesan.
6 Bake in a preheated oven at 190°C (375°F) mark 5 for 20 minutes or until golden brown and bubbling. Serve hot.

SPINACH AND LENTIL ROULADE

SERVES 4

175 g (6 oz) red lentils	salt and pepper
1 small onion, finely chopped	450 g (1 lb) spinach
30 ml (2 tbsp) tomato ketchup	50 g (2 oz) plain flour
	300 ml (½ pint) milk
15 ml (1 tbsp) horseradish sauce	2 eggs, separated
100 g (4 oz) butter	dry breadcrumbs

1 Butter and line a 28 cm (11 inch) Swiss roll tin.
2 Cook the lentils with the onion in a large saucepan of boiling salted water until tender. Drain well, then return to the pan and heat to evaporate excess moisture. Add the tomato ketchup, horseradish and 50 g (2 oz) butter. Rub through a sieve, season to taste and set aside.
3 Trim and wash the spinach but do not dry. Pack into a large saucepan, sprinkle with salt, cover tightly and cook gently for 3–4 minutes.
4 To make the sauce, melt the remaining butter in a saucepan, stir in the flour and cook gently for 1 minute, stirring. Remove from the heat and gradually stir in the milk. Bring to the boil and continue to cook, stirring, until the sauce thickens. Remove from the heat. Stir in the spinach and egg yolks. Season to taste.
5 Whisk the egg whites until stiff and gently fold into the spinach mixture. Spoon into the prepared tin and level the surface. Bake in a preheated oven at 200°C (400°F) mark 6 for 20 minutes or until well risen and golden.
6 Turn out on to a sheet of greaseproof paper sprinkled with the breadcrumbs. Peel off the lining paper. Spread the lentil purée over the surface and roll up Swiss-roll style. Return to the oven to heat through before serving.

SPINACH AND STILTON CRÊPES

SERVES 8

900 g (2 lb) fresh spinach	150 ml (5 fl oz) single cream
salt and pepper	
50 g (2 oz) butter	8 crêpes (see page 119)
50 g (2 oz) salted peanuts, chopped	300 ml (½ pint) milk
2.5 ml (½ tsp) paprika	50 g (2 oz) Blue Stilton cheese, grated
40 ml (8 tsp) plain flour	

1 Tear the stalks off the spinach and wash, but do not dry. Place in a large saucepan, sprinkle with salt, cover tightly and cook for 10 minutes. Drain well and chop.
2 Heat 25 g (1 oz) butter in a small saucepan, add the peanuts and paprika and fry gently for 1 minute. Stir in the spinach, 20 ml (4 tsp) flour and the cream. Season to taste. Bring to the boil and cook for 2–3 minutes, stirring. Divide the filling between the crêpes, roll up and place, side by side, in a buttered ovenproof dish.
3 Melt the remaining butter in a saucepan, stir in the remaining flour and cook for 1 minute, stirring. Remove from the heat and gradually stir in the milk. Bring to the boil, stirring all the time, until the sauce thickens. Stir in the cheese and season to taste. Pour over the crêpes, cover lightly with foil and bake in a preheated oven at 180°C (350°F) mark 4 for 25–30 minutes.

─── **VARIATION** ───
Spinach and Ricotta Crêpes
Ricotta is a fragrant Italian cheese made from the whey left over when producing other cheeses. It has a delicate, smooth flavour and is often mixed with spinach in stuffings for ravioli or cannelloni. It would make an ideal substitute for Stilton in the above recipe.

VEGETARIAN MEDLEY

SERVES 4

25 g (1 oz) butter	100 g (4 oz) lentils, cooked
2 carrots, sliced	15 ml (1 tbsp) raisins
1 large onion, chopped	30 ml (2 tbsp) unsalted peanuts
1 green pepper, sliced	salt and pepper
2 tomatoes, chopped	300 ml (10 fl oz) natural yogurt
1 large cooking apple, peeled, cored and chopped	25 g (1 oz) cream cheese
1 garlic clove, crushed	
15 ml (1 tbsp) chopped fresh sage or 5 ml (1 tsp) dried	

1 Melt the butter in a large frying pan, add the carrots, onion, green pepper, tomatoes, apple, garlic and sage and fry lightly for 15 minutes or until softened

2 Add the lentils, raisins and peanuts. Season to taste. Stir the yogurt into the cream cheese and mix well to blend. Stir into the mixture. Reheat gently for 5 minutes.

—————— **TO MICROWAVE** ——————

Melt the butter in a large bowl on HIGH for 45 seconds. Add the carrots, onion, green pepper, tomatoes, apple, garlic and sage and cook on HIGH for 7 minutes, stirring occasionally. Add the remaining ingredients, as in step 2, and cook on HIGH for 2 minutes. Serve at once.

VEGETABLE CURRY

SERVES 4

30 ml (2 tbsp) vegetable oil	2 potatoes, peeled and roughly chopped
10 ml (2 tsp) ground coriander	2 carrots, sliced
5 ml (1 tsp) ground cumin	1 green pepper, chopped
2.5–5 ml (½–1 tsp) chilli powder	225 g (8 oz) tomatoes, roughly chopped
2.5 ml (½ tsp) ground turmeric	150 ml (5 fl oz) natural yogurt
2 garlic cloves, crushed	salt and pepper
1 medium onion, chopped	
1 small cauliflower, cut into small florets	

1 Heat the oil in a large saucepan, add the coriander, cumin, chilli, turmeric, garlic and onion and fry for 2–3 minutes, stirring continuously.

2 Add the cauliflower, potatoes, carrots and green pepper and stir to coat in the spices. Stir in the tomatoes and 150 ml (¼ pint) water. Bring to the boil, cover and simmer gently for 25–30 minutes or until the vegetables are tender.

3 Remove from the heat, stir in the yogurt and season.

—————— **TO MICROWAVE** ——————

Put the oil, coriander, cumin, chilli, turmeric, garlic and onion in a large bowl and cook on HIGH for 2 minutes, stirring once. Add the cauliflower, potatoes, carrots and green pepper and stir to coat in the spices. Stir in the tomatoes and 150 ml (¼ pint) water. Cover and cook on HIGH for 20 minutes or until the vegetables are tender, stirring occasionally. Complete step 3.

MOONG DAL AND SPINACH

SERVES 6

225 g (8 oz) moong dal (split, washed moong beans)	1 garlic clove, crushed
	10 ml (2 tsp) ground coriander
900 g (2 lb) fresh spinach, washed and trimmed, or 450 g (1 lb) frozen chopped spinach	5 ml (1 tsp) ground turmeric
	2.5 ml (½ tsp) chilli powder
75 g (3 oz) ghee or clarified butter	1.25 ml (¼ tsp) asafoetida (optional)
100 g (4 oz) onion, finely chopped	salt and pepper
15 g (½ oz) fresh root ginger, finely chopped	lemon wedges, to garnish

1 Rinse the dal under cold running water. Place in a bowl, cover with cold water and leave to soak for about 2 hours, then drain.

2 Place the fresh spinach in a saucepan with only the water that clings to the leaves. Cover and cook gently for about 5 minutes or until tender. Drain well and chop roughly. If using frozen spinach, place in a saucepan and cook for 7–10 minutes to thaw and to remove as much liquid as possible.

3 Heat the ghee or butter in a large sauté pan, add the onion, ginger and garlic and fry for 2–3 minutes.

4 Stir in the coriander, turmeric, chilli powder, asafoetida (if using) and the dal. Fry, stirring, for 2–3 minutes.

5 Pour in 300 ml (½ pint) water, season to taste and bring to the boil. Cover and simmer for about 15 minutes or until the dal is almost tender. Add a little more water if necessary, but the mixture should be almost dry.

6 Stir in the spinach and cook, stirring for 2–3 minutes or until heated through. Taste and adjust the seasoning before serving, garnished with lemon wedges.

VEGETABLE BIRYANI

SERVES 4

350 g (12 oz) Basmati rice	2.5 ml (½ tsp) chilli powder
salt and pepper	
50 g (2 oz) ghee or clarified butter	3 medium carrots, thinly sliced
1 large onion, chopped	225 g (8 oz) fresh or frozen green beans, cut in two lengthways
2.5 cm (1 inch) piece of fresh root ginger, grated	
1–2 garlic cloves, crushed	225 g (8 oz) cauliflower florets, divided into small sprigs
5 ml (1 tsp) ground coriander	
10 ml (2 tsp) ground cumin	5 ml (1 tsp) garam masala
	juice of 1 lemon
5 ml (1 tsp) ground turmeric	hard-boiled egg slices and coriander sprigs, to garnish

1 Rinse the rice and put in a saucepan with 600 ml (1 pint) water and 5 ml (1 tsp) salt. Bring to the boil, then simmer for 10 minutes or until only just tender.

2 Meanwhile, heat the ghee or butter in a large heavy-based saucepan, add the onion, ginger and garlic and fry gently for 5 minutes or until soft but not coloured. Add the coriander, cumin, turmeric and chilli powder and fry for 2 minutes more, stirring constantly.

3 Remove the rice from the heat and drain. Add 900 ml (1½ pints) water to the onion and spice mixture and season to taste. Stir well and bring to the boil. Add the carrots and beans and simmer for 15 minutes, then add the cauliflower and simmer for a further 10 minutes. Lastly, add the rice. Fold gently to mix and simmer until reheated.

4 Stir the garam masala and lemon juice into the biryani and simmer for a few minutes more to reheat and allow the flavours to develop. Season, garnish and serve.

VEGETABLE HOT POT
SERVES 4

450 g (1 lb) carrots, thinly sliced	bouquet garni
2 large onions, thinly sliced	salt and pepper
3 celery sticks, thinly sliced	425 g (15 oz) can butter beans, drained
450 g (1 lb) potatoes, peeled and sliced	100 g (4 oz) frozen peas
100 g (4 oz) swede, thinly sliced	175 g (6 oz) fresh breadcrumbs
450 ml (¾ pint) vegetable stock	175 g (6 oz) hard cheese, grated

1 Layer the carrots, onions, celery, potato and swede in a 2.3 litre (4 pint) casserole.
2 Pour the vegetable stock into the casserole and add the bouquet garni. Season to taste.
3 Cover the casserole, and cook in a preheated oven at 180°C (350°F) mark 4 for 1 hour.
4 Remove the bouquet garni. Add the beans and peas to the casserole. Mix the breadcrumbs and cheese together and spoon over the hot pot. Return to the oven and cook, uncovered, for about 20 minutes.

VARIATION

The vegetables used in this satisfying dish can be varied according to the season. Other root vegetables, such as parsnips or turnips could replace the swede, and any canned beans could be used instead of butter beans. When available, replace the frozen peas with fresh.

BUCKWHEAT AND LENTIL CASSEROLE
SERVES 4

salt and pepper	3 bay leaves
150 g (5 oz) buckwheat	30 ml (2 tbsp) lemon juice
30 ml (2 tbsp) vegetable oil	1 garlic clove, crushed
1 red or green pepper, cut into strips	2 rosemary sprigs
1 onion, finely chopped	5 ml (1 tsp) cumin seeds
350 g (12 oz) courgettes, sliced	600 ml (1 pint) vegetable stock
175 g (6 oz) mushrooms, sliced	25 g (1 oz) butter
225 g (8 oz) red lentils	chopped parsley, to garnish

1 Put 450 ml (¾ pint) water in a saucepan, add a pinch of salt, then bring to the boil. Sprinkle in the buckwheat and return to the boil. Boil rapidly for 1 minute, reduce the heat, cover and cook gently for 12 minutes or until the water has been absorbed. Do not stir. Transfer to a buttered casserole.
2 Heat the oil in a flameproof casserole, add the pepper and onion and fry for 5 minutes. Add the courgettes and mushrooms and fry for a further 5 minutes. Stir in the lentils, bay leaves, lemon juice, garlic, rosemary, cumin and stock. Add to the buckwheat and stir well.
3 Simmer for about 45 minutes or until the lentils are cooked, stirring occasionally. Add the butter, adjust the seasoning and sprinkle with parsley. Serve hot.

COUSCOUS

SERVES 6

450 g (1 lb) couscous	salt and pepper
4 courgettes, cut into 1 cm (½ inch) slices	225 g (8 oz) chick-peas, soaked overnight, then drained
1 red pepper, diced	25 g (1 oz) blanched almonds
1 green pepper, diced	
2 onions, diced	5 ml (1 tsp) ground turmeric
2 carrots, diced	10 ml (2 tsp) paprika
225 g (8 oz) turnips, diced	2.5 ml (½ tsp) ground coriander
1 small cauliflower, cut into small florets	75 g (3 oz) butter, melted
4 large tomatoes, skinned and chopped	100 g (4 oz) dried apricots, soaked overnight
2 garlic cloves, crushed	
1.1 litres (2 pints) vegetable stock	

1 Place the couscous in a large bowl with 450 ml (¾ pint) tepid water and leave to soak for 1 hour.

2 Place the prepared vegetables in a large saucepan with the garlic, stock, pepper to taste, chick-peas, almonds and spices. Bring to the boil, cover and simmer for 30 minutes.

3 Drain the couscous and place in a steamer over the vegetables. Cover and cook for a further 40 minutes, then remove the steamer and cover the saucepan.

4 Place the couscous in a large mixing bowl. Beat the butter into the couscous with 50 ml (2 fl oz) salted water.

5 Drain and quarter the apricots, add them to the vegetables and simmer for 15 minutes. Stir the couscous well to remove any lumps, return it to the steamer over the simmering vegetables, cover and cook for 20 minutes.

6 Season the vegetables and serve with the couscous.

VEGETABLE CHILLI

SERVES 4

30 ml (2 tbsp) olive oil	150 ml (¼ pint) dry red wine
1 large onion, chopped	
2 garlic cloves, crushed	30 ml (2 tbsp) chopped fresh oregano or 5 ml (1 tsp) dried
5–10 ml (1–2 tsp) chilli powder	
225 g (8 oz) courgettes, diced	397 g (14 oz) can red kidney beans, drained
100 g (4 oz) carrots, sliced	15 ml (1 tbsp) cornflour
1 red pepper, diced	150 ml (¼ pint) Greek strained yogurt and chopped parsley, to serve
397 g (14 oz) can chopped tomatoes	

1 Heat the oil in a large saucepan, add the onion, garlic and chilli powder and cook for 2–3 minutes or until softened. Add the courgettes and carrots and cook for a further 3–4 minutes.

2 Add the red pepper and chopped tomatoes. Cook for 5 minutes. Stir in the wine, oregano and kidney beans, cover and cook for 25–30 minutes.

3 Mix 45 ml (3 tbsp) water with the cornflour to give a smooth paste. Stir the paste into the chilli and bring to the boil. Simmer for 2–3 minutes, stirring. Serve with yogurt and parsley.

SOUTHERN BAKED BEANS

SERVES 4

275 g (10 oz) dried haricot beans, soaked overnight	30 ml (2 tbsp) treacle
15 ml (1 tbsp) vegetable oil	300 ml (½ pint) tomato juice
2 onions, chopped	45 ml (3 tbsp) tomato purée
225 g (8 oz) carrots, chopped	300 ml (½ pint) beer
15 ml (1 tbsp) mustard powder	salt and pepper

1 Drain the beans, place in a saucepan and cover with fresh water. Bring to the boil and simmer for 25 minutes, then drain.

2 Meanwhile, heat the oil in a flameproof casserole, add the onions and carrots and fry for 5 minutes or until lightly golden.

3 Remove from the heat and add the mustard, treacle, tomato juice, tomato purée, beer and beans. Stir well.

4 Bring to the boil, cover and cook in a preheated oven at 140°C (275°F) mark 1 for about 5 hours or until the beans are tender and the sauce is the consistency of syrup, stirring occasionally. Season well.

—————— VARIATION ——————

If haricot beans are not available, cannellini beans can be used instead.

VEGETARIAN ROAST

SERVES 4–6

175 g (6 oz) long grain brown rice	100 g (4 oz) fresh wholemeal breadcrumbs
15 g (½ oz) butter	100 g (4 oz) almonds, finely chopped
1 medium onion, chopped	100 g (4 oz) mature Cheddar cheese, grated
1 garlic clove, crushed	2 eggs
2 carrots, grated	salt and pepper
100 g (4 oz) button mushrooms, finely chopped	

1 Cook the rice in boiling salted water for 30–35 minutes or until tender. Drain well.

2 Meanwhile, heat the butter in a medium frying pan, add the onion, garlic, carrots and mushrooms and fry for 5–10 minutes or until softened, stirring frequently. Stir in the breadcrumbs, almonds, cooked rice, cheese and eggs. Season to taste and mix thoroughly together.

3 Pack the mixture into a greased 1.7 litre (3 pint) loaf tin and bake in a preheated oven at 180°C (350°F) mark 4 for 1–1¼ hours or until firm to the touch and brown on top. Serve sliced, hot or cold.

—————— VARIATION ——————

Any type of chopped nuts can be used in the above recipe. Try substituting brazils or unsalted peanuts or cashews for the almonds.

CURRIED EGGS

SERVES 4

30 ml (2 tbsp) vegetable oil	15 ml (1 tbsp) tomato purée
1 onion, chopped	2.5 ml (½ tsp) chilli powder
1 medium cooking apple, peeled, cored and chopped	salt and pepper
10 ml (2 tsp) garam masala	300 ml (½ pint) natural yogurt
300 ml (½ pint) vegetable stock or water	4 eggs, hard-boiled
227 g (8 oz) can tomatoes	

1 Heat the oil in a deep, heavy-based saucepan. Add the onion, apple and garam masala and fry gently for about 5 minutes or until soft, stirring frequently.

2 Pour in the stock or water and tomatoes with their juice and bring to the boil, stirring to break up the tomatoes as much as possible. Stir in the tomato purée with the chilli powder. Season to taste. Lower the heat and simmer, uncovered, for 20 minutes to allow the flavours to develop.

3 Cool the sauce slightly, then pour into a blender or food processor. Add half the yogurt and blend to a purée. Return to the rinsed-out pan.

4 Shell the eggs and cut them in half lengthways. Add them to the sauce, cut side up, then simmer very gently for 10 minutes. Taste the sauce and adjust the seasoning if necessary. Serve hot, with the remaining yogurt drizzled over the top.

MIXED VEGETABLE RING

SERVES 4

100 g (4 oz) butter	salt and pepper
1 large onion, sliced	215 ml (7½ fl oz) milk
50 g (2 oz) mushrooms	100 g (4 oz) plain flour
2 courgettes, sliced	3 eggs, beaten
175 g (6 oz) aubergine, quartered and sliced	40 g (1½ oz) walnut pieces, chopped
1 red pepper, sliced	100 g (4 oz) Double Gloucester cheese with chives, grated
3 tomatoes, skinned and chopped	

1 Melt 25 g (1 oz) of the butter in a large saucepan, add the onion and mushrooms and fry lightly for 5 minutes or until softened.

2 Add the courgettes, aubergine and red pepper and cook for 5 minutes, stirring occasionally. Add the tomatoes and season to taste.

3 Melt the remaining butter in a medium saucepan with the milk, then bring to the boil. Remove the pan from the heat, tip in all the flour and beat thoroughly with a wooden spoon. Allow to cool slightly, then beat in the eggs, a little at a time. Stir in the walnuts. Pipe or spoon the mixture around the edge of a well-greased 900 ml (1½ pint) ovenproof serving dish.

4 Fill the centre with the vegetables and bake in a preheated oven at 200°C (400°F) mark 6 for 35–40 minutes or until the pastry is risen and golden. Sprinkle with the cheese, then return to the oven until the cheese has melted. Serve at once.

VEGETABLE JALOUSIE

SERVES 4

SPICED POTATO AND CAULIFLOWER PASTRIES

SERVES 4

550 g (1¼ lb) fresh broad beans, shelled	45 ml (3 tbsp) grated Parmesan cheese
4 new carrots, thinly sliced	1.25 ml (¼ tsp) ground mace
3 medium leeks, thickly sliced	salt and pepper
25 g (1 oz) butter or margarine	400 g (14 oz) frozen puff pastry, thawed
50 g (2 oz) plain flour	10 ml (2 tsp) chopped fresh summer savory or 5 ml (1 tsp) dried
300 ml (½ pint) milk	
100 g (4 oz) Caerphilly or Wensleydale cheese, grated	a little beaten egg, to glaze

1 Parboil the beans for 4 minutes, the carrots for 2 minutes and the leeks for 1 minute. Remove with a slotted spoon and reserve 30 ml (2 tbsp) of the blanching water.

2 Melt the butter in a clean pan, add the flour and cook, stirring, for 1–2 minutes. Off the heat, blend in the milk. Bring to the boil, stirring, then simmer for 3 minutes or until thick. Add the cheese and mace and season.

3 Remove the cheese sauce from the heat and fold in the vegetables. Cover and leave until cold.

4 Roll out half the pastry thinly to a 30.5×23 cm (12× 9 inch) rectangle. Place on a wetted baking sheet.

5 Stir the reserved blanching water and savory into the cold filling, then spread over the pastry.

6 Roll out the remaining pastry to a slightly larger rectangle than the first. Fold in half lengthways. Cut through the double thickness of the pastry six times at 5 cm (2 inch) intervals along the folded edge. Unfold the pastry and place over the top of the filling. Seal the edges firmly.

7 Brush the pastry with beaten egg, then bake in a preheated oven at 220°C (425°F) mark 7 for 30 minutes.

30 ml (2 tbsp) vegetable oil	(6 oz) tiny cauliflower florets
1 onion, finely chopped	100 g (4 oz) potatoes, peeled and diced
2 garlic cloves, crushed	
5 ml (1 tsp) ground turmeric	75 ml (3 fl oz) vegetable stock
15 ml (1 tbsp) ground coriander	350 g (12 oz) frozen wholemeal puff pastry, thawed
10 ml (2 tsp) ground cumin	
15 ml (1 tbsp) mango chutney	beaten egg, to glaze

1 Heat the oil in a large saucepan, add the onion, garlic and spices and cook for 4–5 minutes or until soft, stirring.

2 Add the mango chutney, cauliflower florets and potatoes, stir in the stock and cook for 15–20 minutes or until the liquid has evaporated. Leave to cool.

3 Roll out the pastry on a lightly floured surface and cut out four 18 cm (7 inch) rounds. Divide the filling between the rounds, placing it on one half of each round. Brush beaten egg around the edges of the rounds and fold the pastry over the filling to encase. Seal the edges, then flute.

4 Place on a greased baking sheet and brush with egg. Bake in a preheated oven at 200°C (400°F) mark 6 for 20–25 minutes or until golden. Serve hot or cold.

─── **TO MICROWAVE** ───

Place the oil, onion and garlic in a medium bowl. Cover and cook on HIGH for 3 minutes. Stir in the spices, re-cover and cook on HIGH for a further minute. Add the mango chutney, cauliflower and potatoes with 60 ml (4 tbsp) of the stock. Cook on HIGH for 10–12 minutes or until tender. Cool. Complete steps 3 and 4.

LIGHT MEALS

The recipes in this chapter are ideal for lunches and suppers, when you want something quick and easy yet tasty and satisfying. Soups are included for serving simply with chunks of crusty bread or toast. For cooking in advance, choose from the wide selection of savoury flans and quiches.

COCK-A-LEEKIE SOUP

SERVES 4

15 g (½ oz) butter	1 bouquet garni
275–350 g (10–12 oz) chicken (1 large or 2 small chicken portions)	salt and pepper
	6 prunes, stoned and halved
350 g (12 oz) leeks	
1.1 litres (2 pints) chicken stock	

1 Melt the butter in a large saucepan, add the chicken and fry quickly until golden on all sides.

2 Cut the white parts of the leeks into four lengthways and chop into 2.5 cm (1 inch) pieces. Wash well. Add the white parts to the pan and fry for 5 minutes or until soft.

3 Add the stock and bouquet garni and season to taste. Bring to the boil and simmer for 30 minutes.

4 Shred the green parts of the leeks, then add to the pan with the prunes. Simmer for a further 30 minutes.

5 To serve, remove the chicken from the pan and cut the meat into large pieces, discarding the skin and bones. Put the meat in a warmed soup tureen and pour over the soup.

PEA SOUP

SERVES 6

50 g (2 oz) butter	2 large mint sprigs
1 small onion, finely chopped	salt and pepper
900 g (2 lb) fresh peas, shelled	2 egg yolks, size 2
	150 ml (5 fl oz) double cream
1.1 litres (2 pints) chicken stock	mint sprig, to garnish
2.5 ml (½ tsp) caster sugar	

1 Melt the butter in a large saucepan, add the onion and cook for 5 minutes or until soft. Add the peas, stock, sugar and mint sprigs. Bring to the boil and cook for about 30 minutes.

2 Pass the soup through a fine sieve or purée in a blender or food processor. Return to the pan and season to taste.

3 Beat together the egg yolks and cream and add to the soup. Heat gently, stirring, but do not boil.

4 Transfer to a warmed soup tureen and garnish with mint before serving.

MUSHROOM SOUP

SERVES 4

25 g (1 oz) butter	100 g (4 oz) mushrooms, finely chopped
25 g (1 oz) plain flour	salt and pepper
300 ml (½ pint) chicken stock	15 ml (1 tbsp) lemon juice
300 ml (½ pint) milk	30 ml (2 tbsp) cream
15 ml (1 tbsp) chopped parsley	

1 Place all the ingredients, except the lemon juice and cream, in a large saucepan. Bring to the boil, whisking continuously. Cover and simmer for 10 minutes.
2 Remove from the heat and add the lemon juice and cream, stirring well.
3 Pour into a tureen or individual dishes, and serve immediately with Melba toast.

HARVEST VEGETABLE SOUP

SERVES 4

25 g (1 oz) butter	salt and pepper
450 g (1 lb) carrots, diced	½ bay leaf
1 medium onion, sliced	40 g (1½ oz) plain flour
2 medium potatoes, peeled and diced	450 ml (¾ pint) milk
1 small green pepper, chopped	100 g (4 oz) Cheddar cheese, grated
50 g (2 oz) lentils	croûtons, to garnish

1 Melt the butter and fry the carrots, onion, potatoes and green pepper until soft.
2 Add 450 ml (¾ pint) water, the lentils, salt and pepper to taste and the bay leaf and simmer for 30 minutes.
3 Mix the flour with a little of the milk and gradually blend in the rest. Stir well into the soup until it thickens. Simmer for 5 minutes, then stir in 75 g (3 oz) cheese.
4 Pour into a serving dish, sprinkle with the remaining cheese and garnish with croûtons. Serve immediately.

─── **VARIATION** ───
Vegetable and Oatmeal Broth
Substitute 25 g (1 oz) medium oatmeal and 225 g (8 oz) swede for the lentils and potatoes.

QUICK WINTER SOUP

SERVES 4–6

4 medium carrots, roughly chopped	1 slice of wholemeal bread, crusts removed
2 small white turnips, roughly chopped	2.5 ml (½ tsp) salt
2 small potatoes, peeled and roughly chopped	10 ml (2 tsp) sugar
2 leeks or 1 small onion, roughly chopped (optional)	pepper
1 medium cooking apple, peeled, cored and chopped	2 chicken stock cubes, crumbled

1 Put all the prepared vegetables in a blender or food processor with the apple and bread and blend until finely minced.

2 Transfer to a large saucepan and add 1.1 litres (2 pints) water. Bring slowly to the boil, then add the salt, sugar and pepper and the stock cubes. Simmer for 45–60 minutes.

———— VARIATION ————
Curried Winter Soup
Stir in a little curry powder to taste with the seasoning, sugar and stock cubes.

BROAD BEAN AND BACON SOUP

SERVES 2

225 g (8 oz) shelled broad beans	300 ml (½ pint) vegetable stock
225 g (8 oz) shelled peas	salt and pepper
1 large onion, chopped	2 rashers back bacon, grilled and chopped, to garnish
450 ml (¾ pint) milk	

1 Put the beans, peas and onion in a large saucepan and add the milk and stock. Bring to the boil, then simmer for 20 minutes or until the beans are tender.

2 Leave to cool slightly, then purée one third of the soup in a blender or food processor. Add to the remaining soup, then season to taste. Reheat gently. Serve hot, garnished with chopped bacon.

———— TO MICROWAVE ————
Cook the vegetables, milk and stock in a large bowl on HIGH for 20–25 minutes, stirring occasionally. Complete step 2, reheating on HIGH for 2–3 minutes.

———— VARIATION ————
Use frozen vegetables when fresh broad beans and peas are not available.

MULLIGATAWNY SOUP

SERVES 6

CREAM OF ONION SOUP

SERVES 4

50 g (2 oz) butter	15 ml (1 tbsp) tomato purée
1 medium onion, finely chopped	30 ml (2 tbsp) mango chutney
100 g (4 oz) carrot, finely chopped	1.4 litres (2½ pints) beef stock
100 g (4 oz) swede, finely chopped	5 ml (1 tsp) dried mixed herbs
1 small eating apple, peeled, cored and finely chopped	pinch of ground mace
	pinch of ground cloves
50 g (2 oz) streaky bacon, finely chopped	salt and pepper
25 g (1 oz) plain flour	50 g (2 oz) long grain rice
15 ml (1 tbsp) mild curry paste	150 ml (5 fl oz) double cream

1 Melt the butter in a large saucepan, add the onion, carrot, swede, apple and bacon and fry for 5–10 minutes or until lightly browned.

2 Stir in the flour, curry paste, tomato purée and chutney. Cook for 1–2 minutes before adding the stock, herbs and spices. Season to taste.

3 Bring to the boil, skim, cover and simmer for 30–40 minutes. Sieve the soup or purée in a blender or food processor.

4 Return the soup to the pan, bring to the boil, add the rice and boil gently for about 12 minutes or until the rice is tender.

5 Adjust the seasoning. Stir in the cream, reserving a little for garnish. Heat gently, without boiling, then pour into a warmed soup tureen or individual bowls and swirl with cream.

25 g (1 oz) butter	salt and pepper
450 g (1 lb) onions, thinly sliced	20 ml (4 tsp) cornflour
	45 ml (3 tbsp) single cream
568 ml (1 pint) milk	parsley sprigs, to garnish

1 Melt the butter in a saucepan, add the onions, cover and cook gently for about 5 minutes or until softened, shaking the pan occasionally to prevent browning.

2 Add the milk and 300 ml (½ pint) water, season to taste and bring to the boil, stirring. Reduce the heat, cover and simmer for about 25 minutes or until the onion is tender.

3 Blend the cornflour to a smooth paste with 45 ml (3 tbsp) water, stir into the soup and bring to the boil. Cook gently for a few minutes or until slightly thickened, stirring. Add the cream, adjust the seasoning and reheat without boiling. Garnish with parsley sprigs.

CURRIED PARSNIP SOUP

SERVES 6

40 g (1½ oz) butter	1.4 litres (2½ pints) chicken stock
1 medium onion, sliced	salt and pepper
700 g (1½ lb) parsnips, finely diced	150 ml (5 fl oz) single cream
5 ml (1 tsp) curry powder	paprika, to garnish
2.5 ml (½ tsp) ground cumin	

1 Melt the butter in a large saucepan, add the onion and parsnip and fry for about 3 minutes.

2 Stir in the curry powder and cumin and fry for a further 2 minutes.

3 Add the stock, bring to the boil, reduce the heat, cover and simmer for about 45 minutes or until the vegetables are tender.

4 Cool slightly, then transfer the vegetables to a blender or food processor, using a slotted spoon. Add a little stock and blend to a smooth purée.

5 Return the soup to the pan. Season to taste, add the cream and reheat gently, without boiling. Serve sprinkled with paprika.

CULLEN SKINK

SERVES 4

one 350 g (12 oz) Finnan haddock, skinned	700 g (1½ lb) potatoes
1 medium onion, chopped	knob of butter
568 ml (1 pint) milk	salt and pepper
	chopped parsley, to garnish

1 Put the haddock in a medium saucepan, just cover with 900 ml (1½ pints) boiling water and bring to the boil again. Add the onion, cover and simmer for 10–15 minutes or until tender. Drain off the liquid and reserve.

2 Remove the bones from the haddock and flake the flesh, then set aside. Return the bones and strained stock to the pan with the milk. Cover and simmer for a further hour.

3 Meanwhile, peel and roughly chop the potatoes, then cook in boiling salted water for about 20 minutes or until tender. Drain well, then mash.

4 Strain the liquid from the bones and return it to the pan with the flaked fish. Add the mashed potato and butter and stir well to give a creamy consistency. Season and garnish.

─────────── **TO MICROWAVE** ───────────

Put the haddock, onion and 600 ml (1 pint) boiling water in a large bowl. Cover and cook on HIGH for 10 minutes or until the haddock is cooked. Drain off the liquid and reserve. Remove the bones from the haddock and flake the flesh, then set aside. Return the bones and strained stock to the bowl with the milk, cover and cook on HIGH for 20 minutes. Meanwhile, complete step 3. Strain the liquid from the bones and return it to the bowl with the flaked fish. Add the mashed potato and butter and stir well to give a creamy consistency. Season, garnish and serve.

HADDOCK AND CORN CHOWDER

SERVES 4–6

25–50 g (1–2 oz) butter or margarine	salt and pepper
450 g (1 lb) old potatoes, peeled and cut into 1 cm (½ inch) dice	225 g (8 oz) fresh haddock fillets
2 medium onions, thinly sliced	225 g (8 oz) smoked haddock fillets
2.5 ml (½ tsp) chilli powder	298 g (10½ oz) can cream-style sweetcorn
600 ml (1 pint) fish or vegetable stock	100 g (4 oz) cooked peeled prawns
568 ml (1 pint) milk	chopped parsley

1 Melt the butter or margarine in a large saucepan. Add the vegetables and the chilli powder and stir over a moderate heat for 2–3 minutes.

2 Pour in the stock and milk and season to taste. Bring to the boil, cover and simmer for 10 minutes.

3 Meanwhile, skin the fresh and smoked haddock fillets and divide the flesh into bite-sized pieces, discarding all the bones.

4 Add the haddock to the pan with the corn. Bring back to the boil, cover and simmer until the potatoes are tender and the fish begins to flake apart. Skim the surface of the soup.

5 Stir in the prawns with plenty of parsley. Adjust the seasoning and serve.

DEVONSHIRE CRAB SOUP

SERVES 6

25 g (1 oz) butter	300 ml (½ pint) chicken stock
1 small onion, finely chopped	5 ml (1 tsp) anchovy essence
1 celery stick, chopped	salt and pepper
75 g (3 oz) long grain rice	30 ml (2 tbsp) brandy
568 ml (1 pint) milk	150 ml (5 fl oz) double cream
meat of 1 cooked crab, or 225 g (8 oz) frozen or canned crab meat, drained and flaked	chopped parsley, to garnish

1 Melt the butter in a large saucepan, add the onion and celery and cook for 10 minutes or until soft. Add the rice and milk, cover and cook for 15 minutes or until the rice is cooked. Cool slightly.

2 Pass the soup through a sieve or purée in a blender or food processor. Return to the pan together with the crab meat. Add the stock and anchovy essence, season to taste and reheat.

3 Add the brandy and cream and heat gently without boiling. Transfer to a warmed soup tureen, sprinkle with chopped parsley and serve very hot.

—— COOK'S TIP ——

Melba toast makes a good accompaniment to many soups, including the one above. To make it, simply toast bread slices lightly on both sides, cut off the crusts, then, holding the toast flat, slide a knife between the toasted edges to split the bread. Cut each piece into triangles and toast under the grill, untoasted side uppermost, until golden and the edges curl.

SPAGHETTI BOLOGNESE

SERVES 4

25 g (1 oz) butter or margarine	1 garlic clove, finely chopped
45 ml (3 tbsp) olive oil	1 bay leaf
2 rashers unsmoked streaky bacon, finely chopped	15 ml (1 tbsp) tomato purée
225 g (8 oz) lean minced beef	150 ml (¼ pint) dry white wine
1 small onion, finely chopped	150 ml (¼ pint) beef stock
1 small carrot, finely chopped	salt and pepper
1 small celery stick, finely chopped	450–700 g (1–1½ lb) fresh or dried spaghetti

1 Melt the butter or margarine with the oil in a saucepan, add the bacon and cook for 2–3 minutes or until soft.

2 Add the minced beef and cook for a further 5 minutes or until lightly browned.

3 Add the onion, carrot, celery, garlic and bay leaf. Stir and cook for 2 minutes. Add the tomato purée, wine and stock. Season to taste.

4 Bring to the boil, then simmer, uncovered for 1–1½ hours, stirring occasionally.

5 Cook the spaghetti in a large saucepan of boiling salted water for about 10 minutes for dried pasta, 3 minutes for fresh.

6 Drain the spaghetti well and turn into a warmed serving dish. Top with the sauce and serve immediately.

PAN HAGGERTY

SERVES 4

25 g (1 oz) butter	100 g (4 oz) Cheddar or Lancashire cheese, grated
15 ml (1 tbsp) vegetable oil	salt and pepper
450 g (1 lb) potatoes, peeled and thinly sliced	
2 medium onions, thinly sliced	

1 Heat the butter and oil in a large heavy-based frying pan. Remove the pan from the heat and pour in layers of potatoes, onions and grated cheese, seasoning well with salt and pepper between each layer, and ending with a top layer of cheese.

2 Cover and cook the vegetables gently for about 30 minutes or until the potatoes and onions are almost cooked.

3 Uncover and brown the top of the dish under a hot grill. Serve straight from the pan.

COOK'S TIP

Choose firm-fleshed potatoes for this dish, such as Desirée, Romano or Maris Piper, as they will keep their shape and not crumble into mash at the end of the cooking time.

RED FLANNEL HASH

SERVES 4

450 g (1 lb) potatoes, scrubbed	5 ml (1 tsp) garlic salt
salt and pepper	225 g (8 oz) cooked beetroot, diced
225 g (8 oz) salt beef or corned beef, chopped	30 ml (2 tbsp) chopped parsley
1 medium onion, finely chopped	50 g (2 oz) butter or margarine

1 Cook the potatoes in their skins in lightly salted boiling water for about 20 minutes or until tender.

2 Drain the potatoes, leave until cool enough to handle, then peel off the skins with your fingers. Dice the flesh.

3 Put the diced potatoes in a large bowl, add the beef, onion, garlic salt, beetroot and parsley and toss to combine. Add pepper to taste.

4 Heat the butter or margarine in a heavy-based frying pan until very hot. Add the hash mixture and spread evenly with a fish slice or spatula.

5 Lower the heat to moderate and cook the hash, uncovered, for 10–15 minutes. Break up and turn frequently with the slice or spatula, so that the hash becomes evenly browned. Serve hot.

SPICY SCOTCH EGGS

SERVES 4

25 g (1 oz) butter or margarine	salt and pepper
1 onion, very finely chopped	4 hard-boiled eggs, shelled
10 ml (2 tsp) medium-hot curry powder	plain flour, for coating
450 g (1 lb) pork sausagemeat	1 egg, beaten
100 g (4 oz) mature Cheddar cheese, finely grated	100–175 g (4–6 oz) dried breadcrumbs
	vegetable oil, for deep frying

1 Heat the butter or margarine in a small saucepan, add the onion and curry powder and fry gently for 5 minutes or until soft.

2 Put the sausagemeat and cheese in a bowl, add the onion and season to taste. Mix with your hands to combine the ingredients well.

3 Divide the mixture into four equal portions and flatten out on a floured board or work surface.

4 Place an egg in the centre of each piece. With floured hands, shape and mould the sausagemeat around the eggs. Coat lightly with more flour.

5 Brush each Scotch egg with beaten egg, then roll in the breadcrumbs until evenly coated. Chill for 30 minutes.

6 Heat the oil in a deep-fat fryer to 170°C (325°F). Carefully lower the Scotch eggs into the oil with a slotted spoon and deep-fry for 10 minutes, turning them occasionally until golden brown on all sides. Drain and cool on absorbent kitchen paper.

COLD BEEF IN SOURED CREAM

SERVES 4

30 ml (2 tbsp) vegetable oil	10 ml (2 tsp) chopped fresh thyme or 2.5 ml (½ tsp) dried
450 g (1 lb) lean rump steak in a thin slice, cut into thin strips	1 green eating apple, cored and thinly sliced
salt and pepper	142 ml (5 fl oz) soured cream
1 medium onion, finely chopped	15 ml (1 tbsp) lemon juice
225 g (8 oz) button mushrooms, thinly sliced	crisp lettuce, to serve
5 ml (1 tsp) French mustard	

1 Heat the oil in a large frying pan. When hot, add the steak in a shallow layer and cook over a high heat until browned, turning occasionally. Do not crowd the pan; the meat should remain pink in the centre.

2 Transfer the beef to a bowl using a slotted spoon. Season to taste.

3 Reheat the fat remaining in the pan, add the onion and fry until golden brown. Add the mushrooms, mustard and thyme and fry over a high heat for 1 minute. Add to the beef, cover and leave to cool.

4 Combine the apple with the soured cream and lemon juice.

5 To serve, line a shallow dish with crisp lettuce. Combine the beef mixture with the soured cream, adjust the seasoning and pile into the centre of the lettuce.

CASHEW STUFFED MUSHROOMS

SERVES 4

8 medium flat mushrooms	15 ml (1 tbsp) chopped fresh oregano or 2.5 ml (½ tsp) dried
15 ml (1 tbsp) olive oil	10 ml (2 tsp) tomato purée
2 small onions, finely chopped	30–45 ml (2–3 tbsp) grated Parmesan cheese
2 garlic cloves, crushed	
50 g (2 oz) unsalted cashew nuts, chopped	

1 Remove the stalks from the mushrooms, chop and set aside. Bring a large saucepan of salted water to the boil, add the mushroom caps and cook for 30–60 seconds. Drain, set aside and keep warm.

2 Heat the oil in a medium saucepan, add the onions and garlic and fry gently for 3–5 minutes or until the onions have softened. Stir in the mushroom stalks, cashew nuts and oregano. Cook for 3–5 minutes or until the nuts begin to brown. Stir in the tomato purée.

3 Arrange the mushroom caps on a lightly oiled baking sheet. Divide the topping mixture between them and sprinkle over the Parmesan cheese.

4 Bake in a preheated oven at 190°C (375°F) mark 5 for 10–15 minutes or until golden.

TO MICROWAVE

Complete step 1. Place the oil, onion and garlic in a bowl, cover and cook on HIGH for 2½–3 minutes. Add the chopped mushroom stalks, cashew nuts and oregano. Cover and cook on HIGH for 2–3 minutes. Stir in the tomato purée. Arrange four filled mushrooms in a circle on a plate and cook on HIGH for 3–4 minutes, rearranging occasionally. Repeat with the remaining four mushrooms. Grill to brown, if liked.

GARLIC MUSHROOM PARCELS

SERVES 4–6

15 ml (1 tbsp) olive oil	pepper
1 onion, finely chopped	50 g (2 oz) cream cheese
1–2 garlic cloves, crushed	6 sheets of frozen filo pastry, thawed
225 g (8 oz) button mushrooms, chopped	25 g (1 oz) butter, melted
15 ml (1 tbsp) chopped fresh thyme or 5 ml (1 tsp) dried	

1 Heat the oil in a medium saucepan, add the onion and garlic and cook gently for 3–5 minutes or until the onion has softened. Add the mushrooms, thyme and pepper to taste. Cook for 5–6 minutes, stirring.

2 Drain off any excess juices and add the cheese, stirring continuously until the cheese has melted. Cook for a further 2 minutes, then leave to cool.

3 To make the parcels, lay the first sheet of filo pastry lengthways on a work surface. Brush with butter, then lay a second sheet on top. Brush with butter, then cut into eight equal strips.

4 Place 5 ml (1 tsp) of the cooked filling in one corner of a strip of pastry. Fold this corner over to make a triangle, encasing the filling. Continue to fold in the shape of a triangle, brushing with a little extra melted butter just before the final fold. Repeat to make 24 parcels. Place on a greased baking sheet.

5 Bake in a preheated oven at 200°C (400°F) mark 6 for 10–15 minutes or until golden brown and crisp, turning the parcels over halfway through cooking. Serve hot or cold.

TORTILLA

SERVES 4

30 ml (2 tbsp) olive oil	5 eggs, beaten
225 g (8 oz) potatoes, peeled and thinly sliced	salt and pepper
1 Spanish onion, thinly sliced	15 ml (1 tbsp) chopped fresh parsley or 10 ml (2 tsp) dried
1 red pepper, chopped	

1 Heat the oil in a frying pan, add the potatoes, onion and pepper and fry gently for 20–25 minutes or until the potatoes are golden and cooked.

2 Pour the beaten egg into the pan, season to taste and sprinkle over the parsley.

3 Cook the tortilla over a gentle heat for 7–10 minutes or until golden. Carefully invert the tortilla on to a plate, then slide it back into the frying pan to cook the other side for a further 3–5 minutes.

4 Turn the tortilla on to a warmed serving plate.

TO MICROWAVE

Place the oil, potatoes, onion and pepper in a shallow 20.5 cm (8 inch) dish. Cover and cook on HIGH for 7–10 minutes or until tender, rearranging occasionally. Pour in the beaten eggs, season to taste and sprinkle over the parsley. Cover and cook on HIGH for 3–4 minutes or until almost set. Carefully invert the tortilla on to a plate, then slide back into the dish and cook on HIGH for a further 2–3 minutes or until almost set. Complete step 4 as above.

FARMHOUSE CAULIFLOWER SOUFFLÉS

SERVES 8

225 g (8 oz) small cauliflower florets	15 ml (1 tbsp) whole grain mustard
salt and pepper	100 g (4 oz) farmhouse Cheddar cheese, grated
40 g (1½ oz) butter	4 eggs, separated
45 ml (3 tbsp) plain flour	
200 ml (7 fl oz) milk	

1 Grease eight individual ramekin dishes.
2 Put the cauliflower in a saucepan and just cover with boiling salted water. Cover and simmer until tender, then drain.
3 Meanwhile, prepare a white sauce. Put the butter, flour and milk in a saucepan. Heat, whisking continuously, until the sauce thickens, boils and is smooth. Simmer for 1–2 minutes, then add the mustard and season to taste.
4 Turn the sauce into a blender or food processor. Add the cauliflower and blend to an almost smooth purée.
5 Turn into a large bowl and leave to cool slightly. Stir in the cheese with the egg yolks.
6 Whisk the egg whites until stiff but not dry and fold into the sauce mixture. Spoon into the dishes.
7 Bake in a preheated oven at 180°C (350°F) mark 4 for 25 minutes or until browned and firm. Serve at once.

─────────────── **TO MICROWAVE** ───────────────

The sauce can be prepared in the microwave. Put the butter, flour and milk in a medium bowl. Cook on HIGH for 4–5 minutes or until boiling and thickened, whisking frequently. Add the mustard and season.

OMELETTE ARNOLD BENNETT

SERVES 2

100 g (4 oz) smoked haddock	3 eggs, separated
50 g (2 oz) butter	salt and pepper
150 ml (¼ pint) double cream	50 g (2 oz) Cheddar cheese, grated

1 Put the fish in a saucepan and cover with water. Bring to the boil and simmer gently for 10 minutes. Drain and flake the fish, discarding the skin and bones.
2 Put the fish in a saucepan with half the butter and 30 ml (2 tbsp) cream. Toss over a high heat until the butter melts, then leave to cool.
3 Beat the egg yolks in a bowl with 15 ml (1 tbsp) cream. Season to taste and stir in the fish mixture. Stiffly whisk the egg whites and fold in.
4 Heat the remaining butter in an omelette pan or small frying pan. Pour in the egg mixture and cook gently until beginning to set but still fairly fluid. Do not fold over. Slide the omelette on to a heatproof serving dish.
5 Blend together the cheese and remaining cream and pour over the omelette. Put under a preheated grill until golden and bubbling. Serve immediately.

CHICKEN EGGAH

SERVES 4–6

SMOKED HADDOCK GOUGÈRES

SERVES 4

8 chicken thighs	6 eggs
600 ml (1 pint) chicken stock	50 g (2 oz) butter or margarine
10 ml (2 tsp) ground cumin	1 medium onion, sliced
1.25 ml (¼ tsp) chilli powder	1 garlic clove, crushed
salt and pepper	10 ml (2 tsp) paprika
100 g (4 oz) Chinese egg noodles	

1 Put the chicken thighs in a large saucepan, then add the chicken stock, cumin and chilli powder and season to taste. Simmer for 30 minutes or until the chicken is tender.
2 Remove the chicken from the pan and set aside. Add 1.1 litres (2 pints) water to the pan and bring to the boil. Add the noodles and boil for about 5 minutes, or according to the packet instructions, until tender. Leave to drain thoroughly in a colander or sieve.
3 Remove the chicken flesh from the bones and discard the skin. Cut the meat into small strips.
4 Using kitchen scissors, cut the cooked, drained egg noodles into short lengths.
5 Beat the eggs lightly in a large bowl, then add the noodles and chicken and stir gently to mix. Melt the butter or margarine in a large heavy-based frying pan, add the onion, garlic and paprika and fry gently for about 5 minutes.
6 Pour in the egg mixture and stir lightly with a fork. Cook over a moderate heat for 15 minutes or until set and golden brown underneath.
7 Turn the eggah out on to a plate, then slide back into the pan so that the underside is uppermost. Cook for a further 15 minutes or until golden brown. Serve hot.

90 g (3½ oz) butter	2 tomatoes, skinned, seeded and cut into strips
150 g (5 oz) plain flour	salt and pepper
3 eggs, beaten	lemon juice, to taste
450 g (1 lb) smoked haddock	15 ml (1 tbsp) fresh white breadcrumbs
1 medium onion, chopped	15 g (½ oz) Cheddar cheese, grated
300 ml (½ pint) milk	chopped parsley, to garnish (optional)
10 ml (2 tsp) capers	
2 hard-boiled eggs, shelled and chopped	

1 To make the choux pastry, put 75 g (3 oz) butter and 200 ml (7 fl oz) water in a saucepan and bring to the boil. Add 100 g (4 oz) of the flour, then beat well until the mixture leaves the sides of the pan. Cool for 5 minutes, then gradually beat in the eggs.
2 Using a 1 cm (½ inch) plain nozzle, pipe the mixture in two circles (one on top of the other) inside each of four 200 ml (7 fl oz) ovenproof dishes. Bake at 220°C (425°F) mark 7 for 25 minutes or until risen and golden brown.
3 Meanwhile, poach the haddock for 10 minutes. Drain, flake the flesh and discard the skin and bones.
4 Melt the remaining butter, add the onion and fry for 5 minutes. Add the remaining flour and cook, stirring, for 1–2 minutes. Off the heat, blend in the milk. Bring to the boil, stirring, then simmer for 3 minutes until thick.
5 Stir in the capers, eggs, fish and strips of tomato. Add salt, pepper and lemon juice to taste.
6 Spoon the mixture into the centre of the cooked gougères. Mix together the breadcrumbs and cheese, sprinkle on top and return to the oven for 10 minutes.

HADDOCK AND MUSHROOM PUFFS

SERVES 4

397 g (14 oz) packet puff pastry, thawed if frozen	20 ml (4 tsp) capers, chopped
450 g (1 lb) haddock fillets, skinned	15 ml (1 tbsp) snipped fresh chives or 5 ml (1 tsp) dried
213 g (7½ oz) can creamed mushrooms	salt and pepper
5 ml (1 tsp) lemon juice	1 egg

1 Roll out the pastry on a lightly floured surface into a 40.5 cm (16 inch) square. Using a sharp knife, cut into four squares, trim the edges and reserve the trimmings.

2 Place the squares on dampened baking sheets. Divide the fish into four and place diagonally across the pastry squares.

3 Combine the creamed mushrooms with the lemon juice, capers and chives. Season to taste. Mix well, then spoon over the pieces of haddock fillet.

4 Brush the edges of each square lightly with water. Bring the four points of each square together over the filling and seal the edges to form an envelope-shaped parcel.

5 Decorate with pastry trimmings and make a small hole in the centre of each parcel. Chill in the refrigerator for 30 minutes.

6 Beat the egg with a pinch of salt and use to glaze the pastry. Bake in a preheated oven at 220°C (425°F) mark 7 for about 20 minutes or until the pastry is golden brown and well risen. Serve hot.

─────────────── **VARIATION** ───────────────

Monkfish and Mushrooms Puffs

Substitute monkfish (or any other white fish) for the haddock in the above recipe.

MOCK CRAB

SERVES 2

1 hard-boiled egg, shelled	100 g (4 oz) Red Leicester cheese, grated
15 g (½ oz) butter	2 cooked chicken breast fillets, skinned and finely chopped
7.5 ml (1½ tsp) prepared English mustard	
a few drops of anchovy essence	lettuce leaves, sliced tomato and cucumber, to garnish
pepper	

1 Separate the egg yolks from the whites, sieve the yolks and chop the whites. Reserve a little of the egg yolk and mix the remainder with the butter, mustard, anchovy essence and pepper, to taste.

2 Mix in the cheese with a fork so that it is evenly blended but as many shreds as possible of the cheese remain separate.

3 Mix in the chicken lightly, then taste and adjust the seasoning. Cover and leave in a cool place for at least 2 hours for the flavours to develop.

4 Serve on a small bed of lettuce, in crab shells if available, garnished with the reserved egg yolk, chopped egg white and a little sliced tomato and cucumber.

─────────────── **COOK'S TIP** ───────────────

This was a popular Victorian luncheon dish, cleverly invented to deceive the eye and even the palate. The 'crab' is in fact finely shredded chicken and grated Red Leicester cheese, and the fishy disguise is made all the more convincing with anchovy flavouring.

LEEKS IN CHEESE SAUCE

SERVES 4

8 medium leeks	salt and pepper
50 g (2 oz) butter	8 thin slices of ham or bacon
75 ml (5 tbsp) plain flour	fresh breadcrumbs
568 ml (1 pint) milk	
100 g (4 oz) Cheddar cheese, grated	

1 Put the whole leeks in a saucepan of boiling salted water and boil gently for 20 minutes or until soft. Drain and keep warm.

2 Meanwhile, melt three-quarters of the butter in a pan, stir in the flour and cook gently for 1 minute, stirring. Remove the pan from the heat and gradually stir in the milk. Bring to the boil and continue to cook, stirring, for about 5 minutes, then add 75 g (3 oz) cheese and season to taste.

3 Wrap each leek in a slice of ham or bacon, place in an ovenproof dish and coat with sauce. Top with breadcrumbs and the remaining cheese. Dot with the remaining butter and brown under a preheated grill.

VARIATION

Asparagus in Cheese Sauce
When in season, asparagus would make an interesting substitute for the leeks in the above recipe.

MACARONI AND BROCCOLI CHEESE

SERVES 2

75 g (3 oz) wholewheat macaroni	75 g (3 oz) Red Leicester cheese, grated
salt and pepper	100 g (4 oz) broccoli florets
25 g (1 oz) butter	15 ml (1 tbsp) fresh wholemeal breadcrumbs
25 g (1 oz) plain flour	
300 ml (½ pint) milk	

1 Cook the macaroni in 1.1 litres (2 pints) boiling salted water for 15 minutes, then drain.

2 Put the butter, flour and milk in a saucepan. Heat, whisking continuously, until the sauce boils, thickens and is smooth. Simmer for 1–2 minutes.

3 Remove the pan from the heat, add most of the cheese and stir until melted. Season to taste.

4 Cook the broccoli in boiling water for 7 minutes or until tender. Drain well.

5 Put the broccoli in the base of a 900 ml (1½ pint) heatproof serving dish. Cover with the macaroni and cheese sauce. Sprinkle with the remaining cheese and the breadcrumbs. Brown under a preheated hot grill.

TO MICROWAVE

Put the macaroni in a large bowl. Pour over boiling water to cover the pasta by about 2.5 cm (1 inch). Cover and cook on HIGH for 4 minutes. Stand for 3 minutes. Put the butter, flour and milk in a medium bowl and cook on HIGH for about 4 minutes, until boiling and thickened, whisking frequently. Complete step 3. Cook the broccoli in a large bowl in 45 ml (3 tbsp) water on HIGH for 3½ minutes. Drain well. Complete step 5.

COURGETTE QUICHE

SERVES 4

175 g (6 oz) plain flour	3 eggs
salt and pepper	150 ml (5 fl oz) double cream
100 g (4 oz) butter or margarine	10 ml (2 tsp) chopped fresh basil
100 g (4 oz) grated Cheddar cheese	finely grated rind of 1 lime (optional)
1 egg yolk, beaten	a little egg white
350 g (12 oz) courgettes	

1 To make the pastry, sift the flour into a bowl with a pinch of salt. Rub in the butter or margarine.

2 Stir in the cheese, then the egg yolk. Gather the mixture together with your fingers to make a smooth ball of dough. Wrap the dough and chill for 30 minutes.

3 Meanwhile, prepare the filling. Trim the courgettes, then cut into 2 cm (¾ inch) chunks. Plunge into boiling salted water, bring back to the boil, then simmer for 3 minutes. Drain and set aside.

4 Beat the eggs lightly with the cream. Stir in the basil, lime rind (if using) and season to taste. Set aside.

5 Roll out the chilled dough and use to line a 23 cm (9 inch) loose-bottomed flan tin. Chill for 15 minutes.

6 Prick the base of the dough with a fork, then line with foil and baking beans. Stand the tin on a preheated baking sheet and bake blind in a preheated oven at 200°C (400°F) mark 6 for 10 minutes.

7 Remove the foil and beans and brush the pastry case with egg white. Return to the oven for 5 minutes.

8 Stand the courgette chunks upright in the pastry case and slowly pour in the egg and cream mixture. Return to the oven for 20 minutes.

CAULIFLOWER AND STILTON FLAN

SERVES 4–6

175 g (6 oz) plus 30 ml (2 tbsp) plain flour	200 ml (7 fl oz) milk
1.25 ml (¼ tsp) salt	pepper
100 g (4 oz) butter	100 g (4 oz) Blue Stilton cheese, crumbled
450 g (1 lb) cauliflower florets	25 g (1 oz) Cheddar cheese, grated
225 g (8 oz) onions, chopped	

1 Sift 175 g (6 oz) flour and the salt into a bowl. Add 75 g (3 oz) of the butter and rub in until the mixture resembles fine breadcrumbs. Add a little water and bind to a dough. Chill in the refrigerator for about 10 minutes.

2 Roll out the pastry on a lightly floured surface and use to line a 23 cm (9 inch) flan dish or ring placed on a baking sheet. Chill again for 10–15 minutes.

3 Prick the base of the dough with a fork, then line with foil and baking beans and bake blind in a preheated oven at 200°C (400°F) mark 6 for 10–15 minutes or until set. Remove the foil and beans.

4 Cook the cauliflower florets in boiling salted water for 4–5 minutes or until just tender. Drain well and cool.

5 Melt the remaining butter in a pan, add the onions and cook for about 5 minutes or until soft, then stir in the 30 ml (2 tbsp) flour. Cook gently for 2 minutes, stirring. Remove the pan from the heat and gradually stir in the milk. Bring to the boil and continue to cook, stirring, until the sauce thickens, then add pepper to taste.

6 Sprinkle the Stilton evenly over the base of the flan. Arrange the cauliflower on top. Spoon over the onion sauce and sprinkle with the Cheddar cheese.

7 Bake in the oven at 190°C (375°F) mark 5 for 25–30 minutes or until golden and bubbly. Serve hot.

TARTE À L'OIGNON

SERVES 4–6

50 g (2 oz) butter	50 ml (2 fl oz) milk
700 g (1½ lb) onions, thinly sliced	150 ml (5 fl oz) single cream
175 g (6 oz) frozen shortcrust pastry, thawed	salt and pepper
2 eggs	pinch of grated nutmeg

1 Melt the butter in a large frying pan, add the onions, cover and cook gently for 20 minutes.

2 Roll out the pastry on a lightly floured surface and use to line a 20.5 cm (8 inch) flan dish or ring placed on a baking sheet.

3 Beat together the eggs, milk and cream until smooth. Season to taste and add the nutmeg.

4 Pour a little of the egg mixture into the pastry case. Add the onions, then pour in the remaining egg mixture.

5 Bake in a preheated oven at 200°C (400°F) mark 6 for 30 minutes or until golden brown and set.

SPICED PEPPER AND ONION FLAN

SERVES 4

175 g (6 oz) plus 30 ml (2 tbsp) plain flour	5 ml (1 tsp) ground cumin
salt	150 ml (¼ pint) milk
75 g (3 oz) block margarine	150 ml (5 fl oz) natural yogurt
15 ml (1 tbsp) vegetable oil	2 egg yolks
2 onions, thinly sliced	30 ml (2 tbsp) grated Parmesan cheese
1 red pepper, sliced	
25 g (1 oz) butter	

1 To make the pastry, sift 175 g (6 oz) flour and a pinch of salt into a bowl. Add the margarine and rub in until the mixture resembles breadcrumbs. Bind to a manageable dough with cold water. Knead until smooth.

2 Roll out the dough on a lightly floured surface and use to line a 20.5 cm (8 inch) plain flan ring placed on a baking sheet.

3 Chill for 15–20 minutes, then line with foil and baking beans. Bake blind in a preheated oven at 200°C (400°F) mark 6 for 10–15 minutes or until set but not browned. Remove the foil and beans.

4 Heat the oil in a frying pan, add the sliced onions and pepper, reserving a few slices to garnish, and sauté for 4–5 minutes. Put into the flan case.

5 Melt the butter in a saucepan, stir in the 30 ml (2 tbsp) flour and the cumin. Cook for 2 minutes, stirring, then remove from the heat and gradually stir in the milk and yogurt. Bring to the boil, stirring briskly, and simmer for 2–3 minutes. Beat in the egg yolks.

6 Pour the sauce over the onion and pepper and sprinkle with Parmesan. Cook in the oven at 190°C (375°F) mark 5 for 35–40 minutes. Serve hot garnished with pepper slices.

HOT CRAB AND RICOTTA QUICHES

SERVES 6

175 g (6 oz) plain flour	150 ml (¼ pint) milk
salt and pepper	225 g (8 oz) crab meat, flaked
75 g (3 oz) block margarine	175 g (6 oz) Ricotta cheese, crumbled
2 eggs	
150 ml (¼ pint) single cream	30 ml (2 tbsp) grated Parmesan cheese

1 To make the pastry, sift the flour and a pinch of salt into a bowl. Add the margarine and rub in until the mixture resembles fine breadcrumbs. Add enough cold water to bind to a manageable dough and knead until smooth.

2 Roll out the pastry on a lightly floured surface and use to line six 8.5 cm (3½ inch) fluted, loose-bottomed, flan tins. Line with foil and baking beans and bake blind in a preheated oven at 200°C (400°F) mark 6 for 10–15 minutes. Remove the foil and beans.

3 Meanwhile whisk the eggs, cream and milk together in a bowl and add the crab meat, Ricotta, Parmesan and plenty of salt and pepper. Pour into the flan cases.

4 Reduce the oven temperature to 190°C (375°F) mark 5 and bake the quiches for 35 minutes or until golden.

--- **VARIATION** ---

Make one large quiche instead of six individual ones, if preferred. You will need to use a 20.5 cm (8 inch) flan dish or ring.

SMOKED HADDOCK FLAN

SERVES 4–6

200 g (7 oz) plain flour	1 small bunch of spring onions, chopped
salt and pepper	2 eggs, hard-boiled, shelled and quartered
75 g (3 oz) block margarine	
350 g (12 oz) potatoes, peeled	25 g (1 oz) butter
350 g (12 oz) smoked haddock	25 g (1 oz) Cheddar cheese, grated
300 ml (½ pint) milk	

1 To make the pastry, sift 175 g (6 oz) of the flour into a bowl with a pinch of salt. Rub in the margarine. Add cold water to bind to a dough and knead until smooth.

2 Roll out the pastry and use to line a 20.5 cm (8 inch) flan dish or ring placed on a baking sheet. Bake blind at 200°C (400°F) mark 6 for 10–15 minutes or until set.

3 Cook the potatoes in boiling salted water for about 20 minutes or until tender, then drain and mash. Set aside. Place the fish in a saucepan with the milk, bring to the boil and simmer for 15 minutes.

4 Strain the milk into a bowl. Remove the skin and bones from the fish and flake. Place in the flan case.

5 Plunge the chopped onions into a pan of boiling water, blanch for 1 minute, then drain. Sprinkle the onions over the fish and cover with the eggs.

6 Melt the butter in a saucepan, stir in the remaining flour and cook gently for 1 minute, stirring. Remove from the heat and gradually stir in the reserved milk. Bring to the boil and cook, stirring, until the sauce thickens. Season.

7 Spoon the sauce into the flan case and pipe potato across the top in a lattice design. Sprinkle with cheese and bake in the oven for about 25 minutes or until brown. Serve hot.

SPINACH AND PRAWN QUICHE

SERVES 4–6

200 g (7 oz) plain wholemeal flour	150 ml (¼ pint) milk
salt and pepper	100 g (4 oz) cooked peeled prawns
100 g (4 oz) butter	155 g (5 oz) packet frozen chopped spinach, thawed and drained
1 egg, beaten	

1 Sift the flour into a bowl with a pinch of salt, add the butter and rub in until the mixture resembles fine breadcrumbs. Stir in enough cold water to bind to a manageable dough and knead until smooth.
2 Roll out the pastry on a lightly floured surface and use to line a 20.5 cm (8 inch) flan ring placed on a baking sheet. Line with foil and baking beans and bake blind in a preheated oven at 200°C (400°F) mark 6 for 20 minutes or until set. Remove the foil and beans.
3 Mix the egg, milk, prawns and spinach, season well and pour into the flan case.
4 Bake in the oven at 180°C (350°F) mark 4 for about 40 minutes, until just set. Serve hot.

CURRIED BACON FLAN

SERVES 4–6

175 g (6 oz) plain flour	5 ml (1 tsp) curry powder
salt and pepper	3 eggs, beaten
75 g (3 oz) margarine	150 ml (5 fl oz) natural yogurt
25 g (1 oz) butter	225 g (8 oz) tomatoes, skinned and thinly sliced
100 g (4 oz) celery heart, sliced	
100 g (4 oz) streaky bacon, diced	

1 To make the pastry, sift the flour and a pinch of salt into a bowl. Add the margarine and rub in until the mixture resembles fine breadcrumbs. Add enough cold water to bind to a manageable dough and knead until smooth.
2 Roll out the pastry on a lightly floured surface and use to line a 21.5 cm (8½ inch), loose-bottomed French fluted flan tin. Line with foil and baking beans and bake blind in a preheated oven at 200°C (400°F) mark 6 for 10–15 minutes or until set.
3 Melt the butter in a small frying pan, add the celery and bacon and sauté until golden brown. Stir in the curry powder and cook for 2 minutes.
4 Blend the eggs with the yogurt, add the pan ingredients, season to taste, and turn into the flan case. Top with tomato slices.
5 Bake in the oven at 190°C (375°F) mark 5 for about 25 minutes or until golden brown and set. Serve hot or cold.

FETA CHEESE PUFFS WITH BASIL

MAKES 8

225 g (8 oz) Feta cheese, grated	pepper
150 ml (5 fl oz) natural yogurt	397 g (14 oz) packet frozen puff pastry, thawed
30 ml (2 tbsp) chopped fresh basil or 5 ml (1 tsp) dried	beaten egg
	basil leaves, to garnish

1 Mix the grated cheese with the yogurt, chopped basil and pepper to taste. (Don't add salt as the cheese adds sufficient.)
2 Roll out the pastry thinly on a lightly floured surface and cut out sixteen 10 cm (4½ inch) rounds. Fold and re-roll the pastry as necessary.
3 Place half the rounds on two dampened baking sheets. Spoon some of the cheese mixture into the centre of each one.
4 Brush the pastry edges with egg. Cover with the remaining rounds, knocking up and pressing the pastry edges together to seal. Make a small slit in the top of each pastry puff.
5 Brush with beaten egg. Bake in a preheated oven at 220°C (425°F) mark 7 for about 15 minutes or until well browned and crisp. Serve warm, garnished with basil.

--- COOK'S TIP ---

Feta is a Greek cheese made from goat's or ewe's milk. Vacuum packs, which tend to be rather salty, are available at some large supermarkets, but the best Feta (sold loose in brine) is found in Greek and Middle Eastern stores.

CREAMY HAM AND LEEK PIES

SERVES 4

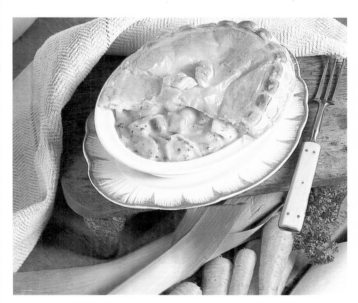

50 g (2 oz) butter	30 ml (2 tbsp) chopped fresh parsley or 10 ml (2 tsp) dried
450 g (1 lb) leeks, thickly sliced	
225 g (8 oz) carrots, sliced	5 ml (1 tsp) grated nutmeg
50 g (2 oz) plain flour	salt and pepper
300 ml (½ pint) vegetable stock	350 g (12 oz) packet puff pastry
300 ml (½ pint) milk	beaten egg, to glaze
225 g (8 oz) cooked ham, diced	

1 Melt the butter in a large saucepan, add the leeks and carrots and fry for 5 minutes. Stir in the flour and cook, stirring continuously, for 1 minute.
2 Gradually stir in the stock, then add the milk. Cook over a medium heat, stirring, until the mixture comes to the boil and thickens. Stir in the ham, parsley and nutmeg. Season to taste, then leave to cool.
3 Roll out the pastry on a lightly floured surface to 0.5 cm (¼ inch) thick. Use a 350 ml (12 fl oz) individual pie dish as a template to cut out four lids for the pies.
4 Divide the ham and leek filling between four 350 ml (12 fl oz) individual pie dishes. Dampen the edges of the dishes with water. Cut the remaining trimmings of pastry into thin strips and place around the rim of each dish. Moisten the strips and lay a lid over each pie. Press the edges to seal, trim and flute.
5 Make a small cut in the top of each pie and brush with beaten egg to glaze. Bake in a preheated oven at 220°C (425°F) mark 7 for 25–30 minutes or until golden brown.

CORNISH PASTIES

SERVES 6

400 g (14 oz) plain flour	175 g (6 oz) swede, diced
salt and pepper	1 medium onion, chopped
225 g (8 oz) butter or margarine	2.5 ml (½ tsp) dried mixed herbs
450 g (1 lb) stewing steak, cut into small pieces	1 egg, beaten
175 g (6 oz) potatoes, peeled and diced	

1 To make the pastry, sift the flour into a bowl with a pinch of salt. Add 200 g (7 oz) of the butter or margarine and rub in until the mixture resembles fine breadcrumbs. Add enough cold water to bind to a manageable dough and knead until smooth.

2 Put the meat, potato, swede and onion in a bowl. Mix in the herbs and season to taste.

3 Divide the pastry into six equal pieces. Roll out each piece on a lightly floured surface to a 20 cm (8 inch) circle.

4 Spoon some of the filling on to half of each pastry circle and top with a little of the remaining butter.

5 Brush the edges of the pastry with water, then fold over and seal the edges firmly together.

6 Place the pasties on a baking sheet and brush with beaten egg. Bake in a preheated oven at 220°C (425°F) mark 7 for 15 minutes. Reduce the heat to 170°C (325°F) mark 3 and cook for a further 1 hour. Serve warm or cold.

CHICKEN PARCELS

SERVES 4

15 g (½ oz) butter	5 ml (1 tsp) lemon juice
1 small onion, chopped	225 g (8 oz) boneless cooked chicken, chopped
2 medium carrots, diced	salt and pepper
15 ml (1 tbsp) plain wholemeal flour	368 g (13 oz) packet frozen puff pastry, thawed
5 ml (1 tsp) mild curry powder	beaten egg, to glaze
300 ml (½ pint) chicken stock	

1 Melt the butter in a large saucepan, add the onion and carrots, cover and cook for 4–5 minutes or until the onion is transparent. Stir in the flour and curry powder and cook, stirring, for 1 minute. Remove from the heat and gradually stir in the stock. Bring to the boil, stirring continuously, then simmer for 2–3 minutes or until thickened.

2 Reduce the heat, add the lemon juice and chicken and season to taste. Leave to cool.

3 When the chicken mixture is cool, roll out the pastry on a lightly floured surface to a 35.5 cm (14 inch) square. Using a sharp knife, cut into four squares.

4 Place the pastry squares on dampened baking sheets, then spoon the chicken mixture on to the pastry, leaving a border round the edges. Brush the edges of each square lightly with water. Fold each square in half and seal and crimp the edges to make a parcel.

5 Make two small slashes in the top of each parcel. Brush with beaten egg to glaze.

6 Bake in a preheated oven at 220°C (425°F) mark 7 for 15–20 minutes or until the pastry is golden brown. Serve hot or cold.

PISSALADIÈRE
SERVES 6

CHILLI PIZZA FINGERS
SERVES 6

100 g (4 oz) plain flour	225 g (8 oz) tomatoes, skinned and sliced
salt and pepper	30 ml (2 tbsp) tomato purée
50 g (2 oz) butter or margarine	5 ml (1 tsp) chopped herbs (marjoram, thyme or sage)
90 ml (6 tbsp) vegetable oil	
450 g (1 lb) onions, finely sliced	anchovy fillets and black olives, to garnish
2 garlic cloves, crushed	

1 To make the pastry, sift the flour and a pinch of salt into a bowl. Add the butter or margarine and rub in until the mixture resembles fine breadcrumbs. Add about 30 ml (2 tbsp) water and mix until it forms a smooth dough. Wrap and chill in the refrigerator for 15 minutes.

2 Roll out the pastry on a lightly floured surface and use to line a 20.5 cm (8 inch) plain flan ring placed on a baking sheet. Line with foil and baking beans and bake blind in a preheated oven at 200°C (400°F) mark 6 for 20 minutes. Remove the foil and beans.

3 Meanwhile, make the filling. Heat the oil in a large saucepan, add the onions and garlic and fry for 10 minutes or until very soft but not brown.

4 Add the tomatoes to the pan and continue cooking for 10 minutes or until the liquid has evaporated. Stir in the tomato purée and herbs and season to taste.

5 Turn the mixture into the flan case. Brush with a little oil and cook in the oven at 200°C (400°F) mark 6 for 20 minutes.

6 To serve, garnish the pissaladière with a lattice of anchovy fillets and the black olives. Serve either hot or cold.

225 g (8 oz) lean minced beef	225 g (8 oz) plain wholemeal flour
2.5 ml (½ tsp) chilli powder	50 g (2 oz) medium oatmeal
1 garlic clove, crushed	15 ml (1 tbsp) baking powder
1 medium onion, chopped	salt and pepper
1 small green pepper, chopped	50 g (2 oz) butter or margarine
100 g (4 oz) mushrooms, sliced	1 egg, beaten
225 g (8 oz) tomatoes, skinned and chopped	60 ml (4 tbsp) milk
213 g (7.51 oz) can red kidney beans, drained	15 ml (1 tbsp) tomato purée
150 ml (¼ pint) beef stock	175 g (6 oz) Mozzarella cheese, thinly sliced

1 First prepare the topping. Put the minced beef, chilli powder and garlic in a saucepan and fry for 3–4 minutes, stirring occasionally. Add the onion, green pepper and mushrooms and fry for a further 1–2 minutes. Stir in the tomatoes, red kidney beans and beef stock. Bring to the boil and simmer for about 15 minutes or until most of the liquid has evaporated, stirring occasionally.

2 Meanwhile, combine the flour, oatmeal, baking powder and a pinch of salt in a bowl. Rub in the butter or margarine. Bind to a soft dough with the egg and milk, then knead lightly until smooth.

3 Roll out the dough to a 25×18 cm (10×7 inch) rectangle. Lift on to a baking sheet, then spread with tomato purée. Pile chilli mixture on top and cover with cheese.

4 Bake at 200°C (400°F) mark 6 for about 30 minutes or until golden and bubbling. Cut into fingers.

PASTA WITH PEAS AND HAM IN CREAM SAUCE

SERVES 4

275–350 g (10–12 oz) tagliatelle	100 g (4 oz) frozen peas, cooked
100 g (4 oz) butter	60 ml (4 tbsp) single cream
1 large onion, sliced	100 g (4 oz) Cheddar cheese, grated
100 g (4 oz) ham, cut into thin strips	salt and pepper

1 Cook the tagliatelle in boiling salted water for about 10 minutes or until tender, but not soft. Drain well.
2 Meanwhile, melt the butter in a pan, add the onion and cook for about 3 minutes or until soft. Add the ham and peas and cook for a further 5 minutes.
3 Add the drained tagliatelle to the pan, stir well and add the cream and most of the cheese. Toss gently, season to taste and serve at once, sprinkled with the remaining cheese.

VARIATION

Spaghetti with Peas and Ham in Cream Sauce
Substitute spaghetti for the tagliatelle in the above recipe.

BACON CAKES

MAKES 8

7 rashers streaky bacon	50 ml (¼ pint) milk
225 g (8 oz) self-raising flour	15 ml (1 tbsp) tomato ketchup
pinch of salt	a dash of Worcestershire sauce
25 g (1 oz) butter	milk, to glaze
75 g (3 oz) Cheddar cheese, grated	

1 Cook three rashers of the bacon under a preheated grill until crisp, then cut into small pieces.
2 Sift the flour and salt together into a bowl, add the butter and rub in until the mixture resembles fine breadcrumbs. Add all but 15 g (½ oz) of the cheese and the crumbled bacon.
3 Mix the milk, tomato ketchup and Worcestershire sauce together and add to the dry ingredients. Mix to a soft dough, roll out to an 18 cm (7 inch) circle, brush with milk and cut into eight wedges.
4 Arrange the wedges on a buttered, floured baking tray in a circle with edges overlapping. Sprinkle with the remaining cheese.
5 Bake in a preheated oven at 200°C (400°F) mark 6 for 30 minutes. Cut the remaining bacon in half and roll up. Place the rolls on a skewer and grill until crisp. Use to garnish the bacon cakes.

FISH CAKES WITH HERBS

SERVES 4

275 g (10 oz) haddock, skinned and boned	15 ml (1 tbsp) snipped chives
15 ml (1 tbsp) lemon juice	15 ml (1 tbsp) chopped parsley
15 ml (1 tbsp) Worcestershire sauce	350 g (12 oz) potatoes, cooked and mashed
15 ml (1 tbsp) horseradish sauce	50 g (2 oz) fresh wholemeal breadcrumbs
100 ml (4 fl oz) milk	

1 Put the fish in a blender or food processor with the lemon juice, Worcestershire sauce and horseradish and blend to a purée. Transfer to a bowl and stir in the milk, chives, parsley and potatoes.

2 Shape the mixture into four fish cakes and coat with breadcrumbs.

3 Cook under a preheated moderate grill for 5 minutes on each side or until browned. Serve immediately.

VARIATION

Cod Fish Cakes with Herbs

The above fish cakes are equally good made with cod instead of haddock.

CHICKEN LIVER SKEWERS

SERVES 4

2 small oranges	1 green pepper, roughly chopped
200 ml (7 fl oz) unsweetened orange juice	100 g (4 oz) onion, roughly chopped
5 ml (1 tsp) chopped fresh tarragon or 2.5 ml (½ tsp) dried	275 g (10 oz) beansprouts
450 g (1 lb) whole chicken livers, thawed if frozen	1 small bunch of chives, snipped
2 slices of bread, crumbed	salt and pepper

1 Finely grate the rind of one of the oranges. Place in a saucepan with the orange juice and tarragon and simmer for 2–3 minutes or until reduced by half.

2 Cut the tops and bottoms off both oranges, then remove the peel by working around the oranges in a spiral.

3 Divide the oranges into segments by cutting through the membranes on either side of each segment.

4 Cut the chicken livers in half and toss lightly in the breadcrumbs. Place in a lightly greased grill pan and cook under a preheated grill for 2 minutes on each side.

5 Thread the pepper and onion on to four oiled kebab skewers alternately with the livers.

6 Place the skewers in the grill pan and spoon over a little of the reduced orange juice. Grill for 2–3 minutes on each side, turning and basting occasionally.

7 Meanwhile, steam the beansprouts for 2–3 minutes. Warm the orange segments in a separate pan with the remaining reduced orange juice.

8 Mix the beansprouts with the chives and season to taste. Arrange on a warmed serving dish. Top with the skewers and spoon over the orange segments and juices.

JANSSON'S TEMPTATION

SERVES 6

4 medium baking potatoes	salt and pepper
two 50 g (2 oz) cans anchovy fillets, soaked in milk for 20 minutes and drained	1 large onion, finely chopped
25 g (1 oz) butter or margarine	450 ml (¾ pint) single cream
	30 ml (2 tbsp) chopped parsley, to garnish

1 Peel the potatoes and cut into very thin matchstick strips. Cut the anchovies into thin strips.

2 Arrange half of the potato strips in a layer in the bottom of a well-buttered ovenproof dish. Sprinkle with a little salt and plenty of pepper.

3 Arrange the strips of anchovy and chopped onion over the potato layer, then top with the remaining potato. Sprinkle with salt and pepper as before.

4 Pour half the cream slowly into the dish, then dot with the remaining butter. Bake in a preheated oven at 180°C (350°F) mark 4 for 30 minutes. Add the remaining cream and bake for a further 1 hour or until the potatoes feel tender when pierced with a skewer. Cover the dish with foil if the potatoes show signs of over-browning during cooking. Serve hot, sprinkled with the parsley.

--- COOK'S TIP ---

In Sweden, this dish is usually served as a starter, but it is easily substantial enough to serve as a main course. To refresh the palate, follow with a crisp green salad tossed in a sharp oil and vinegar dressing.

SALMON KEDGEREE

SERVES 6

350 g (12 oz) salmon	salt and pepper
150 ml (¼ pint) dry white wine	350 g (12 oz) long grain rice
2 small onions, chopped	50 g (2 oz) butter
1 carrot, sliced	7.5 ml (1½ tsp) English mustard powder
1 celery stick, chopped	3 eggs, hard-boiled, shelled and quartered
15 ml (1 tbsp) lemon juice	cayenne, to finish
6 peppercorns	celery leaves or parsley sprigs, to garnish
1 bouquet garni	

1 Put the salmon in a saucepan and pour in the wine and enough water to cover the fish. Add half of the chopped onions, the carrot, celery, lemon juice, peppercorns, bouquet garni and 5 ml (1 tsp) salt. Bring slowly to the boil, then remove from the heat. Cover tightly and cool.

2 Cook the rice in boiling salted water until tender.

3 Meanwhile, remove the salmon from the liquid and flake the flesh, discarding the skin and any bones. Strain the cooking liquid and reserve.

4 Melt half the butter in a large frying pan, add the remaining onion and fry gently for about 5 minutes or until soft. Drain the rice thoroughly, then add to the onion with the remaining butter. Toss to coat and stir in the mustard.

5 Add the flaked salmon and the hard-boiled eggs and a few spoonfuls of the strained cooking liquid to moisten. Heat through. Shake the pan and toss the ingredients gently so that the salmon and eggs do not break up.

6 Transfer to a warmed serving dish and sprinkle with cayenne to taste. Garnish and serve immediately.

PRAWN RISOTTO

SERVES 4

75 g (3 oz) onion, thinly sliced	½ sachet saffron strands
1 garlic clove, crushed	salt and pepper
1 litre (1¾ pints) chicken stock	225 g (8 oz) peeled prawns
225 g (8 oz) long grain brown rice	50 g (2 oz) frozen petits pois
50 g (2 oz) small button mushrooms	12 cooked whole prawns, to garnish

1 Place the onion, garlic, stock, rice, mushrooms and saffron in a large saucepan or flameproof casserole. Season to taste. Bring to the boil and simmer, uncovered, for 35 minutes, stirring occasionally.

2 Stir in the prawns and petits pois. Cook over a high heat for about 5 minutes or until most of the liquid has been absorbed, stirring occasionally.

3 Taste and adjust the seasoning, then turn into a warmed serving dish. Garnish with the whole prawns and serve immediately.

QUICK CHICKEN AND MUSSEL PAELLA

SERVES 4–6

60 ml (4 tbsp) olive oil	1.2 litres (2¼ pints) boiling chicken stock
about 450 g (1 lb) boneless chicken meat, skinned and cut into bite-sized cubes	5 ml (1 tsp) paprika
1 onion, chopped	2.5 ml (½ tsp) saffron powder
2 garlic cloves, crushed	salt and pepper
1 large red pepper, sliced into thin strips	two 150 g (5 oz) jars mussels, drained
3 tomatoes, skinned and chopped	lemon wedges, cooked peeled prawns and fresh mussels (optional), to garnish
400 g (14 oz) Valencia or risotto rice	

1 Heat the oil in a large, deep frying pan, add the cubes of chicken and fry over a moderate heat until golden brown on all sides. Remove from the pan and set aside.

2 Add the onion, garlic and red pepper to the oil remaining in the pan and fry gently for 5 minutes or until softened. Add the tomatoes and fry for a few more minutes or until the juices run, then add the rice and stir to combine.

3 Pour in 1 litre (1¾ pints) of the boiling stock (it will bubble furiously), then add half the paprika and the saffron powder. Season to taste. Stir well and add the chicken.

4 Simmer, uncovered, for 30 minutes or until the chicken is cooked through, stirring frequently during this time to prevent the rice from sticking. When the mixture becomes dry, stir in a few more tablespoons of boiling stock. Repeat as often as necessary to keep the paella moist.

5 To serve, fold in the mussels and heat through. Taste and adjust the seasoning, then garnish with lemon wedges, prawns, mussels and a sprinkling of paprika.

SPAGHETTI ALLA CARBONARA

SERVES 4

4 eggs	350 g (12 oz) spaghetti
150 ml (5 fl oz) single cream	175 g (6 oz) Cheddar cheese, grated
25 g (1 oz) butter	salt and pepper
225 g (8 oz) streaky bacon, chopped	30 ml (2 tbsp) chopped parsley

1 Beat together the eggs and cream. Heat the butter in a frying pan, add the bacon and fry until crisp.

2 Meanwhile, cook the spaghetti in boiling salted water for about 8 minutes or until tender, but not soft. Drain and add it to the bacon in the frying pan.

3 Cook for 1 minute, stirring all the time. Remove from the heat and add the egg mixture. Mix well. (The heat of the spaghetti will be enough to cook the eggs).

4 Stir in 100 g (4 oz) cheese and season to taste. Transfer to a warmed serving dish and serve immediately, sprinkled with the parsley and remaining cheese.

MACARONI CHEESE

SERVES 4

175 g (6 oz) short-cut macaroni	salt and pepper
40 g (1½ oz) butter	175 g (6 oz) mature Cheddar cheese, grated
60 ml (4 tbsp) plain flour	30 ml (2 tbsp) fresh breadcrumbs
568 ml (1 pint) milk	
pinch of nutmeg, or 2.5 ml (½ tsp) prepared mustard	

1 Cook the macaroni in boiling salted water for 10 minutes, then drain well.

2 Meanwhile melt the butter in a saucepan, stir in the flour and cook gently for 1 minute. Remove from the heat and gradually stir in the milk. Bring to the boil and continue to cook, stirring, until the sauce thickens, then remove from the heat, add the nutmeg or mustard and season to taste. Stir in 100 g (4 oz) cheese and the macaroni.

3 Pour into an ovenproof dish and sprinkle with the remaining cheese and the breadcrumbs.

4 Place on a baking sheet and bake in a preheated oven at 200°C (400°F) mark 6 for about 20 minutes or until golden and bubbling.

TUNA AND PASTA IN SOURED CREAM

SERVES 4

225 g (8 oz) pasta spirals or shells	30 ml (2 tbsp) malt vinegar
salt and pepper	198 g (7 oz) can tuna, drained and flaked
5 ml (1 tsp) vegetable oil	4 eggs, hard-boiled, shelled and finely chopped
25 g (1 oz) butter	
150 ml (5 fl oz) soured cream	60 ml (4 tbsp) chopped parsley
5 ml (1 tsp) anchovy essence	

1 Cook the pasta in plenty of boiling salted water to which the oil has been added, for about 15 minutes or until *al dente* (tender but firm to the bite). Drain well.

2 Melt the butter in a deep frying pan and toss in the pasta. Stir in the soured cream, anchovy essence and vinegar.

3 Add the tuna and egg to the pan with the parsley. Season well and warm through over a low heat, stirring occasionally. Serve immediately.

PASTA BAKE

SERVES 4

450 g (1 lb) lean minced beef	100 g (4 oz) wholewheat spaghetti rings
1 red pepper, sliced	300 ml (10 fl oz) natural yogurt
1 onion, chopped	1 egg, beaten
100 g (4 oz) button mushrooms, sliced	50 g (2 oz) plain flour
397 g (14 oz) can tomatoes	2 tomatoes, sliced, and chopped fresh parsley, to garnish
5 ml (1 tsp) Tabasco sauce	
salt and pepper	

1 Put the mince in a saucepan and fry gently in its own fat, until turning brown. Drain off any fat. Add the pepper, onion, mushrooms, tomatoes with their juice and Tabasco sauce. Season to taste and simmer gently for 10 minutes.

2 Meanwhile, cook the pasta in boiling salted water for about 10 minutes or until tender, but not soft. Drain well and place in a 1.4 litre (2½ pint) ovenproof dish. Top with the mince mixture.

3 Beat together the yogurt, egg and flour until smooth and pour over the mince. Bake in a preheated oven at 180°C (350°F) mark 4 for 40 minutes. Serve hot, garnished with tomatoes and chopped parsley.

SESAME CHICKEN PITTAS

SERVES 4

30 ml (2 tbsp) sesame oil	100 g (4 oz) beansprouts
1 onion, sliced	15 ml (1 tbsp) dark soy sauce
100 g (4 oz) broccoli, cut into tiny florets	30 ml (2 tbsp) toasted sesame seeds
1 red pepper, diced	4 large pitta breads
225 g (8 oz) cooked chicken breast, sliced into thin strips	

1 Heat the oil in a large frying pan, add the onion and stir-fry for 2 minutes. Add the broccoli and pepper and cook for 3–4 minutes, stirring frequently.

2 Add the chicken strips to the pan, stir well, then add the beansprouts and soy sauce. Continue to cook for 2–3 minutes. Sprinkle over the sesame seeds and stir to combine. Remove from the heat and keep warm.

3 Cut through a long side of each pitta bread and open the cavity to form a pocket. Place the pitta breads on a baking sheet. Bake in a preheated oven at 200°C (400°F) mark 6 for 5–10 minutes to heat.

4 Using a slotted spoon, fill each pitta pocket with the chicken mixture. Serve immediately.

TO MICROWAVE

Put the oil and onion in a medium bowl. Cover and cook on HIGH for 2–2½ minutes. Add the broccoli and pepper, re-cover and cook on HIGH for 2–2½ minutes. Add the chicken, beansprouts and soy sauce, stir and cook on HIGH for 2–2½ minutes. Stir in the sesame seeds. To warm the pitta breads, place on a double thickness of absorbent kitchen paper and cook on HIGH for 1–1½ minutes or until warm. Complete step 4.

PAN BAGNA WITH AVOCADO

SERVES 6–8

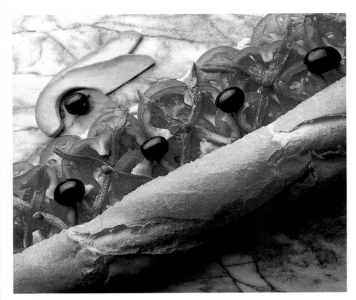

2 ripe avocados	225 g (8 oz) tomatoes, sliced
15 ml (1 tbsp) lemon juice	1 small green pepper, sliced into thin rings
15 ml (1 tbsp) vegetable oil	a few capers and stoned black olives
garlic salt and black pepper	
63 g (2½ oz) can anchovies, drained	
two 35 cm (14 inch) French loaves	

1 Halve the avocados and remove the stones. Mash the flesh with the lemon juice and oil and season to taste with garlic salt and pepper. Cut the anchovies into thin strips.

2 Halve the loaves lengthways. Pull out and discard some of the crumb. Spread the bases with the avocado mixture and top with tomatoes and pepper. Arrange the anchovy strips in a lattice pattern on top and sprinkle with capers and olives. Position the top of the loaf over the filling to make a sandwich, cut the loaf in chunks and serve.

CHICKEN TACOS

SERVES 6

6 Mexican taco shells	salt and pepper
25 g (1 oz) butter or margarine	shredded lettuce
1 medium onion, chopped	100 g (4 oz) Cheddar cheese, grated
450 g (1 lb) cooked chicken meat, diced	Tabasco sauce
4 tomatoes, skinned and chopped	

1 Put the taco shells in the oven to warm according to the instructions on the packet.

2 To make the filling, melt the butter or margarine in a frying pan, add the onion and fry for about 5 minutes or until soft but not coloured. Stir in the chicken and half the tomatoes, season to taste and heat through.

3 Spoon 15–30 ml (1–2 tbsp) filling into each shell. Add a little lettuce, the remaining tomatoes and the cheese with a few drops of Tabasco sauce. Serve immediately.

CRISPY STUFFED POTATO SKINS

SERVES 4–6

4 medium baking potatoes, scrubbed and pricked	25 g (1 oz) fresh breadcrumbs
175 g (6 oz) mature Cheddar cheese, grated	FOR THE DIPPING SAUCE
45 ml (3 tbsp) snipped chives or 15 ml (1 tbsp) dried	30 ml (2 tbsp) snipped chives or 10 ml (2 tsp) dried
salt and pepper	300 ml (10 fl oz) soured cream
vegetable oil, for deep frying	

1 Place the potatoes on a baking sheet and bake in a preheated oven at 220°C (425°F) mark 7 for 1–1½ hours.

2 Cut each potato in half and scoop out the flesh. Chop the flesh into chunks and place in a medium bowl. Add 100 g (4 oz) of the cheese and 30 ml (2 tbsp) of the snipped fresh chives or 10 ml (2 tsp) dried. Season to taste and cover with foil to keep warm.

3 Heat the oil in a deep fat fryer to 190°C (375°F) and deep-fry the potato skins in batches for 3–4 minutes or until crisp. Drain well and arrange, hollow side up, on a baking sheet.

4 Spoon the potato mixture into the skins. Mix the remaining cheese, chives and breadcrumbs together and sprinkle over each stuffed potato skin. Put under a preheated grill until golden. For the dipping sauce, stir the chives into the soured cream and serve with the stuffed potato skins.

—— TO MICROWAVE ——

Place the potatoes on a double thickness of absorbent kitchen paper. Cook on HIGH for 10–15 minutes, rearranging. Stand for 5 minutes. Complete steps 2–4.

SALADS

Needing little or no accompaniment, these salads are complete meals on their own, combining cooked meats, fish, eggs or cheese with dried beans, grains and vegetables as well as more usual salad ingredients. They are the perfect choice for a summer lunch or buffet for family or friends.

CRAB SALAD

SERVES 2

15 ml (1 tbsp) lemon juice	2 tomatoes, skinned and cubed
15 ml (1 tbsp) mayonnaise	50 g (2 oz) pasta shells, cooked
15 ml (1 tbsp) natural yogurt	pepper
225 g (8 oz) cooked crab meat, thawed if frozen	lettuce, shredded
½ cucumber, diced	cucumber and lemon slices, to garnish

1 Mix together the lemon juice, mayonnaise and yogurt.
2 Combine the dressing with the remaining ingredients, except the lettuce. Serve the crab salad on a bed of shredded lettuce, garnished with cucumber and lemon slices.

CHEF'S SALAD

SERVES 4

225 g (8 oz) cooked ham	6 small tomatoes, halved, or 2 large tomatoes, quartered
225 g (8 oz) cold cooked chicken	3 spring onions, finely chopped
225 g (8 oz) Emmenthal cheese	French or blue cheese dressing, to serve
1 Iceberg or Webb's lettuce	
2 eggs, hard-boiled, shelled and quartered	

1 Using a sharp knife, cut the ham and chicken into fine strips and set aside. Remove any rind from the cheese. Carefully cut the cheese into small dice. Wash the lettuce under cold running water and pat it dry.
2 Finely shred the lettuce leaves, or leave them whole, and use to line an oval serving dish.
3 To serve, arrange the meat and cheese alternately around the edge of a large dish. Add the egg and tomatoes and sprinkle over the finely chopped spring onions. Serve the dressing separately.

PORK AND MUSHROOM SALAD

SERVES 6

DEVILLED DUCKLING SALAD

SERVES 6

two 350 g (12 oz) pork fillets (tenderloins)	10 green olives, stoned and chopped
vegetable oil	150 ml (5 fl oz) soured cream
knob of butter	1.25 ml (¼ tsp) mustard powder
225 g (8 oz) small button mushrooms	salt and pepper
juice of ½ lemon	5 ml (1 tsp) chopped marjoram or mint
1 small onion, finely sliced	lemon wedges, to garnish
1 small green pepper, finely shredded	

two 1.4 kg (3 lb) oven-ready ducklings	15 ml (1 tbsp) mild curry paste
salt	salt and pepper
150 ml (5 fl oz) soured cream	50 g (2 oz) cashew nuts
90 ml (6 tbsp) mayonnaise	350 g (12 oz) fresh apricots, stoned and thickly sliced
15 ml (1 tbsp) clear honey	endive leaves, to serve

1 Cut the pork into 1 cm (½ inch) slices on the diagonal, then cut each slice into neat strips.

2 Heat a little oil and the butter in a large frying pan, add half the pork and fry quickly to brown and seal the meal. Repeat with the remaining meat, then return all to the pan. Lower the heat and cook slowly for 10–15 minutes or until very tender. Using a slotted spoon, lift the meat out of the pan and leave to cool.

3 Add the mushrooms to the pan with 50 ml (2 fl oz) water and the lemon juice. Cook, stirring, for 1–2 minutes. Using a slotted spoon, remove from the pan and cool.

4 Put the onion and green pepper in a pan of cold water, bring to the boil and simmer for 1–2 minutes. Drain and cool under cold running water. Stir into the pork with the cooled mushrooms and the olives.

5 Mix the soured cream with the mustard, season to taste and stir into the pork. Cover and chill for at least 3 hours.

6 Stir the salad well before serving sprinkled with marjoram or mint and garnished with lemon wedges.

1 Cut away any surplus fat from the ducklings, then wipe them with a damp cloth. Pat dry.

2 Prick the birds all over with a sharp fork or skewer and sprinkle generously with salt. Place the ducklings, breast-side down, side by side, on a wire rack or trivet in a large roasting tin.

3 Roast in a preheated oven at 180°C (350°F) mark 4 for about 1¾ hours or until the birds are really tender, basting occasionally. Half-way through the cooking time, turn the birds over so they are standing breast-side up.

4 Meanwhile, prepare the dressing. In a large bowl, mix together the soured cream, mayonnaise, honey and curry paste. Season and stir in the cashew nuts and apricots.

5 While the ducklings are still warm, strip off the crisp breast skin and reserve. Remove the meat from the bones.

6 Coarsely shred the meat, discarding all the remaining skin, fat and bones. Fold the shredded duckling meat into the dressing, cover and chill for 2–3 hours.

7 Using a pair of kitchen scissors, cut the reserved duckling skin into strips and quickly crisp it further under a hot grill.

8 To serve, spoon the duckling salad down the centre of a large flat platter, then arrange the crisp duck skin over the top. Serve on a bed of endive leaves.

CHICKEN AND GRAPE SALAD

SERVES 4–6

1.4 kg (3 lb) roasting chicken	150 ml (5 fl oz) whipping cream
1 onion	225 g (8 oz) green grapes, halved and seeded
1 carrot	
1 bay leaf	50 g (2 oz) seedless raisins
6 peppercorns	salt and pepper
2 eggs	lettuce and paprika, to garnish
90 ml (6 tbsp) lemon juice	
45 ml (3 tbsp) clear honey	

1 Put the chicken in a large saucepan with the onion, carrot, bay leaf and peppercorns, cover with water and poach for about 50 minutes or until tender. Leave to cool in the stock.

2 Remove the chicken from the stock and cut all the meat off the bones, discarding the skin. Cut the meat into bite-sized pieces.

3 Beat the eggs with 60 ml (4 tbsp) lemon juice and the honey. Put in the top of a double saucepan or in a heatproof bowl standing over a saucepan of hot water and heat gently, stirring, until thick. Cover with damp greaseproof paper and leave to cool.

4 Whip the cream until softly stiff and fold into the cold lemon mixture.

5 Add the remaining lemon juice to the grapes, then combine with the chicken, raisins and sauce.

6 Serve garnished with lettuce and paprika.

SMOKED CHICKEN AND AVOCADO SALAD

SERVES 4–6

1 kg (2 lb) smoked chicken	2.5 ml (½ tsp) green peppercorn mustard
135 ml (9 tbsp) olive oil	
juice of 1 lemon	2 ripe avocados
5 ml (1 tsp) bottled grated horseradish	salt and pepper
	sprigs of fresh coriander and lemon slices, to garnish

1 Remove all the meat from the chicken carcass, taking care to cut thin, even slices which will look attractive in the finished dish.

2 To make the dressing, whisk together the oil, lemon juice, horseradish and mustard. Add the chicken and coat in the dressing. Cover and leave for 30 minutes to 1 hour.

3 Halve the avocados and remove the stones. Peel off the skin, then cut the flesh lengthways into thin, even slices.

4 Arrange the chicken and avocado slices alternately on a flat, round plate, overlapping them in a 'Catherine-wheel' shape.

5 Chop any remaining oddly-shaped pieces of chicken and avocado and toss them together. Pile this mixture into the centre of the plate.

6 Season the dressing remaining in the bowl and brush over the avocado slices to prevent discoloration.

7 Garnish the centre of the salad with fresh coriander and lemon slices, and serve immediately with the dressing.

CHICKEN WITH CURRIED LEMON MAYONNAISE

SERVES 4

1.4 kg (3 lb) chicken	2 celery sticks, finely chopped
150 ml (¼ pint) dry white wine	175 ml (6 fl oz) thick mayonnaise
1 strip of lemon rind	30 ml (2 tbsp) apricot jam
bouquet garni	finely grated rind and juice of 1 lemon
6 black peppercorns	
salt and pepper	1 red or green pepper, diced
15 g (½ oz) butter	
1 small onion, chopped	2 red-skinned eating apples
15 ml (1 tbsp) curry powder	150 ml (5 fl oz) double or whipping cream
	lettuce, to serve

1 Put the chicken in a deep saucepan with the wine, enough water just to cover, the strip of lemon rind, bouquet garni, peppercorns and a good pinch of salt. Cover and simmer for 1–1¼ hours or until the chicken is tender, then leave to cool in the liquid for about 2 hours.

2 Remove the chicken from the liquid. Strain the liquid into a saucepan, then boil until reduced to a few table-spoons. Cool for 5 minutes. Meanwhile, remove the chicken from the bones and dice the meat, discarding all skin.

3 Melt the butter, add the onion and curry powder and fry for 5 minutes or until soft. Add the celery and fry for 2 minutes, stirring. Cool for 10 minutes.

4 Add the onion and celery to the mayonnaise with the apricot jam, grated lemon rind and juice and the diced pepper. Thin with the reduced cooking liquid. Season.

5 Core and dice or slice the apples. Whip the cream until thick, then fold into the mayonnaise with the apples and chicken. Chill for 30 minutes. Serve on a bed of lettuce.

BEEF AND OLIVE SALAD

SERVES 4

450 g (1 lb) rolled lean brisket	12 black olives
1 bay leaf	450 g (1 lb) French beans
6 peppercorns	salt and pepper
1 large bunch of spring onions	45 ml (3 tbsp) soy sauce
	20 ml (4 tsp) lemon juice

1 Put the beef, bay leaf and peppercorns in a small saucepan and add enough water to cover. Bring to the boil; cover and simmer gently for about 1 hour or until the meat is tender. Leave to cool in the cooking liquid for about 2 hours.

2 Slice the spring onions diagonally into thick pieces. Quarter and stone the olives. Trim and halve the French beans. Cook the beans in boiling salted water for 5–10 minutes or until just tender. Drain well, rinse under cold running water and drain again thoroughly.

3 Drain the beef and trim off the fat. Slice thinly and cut into 4 cm (1½ inch) long shreds.

4 Put the beef in a bowl, add the spring onions, olives, beans, soy sauce and lemon juice. Toss well together, then season with pepper. (The soy sauce should provide sufficent salt.) Cover and chill in the refrigerator for about 30 minutes before serving.

AVOCADO AND LEMON SALAD WITH OMELETTE RINGS

SERVES 4–6

4 eggs	5 ml (1 tsp) coriander seeds
50 g (2 oz) Cheddar cheese, grated	90 ml (6 tbsp) olive or vegetable oil
salt and pepper	45 ml (3 tbsp) lemon juice
25 g (1 oz) butter or margarine	2 ripe avocados
5 ml (1 tsp) black peppercorns	parsley sprigs, to garnish (optional)

1 Put the eggs in a bowl with the cheese and 15 ml (1 tbsp) water. Season to taste and whisk together.

2 Melt a quarter of the butter or margarine in an omelette pan or small non-stick frying pan. When foaming, pour in a quarter of the egg mixture. After a few seconds, push the set egg mixture into the centre of the pan and tilt the pan to allow the egg to run to the edges. Cook until just set.

3 Brown the omelette under a preheated hot grill. Turn out on to a plate. Repeat with the remaining egg mixture to make another three omelettes.

4 While the omelettes are still warm, roll them up loosely. Wrap in greaseproof paper and leave to cool.

5 Meanwhile, crush the peppercorns and coriander seeds coarsely with a pestle and mortar, or with the end of a rolling pin in a strong bowl.

6 Whisk together the oil, lemon juice and crushed spices and season to taste. Halve, stone and peel the avocados, then slice thickly into the dressing. Toss gently to coat.

7 Slice the rolled omelettes thinly. Arrange the omelette rings and avocado slices in individual serving plates. Spoon over the dressing and garnish with sprigs of parsley, if liked. Serve immediately.

CHEESE AND CHICORY SALAD

SERVES 4

2 large heads of chicory, trimmed	45 ml (3 tbsp) white wine vinegar
100 g (4 oz) Cotswold or Cheddar cheese, cubed	5–10 ml (1–2 tsp) soft brown sugar
1 green pepper, chopped	1 small garlic clove, crushed
2 celery sticks, chopped	salt and pepper
100 g (4 oz) radishes, sliced	100 g (4 oz) walnut halves
30 ml (2 tbsp) beef stock	
90 ml (6 tbsp) vegetable oil	

1 Chop the chicory coarsely. Place the cheese cubes in a salad bowl with the chicory. Add the pepper, celery and radishes and mix together.

2 Place the stock, oil, vinegar, sugar and garlic in a screw-topped jar, season to taste, and shake well to combine. Pour over the salad and stir in the walnuts.

--- **COOK'S TIP** ---

Cotswold cheese is a variety of Double Gloucester flavoured with chopped chives and onion.

CHEDDAR CHEESE AND APPLE SALAD

SERVES 4

½ round lettuce	2 eating apples, peeled, cored and diced
150 ml (5 fl oz) soured cream	225 g (8 oz) Cheddar cheese, diced
45 ml (3 tbsp) milk	2 canned pineapple rings, coarsely chopped
5 ml (1 tsp) lemon juice	4 orange slices and 8 black olives, to garnish
5 ml (1 tsp) icing or caster sugar	
1.25 ml (¼ tsp) salt	

1 Tear the lettuce leaves into bite-sized pieces and use to cover the base of a serving dish.
2 Combine the soured cream with the milk, lemon juice, sugar and salt.
3 Add the apples, cheese and pineapple to the soured cream mixture and toss lightly together. Pile on to the lettuce and garnish with orange slices and olives.

GOAT'S CHEESE WITH PEAR AND WALNUT SALAD

SERVES 2

a few lettuce leaves, such as Webb's and radicchio, torn into pieces	50 g (2 oz) walnuts, chopped
100 g (4 oz) goat's cheese, halved into 2 discs	½ bunch of watercress
2 ripe pears, cored and cut into chunks	30 ml (2 tbsp) lemon juice
	45 ml (3 tbsp) vegetable oil

1 Arrange the lettuce on two serving plates and top with the goat's cheese. Mix together the pears, walnuts and watercress.
2 Blend the lemon juice and oil together, add to the pear mixture and toss to coat. Spoon on to the cheese to serve.

─── **VARIATION** ───

Caerphilly with Pear and Walnut Salad
If you prefer not to use goat's cheese, Caerphilly makes a delicious substitute, as do other white cheeses, such as Lancashire, Wensleydale or white Stilton.

WHOLE WHEAT BRAZIL NUT SALAD

SERVES 4–6

75 g (3 oz) dried black-eyed beans, soaked in cold water overnight	45 ml (3 tbsp) chopped mint
	salt and pepper
100 g (4 oz) whole wheat grain, soaked in cold water overnight	½ cucumber, diced
	225 g (8 oz) tomatoes, skinned and roughly chopped
90 ml (6 tbsp) natural yogurt	
	100 g (4 oz) cheese, grated
30 ml (2 tbsp) olive oil	
45 ml (3 tbsp) lemon juice	100 g (4 oz) Brazil nuts, chopped

1 Drain the beans and place in a saucepan of water. Bring to the boil and simmer gently for 1½ hours or until tender.
2 Meanwhile, drain the whole wheat and place in a saucepan of water. Bring to the boil and simmer gently for 20–25 minutes or until tender. Drain, rinse well with cold water and cool for 30 minutes. When the beans are cooked, drain and cool for 30 minutes.
3 Whisk the yogurt and olive oil together with the lemon juice and mint. Season to taste.
4 Put the whole wheat, beans, cucumber, tomatoes, cheese and Brazil nuts in a bowl. Pour over the dressing and mix well.
5 Garnish and chill before serving.

WINTER SALAD

SERVES 4–6

1 eating apple, cored and chopped	2.5 ml (½ tsp) sugar
	60 ml (4 tbsp) single cream
1 head of celery, sliced	10 ml (2 tsp) white wine vinegar
1 cooked beetroot, peeled and sliced	
	salt and pepper
2 heads of chicory, trimmed and sliced	3 eggs, hard-boiled, shelled and cut into wedges
1 punnet of salad cress	
2.5 ml (½ tsp) prepared English mustard	

1 Lightly mix the apple, celery, beetroot and chicory together with the cress in a large salad bowl.
2 To make the dressing, whisk the mustard, sugar, cream and vinegar together. Season to taste. Pour over the salad and toss together so that everything is coated in the dressing. Add the eggs, then serve at once.

BEAN, CHEESE AND AVOCADO SALAD

SERVES 4

225 g (8 oz) dried red kidney beans, soaked in cold water overnight	1 small onion, finely chopped
90 ml (6 tbsp) olive oil	2 celery sticks, finely chopped
juice and finely grated rind of 1 lemon	2 tomatoes, skinned and chopped
1.25 ml (¼ tsp) Tabasco sauce	1 ripe avocado
salt and pepper	celery leaves, to garnish
175 g (6 oz) Edam cheese, diced	

1 Drain the kidney beans and rinse under cold running water. Put in a saucepan, cover with fresh cold water and bring to the boil. Boil rapidly for 10 minutes, then simmer for 1–1½ hours or until tender.
2 Drain the beans and put in a bowl. Add the oil, lemon juice and rind and Tabasco. Season to taste. Toss well, then leave until cold.
3 Add the cheese, onion, celery and tomatoes to the beans and toss again to mix the ingredients together. Cover and chill.
4 When ready to serve, cut the avocado in half and remove the stone. Peel and chop the flesh into chunky pieces. Fold the avocado pieces gently into the bean salad and taste and adjust the seasoning. Garnish and serve.

MIXED BEAN SALAD

SERVES 4

450 g (1 lb) broad beans	15 ml (1 tbsp) lemon juice
salt and pepper	397 g (14 oz) can red kidney beans, drained and rinsed
225 g (8 oz) French beans	
15 ml (1 tbsp) vegetable oil	
150 ml (5 fl oz) natural yogurt	225 g (8 oz) Charnwood or Applewood cheese, cubed
15 ml (1 tbsp) mild whole grain mustard	chopped parsley, to garnish

1 Shell the broad beans and cook in boiling salted water for 10 minutes. Add the French beans and continue to cook for 5–10 minutes or until both are tender.
2 Meanwhile, mix together the oil, yogurt, mustard and lemon juice. Season to taste and beat until well blended.
3 Drain the cooked beans and, while still hot, combine with the kidney beans and dressing. Leave to cool.
4 Toss in the cubes of cheese and garnish with chopped fresh parsley just before serving.

TO MICROWAVE

Put the broad beans in a small bowl with 30 ml (2 tbsp) water. Cover and cook on HIGH for 10–12 minutes or until tender. Put the French beans and 15 ml (1 tbsp) water in a small bowl, cover and cook on HIGH for 4–5 minutes or until tender, stirring once. Complete steps 2, 3 and 4.

COOK'S TIP

Charnwood or Applewood cheeses are varieties of mature Cheddar, smoked and coated with paprika.

SMALL CAKES & BISCUITS

A tempting collection of recipes for teatime treats and lunchboxes, featuring traditional small cakes, children's favourites, moist chewy traybakes and crunchy cookies. Quick and easy griddle pancakes, irresistible muffins and melt-in-the-mouth shortbread are also included.

MADELEINES

MAKES 10

100 g (4 oz) butter or block margarine	30 ml (2 level tbsp) red jam, sieved and melted
100 g (4 oz) caster sugar	50 g (2 oz) desiccated coconut
2 eggs, beaten	5 glacé cherries, halved
100 g (4 oz) self-raising flour	angelica leaves

1 Grease 10 dariole moulds. Cream the fat and sugar until pale and fluffy. Add the eggs, a little at a time, beating well after each addition before adding more.
2 Fold in the flour, using a metal spoon, then three-quarters fill the moulds.
3 Bake in the oven at 180°C (350°F) mark 4 for about 20 minutes, or until firm and browned. Turn them out of the moulds and leave to cool on a wire rack.
4 Trim off the bottoms, so that the cakes stand firmly and are of even height. When they are nearly cold, brush with melted jam, then holding them on a skewer, roll in coconut.
5 Top each madeleine with a glacé cherry half and two angelica leaves.

MAIDS OF HONOUR

MAKES 12

600 ml (1 pint) milk	1 egg, beaten
15 ml (1 tbsp) rennet	15 g (½ oz) butter or margarine, melted
212 g (7½ oz) packet frozen puff pastry, thawed	50 g (2 oz) caster sugar

1 Gently heat the milk in a saucepan until just warm to the finger. Remove from the heat and stir in the rennet. Leave for 1½-2 hours until set.
2 When set, put the junket into a muslin bag and leave to drain overnight. Next day, chill the curd for several hours or until very firm.
3 Grease twelve 6 cm (2½ inch) patty tins. On a lightly floured surface, roll out the pastry very thinly and using a 7.5 cm (3 inch) plain cutter, cut out 12 rounds. Line the patty tins with the pastry rounds and prick well.
4 Stir the egg, butter and sugar into the drained curd. Divide the mixture between the pastry cases and bake in the oven at 200°C (400°F) mark 6 for 30 minutes, until well risen and just firm to the touch. Serve warm.

QUEEN CAKES

MAKES 16

100 g (4 oz) butter	100 g (4 oz) self-raising flour
100 g (4 oz) caster sugar	50 g (2 oz) sultanas
2 eggs, beaten	

1 Spread out 16 paper cases on baking sheets, or put them into patty tins.
2 Cream the butter and sugar together until pale and fluffy. Gradually beat in the eggs, a little at a time, beating well after each addition. Fold in the flour, then the fruit.
3 Fill the paper cases half full. Bake at 190°C (375°F) mark 5 for 15-20 minutes, until golden brown. Transfer to a wire rack to cool.

VARIATIONS

Replace the sultanas with one of the following: 50 g (2 oz) chopped dates; 50 g (2 oz) chopped glacé cherries; 50 g (2 oz) chocolate chips.

MINI CHERRY BUNS

MAKES ABOUT 36

50 g (2 oz) soft margarine	1 ripe banana, peeled and mashed
50 g (2 oz) caster sugar	125 g (4 oz) icing sugar, sifted
1 egg, beaten	about 15 ml (1 tbsp) orange juice
50 g (2 oz) self-raising flour	red glacé cherries or red spherical sweets
1.25 ml (¼ level tsp) baking powder	

1 Put the margarine, sugar, egg, flour and baking powder in a food processor and process until smooth and well mixed. Add the banana and process for 1 minute.
2 Put a teaspoonful of the mixture into about 36 small petits fours cases. Arrange the filled cases on a baking sheet and bake in the oven at 190°C (375°F) mark 5 for about 12-15 minutes or until golden brown. Cool on a wire rack.
3 When the buns are cold, make the glacé icing by mixing the icing sugar with the orange juice until smooth and just thick enough to coat the back of a spoon. Top each bun with a small blob of icing and stick half a cherry or a sweet onto each. Leave to set.

CINNAMON CHERRY BARS

MAKES 24

125 g (4 oz) ground almonds	5 ml (1 level tsp) ground cinnamon
1 egg	finely grated rind of 1 lemon
225 g (8 oz) plain flour	125 g (4 oz) black cherry jam
225 g (8 oz) caster sugar	icing sugar, for dredging
175 g (6 oz) butter or margarine	

1 Lightly grease a 28 x 18 cm (11 x 7 inch) shallow tin.
2 Put the first seven ingredients into a large bowl and beat well.
3 Knead lightly. Cover and refrigerate for at least 30 minutes. Press half of the dough evenly into the prepared tin. Spread the jam over the surface.
4 On a lightly floured work surface, lightly knead the remaining dough. With well-floured hands, roll into pencil-thin strips. Arrange over the jam to form a close lattice pattern. Refrigerate for 30 minutes.
5 Bake at 180°C (350°F) mark 4 for 40 minutes or until golden brown and firm to the touch. Leave to cool then dredge with icing sugar. Cut into 24 bars and ease out of the tin.

COOK'S TIP

If you haven't got the right size tin use two small sandwich tins instead and cut the baked mixture into wedges.

LAMINGTONS

MAKES 12

	FOR THE TOPPING
40 g (1½ oz) butter or margarine	450 g (1 lb) icing sugar
65 g (2½ oz) plain flour	75 g (3 oz) cocoa powder
15 ml (1 level tbsp) cornflour	15 g (½ oz) butter
3 eggs, size 2	100 ml (4 fl oz) milk
75 g (3 oz) caster sugar	75 g (3 oz) desiccated coconut

1 Grease a 28 x 18 cm (11 x 7 inch) cake tin. Line with greased greaseproof paper.
2 To make the cakes, melt the butter and let it stand for a few minutes for the salt and any sediment to settle. Sift the flour and cornflour.
3 Put the eggs and sugar into a deep bowl, place over a pan of simmering water and whisk until light and creamy – the mixture should leave a trail on the surface for a few seconds when the whisk is lifted. Remove from the heat and whisk for 5-10 minutes until cool.
4 Re-sift the flours and fold half into the egg mixture with a metal spoon.
5 Pour the cooled but still flowing butter round the edge of the mixture, taking care not to let the sediment run in.
6 Fold the butter very lightly into the mixture, alternating with the rest of the flour.
7 Turn the mixture into the prepared tin. Bake in the oven at 190°C (375°F) mark 5 for 20-25 minutes until firm to the touch. Turn out on to a wire rack and leave to cool.
8 Meanwhile, make the icing. Sift the icing sugar and cocoa into a heatproof bowl placed over a pan of simmering water. Add the butter and the milk and stir over a gentle heat to a coating consistency.
9 Cut the cake into twelve even-sized pieces. Place on a wire cooling rack and stand the rack on a baking sheet. Spoon the icing over each cake to cover completely. Sprinkle the tops with coconut. Leave until set.

ORANGE AND CARAWAY CASTLES

MAKES 10

75 g (3 oz) butter or margarine	2 eggs, beaten
50 g (2 oz) caster sugar	125 g (4 oz) self-raising flour
120 ml (8 level tbsp) fine shred marmalade	pinch of salt
	2.5-5 ml (½-1 level tsp) caraway seeds
finely grated rind of 1 orange	125 g (4 oz) toasted flaked almonds, roughly chopped

1 Grease 10 small dariole moulds and stand them on a baking sheet.

2 Cream together the butter and sugar until pale and fluffy. Beat in 30 ml (2 level tbsp) marmalade and the orange rind. Gradually beat in the eggs, then fold in the flour, salt and caraway seeds.

3 Divide the mixture between the prepared dariole moulds and bake at 170°C (325°F) mark 3 for 25 minutes or until well risen and firm to the touch. Turn out and cool on a wire rack.

4 Trim the bases of the cakes so that they stand level. Heat the remaining marmalade gently in a saucepan until melted. Spread the nuts out on a large plate. Spear each cake on a skewer, brush the tops and sides with marmalade, then roll in the nuts to coat.

COOK'S TIP

We used dariole moulds with a capacity of 75 ml (3 fl oz). If yours are slightly larger you can still use them but you will make fewer cakes.

UPSIDE DOWN CURRANT BUNS

MAKES 15

30 ml (2 tbsp) currants	2 eggs, beaten
30 ml (2 tbsp) nibbed almonds	2.5 ml (½ tsp) vanilla flavouring
150 g (5 oz) butter or margarine	finely grated rind of 1 lemon
150 g (5 oz) caster sugar	100 g (4 oz) plain flour

1 Grease 15 fluted bun tins and divide the currants and almonds between the bases.

2 Cream together the butter and sugar until light and fluffy. Gradually beat in the eggs, vanilla flavouring and grated lemon rind. Sift over the flour and fold in.

3 Divide the mixture evenly between the tins and level with a knife.

4 Bake at 190°C (375°F) mark 5 for 25-30 minutes or until firm to the touch and golden brown. Ease out of the tins immediately and cool on a wire rack.

COOK'S TIP

Try other combinations of dried fruit and chopped nuts such as pistachios and apricots, or pecans and raisins.

ECCLES CAKES

MAKES 8-10

212 g (7½ oz) packet frozen puff pastry, thawed	25 g (1 oz) finely chopped mixed peel
25 g (1 oz) butter or block margarine, softened	50 g (2 oz) currants
25 g (1 oz) soft dark brown sugar	caster sugar, to sprinkle

1 Roll out the pastry on a lightly floured surface and cut into eight to ten 9 cm (3½ inch) rounds.
2 Mix the butter, sugar, mixed peel and currants in a bowl.
3 Place 5 ml (1 tsp) of the fruit and butter mixture in the centre of each pastry round. Draw up the edges of each pastry round to enclose the filling, then re-shape.
4 Turn each round over and roll lightly until the currants just show through. Prick the top of each with a fork. Leave to 'rest' for about 10 minutes in a cool place.
5 Transfer the rounds to a dampened baking sheet. Bake in the oven at 230°C (450°F) mark 8 for about 15 minutes until golden. Transfer to a wire rack to cool. Sprinkle with sugar while warm.

TRADITIONAL CAKE-IN-THE-PAN

MAKES 4

225 g (8 oz) wholemeal self-raising flour	50 g (2 oz) lard, cut into pieces
pinch of salt	50 g (2 oz) caster sugar
pinch of freshly grated nutmeg	100 g (4 oz) seedless raisins

1 Sift the flour, salt and nutmeg together into a bowl. Rub in the lard, then add the caster sugar and seedless raisins.
2 Mix in 150 ml (¼ pint) cold water to make a soft dough and divide into four equal pieces.
3 Form each quarter of dough into a ball and roll out on a lightly floured surface into a round about 12 cm (5 inches) in diameter.
4 Lightly grease a griddle or frying pan and place over a low heat. Cook the rounds for about 10 minutes on each side. Serve at once.

GRIDDLE PANCAKES

MAKES 15-18

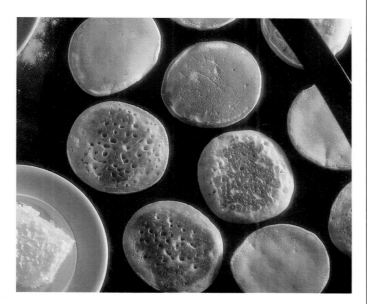

100 g (4 oz) self-raising flour	1 egg, beaten
30 ml (2 tbsp) caster sugar	150 ml (¼ pint) milk

1 Mix the flour and sugar in a bowl. Make a well in the centre and stir in the egg, with enough of the milk to make a batter the consistency of thick cream; the mixing should be done as quickly and lightly as possible.
2 Drop the mixture in spoonfuls on to a greased hot griddle or heavy-based frying pan. For round pancakes, drop it from the point of the spoon; for oval ones, drop from the side.
3 Keep the griddle at a steady heat and when bubbles rise to the surface of the pancakes and burst, after 2-3 minutes, turn the pancakes over with a palette knife. Continue cooking for a further 2-3 minutes.

COOK'S TIP

Today's cookers make cooking on a griddle much less of a hit and miss business than when the griddle or bakestone was perched over the coals of the fire. These pancakes or drop scones should be eaten as soon as they are cooked. They are quick and easy to make but don't reheat well.

TRADITIONAL MUFFINS

MAKES ABOUT 14

5 ml (1 level tsp) caster sugar	5 ml (1 level tsp) salt
300 ml (½ pint) warm milk	5 ml (1 level tsp) plain flour, for dusting
10 ml (2 level tsp) dried yeast	
450 g (1 lb) strong plain flour	5 ml (1 level tsp) fine semolina

1 Dissolve the sugar in the milk, sprinkle the yeast over the surface and leave in a warm place for about 20 minutes or until frothy.
2 Sift the flour and salt together. Form a well in the centre. Pour the yeast liquid into the well, draw in the flour and mix to a smooth dough.
3 Knead the dough on a lightly floured surface for about 10 minutes until smooth and elastic. Place in a clean bowl, cover with a tea towel and leave in a warm place until doubled in size.
4 Roll out the dough on a lightly floured surface, using a lightly floured rolling pin, to about 5-10 mm (¼-½ inch) thick. Leave to rest, covered, for 5 minutes, then cut into rounds with a 7.5 cm (3 inch) plain cutter.
5 Place the muffins on a well-floured baking sheet. Mix together the flour and semolina and use to dust the tops. Cover with a tea towel and leave in a warm place until doubled in size.
6 Heat a griddle or heavy-based frying pan and grease lightly. Cook the muffins on the griddle or frying pan for about 7 minutes each side. Cool on a wire rack.

COOK'S TIP

The correct way to toast muffins is not to split them and toast the two halves separately, as this makes them tough. Instead, cut them open, then close together again and toast slowly until warm right through, before opening out and buttering generously.

PECAN AND RAISIN MUFFINS

MAKES 12

350 g (12 oz) plain flour	150 ml (¼ pint) milk
15 ml (1 level tbsp) baking powder	60 ml (2 fl oz) corn oil
salt	1.25 ml (¼ tsp) vanilla flavouring
125 g (4 oz) caster sugar	75 g (3 oz) pecan nuts, roughly chopped
2 eggs	75 g (3 oz) raisins

1 Line 12 deep bun or patty tins with paper cake cases, or grease 12 muffin tins.
2 Sift the flour, baking powder and a pinch of salt into a bowl. Mix in the sugar and make a well in the centre.
3 Lightly beat the eggs with the milk, oil and vanilla flavouring and pour into the centre of the dry ingredients. Mix quickly to blend the flour with the liquid. Do not over-mix, the mixture should look slightly lumpy. Lightly stir in the nuts and raisins.
4 Divide the mixture equally between the paper cake cases or muffin tins. Bake in the oven at 190°C (375°F) mark 5 for 25-27 minutes or until well risen, golden brown and cooked through. Leave in the tins to cool for a few minutes. Serve warm or cold.

VARIATION

Blueberry Muffins
Use one third wholemeal flour and two thirds plain white flour. Replace the pecan nuts and raisins with 225 g (8 oz) blueberries. (Illustrated above right.)

DOUBLE CHOCOLATE MUFFINS

MAKES 12

100 g (4 oz) plain chocolate, broken into pieces	pinch of salt
50 g (2 oz) cocoa powder	100 g (4 oz) plain chocolate polka dots
225 g (8 oz) self-raising flour	225 ml (8 fl oz) milk
5 ml (1 level tsp) baking powder	60 ml (4 tbsp) vegetable oil
50 g (2 oz) dark brown soft sugar	5 ml (1 tsp) vaniila flavouring
	1 egg

1 Thoroughly grease 12 deep muffin or bun tins. Place a large paper cake case in each.
2 Put the chocolate into a large bowl and stand over a saucepan of simmering water. Heat gently until the chocolate melts.
3 Remove from the heat and stir in the remaining ingredients. Beat thoroughly together.
4 Spoon the mixture into the paper cases. Bake in the oven at 220°C (425°F) mark 7 for 15 minutes until well risen and firm to the touch. Serve warm.

COOK'S TIP

It's important to use deep bun tins to make muffins. They are quick to make and taste delicious, especially if served fresh from the oven.

EASTER BISCUITS

MAKES ABOUT 30

100 g (4 oz) butter	2.5 ml (½ level tsp) ground cinnamon
75 g (3 oz) caster sugar	50 g (2 oz) currants
1 egg, separated	15 ml (1 tbsp) chopped mixed peel
200 g (7 oz) plain flour	15-30 ml (1-2 tbsp) brandy or milk
pinch of salt	caster sugar for sprinkling
2.5 ml (½ level tsp) ground mixed spice	

1 Cream the butter and sugar together until pale and fluffy, then beat in the egg yolk. Sift in the flour, salt and spices and mix well. Add the fruit and peel and enough brandy or milk to give a fairly soft dough.

2 Knead lightly on a lightly floured surface and roll out until about 5 mm (¼ inch) thick. Cut into 6 cm (2 inch) rounds using a fluted cutter. Place on greased baking sheets and bake at 200°C (400°F) mark 6 for 10 minutes.

3 Remove from the oven, brush with the lightly beaten egg white, sprinkle with a little caster sugar and return to the oven to bake for about 5 minutes longer, until the tops are golden brown. Transfer to a wire rack to cool. Store in an airtight container.

SHREWSBURY BISCUITS

MAKES 20-24

125 g (4 oz) butter or block margarine	225 g (8 oz) plain flour
150 g (5 oz) caster sugar	grated rind of 1 lemon or orange
2 egg yolks	

1 Grease two large baking sheets.

2 Cream the butter and sugar until pale and fluffy. Add the egg yolks and beat well.

3 Stir in the flour and grated lemon rind and mix to a fairly firm dough with a round-bladed knife.

4 Turn out on to a lightly floured surface and knead lightly.

5 Roll out to about 5 mm (¼ inch) thick. Cut into rounds with a 6 cm (2½ inch) fluted cutter and place on the baking sheets.

6 Bake in the oven at 180°C (350°F) mark 4 for about 15 minutes, until firm and a very light brown colour.

VARIATION

Add 50 g (2 oz) chopped dried fruit to the mixture with the flour.

ALMOND CRISPS

MAKES 24

125 g (4 oz) butter or block margarine	few drops of almond flavouring
75 g (3 oz) caster sugar	150 g (5 oz) self-raising flour
1 egg yolk	75 g (3 oz) chopped almonds

1 Grease two or three baking sheets.
2 Cream together the butter and sugar until pale and fluffy. Beat in the egg yolk and almond flavouring and then the flour to give a smooth dough.
3 Form into a neat log shape and cut into twenty-four even slices. Shape each into a barrel, then roll in chopped almonds.
4 Place well apart on the baking sheets and bake in the oven at 190°C (375°F) mark 5 for 15-20 minutes. Cool on a wire rack.

REFRIGERATOR BISCUITS

MAKES ABOUT 32

150 g (5 oz) caster sugar	grated rind of 1 lemon
150 g (5 oz) soft tub margarine	1 egg, beaten
few drops of vanilla flavouring	225 g (8 oz) plain flour

1 Lightly grease two baking sheets.
2 Cream together the sugar and margarine until pale and fluffy. Beat in the vanilla flavouring, lemon rind and egg.
3 Stir in the flour and mix to a firm paste. Knead lightly, wrap and chill in the refrigerator for 30 minutes.
4 Roll the dough to a sausage shape about 5 cm (2 inches) in diameter and 20 cm (8 inches) long. Wrap in greaseproof paper. Refrigerate for at least 30 minutes.
5 When required, cut off 5 mm (¼ inch) slices, place on the baking sheets and bake at 190°C (375°F) mark 5 for 12-15 minutes. Cool the biscuits on a wire rack.

VARIATION

Honey Jumbles

Follow the basic recipe above as far as the end of stage 4. Slice off 5 mm (¼ inch) rounds. Roll into pencil-thin strips 10 cm (4 inches) long. Twist into 'S' shapes and place on lightly greased baking sheets. Chill for 30 minutes. Bake as above. While still warm, glaze with thin honey, sprinkle with demerara sugar and grill for 1-2 minutes until caramelised. Cool.

PECAN COOKIES

MAKES ABOUT 24

125 g (4 oz) plain flour	50 g (2 oz) pecan nuts, finely chopped
50 g (2 oz) cornflour	75 g (3 oz) butter
3.75 ml (¾ level tsp) baking powder	50 g (2 oz) light soft brown sugar
pinch of salt	25 g (1 oz) dark muscovado sugar
10 ml (2 level tsp) ground ginger	40 g (1½ oz) golden syrup
5 ml (1 level tsp) ground mixed spice	30 pecan nut halves, to decorate
5 ml (1 level tsp) ground cinnamon	

1   Lightly grease several baking sheets. Sift the flour, cornflour, baking powder, salt and the spices into a bowl. Stir in the chopped pecans.
2   Beat the butter with the sugars until very soft, light and fluffy. Beat in the golden syrup, then mix in the flour and nut mixture. Knead the dough very lightly on a floured surface until smooth.
3   Divide the dough into walnut-sized pieces. Roll each one into a ball and place on the greased baking sheets, spacing the balls well apart. Flatten each ball of dough with a fork, then press a pecan nut half into the centre of each one.
4   Bake at 180°C (350°F) mark 4 for 15-20 minutes, until just lightly browned around the edges. Allow to cool slightly on the baking sheets, then remove with a palette knife to cooling racks to cool completely.

COOK'S TIP

Pecan nuts belong to the walnut family and are grown in North America where they are known as hickory nuts. They are available in their shells, which are smooth and reddish-brown, or shelled, looking like narrow, elongated walnuts. If pecans are unavailable, walnuts may be used.

CINNAMON BISCUITS

MAKES ABOUT 24

275 g (10 oz) plain flour	225 g (8 oz) butter
90 ml (6 level tbsp) ground almonds	egg yolk, to glaze
10 ml (2 level tsp) ground cinnamon	flaked almonds
125 g (4 oz) caster sugar	icing sugar and drinking chocolate, for dredging

1   Sift the flour into a bowl. Add the almonds, cinnamon and sugar and mix together. Work in the butter with your fingertips. Knead well.
2   Roll out on a surface dusted with icing sugar until about 2.5 cm (½ inch) thick. Cut out heart or flower shapes with small pastry cutters. Brush with egg yolk and sprinkle with a few almonds.
3   Bake in the oven at 170°C (325°F) mark 3 for about 40 minutes, until firm and pale golden brown. Cool on a wire rack. Dredge a few biscuits with sifted icing sugar and a few with drinking chocolate powder.

LEMON AND LIME COOKIES

MAKES ABOUT 24

100 g (4 oz) butter or margarine	175 g (6 oz) plain flour
100 g (4 oz) caster sugar	finely grated rind of 1 small lemon
1 egg yolk	15 ml (1 tbsp) lemon juice
50 g (2 oz) full-fat soft cheese	20 ml (4 tsp) lime marmalade

1 Put the butter and caster sugar in a bowl and beat together until light and fluffy.
2 Beat in the egg yolk, cheese, flour, lemon rind and juice, until a soft mixture is formed.
3 Place small spoonfuls of the mixture on to greased baking sheets, allowing room for spreading.
4 Bake in the oven at 190°C (375°F) mark 5 for about 17 minutes or until light brown. Transfer to a wire rack to cool.
5 Melt the marmalade in a small saucepan and brush over the cookies, to glaze. Leave to set.

COOK'S TIP

These cookies are simplicity itself to make, almost like craggy, flat rock cakes. If you have a food processor, steps 1 and 2 can be made in moments, by working all the ingredients together in one go.

FLORENTINES

MAKES ABOUT 12

90 g (3½ oz) butter or margarine	5 glacé cherries, chopped
100 g (4 oz) caster sugar	25 g (1 oz) chopped mixed peel
100 g (4 oz) flaked almonds, roughly chopped	15 ml (1 tbsp) single cream
25 g (1 oz) sultanas	175 g (6 oz) plain chocolate

1 Line 3 baking sheets with non-stick paper.
2 Melt the butter in a saucepan over a low heat, add the sugar and boil the mixture for 1 minute.
3 Remove pan from the heat and add the remaining ingredients, except chocolate, stirring well to mix.
4 Drop the mixture in small, well-rounded heaps on to the prepared sheets, allowing enough room between each for the mixture to spread.
5 Bake the biscuit rounds in the oven at 180°C (350°F) mark 4 for 10 minutes until golden brown.
6 Remove from the oven and press around the edges of the biscuits with the blade of a knife to neaten the shape. Leave on the baking sheets for 5 minutes until beginning to firm, then lift on to a wire rack to cool for 20 minutes.
7 Break the chocolate into a heatproof bowl and place over simmering water. Stir until the chocolate is melted, then remove from the heat and leave to cool for 10-15 minutes.
8 Just as the chocolate is beginning to set, spread it over the backs of the biscuits. Draw the prongs of a fork across the chocolate to mark wavy lines and leave to set.

COOK'S TIP

If chocolate is overheated, it may curdle or thicken instead of melting smoothly. To guard against this, either melt it in a bowl placed over a pan of hot water, as suggested here, or use a double saucepan. If the chocolate does curdle, add a little blended white vegetable fat in small pieces, stirring into the chocolate until it reaches the desired consistency.

PISTACHIO RINGS

MAKES ABOUT 20

	FOR THE ICING
175 g (6 oz) butter	125 g (4 oz) icing sugar, sifted
50 g (2 oz) caster sugar	30 ml (2 tbsp) fresh lime juice
225 g (8 oz) plain flour, sifted	40 g (1½ oz) shelled pistachio nuts, skinned and chopped
15 ml (1 tbsp) milk	

1 Cream the butter and sugar together until light and creamy. Stir in the flour and milk and mix to form a fairly soft dough.

2 Put the mixture into a piping bag fitted with a 1 cm (½ inch) star nozzle. Pipe the mixture into 5.5 cm (2¼ inch) diameter rings, spaced well apart, on greased baking sheets.

3 Bake at 180°C (350°F) mark 4 for 8-10 minutes until lightly golden and cooked through. Transfer to wire racks to cool slightly.

4 To make the icing, blend the icing sugar with the lime juice to make a thin consistency. Brush over the rings while still warm to glaze and sprinkle at once with chopped nuts. Leave to set before serving.

BRANDY SNAPS

MAKES 10

50 g (2 oz) butter or block margarine	2.5 ml (½ level tsp) ground ginger
50 g (2 oz) caster sugar	5 ml (1 tsp) brandy
30 ml (2 level tbsp) golden syrup	grated rind of ½ a lemon
50 g (2 oz) plain flour, sifted	150 ml (¼ pint) double cream

1 Grease the handles of several wooden spoons and line two or three baking sheets with non-stick baking parchment.

2 Melt the butter with the sugar and syrup in a saucepan over low heat. Remove from the heat. Stir in the flour and ginger, brandy and lemon rind.

3 Put small spoonfuls of the mixture about 10 cm (4 inches) apart on the baking sheets, to allow plenty of room for spreading.

4 Bake one sheet at a time in the oven at 180°C (350°F) mark 4 for 7-10 minutes, until bubbly and golden. Allow to cool for 1-2 minutes, then loosen with a palette knife and roll them round the spoon handles.

5 Leave until set, then twist gently to remove. (If the biscuits cool too much whilst still on the sheet and become too brittle to roll, return the sheet to the oven for a moment to soften them.) Before serving, whisk the cream until thick and fill the brandy snaps.

GINGERBREAD MEN

MAKES 12

350 g (12 oz) plain flour	175 g (6 oz) light soft brown sugar
5 ml (1 level tsp) bicarbonate of soda	60 ml (4 level tbsp) golden syrup
10 ml (2 level tsp) ground ginger	1 egg, beaten
100 g (4 oz) butter or block margarine	currants, to decorate

1 Grease three baking sheets.
2 Sift the flour, bicarbonate of soda and ginger into a bowl. Rub the butter into the flour until the mixture looks like fine crumbs. Stir in the sugar. Beat the syrup into the egg and stir into the bowl.
3 Mix to form a dough and knead until smooth.
4 Divide into two and roll out on a lightly floured surface to about 5 mm (¼ inch) thick. Using a gingerbread man cutter, cut out figures and place them on the baking sheets. Decorate with currants. Bake in the oven at 190°C (375°F) mark 5 for 12-15 minutes, until golden. Cool slightly, then place on a wire rack.

HARLEQUIN BISCUITS

MAKES 30

75 g (3 oz) plain flour	15 ml (1 tbsp) golden syrup
1.25 ml (¼ level tsp) bicarbonate of soda	1 egg, size 6, beaten
2.5 ml (½ level tsp) ground ginger	227 g (8 oz) packet ready-to-roll icing
25 g (1 oz) butter or block margarine	liquid food colourings
40 g (1½ oz) light soft brown sugar	juice of ½ small orange
	edible silver balls, to decorate

1 Grease two large baking sheets. Sift the flour, bicarbonate of soda and ginger into a bowl. Rub the fat into the flour and stir in the sugar. Add the syrup with enough egg to form a soft dough, then turn onto a lightly floured surface and knead until smooth.
2 Using a floured rolling pin, roll out the dough to a 25 cm (10 inch) square. Cut into 2.5 cm (1 inch) wide strips. Separate the strips then, cutting at an angle, cut off pieces to make diamond shapes.
3 Place the biscuits on the prepared baking sheets and bake in the oven at 190°C (375°F) mark 5 for 8-10 minutes until golden brown. Cool slightly then transfer to a wire rack.
4 When the biscuits are completely cold, roll out the icing on a surface dusted with icing sugar. Cut the icing into strips (as when making the biscuits). Paint each strip a different colour using a little food colouring. Wash and dry your brush between each colour. Cut off diamond shapes. Moisten the surface of each biscuit with a little orange juice and top each biscuit with a piece of icing and three edible silver balls. Leave to set.
5 Serve the biscuits on a platter, decoratively arranged in a harlequin pattern.

CHOCOLATE VIENNESE FINGERS

MAKES ABOUT 26

125 g (4 oz) butter or margarine	few drops of vanilla flavouring
25 g (1 oz) icing sugar	50 g (2 oz) plain chocolate or plain chocolate flavour cake covering
125 g (4 oz) plain flour	
1.25 ml (¼ level tsp) baking powder	icing sugar, to decorate (optional)

1 Beat the butter until smooth, then beat in the icing sugar until pale and fluffy.
2 Sift in the flour and baking powder. Beat well, adding the vanilla flavouring.
3 Put into a piping bag fitted with a medium star nozzle. Pipe out finger shapes, about 7.5 cm (3 inch) long, on to two greased baking sheets, spacing them well apart.
4 Bake in the oven at 190°C (375°F) mark 5 for 15-20 minutes. Cool on a wire rack.
5 Break up the chocolate and place in a bowl over a pan of simmering water. Heat gently until the chocolate melts. Dip the ends of each Viennese Finger in the melted chocolate to coat. Leave to set on the wire rack.
6 Dredge with icing sugar to serve if wished.

PETTICOAT TAIL SHORTBREAD

MAKES 8

100 g (4 oz) butter, softened	150 g (5 oz) plain flour
50 g (2 oz) caster sugar, plus extra for dredging	50 g (2 oz) ground rice

1 In a medium bowl, cream the butter and sugar together until pale and fluffy.
2 Gradually stir in the flour and ground rice. Draw the mixture together and press into an 18 cm (7 inch) round sandwich tin.
3 Prick well all over, pinch up the edges with a finger and thumb. Mark into 8 triangles with a sharp knife. Bake at 170°C (325°F) mark 3 for about 40 minutes, until pale straw in colour.
4 Leave in the tin for 5 minutes, cut into 8 triangles, then dredge with caster sugar. Remove from the tin when cold. Store in an airtight container.

COOK'S NOTE

These traditional Scottish shortbread biscuits date back beyond the 12th century. The triangles fit together into a circle and were the same shape as the pieces of fabric used to make a full-gored petticoat in Elizabethan times. The biscuits got their name because in those days the word for a pattern was a 'tally', and so the biscuits became known as 'petticote tallis'.

INVERNESS GINGERNUTS

MAKES ABOUT 36

225 g (8 oz) plain flour	75 g (3 oz) caster sugar
10 ml (2 level tsp) ground ginger	2.5 ml (½ level tsp) bicarbonate of soda
5 ml (1 level tsp) ground mixed spice	175 g (6 oz) treacle
75 g (3 oz) fine oatmeal	50 g (2 oz) butter

1 Put the flour, ginger, spice, oatmeal, sugar and bicarbonate of soda in a bowl and mix together.
2 Heat the treacle and butter in a small pan until melted. Pour on to the dry ingredients and mix to make a smooth dough. Knead well.
3 Roll the dough out until about 5 mm (¼ inch) thick. Prick with a fork and cut out 6.5 cm (2½ inch) rounds with a plain cutter. Place on greased baking sheets and bake at 170°C (325°F) mark 3 for 20-25 minutes, until firm to the touch. Transfer to wire racks to cool.

TONBRIDGE BISCUITS

MAKES ABOUT 24

75 g (3 oz) butter, diced	1 egg, beaten
225 g (8 oz) plain flour	1 egg white, beaten, to glaze
75 g (3 oz) caster sugar	caraway seeds, for sprinkling

1 Rub the butter into the flour until the mixture resembles fine breadcrumbs, then stir in the sugar. Add the egg and mix to a stiff paste.
2 Roll out on a lightly floured surface, until about 5 mm (¼ inch) thick, prick the top with a fork and cut into rounds with a 5 cm (2 inch) plain cutter. Brush with egg white and sprinkle on a few caraway seeds.
3 Put on to greased baking sheets and bake at 180°C (350°F) mark 4 for about 10 minutes or until light brown. Transfer to wire racks to cool. Store in an airtight container.

FRUIT CAKES & TEABREADS

Fruit cakes and teabreads have the advantage that they keep much better than other cakes. Indeed, many actually improve in flavour and are easier to slice after storing closely wrapped, in an airtight tin for 2-3 days.

SAFFRON CAKE

MAKES 8-10 SLICES

2.5 ml (½ tsp) saffron strands	50 g (2 oz) butter, in pieces
7.5 ml (1½ tsp) dried yeast plus a pinch of sugar	50 g (2 oz) lard, in pieces
150 ml (¼ pint) tepid milk	175 g (6 oz) currants
450 g (1 lb) strong plain flour	grated rind of ½ a lemon
5 ml (1 tsp) salt	25 g (1 oz) caster sugar

1 Infuse saffron in 150 ml (¼ pint) boiling water for 2 hours. Grease a 20 cm (8 inch) round cake tin. Sprinkle the yeast and sugar into the milk and leave in a warm place for 15 minutes until frothy.
2 Sift the flour and salt into a bowl. Rub in the butter and lard until the mixture resembles fine breadcrumbs. Stir in the currants, lemon rind and sugar.
3 Strain the saffron infusion; warm slightly. Add to the dry ingredients with the yeast liquid and beat well.
4 Turn the dough into the prepared tin, cover with a clean cloth and leave to rise in a warm place for about 1 hour until the dough comes to the top of the tin.
5 Bake in oven at 200°C (400°F) mark 6 for 30 minutes. Lower temperature to 180°C (350°F) mark 4 and bake for a further 30 minutes. Turn out on to a wire rack to cool.

FRUIT BRAZIL CAKE

MAKES ABOUT 12 SLICES

175 g (6 oz) butter	125 g (4 oz) no-soak dried apricots, chopped
175 g (6 oz) caster sugar	125 g (4 oz) sultanas
3 eggs, size 2, beaten	2 tablespoons apricot jam, sieved and melted
125 g (4 oz) plain white flour	225 g (8 oz) marzipan
125 g (4 oz) self-raising flour	few Brazil nuts, to decorate
125 g (4 oz) Brazil nuts	
50 g (2 oz) candied lemon peel, chopped	

1 Grease a deep 20 cm (8 inch) round cake tin or a 1.7 litre (3 pint) loaf tin and line with greaseproof paper.
2 Put the butter and sugar in a bowl and cream together until light and fluffy. Gradually beat in the eggs.
3 Sift the flours together and fold into the creamed mixture, followed by the chopped nuts, peel and fruit.
4 Spoon into the prepared tin, level surface and bake in the oven at 180°C (350°F) mark 4 for 1¼ hours. Leave in tin for 10 minutes, then turn out and cool on a wire rack.
5 Brush the top of the cake with the apricot jam. Roll out the marzipan to fit the cake and press on top. Crimp the edges and score the top in a diamond pattern. Decorate with the nuts. Grill the cake to brown the top.

FRUIT-CRUSTED CIDER CAKE

MAKES 8-10 SLICES

45 ml (3 tbsp) golden syrup	50 g (2 oz) cornflakes, crushed
150 g (5 oz) butter or margarine	125 g (4 oz) caster sugar
350 g (12 oz) cooking apples, peeled, cored and finely chopped	2 eggs, beaten
	125 g (4 oz) self-raising flour
45 ml (3 tbsp) mincemeat	45 ml (3 tbsp) dry cider

1 Line a 35 x 11 cm (14 x 4½ inch) tart frame with foil. Grease the foil.
2 Put the syrup into a pan with 25 g (1 oz) butter and heat until melted. Add the apple, mincemeat and cornflakes and mix together.
3 Put the remaining butter and the sugar into a bowl and beat together until pale and fluffy. Gradually beat in the eggs. Fold in the flour and cider.
4 Turn into the frame and level the surface. Spread the apple mixture on top.
5 Bake in the oven at 170°C (325°F) mark 3 for 45-50 minutes or until firm to the touch. Cool in the tin for 1 hour, then cut into bars.

COOK'S TIP

If you don't own a tart frame, use a 20 cm (8 inch) square cake tin instead.

FARMHOUSE SULTANA CAKE

MAKES ABOUT 16 SLICES

225 g (8 oz) plain white flour	175 g (6 oz) butter or block margarine
10 ml (2 level tsp) ground mixed spice	225 g (8 oz) soft brown sugar
5 ml (1 level tsp) bicarbonate of soda	225 g (8 oz) sultanas
	1 egg, beaten
225 g (8 oz) plain wholemeal flour	about 300 ml (½ pint) milk
	10 sugar cubes (optional)

1 Grease and base-line a 20 cm (8 inch) square cake tin.
2 Sift the plain flour with the spice and soda into a large mixing bowl; stir in the wholemeal flour.
3 Rub in the butter until the mixture resembles fine breadcrumbs, then stir in the sugar and sultanas.
4 Make a well in the centre of the dry ingredients and add the egg and milk. Beat gently until well mixed and of a soft dropping consistency, adding more milk if necessary. Turn into the prepared tin.
5 Roughly crush the sugar cubes with the end of a rolling pin and scatter over the cake, if liked.
6 Bake in the oven at 170°C (325°F) mark 3 for about 1 hour 40 minutes, until cooked. When a fine skewer is inserted into the centre, no traces of moist cake should remain. Turn out and cool on a wire rack.

HALF-POUND CAKE

MAKES ABOUT 16 SLICES

225 g (8 oz) butter or block margarine, softened	100 g (4 oz) glacé cherries, halved
225 g (8 oz) caster sugar	225 g (8 oz) plain flour
4 eggs, beaten	2.5 ml (½ level tsp) salt
225 g (8 oz) seedless raisins	2.5 ml (½ level tsp) ground mixed spice
225 g (8 oz) mixed currants and sultanas	15 ml (1 tbsp) brandy
	few walnut halves

1 Line a 20 cm (8 inch) round cake tin with greased greaseproof paper.
2 Cream the fat and sugar until pale and fluffy. Add the eggs, a little at a time, beating well after each addition.
3 Mix together the fruit, flour, salt and spice and fold into the creamed mixture, using a metal spoon. Add the brandy and mix to a soft dropping consistency.
4 Turn the mixture into the tin, level the top and arrange the nuts on top. Bake in the oven at 150°C (300°F) mark 2 for about 2½ hours, until a fine warmed skewer inserted in the centre comes out clean. Turn out and cool on a wire rack.

COOK'S TIP

This recipe is so named because the main ingredients are added in 225 g (8 oz) or half pound quantities, making it an easy one to remember.

DUNDEE CAKE

MAKES ABOUT 16 SLICES

100 g (4 oz) currants	225 g (8 oz) butter or block margarine, softened
100 g (4 oz) seedless raisins	225 g (8 oz) light soft brown sugar
50 g (2 oz) blanched almonds, chopped	finely grated rind of 1 lemon
100 g (4 oz) chopped mixed peel	4 eggs, beaten
275 g (10 oz) plain flour	25 g (1 oz) split almonds, to decorate

1 Line a 20 cm (8 inch) round cake tin with greased greaseproof paper. Combine the fruit, chopped nuts and mixed peel in a bowl. Sift in a little flour and stir until the fruit is evenly coated.
2 Cream the butter and sugar until pale and fluffy, then beat in the lemon rind. Add the eggs, a little at a time, beating well after each addition.
3 Sift the remaining flour over the mixture and fold in lightly with a metal spoon, then fold in the fruit and nut mixture.
4 Turn the mixture into the tin and make a slight hollow in the centre with the back of a metal spoon. Arrange the split almonds on top.
5 Bake in the oven at 170°C (325°F) mark 3 for about 2½ hours until a fine warmed skewer inserted in the centre comes out clean. Check near the end of the cooking time and cover with several layers of greaseproof paper if it is over-browning.
6 Cool in the tin for 15 minutes, before turning out on to a wire rack to cool completely for 2 hours. Wrap in greaseproof paper and foil and store in an airtight tin for at least 1 week to mature.

CHERRY AND COCONUT CAKE

MAKES ABOUT 10 SLICES

250 g (9 oz) self-raising white flour	125 g (4 oz) caster sugar
1.25 ml (¼ level tsp) salt	125 g (4 oz) glacé cherries, finely chopped
125 g (4 oz) butter or margarine	2 eggs, size 6, beaten
75 g (3 oz) desiccated coconut	225 ml (8 fl oz) milk
	25 g (1 oz) shredded coconut

1   Grease a 1.3 litre (2¼ pint) loaf tin. Line the base with greaseproof paper, grease the paper and dust with flour.
2   Put the flour and salt into a bowl and rub in the fat until the mixture resembles fine breadcrumbs. Stir in the desiccated coconut, sugar and cherries.
3   Whisk together the eggs and milk and beat into the dry ingredients. Turn the mixture into the tin, level the surface and scatter over the shredded coconut.
4   Bake in the oven at 180°C (350°F) mark 4 for 1½ hours until a fine warmed skewer inserted in the centre comes out clean. Check after 40 minutes and cover with greaseproof paper if overbrowning. Turn out on to a wire rack to cool.

COOK'S TIP

Wash any excess syrup from glacé cherries before use and dry thoroughly, then toss in a little flour.

CUT-AND-COME-AGAIN FRUIT CAKE

MAKES ABOUT 16 SLICES

100 g (4 oz) plain flour	175 g (6 oz) caster sugar
100 g (4 oz) self-raising flour	4 eggs, beaten
2.5 ml (½ level tsp) ground nutmeg	350 g (12 oz) mixed dried fruit
2.5 ml (½ level tsp) ground ginger	100 g (4 oz) glacé cherries, halved
finely grated rind of ½ lemon	15 ml (1 tbsp) milk
50 g (2 oz) ground almonds	25 g (1 oz) slivered almonds
175 g (6 oz) butter or margarine	

1   Grease and line a 20 cm (8 inch) round cake tin. Sift the flours, nutmeg and ginger into a bowl. Add the lemon rind and almonds and stir well to mix.
2   In a separate bowl, cream the butter and sugar together until pale and fluff. Add the eggs a little at a time, beating well after each addition. Fold in the flour mixture with a metal spoon, then the mixed dried fruit, halved glacé cherries and milk.
3   Turn the mixture into the prepared tin and make a slight hollow in the centre. Scatter the almonds on top.
4   Bake the cake in the oven at 180°C (350°F) mark 4 for 1 hour, then lower the temperature to 170°C (325°F) mark 3 and bake for a further 30 minutes.
5   Remove from the oven and allow to cool slightly for 15 minutes in the tin, then transfer to a wire rack to cool completely for at least 2 hours. Double wrap in greaseproof and foil and store in an airtight tin.

COOK'S TIP

This fruit cake improves with keeping and should be stored for at least 24 hours before being cut. It is perfect for teatime snacks or if visitors call unexpectedly, because it will keep for several months if wrapped in greaseproof paper and foil and stored in a tin.

MIXED FRUIT TEABREAD

MAKES 8-10 SLICES

175 g (6 oz) raisins	1 egg, beaten
125 g (4 oz) sultanas	225 g (8 oz) plain wholemeal flour
50 g (2 oz) currants	7.5 ml (1½ level tsp) baking powder
175 g (6 oz) soft brown sugar	2.5 ml (½ level tsp) ground mixed spice
300 ml (½ pint) strained cold tea	

1 Place the dried fruit and the sugar in a large bowl. Pour over the tea, stir well to mix and leave to soak overnight.

2 The next day, add the egg, flour, baking powder and mixed spice to the fruit and tea mixture. Beat thoroughly with a wooden spoon until all the ingredients are evenly combined.

3 Spoon the cake mixture into a greased and base-lined 900 g (2 lb) loaf tin. Level the surface.

4 Bake in the oven at 180°C (350°F) mark 4 for about 1¼ hours until the cake is well risen and a skewer inserted in the centre comes out clean.

5 Turn the cake out of the tin and leave on a wire rack until completely cold. Wrap in greaseproof paper and foil. Store in an airtight container for 1-2 days before slicing and eating.

SERVING SUGGESTION

Serve this moist, fruity teabread sliced and buttered at tea-time. Or serve with thin wedges of sharp Cheddar cheese for a snack at any time of day.

PRUNE AND NUT LOAF

MAKE 8-10 SLICES

275 g (10 oz) self-raising flour	1 egg
pinch of salt	100 ml (4 fl oz) milk
7.5 ml (1½ level tsp) ground cinnamon	50 g (2 oz) shelled walnuts, chopped
75 g (3 oz) butter or margarine	100 g (4 oz) no-soak prunes, chopped
75 g (3 oz) demerara sugar	15 ml (1 tbsp) clear honey

1 Grease a 2 litre (3½ pint) loaf tin, line with greaseproof paper and grease the paper.

2 Sift the flour and salt into a bowl and add the cinnamon. Rub in the fat until the mixture resembles fine breadcrumbs.

3 Stir in the sugar, and make a well in the centre. Add the egg and milk and gradually draw in the dry ingredients to form a smooth dough.

4 Using floured hands shape the mixture into sixteen even-sized rounds. Place eight in the base of the tin. Sprinkle over half of the nuts and all of the prunes.

5 Arrange the remaining dough rounds on top and sprinkle over the remaining chopped walnuts.

6 Bake in the oven at 190°C (375°F) mark 5 for about 50 minutes or until firm to the touch. Check near the end of the cooking time and cover with greaseproof paper if it is overbrowning.

7 Turn out on to a wire rack and leave to cool for 1 hour. When cold brush with the honey to glaze. Wrap and store for 1-2 days in an airtight tin before slicing and buttering.

COOK'S TIP

This fruity teabread improves as it matures, the flavour and moisture from the fruit penetrating the cake and mellowing it over a number of days.

WHOLEMEAL DATE AND BANANA BREAD

MAKES 10-12 SLICES

225 g (8 oz) stoned dates, roughly chopped	100 g (4 oz) butter or margarine
5 ml (1 level tsp) bicarbonate of soda	75 g (3 oz) shelled hazelnuts, chopped
300 ml (½ pint) milk	2 medium ripe bananas
275 g (10 oz) self-raising wholemeal flour	1 egg, beaten
	30 ml (2 tbsp) clear honey

1 Grease a 1.3 litre (2¼ pint) loaf tin and line with greaseproof paper.
2 Put the dates in a pan with the soda and milk. Bring slowly to boiling point, stirring, then remove from the heat and leave until cold.
3 Put the flour in a large bowl and rub in the butter. Stir in the hazelnuts, reserving 30 ml (2 tbsp) for the decoration.
4 Peel and mash the bananas, then add to the flour mixture with the dates and the egg. Beat well to mix.
5 Spoon the mixture into the prepared tin and bake in the oven at 180°C (350°F) mark 4 for 1-1¼ hours until a skewer inserted in the centre comes out clean.
6 Leave the loaf to cool in the tin for about 5 minutes. Turn out, peel off the lining paper and place on a wire rack.
7 Heat the honey gently, then brush over the top of the loaf. Sprinkle with the reserved hazelnuts and leave until cold.

COOK'S TIP

It may seem unusual to have a cake made entirely without sugar, but this is because of the high proportion of dates used in this recipe. Dates have the highest natural sugar content of all dried fruit and if used in cakes such as this one there is no need to add extra sugar.

BANANA AND BRAZIL NUT LOAF

MAKES 8-10 SLICES

75 g (3 oz) soft margarine	225 g (8 oz) self-raising flour
175 g (6 oz) caster sugar	Brazil nuts and icing sugar, to decorate
3 eggs	
450 g (1 lb) ripe bananas	
50 g (2 oz) Brazil nuts, roughly chopped	

1 Grease a 900 g (2 lb)/1.4 litre (2 pint) loaf tin and line the base with greaseproof paper.
2 Cream together the margarine and sugar until light and fluffy. Gradually add the eggs, beating well after each addition.
3 Peel and mash the bananas with a fork, then stir into the creamed mixture. Add the chopped nuts. Sift the flour over the mixture and fold in lightly. Turn the mixture into the prepared tin and smooth the surface. Decorate with a few Brazil nuts.
4 Bake at 180°C (350°F) mark 4 for about 1½ hours until golden brown, firm to the touch and cooked through. Cover with foil if the loaf becomes too brown. Leave to cool in the tin. Sift icing sugar over the loaf to decorate just before serving.

GINGER MARMALADE TEABREAD

MAKES 8-10 SLICES

200 g (7 oz) plain flour	60 ml (4 tbsp) ginger marmalade
5 ml (1 level tsp) ground ginger	1 egg, beaten
5 ml (1 level tsp) baking powder	60 ml (4 tbsp) milk
40 g (1½ oz) block margarine	40 g (1½ oz) stem ginger, chopped
65 g (2½ oz) light soft brown sugar	

1 Grease a 900 ml (1½ pint) loaf tin with melted lard. Base-line with greaseproof paper and grease the paper.
2 Put the flour, ginger and baking powder into a bowl and rub in the fat until the mixture resembles fine breadcrumbs. Stir in the sugar.
3 Mix together the marmalade, egg and most of the milk. Stir into the dry ingredients and add the rest of the milk, if necessary, to mix to a soft dough.
4 Turn the mixture into the prepared tin, level the surface and press pieces of ginger on top. Bake in the oven at 170°C (325°F) mark 3 for about 1 hour or until golden. Turn out on to a wire rack for 1 hour to cool.

VARIATION

Use coarse-cut orange marmalade instead of ginger marmalade, and replace the stem ginger with chopped candied orange peel.

MARBLED CHOCOLATE TEABREAD

MAKES ABOUT 10 SLICES

225 g (8 oz) butter	15 ml (1 tbsp) orange juice
225 g (8 oz) caster sugar	few drops of orange flower water (optional)
4 eggs, beaten	75 g (3 oz) plain chocolate
225 g (8 oz) self-raising flour	15 ml (1 level tbsp) cocoa powder
finely grated rind of 1 large orange	

1 Grease a 900 ml (2 pint) loaf tin and line the base and sides with greaseproof paper.
2 Cream the butter and sugar together until pale and fluffy, then gradually beat in the eggs, beating well after each addition. Fold in the flour.
3 Transfer half of the mixture to another bowl and beat in the orange rind, juice and orange flower water, if using.
4 Break the chocolate into pieces, put into a small bowl and place over a pan of simmering water. Stir until the chocolate melts. Stir into the remaining cake mixture with the cocoa powder.
5 Put alternate spoonfuls of the two mixtures into the prepared tin. Use a knife to swirl through the mixture to make a marbled effect, then level the surface.
6 Bake at 180°C (350°F) mark 4 for 1¼-1½ hours, until well risen and firm to the touch. Turn out on to a wire rack to cool. Serve cut in slices.

DATE AND ORANGE BARREL TEABREAD

MAKES 8-10 SLICES

200 g (7 oz) plain flour	75 g (3 oz) stoned dates, snipped
5 ml (1 level tsp) baking powder	finely grated rind of 1 orange
5 ml (1 level tsp) bicarbonate of soda	45 ml (3 tbsp) orange juice
65 g (2½ oz) butter or block margarine, cut into pieces	about 90 ml (6 tbsp) milk
65 g (2½ oz) light soft brown sugar	TO DECORATE
	½ quantity orange buttercream (see page 328)
	candied orange peel

1   Grease and flour a 25 cm (10 inch) Balmoral tin or a 900 ml (1½ pint) loaf tin.
2   Sift the flour, baking powder and bicarbonate of soda into a bowl. Rub in the butter until the mixture resembles fine breadcrumbs. Stir in the sugar and mix well until evenly incorporated.
3   Stir in the dates and orange rind. Add the orange juice and enough milk to make a soft dough.
4   Carefully turn the mixture into the prepared tin. Stand it on a baking sheet, grease another baking sheet and place it, greased side down, on top of the tin. Bake in the oven at 180°C (350°F) mark 4 for 1 hour or until a fine warmed skewer inserted in the centre comes out clean and dry.
5   Turn out on to a wire rack to cool for 1 hour. Wrap and store for 1 day in an airtight tin before eating. To serve, pipe buttercream along the top of the cake. Decorate with small diamonds of cut orange peel.

COOK'S TIP

You may think this is a strange way to bake a cake, covered with a baking sheet, but it achieves a special effect. Being totally surrounded by tin, the cake forms no crust and the inside stays particularly moist. A fluted Balmoral tin gives the full 'barrel' effect, but a loaf tin can be used instead.

PEANUT AND ORANGE TEABREAD

MAKES 12 SLICES

225 g (8 oz) chunky peanut butter	2 eggs
50 g (2 oz) butter or margarine	finely grated rind and juice of 1 orange
225 g (8 oz) self-raising flour	about 150 ml (¼ pint) milk
100 g (4 oz) light soft brown sugar	50 g (2 oz) unsalted peanuts

1   Grease a 1.7 litre (3 pint) loaf tin and line with greaseproof paper.
2   Put the peanut butter, fat, flour, salt, sugar, eggs and grated orange rind in a large bowl. Squeeze the juice from the orange and make up to 225 ml (8 fl oz) with milk. Add to the bowl and beat all together with a wooden spoon for about 3 minutes.
3   Turn into the prepared loaf tin. Level the surface, sprinkle with the peanuts and press them in lightly. Bake in the oven at 180°C (350°F) mark 4, for about 1¼ hours or until well risen and firm to the touch. Leave in the tin for 10 minutes before turning out to cool on a wire rack.

COOK'S TIP

Chunky peanut butter gives the best flavour and texture. If you only have the smooth variety, roughly chop a few nuts and stir into the cake mixture.

LARGE CAKES & SPONGES

There is nothing quite as tempting as a freshly baked cake and in this chapter you have a variety to choose from. Ideas range from classic sponges and spiced cakes to delicious moist cakes featuring fresh fruit, such as apples and pears. Irresistible chocolate cakes will satisfy all passionate chocolate lovers.

MADEIRA CAKE

MAKES ABOUT 12 SLICES

100 g (4 oz) plain flour	5 ml (1 tsp) vanilla flavouring
100 g (4 oz) self-raising flour	3 eggs, beaten
175 g (6 oz) butter or block margarine, softened	15-30 ml (1-2 tbsp) milk (optional)
175 g (6 oz) caster sugar	2-3 thin slices citron peel

1 Grease and line an 18 cm (7 inch) round cake tin with greaseproof paper.
2 Sift the plain and self-raising flours together. Cream the butter and the sugar together in a bowl until pale and fluffy, then beat in the vanilla flavouring. Add the eggs, a little at a time, beating well after each addition.
3 Fold in the sifted flour with a metal spoon, adding a little milk if necessary to give a dropping consistency.
4 Turn the mixture into the tin and bake in the oven at 180°C (350°F) mark 4 for 20 minutes.
5 Lay the citron peel on top of the cake, return it to the oven and bake for a further 40 minutes until firm. Turn out and cool on a wire rack.

VICTORIA SANDWICH CAKE

MAKES ABOUT 8 SLICES

175 g (6 oz) butter or block margarine, softened	175 g (6 oz) self-raising flour
175 g (6 oz) caster sugar	45-60 ml (3-4 level tbsp) jam
3 eggs, beaten	caster sugar, for sprinkling

1 Grease and base-line two 18 cm (7 inch) sandwich tins.
2 Beat the butter and sugar together until pale and fluffy. Add the eggs, a little at a time, beating well after each addition. Fold in half the flour, using a metal spoon, then fold in the rest.
3 Divide the mixture evenly between the tins and level with a knife. Bake in the oven at 190°C (375°F) mark 5 for about 20 minutes until they are well risen, firm to the touch and beginning to shrink away from the sides of the tins. Turn out and cool on a wire rack.
4 When the cakes are cool, sandwich them together with the jam and sprinkle the top with caster sugar.

VARIATION

Chocolate Sandwich Cake
Replace 45 ml (3 tbsp) flour with cocoa powder. Sandwich cakes together with buttercream (see page 328).

VICTORIAN SEED CAKE

MAKES 8-10 SLICES

175 g (6 oz) butter	110 g (4 oz) plain flour
175 g (6 oz) caster sugar	110 g (4 oz) self-raising flour
5 ml (1 tsp) vanilla flavouring	10 ml (2 level tsp) caraway seeds
3 eggs, beaten	15-30 ml (1-2 tbsp) milk (optional)

1 Grease an 18 cm (7 inch) round cake tin. Line with greaseproof paper and grease the paper.
2 Put the butter, sugar and vanilla flavouring into a bowl and beat until pale and fluffy. Beat in the eggs a little at a time.
3 Fold in the flours with the caraway seeds, adding a little milk if necessary to give a dropping consistency.
4 Turn the mixture into the prepared tin. Bake in the oven at 180°C (350°F) mark 4 for about 1 hour until firm to the touch. Turn out on to a wire rack to cool for 1-2 hours.

COOK'S TIP

Seed cake is one of the oldest traditional English cakes. It is said to have been made on the farms to celebrate the completion of sowing in the spring.

GUERNSEY APPLE CAKE

MAKES 8 SLICES

225 g (8 oz) wholemeal flour	125 g (4 oz) butter
10 ml (2 level tsp) freshly grated nutmeg	225 g (8 oz) dark soft brown sugar
5 ml (1 level tsp) ground cinnamon	2 eggs, beaten
10 ml (2 level tsp) baking powder	a little milk (optional)
225 g (8 oz) cooking apples, peeled, cored and chopped	15 ml (1 tbsp) clear honey
	15 ml (1 tbsp) demerara sugar

1 Grease an 18 cm (7 inch) deep round cake tin. Line with greaseproof paper and grease the paper.
2 Put the wholemeal flour, nutmeg, cinnamon and baking powder into a bowl and stir well. Mix in the chopped cooking apples.
3 Put the butter and sugar into a bowl and beat until pale and fluffy. Add the eggs, a little at a time, and continue to beat.
4 Fold the flour mixture into the creamed mixture with a little milk, if necessary, to give a dropping consistency.
5 Turn the mixture into the prepared tin. Bake in the oven at 170°C (325°F) mark 3 for about 1½ hours. Turn out on to a wire rack to cool for 1-2 hours. Brush with honey and sprinkle with the demerara sugar to decorate. Eat within 1-2 days.

GENOESE APPLE CAKE

MAKES 8-10 SLICES

4 eggs	finely grated rind of 1 lemon
150 g (5 oz) caster sugar	700 g (1½ lb) Golden Delicious apples, peeled, cored and thinly sliced
150 g (5 oz) plain flour	
5 ml (1 tsp) baking powder	5-10 ml (1-2 tsp) vegetable oil
pinch of salt	
100 g (4 oz) butter, melted and cooled	15-30 ml (1-2 tbsp) dried breadcrumbs
90 ml (6 tbsp) milk	icing sugar, to finish

1 Put the eggs and sugar in a heatproof bowl standing over a pan of gently simmering water.

2 Whisk for 10-15 minutes until the mixture is thick and pale and holds a ribbon trail when the beaters are lifted. (Alternatively, if you have a table top electric mixer, this can be used instead of whisking over hot water.)

3 Remove the bowl from the heat and continue whisking until the mixture is cool.

4 Sift the flour with the baking powder and salt. Fold half of this mixture into the whisked eggs and sugar.

5 Slowly trickle the melted butter around the edge of the bowl and fold it in gently. Take care not to stir too heavily or the mixture will lose air.

6 Fold in the remaining flour mixture, then the milk and lemon rind. Fold in the apples.

7 Brush the inside of a 23 cm (9 inch) round cake tin with oil. Sprinkle with breadcrumbs, then shake off the excess.

8 Pour the cake mixture into the tin and bake in the oven at 180°C (350°F) mark 4 for about 40 minutes until a skewer inserted in the centre comes out clean.

9 Leave the cake to rest in the tin for about 5 minutes, then turn out on to a wire rack and leave for 2-3 hours to cool completely. Sift icing sugar over the top of the cake just before serving.

ORANGE-GLAZED GINGER CAKE

MAKES ABOUT 12 SLICES

125 g (4 oz) lard	5 ml (1 level tsp) ground ginger
125 g (4 oz) caster sugar	
1 egg, beaten	100 g (4 oz) golden syrup
275 g (10 oz) plain white flour	100 g (4 oz) black treacle
	FOR THE TOPPING
7.5 ml (1½ level tsp) bicarbonate of soda	pared rind and juice of 1 orange
2.5 ml (1½ level tsp) salt	100 g (4 oz) icing sugar
5 ml (1 level tsp) ground cinnamon	

1 Grease a deep 23 cm (9 inch) round cake tin. Line with greaseproof paper and then grease the paper.

2 Put the lard and sugar into a bowl and beat together until pale and fluffy. Beat in the egg, then the flour, bicarbonate of soda, salt and spices.

3 Put the golden syrup, black treacle and 225 ml (8 fl oz) water in a pan and bring to the boil. Stir into the lard mixture, beating all the time until completely incorporated.

4 Turn the mixture into the prepared tin. Bake in the oven at 180°C (350°F) mark 4 for about 50 minutes or until a fine warmed skewer inserted in the centre comes out clean. Cool in the tin for about 10 minutes before turning out on to a wire rack to cool completely. Wrap and store in an airtight tin for 2 days.

5 Cut the orange rind into strips, put into a pan and cover with water. Boil until tender, about 10 minutes, and drain well.

6 Make an orange glacé icing by sifting the icing sugar into a basin, then beating in enough orange juice to make a smooth, fairly thick icing.

7 Evenly coat the top of the cake with the orange icing and leave to set for 1 hour. Sprinkle the orange strips around the top to decorate.

SWEDISH GINGER CAKE

MAKES ABOUT 10 SLICES

100 g (4 oz) butter or margarine	5 ml (1 level tsp) ground mixed spice
175 g (6 oz) caster sugar	150 ml (¼ pint) soured cream
3 eggs, beaten	25 g (1 oz) stem ginger, chopped
200 g (7 oz) plain flour	15 ml (1 tbsp) stem ginger syrup
5 ml (1 level tsp) bicarbonate of soda	15 ml (1 tbsp) black treacle
7.5 ml (1½ level tsp) ground ginger	

1   Grease an 18 cm (7 inch) square cake tin, line with greaseproof paper and grease the paper.
2   Put the butter in a bowl and beat until soft. Gradually add the sugar and beat until fluffy. Add the eggs, a little at a time, beating well after each addition until thoroughly incorporated.
3   Sift together the flour, bicarbonate of soda, ground ginger and mixed spice. Fold half into the creamed mixture. Add the soured cream, stem ginger and syrup, black treacle and remaining flour. Fold in until well mixed.
4   Spoon the mixture into the prepared tin. Bake in the oven at 170°C (325°F) mark 3 for about 1¼ hours until the centre is firm to the touch.
5   Leave the cake to cool in the tin for about 15 minutes, then turn out on to a wire rack and leave to cool completely. Store in an airtight container for up to 2 weeks. Serve with butter.

SERVING SUGGESTION

Swedish Ginger Cake is moist, dark and spicy. Serve it with coffee and sherry when visitors call during the festive season.

GINGERBREAD SLAB CAKE

MAKES 20-24 SLICES

125 g (4 oz) black treacle	5 ml (1 level tsp) ground mixed spice
125 g (4 oz) golden syrup	5 ml (1 level tsp) ground ginger
50 g (2 oz) butter or margarine	100 g (4 oz) dark soft brown sugar
50 g (2 oz) lard	150 ml (¼ pint) milk
225 g (8 oz) plain white flour	
1.25 ml (¼ level tsp) bicarbonate of soda	

1   Grease a deep 18 cm (7 inch) square cake tin. Line with greaseproof paper and then grease the paper.
2   Put the black treacle, golden syrup, butter and lard into a saucepan and heat gently until melted.
3   Sift the flour, bicarbonate of soda and spices into a bowl and stir in the sugar. Make a well in the centre and pour in the milk and treacle mixture. Beat well until smooth and of a thick pouring consistency.
4   Pour into the prepared tin and bake in the oven at 170°C (325°F) mark 3 for 1-1¼ hours or until a fine warmed skewer inserted in the centre of the cake comes out clean. Cool in the tin for 1 hour then turn out and cool completely on a wire rack.
5   Wrap in greaseproof paper and foil and store in an airtight tin for 2 days before eating.

COOK'S TIP

Gingerbread should always be wrapped tightly in greaseproof paper and foil, then stored in an airtight tin for 2 days before eating. This allows the cake to mature and become moist and sticky.

APPLE GINGERBREAD

MAKES 12 SLICES

225 g (8 oz) plain flour	75 g (3 oz) butter or margarine
2.5 ml (½ level tsp) salt	75 g (3 oz) black treacle
15 ml (1 level tbsp) ground ginger	75 g (3 oz) golden syrup
7.5 ml (1½ level tsp) baking powder	150 ml (¼ pint) milk
7.5 ml (1½ level tsp) bicarbonate of soda	1 egg, size 4, beaten
100 g (4 oz) demerara sugar	1 eating apple, cored and roughly chopped

1　Grease and line a 900 g (2 lb) loaf tin. Sift the plain flour into a large bowl with the salt, ginger, baking powder and bicarbonate of soda.

2　Put the sugar, butter, treacle and syrup in a saucepan and warm gently over low heat until melted and well blended. Do not allow the mixture to boil. Remove from the heat and leave to cool slightly, until you can hold your hand comfortably against the side of the pan.

3　Mix in the milk and egg. Make a well in the centre of the dry ingredients, pour in the liquid and mix thoroughly. Stir in the chopped apple.

4　Turn into the tin and bake in the oven at 170°C (325°F) mark 3 for about 1½ hours, or until firm to the touch.

5　Turn out on to a wire rack to cool for at least 1 hour. Wrap in foil, then store in an airtight container for at least 2-3 days before eating.

SERVING SUGGESTION

Gingerbread can be served plain, but it tastes even better when spread with butter. It is the perfect cake to include in a lunch box because it keeps so well, and it tastes particularly good with cheese and apple.

LEMON SEED CAKE

MAKES 8-10 SLICES

325 g (11 oz) butter	250 g (9 oz) self-raising flour
175 g (6 oz) soft brown sugar	10 ml (2 level tsp) caraway seeds
finely grated rind and juice of 2 large lemons	175 g (6 oz) icing sugar, plus a little extra to decorate
3 eggs, separated	

1　Grease and base-line an 18 cm (7 inch) round cake tin. In a bowl, cream together 175 g (6 oz) butter, the brown sugar and the rind from one lemon, until fluffy.

2　Beat in the egg yolks, then stir in the flour, caraway seeds and 45 ml (3 tbsp) lemon juice.

3　Fold in the stiffly whisked egg whites. Turn into the prepared cake tin. Bake in the oven at 180°C (350°F) mark 4 for 1 hour. Turn out onto a wire rack and leave to cool for 1 hour.

4　To make the butter icing, cream the remaining butter until fluffy. Gradually sift in the icing sugar, beating until smooth. Beat in 15 ml (1 tbsp) lemon juice and the remaining grated lemon rind.

5　Use the lemon butter icing to completely coat the cake and then swirl using a small palette knife. Dust lightly with sifted icing sugar. This cake is best stored in an airtight tin and eaten the next day.

MARMALADE SPICE CAKE

MAKES ABOUT 12 SLICES

175 g (6 oz) butter or block margarine, at room temperature	5 ml (1 level tsp) grated nutmeg
120 ml (8 tbsp) golden syrup	5 ml (1 level tsp) ground cinnamon
2 eggs, size 2, beaten	1.25 ml (¼ level tsp) ground cloves
150 ml (10 tbsp) medium cut orange marmalade	about 150 ml (¼ pint) milk
350 g (12 oz) self-raising flour	50 g (2 oz) cornflakes
5 ml (1 level tsp) baking powder	

1 Grease and base-line a 20 cm (8 inch) square or 23 cm (9 inch) round cake tin.

2 In a bowl, beat the butter with 90 ml (6 tbsp) of the golden syrup until well mixed. Gradually beat in the eggs, keeping the mixture stiff.

3 Chop the marmalade and stir half into the cake mixture. Mix in the flour sifted with the baking powder and spices, adding sufficient milk to give a fairly stiff consistency. Turn into the prepared cake tin and level the surface.

4 Crush the cornflakes and mix with the remaining syrup and marmalade. Carefully spread over the cake mixture.

5 Bake in the oven at 180°C (350°F) mark 4 for about 1 hour until well risen and firm. Turn out and cool on a wire rack for 1-2 hours before serving.

MARZIPAN PINEAPPLE CAKE

MAKES 12-14 SLICES

175 g (6 oz) butter	50 g (2 oz) cornflour
150 g (5 oz) light soft brown sugar	pinch of salt
finely grated rind of 1 lemon plus 15 ml (1 tbsp) juice	75 g (3 oz) glacé pineapple, thinly sliced
finely grated rind of 1 orange plus 15 ml (1 tbsp) juice	75 g (3 oz) firm bought marzipan, cut into small cubes
2 eggs, size 2	FOR THE GLACÉ ICING
2 egg yolks	75 g (3 oz) icing sugar
125 g (4 oz) self-raising flour	15-30 ml (1-2 tbsp) lemon juice

1 Grease a 24 x 18 cm (9½ x 7inch) cake or roasting tin. Line with greaseproof paper and grease the paper.

2 Put the butter and sugar into a bowl and beat together until pale and fluffy. Stir in the lemon and orange rind.

3 Lightly beat in the whole eggs and the yolks. Lightly beat in the self-raising flour, cornflour and salt with the orange and lemon juice. Fold in the pineapple.

4 Turn the mixture into the prepared tin, level the surface and scatter with marzipan cubes.

5 Bake in the oven at 180°C (350°F) mark 4 for about 45 minutes or until a fine warmed skewer inserted in the centre comes out clean.

6 Meanwhile, make the glacé icing. Sift the icing sugar into a bowl and beat in enough lemon juice to make a smooth, fairly thick icing.

7 When the cake is baked, turn it out on to a wire rack and immediately coat the top with the glacé icing. Leave to cool completely for about 1 hour before serving.

HONEY CAKE

MAKES 12-16 SLICES

225 ml (8 fl oz) clear honey plus 45 ml (3 tbsp)	50 g (2 oz) glacé cherries, halved
75 g (3 oz) butter	50 g (2 oz) chopped mixed peel
350 g (12 oz) plain wholemeal flour	3 eggs
pinch of salt	45 ml (3 tbsp) milk
5 ml (1 level tsp) ground mixed spice	grated rind of 1 large lemon
5 ml (1 level tsp) bicarbonate of soda	25 g (1 oz) flaked almonds

1 Grease a 20 cm (8 inch) square cake tin and line the base and sides with greaseproof paper.

2 Put 225 ml (8 fl oz) honey in a saucepan, add the butter and heat gently, stirring, until smooth.

3 Sift the flour, salt, spice and bicarbonate of soda into a large bowl, stirring in any bran left in the sieve. Add the cherries and peel.

4 Beat the eggs and the milk together and stir into the honey mixture with the lemon rind. Pour gradually on to the dry ingredients, beating well after each addition, until well blended.

5 Turn the mixture into the prepared tin and sprinkle with flaked almonds. Bake at 170°C (325°F) mark 3 for about 1¼ hours, until the cake is firm to the touch or a skewer inserted in the centre of the cake comes out clean.

6 Using a skewer, prick the top of the cake all over and spoon over the remaining honey. Turn out and leave to cool on a wire rack. Do not remove the greaseproof lining paper until the cake is cold.

CARROT CAKE

MAKES 8 SLICES

225 g (8 oz) butter	50 g (2 oz) ground almonds
225 g (8 oz) light soft brown sugar	150 g (5 oz) walnut pieces, chopped
4 eggs, separated	350 g (12 oz) young carrots, peeled and grated
finely grated rind of ½ orange	225 g (8 oz) cream cheese
20 ml (4 tsp) lemon juice	10 ml (2 level tsp) clear honey
175 g (6 oz) self-raising flour	
5 ml (1 level tsp) baking powder	

1 Grease and line a deep 20 cm (8 inch) round cake tin.

2 Cream the butter and sugar together in a bowl until pale and fluffy. Beat in the egg yolks, then stir in the orange rind and 15 ml (3 tsp) of the lemon juice.

3 Sift in the flour and baking powder, then stir in the ground almonds and 125 g (4 oz) of the walnuts.

4 Whisk the egg whites until stiff, then fold into the cake mixture with the carrots. Pour into the prepared tin and hollow the centre slightly.

5 Bake at 180°C (350°F) mark 4 for about 1½ hours. Cover the top with foil after 1 hour if it starts to brown.

6 Leave to cool slightly, then turn out on to a wire rack and remove the lining paper. Leave to cool.

7 To make the topping, beat together the cream cheese, honey and remaining lemon juice and spread over the top of the cake. Sprinkle the topping with the remaining walnuts to decorate.

TODDY CAKE

MAKES 6-8 SLICES

225 g (8 oz) butter	60 ml (4 tbsp) whisky
175 g (6 oz) soft brown sugar	30 ml (2 level tbsp) thick honey
finely grated rind of 1 lemon	175 g (6 oz) icing sugar, sifted
3 eggs, beaten	
175 g (6 oz) self-raising flour, sifted	a few walnut halves

1 Butter and base-line two 18 cm (7 inch) straight-sided sandwich tins.

2 Beat 175 g (6 oz) of the butter until soft. Add the sugar and lemon rind. Continue to beat until pale and fluffy. Gradually beat in the eggs, keeping the mixture stiff.

3 Fold in half the sifted flour, then the whisky and lastly the remaining flour. Spoon into the prepared tins.

4 Bake in the oven at 190°C (375°F) mark 5 for 20-25 minutes. Turn out and cool on a wire rack.

5 Beat the remaining butter with the honey until smooth, then gradually work in the icing sugar and 15 ml (1 tbsp) lemon juice.

6 Sandwich the cake together with half the butter cream and swirl the rest over the top. Decorate with walnuts.

COOK'S TIP

To test whether the cake is cooked, press the centre very lightly with the fingertip. The cake should be spongy and should give only very slightly to pressure, then rise again immediately, retaining no impression.

BALMORAL ALMOND CAKE

MAKES ABOUT 8 SLICES

	FOR THE ICING AND DECORATION
125 g (4 oz) butter or margarine	50 g (2 oz) butter
125 g (4 oz) caster sugar	125 g (4 oz) icing sugar
almond flavouring	almond flavouring
2 eggs, beaten	toasted flaked almonds, to decorate
50 g (2 oz) ground almonds	
125 g (4 oz) self-raising flour	icing sugar, for dredging
30 ml (2 tbsp) milk	

1 Grease a 900 ml (1½ pint) Balmoral cake tin or use a 900 ml (1½ pint) loaf tin.

2 Cream together the butter and the caster sugar until light and fluffy. Add a few drops of almond flavouring. Beat in the eggs a little at a time. Fold in the ground almonds and flour with the milk. Spoon into the prepared tin and bake in the oven at 170°C (325°F) mark 3 for 45-50 minutes or until risen and firm to the touch. Turn out on to a wire rack to cool.

3 To make the icing, cream the butter and icing sugar together and flavour with one or two drops of almond flavouring. Pipe down the centre of the cake, decorate with the almonds and dust lightly with icing sugar.

PINEAPPLE
AND CHERRY RING

MAKES 6-8 SLICES

175 g (6 oz) butter	25 g (1 oz) glacé pineapple, chopped
175 g (6 oz) caster sugar	
2 eggs, beaten	TO FINISH
225 g (8 oz) self-raising flour, sifted	1 quantity glacé icing (see page 328)
45 ml (3 tbsp) milk	8 pieces glacé pineapple
65 g (2½ oz) glacé cherries, quartered	8 glacé cherries

1 Butter and line a 1.4 litre (2½ pint) ring mould.
2 Beat together the butter and sugar in a bowl until pale and fluffy. Beat in the eggs, a little at a time, beating well after each addition, and add 15 ml (1 level tbsp) flour with last amount of egg. Fold the remaining flour into the mixture, then add the milk, cherries and pineapple.
3 Turn the mixture into the prepared tin and bake in the oven at 180°C (350°F) mark 4 for 55-60 minutes. Turn out and cool on a wire rack.
4 Spread a layer of glacé icing on top of the ring. Decorate with the pineapple and cherries, then trickle the remaining icing over the fruit, letting some run down the sides.

COOK'S TIP

Wash any excess syrup from glacé cherries before use and dry thoroughly, then toss in a little flour.

CHERRY
AND ALMOND CAKE

MAKES ABOUT 12 SLICES

275 g (10 oz) glacé cherries	pinch of salt
225 g (8 oz) butter, softened	175 g (6 oz) ground almonds
225 g (8 oz) caster sugar	2.5 ml (½ tsp) almond flavouring
6 eggs, beaten	icing sugar, to decorate
65 g (2½ oz) self-raising flour	

1 Grease a deep 23 cm (9 inch) loose-bottomed round cake tin and line the base and sides with greaseproof paper. Grease the paper.
2 Arrange the cherries in the bottom of the tin.
3 Cream the butter and sugar together until pale and fluffy. Beat in the eggs a little at a time, adding a little of the flour if the mixture shows signs of curdling.
4 Sift in the remaining flour and salt, then add the ground almonds and almond flavouring.
5 Turn the mixture into the prepared tin and bake at 180°C (350°F) mark 4 for 1 hour, until firm to the touch. Cover with greaseproof paper if browning too quickly. Leave in the tin to cool.
6 When the cake is cold, remove from the tin and dredge the top with icing sugar to decorate.

COFFEE BATTENBERG

MAKES ABOUT 8 SLICES

175 g (6 oz) butter	150 ml (10 level tbsp) ginger marmalade or apricot jam
175 g (6 oz) caster sugar	
3 eggs, beaten	450 g (1 lb) bought marzipan
175 g (6 oz) self-raising flour	crystallised ginger, roughly chopped, to decorate (optional)
20 ml (4 tsp) coffee essence	
15 ml (1 tbsp) milk	

1 Butter a 20 cm (8 inch) square cake tin. Divide the tin in half by making a pleat, the height of the tin, in the centre of a piece of foil. Use the foil to base-line the tin, sliding a piece of cardboard inside the pleat to support it.

2 Cream the butter and sugar together in a bowl, then gradually beat in the eggs, keeping the mixture fairly stiff. Lightly fold in the flour.

3 Divide the mixture in half and fold the coffee essence into one portion and the milk into the other.

4 Spoon one flavour into each side of the tin and bake in the oven at 190°C (375°F) mark 5 for about 30 minutes. Turn out and cool on a wire rack.

5 Trim each piece of cake and divide in half lengthwise. Sandwich together alternately with half the marmalade or apricot jam.

6 Cut out a sheet of non-stick paper to exactly cover the cake, leaving the ends bare, and roll out the marzipan on top to just fit it. Spread the remaining jam over the marzipan and wrap closely around the Battenberg. Remove the paper. Crimp the top edges and press the roughly chopped ginger along the middle of the cake.

LEMON SWISS ROLL

MAKES 6-8 SLICES

3 eggs, size 2	about 275 g (10 oz) lemon curd
100 g (4 oz) caster sugar	
100 g (4 oz) plain flour	1 quantity glacé icing (see page 328)
150 ml (5 fl oz) double cream	

1 Grease a 33 x 23 cm (13 x 9 inch) Swiss roll tin. Line the base with greaseproof paper and grease the paper. Dust with caster sugar and flour.

2 Whisk the eggs and sugar in a bowl until thick enough to leave a trail on the surface when the whisk is lifted. Sift in the flour and fold gently through the mixture.

3 Turn the mixture into the prepared tin and level the surface. Bake in the oven at 200°C (400°F) mark 6 for 10-12 minutes or until the cake springs back when pressed lightly with a finger and has shrunk away a little from the sides of the tin.

4 Sprinkle a sheet of greaseproof paper with caster sugar and turn the cake out on to it. Roll up with the paper inside. Transfer to a wire rack and leave to cool for 30 minutes.

5 Whip the cream until it just holds its shape. Unroll the Swiss roll and spread with three quarters of the lemon curd. Top with cream then roll up again and place on a serving plate.

6 Spoon glacé icing on to the Swiss roll. Immediately, using the point of a teaspoon, draw rough lines of lemon curd across the icing and pull a skewer through to form a feather pattern. Leave to set, for about 1 hour.

WALNUT
LAYER CAKE

MAKES 8 SLICES

4 eggs, separated	½ quantity coffee butter cream (see page 328)
100 g (4 oz) caster sugar	10 ml (2 tsp) coffee essence
75 g (3 oz) walnuts, finely chopped	1 quantity American frosting (see page 211)
25 g (1 oz) fresh brown breadcrumbs	walnut halves, to decorate
25 g (1 oz) plain flour	

1 Grease and base-line two 18 cm (7 inch) sandwich tins. Dust with caster sugar and flour.

2 Whisk together the egg yolks and caster sugar until very pale. Fold in the chopped walnuts, breadcrumbs and flour.

3 Whisk the egg whites until stiff. Stir one large spoonful into the egg yolk mixture, then fold in the remainder.

4 Divide the mixture equally between the tins and level the surface. Bake at 180°C (350°F) mark 4 for about 30 minutes. Turn out and cool on a wire rack.

5 When the cakes are cold, sandwich them together with the butter cream.

6 Coat the cake completely with the American frosting, working quickly to ensure an even glossy frosting. Decorate at once with the walnut halves.

FROSTED
COCONUT CAKE

MAKES 8 SLICES

50 g (2 oz) shelled hazelnuts	125 g (4 oz) plain flour
225 g (8 oz) butter or block margarine, softened	125 g (4 oz) self-raising flour
225 g (8 oz) caster sugar	40 g (1½ oz) desiccated coconut
5 eggs	75 g (3 oz) icing sugar
2.5 ml (½ tsp) vanilla flavouring	shredded coconut, to decorate

1 Grease and base-line a 20 cm (8 inch) spring-release cake tin with greaseproof paper. Spread the hazelnuts in a grill pan and brown them under a hot grill. Place in a clean tea towel and rub off the skins. Leave to cool, then finely chop.

2 Cream the fat and sugar together until pale and fluffy. Whisk 4 whole eggs and 1 egg yolk together and gradually beat into the creamed mixture with the vanilla flavouring.

3 Sift the flours together into a large mixing bowl. Fold into the mixture with 25 g (1 oz) of the desiccated coconut, and half the nuts. Spoon into the prepared tin and bake in the oven at 180°C (350°F) mark 4 for 45 minutes.

4 Meanwhile, in a bowl whisk the egg white until stiff. Whisk in half the sifted icing sugar, then fold in the remaining icing sugar, desiccated coconut and hazelnuts.

5 Spoon the meringue topping on to the partially baked cake and scatter with shredded coconut.

6 Return to the oven for 20-30 minutes, or until a fine warmed skewer inserted in the centre comes out clean. Cover lightly with a double layer of greaseproof paper after 15 minutes if necessary. Cool on a wire rack.

SPICED APPLE TORTE

MAKES 6 SLICES

175 g (6 oz) butter or margarine	finely grated rind of 1 lemon
175 g (6 oz) light soft brown sugar	45 ml (3 tbsp) lemon juice
75 g (3 oz) oat flakes	2 eggs, beaten
5 ml (1 level tsp) ground cinnamon	125 g (4 oz) self-raising flour
450 g (1 lb) cooking apples	5 ml (1 level tsp) ground mixed spice
	icing sugar, for dusting

1 Melt 50 g (2 oz) of the butter or margarine in a saucepan. Add 50 g (2 oz) of the sugar and the oats and cinnamon and fry gently stirring, until golden.
2 Spoon the mixture into a greased and lined 18 cm (7 inch) round cake tin.
3 Peel and core the apples, then slice them thinly into a bowl. Stir in the lemon rind and juice. Set aside.
4 Put the remaining butter or margarine in a separate bowl, add the remaining sugar and beat together until light and fluffy. Beat in the eggs gradually. Sift in the flour with the spice and stir in, followed by the apple mixture.
5 Spoon the mixture into the cake tin and level the surface. Bake in the oven at 180°C (350°F) mark 4 for about 50 minutes. Turn out on to a baking sheet lined with non-stick paper. Leave to cool completely for about 1 hour. Cover and chill until required or for up to 2 days.
6 Unwrap, cut into wedges and serve with single cream.

APPLE HAZELNUT GENOESE

MAKES 6-8 SLICES

3 eggs	FOR THE FROSTING
100 g (4 oz) caster sugar	1 egg white
50 g (2 oz) plain flour	175 g (6 oz) caster sugar
15 ml (1 tbsp) cornflour	pinch of salt
25 g (1 oz) ground hazelnuts	pinch of cream of tartar
75 g (3 oz) butter, melted and cooled	FOR THE FILLING AND DECORATION
90 ml (6 tbsp) apple jelly or purée	30 ml (2 tbsp) thick apple purée
	about 12 hazelnuts

1 Grease two 18 cm (7 inch) sandwich tins, line the bases with greaseproof paper and grease the paper.
2 Whisk the eggs and sugar together in a bowl until very thick. Sift in the flour and cornflour. Add the hazelnuts, then fold in the butter. Turn the mixture into the prepared cake tins.
3 Bake in the oven at 180°C (350°F) mark 4 for about 25 minutes or until the sponge springs back when pressed lightly with a finger and has shrunk away a little from the tins. Turn out on to a wire rack and leave to cool for 1-2 hours.
4 Sandwich the layers together with apple jelly. To prepare the seven-minute frosting put all the ingredients into a bowl and whisk lightly. Place the bowl over a pan of hot water and heat, whisking continuously, until the mixture thickens sufficiently to stand in peaks. This will take about 7 minutes.
5 Cover the cake with the frosting, peaking up the surface and decorate with hazelnuts. Leave for 2-3 hours before serving to allow the frosting to firm up.

COOK'S TIP

Home-made apple jelly or purée gives the best flavour, but do not add too much sugar; the frosting is very sweet.

PEAR SPONGE

MAKES ABOUT 12 SLICES

1¼ quantity shortcrust pastry (see page 327)	100 g (4 oz) self-raising flour
FOR THE FILLING	75 g (3 oz) cornflour
150 g (5 oz) butter or margarine	5 ml (1 level tsp) baking powder
150 g (5 oz) caster sugar	75 g (3 oz) ground almonds
few drops of almond flavouring	30 ml (2 tbsp) milk
	3 small ripe, even-sized pears
3 eggs	icing sugar, for dusting

1 Grease a 24 cm (9½ inch) round spring-release cake tin.
2 Roll out the pastry and use to line the tin. Chill.
3 To make the filling, cream the butter and sugar together in a bowl until pale and fluffy. Beat in a few drops of almond flavouring, then add the eggs, one at a time. Fold in the flours, baking powder and ground almonds, then fold in the milk. Spoon the mixture into the pastry case and level the surface.
4 Peel, core and halve the pears. Make a series of parallel cuts across the width of each pear half, but do not cut right through. Arrange the pear halves, rounded sides up, on top of the filling.
5 Bake in the oven at 190°C (375°F) mark 5 for 1¼ hours or until a skewer inserted into the centre comes out clean. Cool in the tin for 15 minutes, then carefully remove the sides of the tin. Serve the sponge flan warm or cold, dusted with icing sugar.

COOK'S TIP

Make sure you use ripe even-sized pears or the appearance of the finished flan will be spoilt.

CARAMEL BANANA TORTE

MAKES 8 SLICES

175 g (6 oz) self-raising flour	TO FINISH
1.25 ml (¼ level tsp) each baking powder and bicarbonate of soda	75 g (3 oz) sugar
	175 g (6 oz) full-fat soft cheese
50 g (2 oz) butter, in pieces	30 ml (2 tbsp) lemon juice
150 g (5 oz) caster sugar	30 ml (2 level tbsp) icing sugar
175 g (6 oz) ripe bananas	
2.5 ml (½ level tsp) freshly grated nutmeg	175 g (6 oz) ripe bananas
45 ml (3 tbsp) milk	50 g (2 oz) flaked almonds, toasted
1 egg, beaten	

1 Grease a 20 cm (8 inch) round cake tin, line the base with greaseproof paper and grease the paper.
2 Sift the flour, baking powder and bicarbonate of soda into a bowl. Rub in the butter until the mixture resembles fine breadcrumbs, then stir in the caster sugar.
3 Peel the bananas and mash them in a bowl, then beat in the nutmeg, milk and egg. Stir the banana mixture into the dry ingredients.
4 Turn into the prepared tin and level the surface. Bake in the oven at 180°C (350°F) mark 4 for about 40 minutes. Leave in the tin for 5 minutes before turning out on to a wire rack to cool. Cut the cake in half horizontally.
5 To make the caramel, dissolve the sugar in a small saucepan without stirring, over gentle heat, then boil until a rich brown colour. Immediately pour on to the cake and spread with an oiled knife to cover the top. Mark into 8 portions.
6 Beat the cheese, lemon juice and icing sugar together. Peel and chop the bananas; add to half of the cheese mixture. Use this to sandwich the cakes together.
7 Use remaining cheese mixture to coat sides and decorate top. Finish with the almonds.

MARBLED CHOCOLATE CAKE

MAKES ABOUT 8 SLICES

50 g (2 oz) plain chocolate	10 ml (2 level tsp) baking powder
5 ml (1 tsp) vanilla flavouring	50 g (2 oz) ground almonds
225 g (8 oz) butter or block margarine	30 ml (2 tbsp) milk
225 g (8 oz) caster sugar	FOR THE FROSTING
4 eggs, beaten	150 g (5 oz) plain chocolate
225 g (8 oz) plain flour	100 g (4 oz) butter

1 Grease a 1.7 litre (3 pint) ring mould. Melt the chocolate with the vanilla flavouring and 15 ml (1 tbsp) water in a bowl placed over a pan of simmering water. Remove from the heat.

2 Cream together the fat and caster sugar until pale and fluffy. Add the eggs, a little at a time, beating well after each addition.

3 Fold the flour, baking powder and ground almonds into the creamed mixture. Stir in the milk. Spoon half the mixture evenly into the base of the prepared tin.

4 Stir the cooled but still soft chocolate into the remaining mixture. Spoon into the tin. Draw a knife through the cake mixture in a spiral. Level the surface.

5 Bake in the oven at 180°C (350°F) mark 4 for about 55 minutes, until well risen, firm to touch and beginning to shrink from sides of tin. Turn out and cool on a wire rack.

6 To make the chocolate frosting, melt the chocolate and butter with 30 ml (2 tbsp) water in a bowl over a pan of hot water. Stir until smooth, then pour over the cooled cake, working quickly to coat top and sides. Leave to set.

COOK'S TIP

For a decorative finish, drizzle a little melted chocolate over the top of the ring cake.

CHOCOLATE BISCUIT CAKE

MAKES ABOUT 8 SLICES

125 g (4 oz) plain chocolate or plain chocolate flavoured cake covering	25 g (1 oz) seedless raisins
15 ml (1 tbsp) golden syrup	25g (1 oz) glacé cherries, halved
125 g (4 oz) butter or block margarine	50 g (2 oz) flaked almonds, toasted
125 g (4 oz) digestive biscuits, broken up	

1 Grease a loose-based 18 cm (7 inch) flan tin.

2 Break the chocolate into a bowl and place over a pan of simmering water. Add the syrup and butter and stir until the chocolate and butter have melted. Remove from the heat and cool slightly.

3 Mix the biscuits, fruit and almonds into the chocolate mixture. Turn the mixture into the tin, lightly level the top, then chill for at least 1 hour before serving.

VARIATION

Vary this simple no-bake cake by using different biscuits, such as petit beurre biscuits or ratafias.

RICH CHOCOLATE CAKE

MAKES 6-8 SLICES

100 g (4 oz) plain flour	150 g (5 oz) butter or margarine
45 ml (3 level tbsp) cocoa powder	75 g (3 oz) light soft brown sugar
2.5 ml (¼ level tsp) baking powder	1 egg, size 4, beaten
large pinch of bicarbonate of soda	75 ml (5 tbsp) natural yogurt
large pinch of salt	few drops of vanilla flavouring
100 g (4 oz) plain chocolate, in pieces	150 g (5 oz) icing sugar

1 Grease and line a 15 cm (6 inch) round cake tin with greaseproof paper.
2 Sift the flour into a bowl with 15 ml (1 tbsp) of the cocoa powder, the baking powder, bicarbonate of soda and salt.
3 Put half of the chocolate in a bowl with 15 ml (1 tbsp) water. Place over a pan of hot water and heat gently, stirring, until melted. Remove and cool.
4 Put 50 g (2 oz) of the butter in a separate bowl. Add the brown sugar and beat until fluffy. Beat in the egg, then fold in the melted chocolate, yogurt, vanilla flavouring and the sifted ingredients.
5 Turn the mixture into the prepared tin and level the surface. Bake in the oven at 190°C (375°F) mark 5 for 45 minutes until risen and firm to the touch. Turn out on to a wire rack and leave to cool for at least 1 hour.
6 To make the chocolate frosting, cream the remaining butter with the sifted icing sugar and remaining cocoa powder. Melt the remaining chocolate in a small bowl over a pan of hot water, leave to cool, then beat into the creamed mixture until evenly mixed.
7 Split the cake into two halves. Use half the frosting to sandwich the cakes together and smooth the remainder over the top. Allow to set for at least 30 minutes.

DEVIL'S FOOD CAKE

MAKES 8 SLICES

75 g (3 oz) plain chocolate	175 g (6 oz) plain flour
250 g (9 oz) light soft brown sugar	3.75 ml (¾ level tsp) bicarbonate of soda
200 ml (7 fl oz) milk	FOR THE AMERICAN FROSTING
75 g (3 oz) butter or block margarine, softened	450 g (1 lb) caster sugar
2 eggs, beaten	2 egg whites

1 Grease and base-line two 19 cm (7½ inch) sandwich tins. Grease the paper and dust with caster sugar and flour.
2 Break the chocolate into a small saucepan, add 75 g (3 oz) brown sugar and the milk and heat very gently, stirring. Remove from the heat and leave to cool.
3 Cream the butter with the remaining brown sugar. Gradually beat in the eggs, then slowly pour in the chocolate mixture and beat until well combined.
4 Sift together the flour and bicarbonate of soda and gently fold into the cake mixture, using a metal spoon.
5 Turn the mixture into the prepared tins and tilt to spread evenly. Bake in the oven at 180°C (350°F) mark 4 for about 35 minutes, until the cakes spring back when lightly pressed. Turn out on to a wire rack to cool.
6 Meanwhile, make the frosting. Place sugar in a large heavy-based saucepan with 135 ml (4½ fl oz) water and heat gently until dissolved. Bring to the boil and boil to 115°C (240°F) as registered on a sugar thermometer.
7 Meanwhile, whisk the egg whites in a large deep bowl until stiff. Allow the bubbles to settle, then slowly pour the hot syrup on to the egg whites, whisking constantly. When all the sugar syrup is added, continue whisking until the mixture stands in peaks and just starts to become matt around the edges. The icing sets quickly, so work rapidly.
8 Sandwich cakes together with frosting; spread remainder over top and sides using a palette knife and pull up into peaks. Leave to set in a cool place, not the refrigerator.

CHOCOLATE BRAZIL CAKE

MAKES 8 SLICES

100 g (4 oz) plus a knob of butter	30 ml (2 tbsp) cornflour
300 g (11 oz) plain chocolate	175 g (6 oz) Brazil nuts, ground
100 g (4 oz) caster sugar	100 g (4 oz) icing sugar
4 eggs, separated	chocolate caraque, to decorate

1 Grease a 1.7 litre (3 pint) ring tin. Dust with flour.

2 Break 200 g (7 oz) chocolate into a small bowl. Add 30 ml (2 tbsp) water. Place over a saucepan of gently simmering water until melted. Remove from the heat and stir until smooth.

3 Cream 100 g (4 oz) of the butter with the caster sugar until pale and fluffy. Gradually beat in the egg yolks and cornflour. Fold in the melted chocolate and nuts.

4 Whisk the egg whites until stiff but not dry. Stir one spoonful of egg white into the mixture to loosen it. Gently fold in the remainder. Spoon into the tin.

5 Bake in the oven at 170°C (325°F) mark 3 for about 1 hour 20 minutes or until a skewer inserted into the centre comes out clean. Leave to cool in the tin for 5 minutes before turning out on to a wire rack to finish cooling.

6 Place the remaining chocolate in a bowl with the knob of butter and 60 ml (4 tbsp) water. Melt over a saucepan of simmering water as in stage 2. Beat in the sifted icing sugar until smooth. Cool, then chill in the refrigerator for about 15 minutes until the consistency of lightly whipped cream.

7 Place the cake on its rack over a baking sheet. Spread over the chocolate icing until thinly coated. Decorate with chocolate caraque. Leave to set.

COOK'S TIP

To make chocolate caraque, spread the melted chocolate thinly on a cold surface. When it is just on the point of setting, shave it off in curls, with a thin, sharp knife.

CHOCOLATE FUDGE CAKE

MAKES ABOUT 8 SLICES

325 g (12 oz) plain chocolate flavoured cake covering	10 ml (2 tsp) vanilla flavouring
275 g (10 oz) butter	100 g (4 oz) icing sugar, sifted
175 g (6 oz) caster sugar	10-15 ml (2-3 tsp) coffee essence
4 eggs, size 2, beaten	toasted almonds, half dipped in melted chocolate, to decorate
175 g (6 oz) self-raising flour	
50 g (2 oz) ground rice	

1 Grease and line a 23 cm (9 inch) round cake tin with greaseproof paper. Melt half the chocolate cake covering in a bowl over a pan of hot water.

2 Whisk 225 g (8 oz) butter and caster sugar together in a bowl until pale and fluffy then gradually beat in the eggs, keeping the mixture stiff. Lightly beat in the flour with the ground rice, vanilla and cool, but still liquid, chocolate cake covering.

3 Turn the mixture into the cake tin. Bake in the oven at 180°C (350°F) mark 4 for about 1¼ hours. Cool in the tin for 30 minutes before turning out on to a wire rack.

4 Melt the remaining chocolate cake covering and use to coat the top and sides of the cake.

5 Cream the remaining butter in a bowl, then beat in the icing sugar and coffee essence. Pipe around the top of the cake, using a piping bag fitted with a 1 cm (½ inch) star nozzle. Decorate with chocolate toasted almonds.

SPECIAL OCCASION CAKES

You will find plenty of ideas for special occasion baking in this chapter. Sumptuous cream filled gâteaux flavoured with summer fruits contrast with wickedly rich chocolate and coffee concoctions. Festive and celebration cakes – such as Simnel cake, stollen and traditional Christmas cakes – are included, too.

CHOCOLATE AND ORANGE GATEAU

SERVES 6-8

100 g (4 oz) butter	175 ml (6 fl oz) milk
100 g (4 oz) sugar	300 ml (10 fl oz) whipping cream
1 egg, beaten	10 ml (2 tsp) orange-flavoured liqueur
175 g (6 oz) self-raising flour	
30 ml (2 tbsp) cocoa powder	finely pared rind and segments of 1 orange
5 ml (1 level tsp) bicarbonate of soda	

1   Lightly grease two 15 cm (6 inch) cake tins. Melt the butter and sugar in a saucepan over a low heat. Leave to cool for 2 minutes. Add the egg and beat well. Fold in the flour and cocoa powder. Mix the bicarbonate of soda and milk together, then slowly add to the mixture.
2   Pour into the prepared cake tins and bake at 180°C (350°F) mark 4 for 25 minutes, until cooked and risen.
3   Leave in the tins for 2 minutes, then turn out and leave to cool on a wire rack.
4   Whip the cream stiffly, then fold in the liqueur. Use to sandwich the cakes together, reserving some for the top. Decorate with the remaining cream mixture, orange rind and orange segments.

STRAWBERRY GATEAU

SERVES 12-16

225 g (8 oz) butter	300 ml (10 fl oz) double cream
225 g (8 oz) caster sugar	225 g (8 oz) strawberries, sliced
4 eggs, beaten	
350 g (12 oz) self-raising flour	icing sugar, to decorate
30-45 ml (2-3 tbsp) milk	

1   Grease and line the bases of three 18 cm (7 inch) round cake tins.
2   Cream the butter and the sugar together until pale and fluffy. Gradually add the eggs, a little at a time, beating well after each addition. Fold in the flour, then add enough milk to give a soft dropping consistency.
3   Divide the mixture evenly between the prepared tins and bake at 190°C (375°F) mark 5 for 25-30 minutes, until well risen and firm to the touch, swapping the position of the top and bottom cakes halfway through cooking. Turn out and leave to cool on a wire rack.
4   Whip the cream until it just holds its shape. Sandwich the cakes together with the cream and the strawberries, reserving a few for decoration. Dredge the top with icing sugar and decorate with the reserved strawberries.

CHOCOLATE COFFEE REFRIGERATOR SLICE

SERVES 6

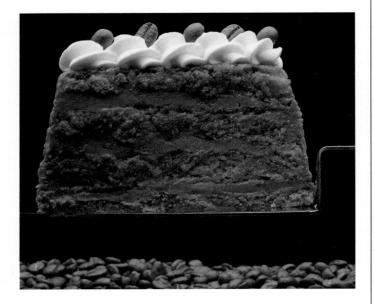

30 ml (2 tbsp) instant coffee granules	2 egg yolks
45 ml (3 tbsp) brandy	300 ml (½ pint) whipping cream
100 g (4 oz) plain chocolate	50 g (2 oz) chopped almonds, toasted
50 g (2 oz) icing sugar	about 30 sponge fingers
100 g (4 oz) unsalted butter, softened	coffee beans, to decorate

1   Grease a 22 x 11.5 cm (8½ x 4½ inch) top measurement loaf tin and line the base with greaseproof paper. Grease the paper.
2   Make up the coffee granules with 250 ml (8 fl oz) boiling water and stir in the brandy. Set aside to cool for 15 minutes.
3   Break the chocolate into small pieces. Place in a heatproof bowl with 15 ml (1 tbsp) water. Stand the bowl over a pan of simmering water and heat gently until the chocolate melts. (Alternatively microwave on LOW for 4-5 minutes or until melted, stirring occasionally.) Remove from the heat and leave to cool for about 5 minutes.
4   Sift the icing sugar into a bowl. Add the butter and beat together until pale and fluffy. Add the egg yolks, beating well.
5   Lightly whip the cream and chill half of it. Stir the remaining cream, the cooled chocolate and the nuts into the butter and egg yolk mixture.
6   Line the bottom of the prepared tin with sponge fingers, cutting to fit if necessary. Spoon over one third of the coffee and brandy mixture.
7   Layer the chocolate mixture and sponge fingers in the tin, soaking each layer with coffee and ending with soaked sponge fingers. Weight down lightly and chill for 3-4 hours until set.
8   Turn out, remove the paper and decorate with the reserved whipped cream and the coffee beans.

BLACK FOREST GATEAU

SERVES 10

100 g (4 oz) butter	two 425 g (15 oz) cans stoned black cherries, drained and syrup reserved
6 eggs	
225 g (8 oz) caster sugar	60 ml (4 tbsp) kirsch
75 g (3 oz) plain flour	600 ml (20 fl oz) whipping cream, whipped
50 g (2 oz) cocoa powder	
2.5 ml (½ tsp) vanilla flavouring	chocolate caraque
	5 ml (1 level tsp) arrowroot

1   Grease and base-line a 23 cm (9 inch) round cake tin. Beat butter in a bowl over a pan of warm water until soft.
2   Put the eggs and sugar in a large bowl over a pan of hot water and whisk until pale and creamy and thick enough to leave a trail on the surface when the whisk is lifted.
3   Sift the flour and cocoa together, then lightly fold into the mixture. Fold in the vanilla and softened butter.
4   Turn mixture into the tin and tilt to spread evenly. Bake in the oven at 180°C (350°F) mark 4 for about 40 minutes, until well risen, firm to the touch and beginning to shrink away from sides of tin. Turn out and cool on a wire rack.
5   Cut the cake into three horizontally. Place a layer on a flat plate. Mix together 75 ml (5 tbsp) cherry syrup and the kirsch. Spoon 45 ml (3 tbsp) over the cake. Spread with a thin layer of cream. Reserve a quarter of the cherries for decoration; scatter half the remainder over the cream.
6   Repeat layers of sponge, syrup, cream and cherries. Top with the third cake round and spoon over remaining kirsch-flavoured syrup. Spread a thin layer of cream around side of cake and coat with chocolate caraque.
7   Decorate top edge with cream whirls and caraque. Fill the centre with the reserved cherries. Blend the arrowroot with 45 ml (3 tbsp) cherry syrup, place in a small saucepan, bring to the boil and boil, stirring, for a few minutes until the mixture is thickened and clear. Brush the glaze over the cherries.

DOBOS TORTE

SERVES 8

4 eggs	FOR THE FILLING
275 g (10 oz) caster sugar	3 egg whites
150 g (5 oz) plain flour	175 g (6 oz) icing sugar
100 g (4 oz) chopped nuts, for coating	225 g (8 oz) butter
	100 g (4 oz) plain chocolate, melted

1   Line 2 baking sheets with non-stick baking parchment.

2   Whisk the eggs and 175 g (6 oz) of the caster sugar in a bowl standing over a pan of hot water. Whisk until the mixture is thick enough to leave a trail on the surface when the whisk is lifted. Remove from the heat.

3   Sift half the flour over the mixture and fold in lightly with a metal spoon. Add the remaining flour in the same way. Carefully spread some of the mixture into 20 cm (8 inch) rounds on the prepared baking sheets.

4   Bake in the oven at 190°C (375°F) mark 5 for 7-10 minutes until golden brown. Loosen from baking sheets and trim to neaten. Transfer to wire racks to cool.

5   Repeat to make six or seven rounds. Select the round with the best surface and lay it on an oiled baking sheet.

6   Dissolve the remaining caster sugar in a small, heavy-based saucepan, without stirring, over a gentle heat, then boil steadily to a rich brown. Pour over the round on the baking sheet, spreading it with a knife brushed with oil. Mark into eight sections and trim round the edge.

7   To make the filling, whisk egg whites and sifted icing sugar in a heatproof bowl standing over a pan of simmering water until very thick, then remove from heat.

8   Put the butter into a bowl and beat until pale and soft. Gradually beat in the egg and sugar mixture, then stir in the melted chocolate.

9   Sandwich the remaining biscuit rounds together with some of filling and put the caramel-covered one on top.

10   Spread the sides of the torte with the remaining filling and press the chopped nuts round the sides.

WHITE CHOCOLATE GATEAU

SERVES 12-16

23 cm (9 inch) Genoese cake (see page 326)	300 ml (½ pint) double cream
FOR THE FILLING	5 ml (1 level tsp) powdered gelatine
175 g (6 oz) plain chocolate, in pieces	TO DECORATE
30 ml (2 tbsp) brandy	275 g (10 oz) white chocolate
2 eggs, separated	150 ml (¼ pint) double cream
	icing sugar, for dusting

1   To make the filling, put the chocolate into a heatproof bowl standing over a pan of simmering water and heat gently until the chocolate melts. Remove from the heat and stir in the brandy and egg yolks. Whip cream until it stands in soft peaks, then fold into the mixture.

2   Sprinkle the gelatine over 15 ml (1 tbsp) water in a small bowl; soak for 2-3 minutes. Place bowl over a pan of simmering water until dissolved. Cool, then stir into the chocolate mixture. Whisk egg whites until stiff, then fold in.

3   Cut the cake into two layers. Put one piece of sponge back in the tin. Pour the mousse filling on top. Put the second piece of sponge on top. Leave to set.

4   While the filling is setting, make the decoration. Melt the white chocolate as in step 1. Spread out thinly on a marble slab or a clean, smooth work surface. Leave until set. When the chocolate is set, push a clean stripping knife (see below) across the chocolate at an angle of about 25° to create large thick chocolate curls. Chill until required.

5   When mousse is set, whip cream until it holds its shape. Ease cake out of tin and cover with cream. Coat with the chocolate curls and dust lightly with icing sugar.

COOK'S TIP

A stripping knife is a decorator's tool used for scraping off wallpaper! It has a sharp flexible blade and is ideal for making large chocolate curls. Buy one and keep it specifically for this purpose.

CHOCOLATE AND HAZELNUT GATEAU

SERVES 10

275 g (10 oz) unsalted butter, softened	100 g (4 oz) plain chocolate, finely grated
225 g (8 oz) soft light brown sugar	225 g (8 oz) icing sugar
4 eggs, separated	50 g (2 oz) cocoa powder
100 g (4 oz) self-raising flour	30 ml (2 tbsp) milk
pinch of salt	25 g (1 oz) chopped hazel-nuts, to decorate
100 g (4 oz) ground hazel-nuts	

1 Grease and line a 23 cm (9 inch) round cake tin. Put 225 g (8 oz) of the butter and the sugar into a bowl and beat together until pale and fluffy. Beat in the egg yolks one at a time, then fold in the flour and salt. Stir in the hazelnuts and chocolate.

2 Whisk the egg whites until stiff, then fold into the cake mixture. Pour into the prepared tin and bake in the oven at 170°C (325°F) mark 3 for 1-1¼ hours or until a fine warmed skewer inserted in the centre comes out clean. Leave to cool in the tin for 45 minutes.

3 Make the fudge icing. Sift the icing sugar and cocoa powder together, then put into a heavy-based pan with the remaining butter and the milk. Heat gently until the butter has melted; beat until smooth. Remove from heat.

4 Cut the cake in half horizontally. Spread a little icing over one half, then top with the other. Swirl remaining icing over and sprinkle with nuts.

CHOCOLATE MOUSSE CAKE

SERVES 8

450 g (1 lb) plain chocolate	100 g (4 oz) unsalted butter, softened
45 ml (3 tbsp) orange-flavoured liqueur	TO DECORATE
9 eggs, 5 of them separated	blanched julienne strips of orange rind
150 g (5 oz) caster sugar	

1 Grease a 20 cm (8 inch) spring-release cake tin, line with greaseproof paper and grease the paper.

2 Break 225 g (8 oz) of the chocolate into small pieces. Place in a heatproof bowl standing over a pan of simmering water and heat gently until the chocolate melts. Stir in 15 ml (1 tbsp) of the liqueur, then remove from the heat.

3 Using an electric whisk, whisk 5 egg yolks and the sugar together in a bowl until thick and creamy. Beat in the butter, a little at a time, until smooth. Beat in the melted chocolate until smooth.

4 Whisk the 5 egg whites until stiff, then fold into the chocolate mixture. Turn into the prepared tin.

5 Bake in the oven at 180°C (350°F) mark 4 for 40 minutes until risen and firm. Leave to cool in the tin for 1 hour.

6 To make the top layer, melt the remaining chocolate as before, then stir in the remaining liqueur. Remove from the heat and cool for 1-2 minutes. Separate the remaining eggs and beat the egg yolks into the chocolate mixture. Whisk the egg whites until stiff, then fold into the chocolate mixture.

7 Press the crust down on the baked cake with your fingers and pour the top layer over it. Chill overnight.

8 The next day, remove the cake carefully from the tin and put on to a serving plate. Arrange strips of orange rind around the edge to decorate.

DARK AND SINFUL CHOCOLATE CAKE

SERVES 8

	FOR THE ICING
125 g (4 oz) unsalted butter	175 g (6 oz) plain chocolate, broken into pieces
3 eggs, separated	
125 g (4 oz) dark soft brown sugar	25 g (1 oz) unsalted butter
50 ml (2 fl oz) brandy	175 g (6 oz) icing sugar, sifted
2.5 ml (½ tsp) vanilla flavouring	45 ml (3 tbsp) warm water
200 g (7 oz) plain chocolate, melted	TO DECORATE
75 g (3 oz) plain flour	300 ml (½ pint) double cream, stiffly whipped
50 g (2 oz) ground almonds	grated chocolate

1 Grease and flour a deep 20 cm (8 inch) round cake tin and line the base with greaseproof paper.
2 Whisk the egg yolks and sugar in a large bowl over a pan of hot water until very pale and creamy and thick enough to leave a trail on the surface when the whisk is lifted. Remove from the heat and whisk until cool.
3 Add the brandy and vanilla flavouring and whisk in the melted chocolate and butter mixture. Add the sifted flour and the ground almonds and fold in gently using a metal spoon. Whisk the egg whites until stiff then lightly fold into the mixture, a little at a time.
4 Pour into the tin and bake at 180°C (350°F) mark 4 for 45-50 minutes or until firm to the touch. Leave in the tin for 10 minutes, then turn out onto a wire rack to cool.
5 To make the icing, melt chocolate and butter in a bowl over a pan of hot water. Remove from heat and gradually stir in the icing sugar and water to make a thick icing.
6 Cut the cake in half and spread one third of the icing over one half; cool, then top with one third of the whipped cream. Put the remaining cake on top. Spoon the rest of the icing over the cake and swirl quickly with a knife to completely coat the top and sides. Leave to set.
7 Decorate with cream and grated chocolate.

CHOCOLATE-WRAPPED ORANGE GATEAU

SERVES 12

	FOR THE LIQUEUR SYRUP
200 g (7 oz) self-raising flour	100 g (4 oz) granulated sugar
50 g (2 oz) cornflour	finely grated rind and juice of 1 orange
7.5 ml (1½ level tsp) baking powder	
175 g (6 oz) caster sugar	45 ml (3 tbsp) orange-flavoured liqueur
3 eggs, separated	TO DECORATE
finely grated rind and juice of 1 small orange	2 large oranges, peeled segmented and chopped
105 ml (7 tbsp) oil	300 ml (½ pint) whipped cream
45 ml (3 tbsp) milk	225 g (8 oz) plain chocolate, melted
	cocoa powder, for dusting

1 Grease a deep 22 cm (8½ inch) spring-release cake tin and line the base with greaseproof paper.
2 To make the sponge, mix the flours, baking powder and sugar together in a bowl. Blend the egg yolks with the orange rind and juice, oil and milk, then mix into the dry ingredients. Beat thoroughly to a smooth batter. Whisk the egg whites until stiff, then fold in. Pour into the tin.
3 Bake in the oven at 180°C (350°F) mark 4 for about 55 minutes or until well risen and firm to the touch.
4 Meanwhile to make the syrup, gently heat the sugar, orange rind and juice and 60 ml (4 tbsp) water in a heavy-based saucepan until the sugar has dissolved. Bring to the boil and boil rapidly for 2 minutes. Stir in the liqueur.
5 Prick the hot cake all over, then spoon over the hot syrup. Leave to cool, then top with the oranges. Spread the cream over the top and sides.
6 Meanwhile, spread the melted chocolate over a strip of greaseproof paper, long enough to go round the side and wide enough to extend above the cake. Leave until setting, then wrap around the gâteau. Dust the top with cocoa.

CHOCOLATE MACAROON LOG

SERVES 10

FOR THE MACAROONS	300 ml (½ pint) double cream
3 egg whites, size 6	45 ml (3 tbsp) almond-flavoured liqueur
175 g (6 oz) ground almonds	
275 g (10 oz) caster sugar	TO DECORATE
7.5 ml (1½ tsp) almond flavouring	icing sugar, for dusting
FOR THE FILLING	cocoa powder, for dusting
100 g (4 oz) hazelnuts	chocolate leaves or curls
100 g (4 oz) plain chocolate, in pieces	hazelnuts

1 To make the macaroons, line two baking sheets with non-stick baking paper. Whisk the egg whites in a bowl until stiff, then fold in the ground almonds, sugar and almond flavouring.

2 Spoon the mixture into a piping bag fitted with a 1 cm (½ inch) plain nozzle and pipe 30 small rounds on to the prepared baking sheets, allowing room for spreading.

3 Bake in the oven at 180°C (350°F) mark 4 for about 20 minutes. Transfer to a wire rack to cool for 20 minutes.

4 To make filling, spread the nuts on a baking sheet. Brown in the oven at 200°C (400°F) mark 6 for 5-10 minutes. Tip on to a cloth and rub off skins. Chop finely.

5 Place the chocolate in a heatproof bowl standing over a pan of simmering water and heat gently until melted. Leave to cool for 5 minutes.

6 Whip the cream until it holds its shape. Gradually beat in the cooled chocolate, nuts and liqueur.

7 Use some of the chocolate cream to sandwich the macaroons together. Place side by side on a serving plate to form a double log. Spread chocolate cream on top and add a further layer of macaroons. Spread remaining chocolate cream over the top and sides. Chill overnight.

8 To serve, dust with icing sugar and cocoa, then decorate with chocolate leaves or curls and whole hazelnuts.

CINNAMON CHOCOLATE TORTE

SERVES 6-8

175 g (6 oz) plain chocolate	75 g (3 oz) ground almonds
175 g (6 oz) butter	FOR THE FILLING
200 g (7 oz) caster sugar	90 ml (6 tbsp) apricot jam
5 eggs, separated	30 ml (2 tbsp) lemon juice
150 g (5 oz) plain flour	300 ml (½ pint) whipping cream, whipped
15 ml (3 level tsp) ground cinnamon	icing sugar, for dusting

1 Grease and line two 19 cm (7½ inch) sandwich tins.

2 To make the cake, first break the chocolate into small pieces. Place in a heatproof bowl with 45 ml (3 tbsp) water. Stand the bowl over a pan of simmering water and heat gently until the chocolate melts. Leave to cool.

3 Cream the butter and sugar together in a bowl until light. Beat in the egg yolks. Add the cooled chocolate, mixing well.

4 Whisk the egg whites. Sift the flour with 10 ml (2 tsp) of the cinnamon and fold into the creamed mixture with the ground almonds and egg whites. Spoon the mixture into the prepared tins.

5 Bake in the oven at 190°C (375°F) mark 5 for 35-40 minutes or until a skewer inserted into the centre comes out clean. Turn out on to a wire rack and leave to cool for about 2 hours. Cut each cake into two layers.

6 To make the filling, put the apricot jam in a small pan with the lemon juice and remaining cinnamon, then heat gently. Cool and spread on the cakes. Layer up with cream and dust the top with icing sugar before serving.

COOK'S TIP

Use quality French, Swiss or Belgian chocolate, available from most supermarkets and delicatessens.

SACHERTORTE

SERVES 8-10

150 g (5 oz) plain chocolate, in pieces	50 g (2 oz) fresh brown breadcrumbs
100 g (4 oz) unsalted butter or margarine, softened	30 ml (2 level tbsp) apricot jam, melted
100 g (4 oz) caster sugar	FOR THE ICING
100 g (4 oz) ground almonds	200 g (7 oz) plain chocolate, in pieces
4 eggs, separated	200 ml (7 fl oz) double cream

1 Grease a 23 cm (9 inch) spring-release cake tin, line with greaseproof paper and grease the paper.
2 Melt the chocolate in a heatproof bowl over a pan of simmering water. Remove from the heat.
3 Cream the butter and sugar together in a bowl until pale and fluffy. Stir in the ground almonds, egg yolks, breadcrumbs and melted chocolate, then beat until well combined.
4 Whisk the egg whites until stiff and fold half into the chocolate mixture, then fold in the other half. Pour the mixture into the prepared tin and level the surface.
5 Bake in the oven at 180°C (350°F) mark 4 for 40-45 minutes until firm to the touch.
6 Cover with a damp tea towel, leave for 5 minutes to cool slightly, then transfer on to a wire rack to cool. When cold, brush the top with the melted apricot jam.
7 To make the icing, place the chocolate in a heatproof bowl with the cream. Stand the bowl over a pan of simmering water and heat until the chocolate melts and blends with the cream. Cool for a few minutes until the icing just coats the back of a spoon.
8 Stand the cake on the wire rack on a baking sheet and pour over the icing. Gently shake the cake to spread the icing evenly and use a palette knife, if necessary to ensure that the sides are completely covered. Leave in a cool place, but not the refrigerator, to set.

RASPBERRY TORTE

SERVES 12

1½ quantity Genoese sponge mixture (see page 326)	225 ml (8 fl oz) milk
1 quantity pâte sucrée (see page 327)	300 ml (½ pint) double cream
15 ml (1 tbsp) raspberry conserve, sieved	30 ml (2 tbsp) icing sugar
FOR THE BAVAROIS	225 g (8 oz) raspberries, sieved
20 ml (4 level tsp) gelatine	TO DECORATE
4 egg yolks	450 ml (¾ pint) double cream, whipped
25 g (1 oz) caster sugar	toasted flaked almonds
	few raspberries

1 Grease and line a 25 cm (10 inch) round cake tin. Turn the genoese into the prepared tin and bake in the oven at 180°C (350°F) mark 4 for 30-35 minutes until well risen and firm to the touch. Turn out and cool on a wire rack.
2 Roll out pastry on a baking sheet and trim to a 25 cm (10 inch) round. Prick all over and chill for 30 minutes. Bake in the oven at 220°C (425°F) mark 7 for 20 minutes.
3 To make the bavarois, soak gelatine in 45 ml (3 tbsp) water. Lightly whisk egg yolks and caster sugar together. Heat milk until almost boiling, then whisk into the egg yolks. Stir over a pan of hot water until custard is thick enough to coat back of spoon. Strain into a bowl, add gelatine and stir until dissolved. Cool, stirring often.
4 Softly whip cream with icing sugar. Mix custard and raspberry purée together, then fold in the cream.
5 Cut the sponge into two layers. Place pastry base on a plate, then spread with the raspberry conserve. Cover with a layer of sponge. Trim pastry base to the same size as the sponge and place a torten ring or a length of flexible card around them to fit snugly. Pour bavarois on to sponge, then chill until beginning to set. Place the other sponge layer on top and chill until very firm. Remove ring or card. Coat with a layer of cream, then cover sides with almonds. Decorate with remaining cream and raspberries.

PINEAPPLE GRIESTORTE

SERVES 6-8

3 eggs, separated	75 g (3 oz) semolina
125 g (4 oz) caster sugar	300 ml (10 fl oz) whipping cream
376 g (13¼ oz) can pineapple pieces, drained and juice reserved	100 g (4 oz) chopped mixed nuts, toasted

1 Grease a 20 cm (8 inch) round cake tin. Base-line with greaseproof paper and grease the paper.
2 Whisk the egg yolks and sugar in a bowl until pale and really thick. Stir in 30 ml (2 tbsp) of the reserved pineapple juice together with the semolina.
3 Whisk the egg whites until stiff, then gently fold into the yolks and sugar mixture.
4 Turn into the prepared tin. Bake in the oven at 180°C (350°F) mark 4 for about 40 minutes or until the sponge springs back when pressed lightly with a finger and has shrunk away a little from the tin. Turn out on to a wire rack and leave for 30 minutes to cool.
5 Roughly chop the pineapple pieces. Lightly whip the cream. Split the cake in half and fill with half the cream and half the pineapple. Spread a little of the cream around the sides and top of the cake and press the nuts on the side. Pipe the remaining cream in whirls on top of the cake and decorate with the remaining nuts and pineapple.

LEMON AND PASSION FRUIT GATEAU

SERVES 8-10

50 g (2 oz) butter	50 g (2 oz) icing sugar
4 eggs	3 passion fruit
125 g (4 oz) caster sugar	150 ml (5 fl oz) whipping cream
finely grated rind and juice of 1 lemon	150 ml (5 fl oz) soured cream
125 g (4 oz) plain flour	lemon slice and strawberry, to decorate
225 g (8 oz) strawberries, hulled and thinly sliced	

1 Grease a deep 20 cm (8 inch) round cake tin. Base-line with greaseproof paper. Grease paper, then dust with sugar and flour.
2 Melt the butter in a small saucepan, remove from the heat and cool for 10 minutes.
3 In another bowl, whisk together the eggs, caster sugar and lemon rind until very pale and thick enough to leave a trail. Sift the flour over the egg mixture.
4 Drizzle over the butter. Fold in thoroughly. Turn the mixture into the prepared tin.
5 Bake in the oven at 190°C (375°F) mark 5 for 35-40 minutes or until a fine warmed skewer inserted in the centre comes out clean. Turn out on to a wire rack and cool for 1-2 hours.
6 Meanwhile, put the strawberries into a bowl with the lemon juice and 25 g (1 oz) icing sugar and leave to macerate for 2-3 hours. When the cake is cold, split in half and drizzle both halves with the juices from the fruit.
7 Using a sharp knife, cut the passion fruit in half and scoop out the pulp. Discard the skin. Lightly whip the cream, fold in the soured cream and passion fruit seeds.
8 Sandwich the cakes together with the strawberries and cream mixture and dust the top with the remaining icing sugar. Decorate with a lemon slice and a strawberry.

CHOCOLATE AND COCONUT ROULADE

SERVES 8

165 g (5½ oz) plain chocolate, broken into pieces	caster sugar, for dusting
5 eggs, separated	300 ml (½ pint) double cream
175 g (6 oz) caster sugar	50 g (2 oz) creamed coconut, grated or finely chopped
15 ml (1 tbsp) water	25 g (1 oz) flaked or shredded coconut, toasted
15 g (½ oz) cocoa powder, sifted	

1 Grease a 33 x 23 cm (13 x 9 inch) Swiss roll tin and line with greased greaseproof paper.
2 Melt 125 g (4 oz) chocolate in a heatproof bowl set over a saucepan of hot water. Leave the chocolate to cool.
3 Whisk the egg yolks with the sugar until pale and fluffy. Add the water, melted chocolate and cocoa and whisk well to combine.
4 Stiffly whisk the egg whites and lightly fold into the mixture. Turn the mixture into the prepared tin and level the surface.
5 Bake at 180°C (350°F) mark 4 for 20 minutes until well risen and firm to the touch. Remove from the oven, but do not turn out of the tin. Cover with a sheet of greaseproof paper and a damp tea towel and leave at room temperature overnight.
6 The next day, have ready a large sheet of greaseproof paper dusted with caster sugar. Turn the cake out on to the paper and remove the lining paper.
7 Stiffly whip the cream and fold in the creamed coconut. Spread half of the cream over the chocolate mixture and roll up, like a Swiss roll. (Don't worry when it cracks during rolling, as this won't show once the roll is complete).
8 Cover the roll with the remaining coconut cream and arrange the toasted coconut down the centre. Melt the remaining chocolate and drizzle over the roll. Leave to set before serving.

COFFEE PRALINE GATEAU

SERVES 8

75 g (3 oz) caster sugar	PRALINE
3 eggs	50 g (2 oz) unblanched almonds
100 g (3½ oz) plain flour	
1½ quantity coffee butter cream (see page 328)	50 g (2 oz) caster sugar

1 Grease a 33 x 23 cm (13 x 9 inch) Swiss roll tin and line the base and sides with greaseproof paper.
2 To make the sponge, whisk the sugar and eggs in a bowl over a pan of hot water, using an electric whisk until pale and creamy and thick enough to leave a trail on the surface when the whisk is lifted. Remove the bowl from the heat and whisk until cool.
3 Sift the flour over the mixture and fold in lightly using a metal spoon. Turn the mixture into the prepared tin and gently level the surface.
4 Bake in the oven at 190°C (375°F) mark 5 for 10-12 minutes until well risen and golden brown. Have ready a large sheet of greaseproof paper, sprinkled with a little caster sugar. Turn the sponge out on to the paper, remove the lining paper and leave to cool.
5 To make the praline, gently heat the almonds and sugar in a non-stick frying pan until the sugar melts and turns a rich dark golden brown. Carefully pour on to a well-buttered baking sheet. Quickly coat and separate 8 almonds and leave to one side to set individually; leave the rest of the praline to cool and set.
6 Roughly crush the praline in a blender, or between two sheets of greaseproof paper with a rolling pin.
7 Cut sponge crossways into 3 equal strips. Sandwich together with half of the butter cream. Spread remainder over the top and sides of the gâteau. Cover sides with the crushed praline. Put the remaining butter cream in a piping bag fitted with a small star nozzle and pipe on top of the gâteau. Decorate with the caramel coated almonds.

CELEBRATION CAKE

MAKES 20-24 SLICES

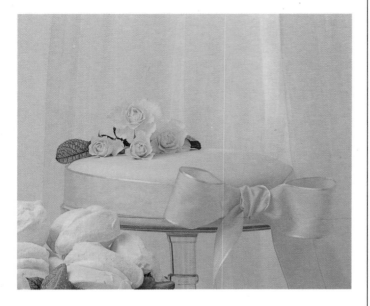

225 g (8 oz) butter or margarine	three 225 g (8 oz) packets ready-to-roll fondant icing
225 g (8 oz) caster sugar	300 ml (10 fl oz) double cream
4 eggs, beaten	120 ml (8 level tbsp) black cherry conserve or 50 g (2 oz) sliced strawberries
225 g (8 oz) self-raising flour	
grated rind and juice of 1 lemon	icing sugar for dusting
red, blue or yellow edible food colouring	fresh flowers and ribbon, to decorate

1 Grease and base-line a 23 cm (9 inch) round cake tin.
2 Cream the butter and sugar together until pale and fluffy. Add the eggs a little at a time, beating well after each addition.
3 Sift the flour and fold into the mixture with the grated lemon rind and juice. Spoon into the prepared tin and level the surface.
4 Bake in the oven at 180°C (350°F) mark 4 for about 1-1½ hours or until golden and firm to the touch. Cover the top with greaseproof paper, if necessary, towards the end of cooking time. Turn out on to a wire rack to cool.
5 Meanwhile tint the ready-to-roll icing a pale shade by kneading in a little colouring until evenly blended. Wrap tightly in greaseproof paper.
6 Split the cake in half horizontally. Whip the cream until it just holds its shape. Sandwich the cake layers together with jam or fruit and all but 45 ml (3 level tbsp) cream. Place on a serving plate. Spread the reserved cream thinly around the sides and over the top of the cake.
7 Dust the work surface lightly with icing sugar and roll out the icing large enough to cover the cake completely. Fold icing over a rolling pin and carefully lift it onto the cake; gently smooth the sides. Trim excess icing from base.
8 Decorate with a broad ribbon and fresh flowers just before serving.

SIMNEL CAKE

MAKES ABOUT 20 SLICES

175 g (6 oz) butter	100 g (4 oz) sultanas
175 g (6 oz) caster sugar	50 g (2 oz) chopped mixed peel
3 whole eggs and 1 egg white	100 g (4 oz) glacé cherries, quartered
225 g (8 oz) plain flour	finely grated rind of 1 lemon
pinch of salt	15-30 ml (1-2 tbsp) milk
2.5 ml (½ level tsp) each ground cinnamon and grated nutmeg	450 g (1 lb) almond paste
250 g (9 oz) currants	glacé icing (see page 328)

1 Grease an 18 cm (7 inch) round cake tin. Line with greaseproof paper and grease the paper.
2 Cream the butter and sugar until pale and fluffy. Gradually beat in the lightly whisked whole eggs.
3 Sift the flour, salt and spices over the surface and fold into the mixture with a metal spoon. Fold in the fruit, peel, lemon rind and milk to give a dropping consistency.
4 Divide the almond paste in half and roll out one half to a 16 cm (6½ inch) circle on a sugared surface.
5 Spoon half the cake mixture into the prepared tin. Place the round of almond paste on top and cover with the remaining cake mixture. Level the surface.
6 Tie a double thickness of brown paper round the outside of the tin. Bake in the oven at 170°C (325°F) mark 3 for 1 hour, then lower the heat to 150°C (300°F) mark 2 and bake for a further 2 hours. Leave in the tin for about 1 hour, then turn out and cool on a wire rack.
7 Divide remaining almond paste in two. Roll out one half to an 18 cm (7 inch) circle and the rest into 11 small balls and a rope edging. Brush the top of the cake with lightly beaten egg white. Place the circle on top and apply the edging and balls, securing with a little egg white.
8 Brush the almond paste with egg white and place under a hot grill for 1-2 minutes until browned. Coat the top of the cake with glacé icing and apply any decorations.

TRADITIONAL CHRISTMAS CAKE

MAKES ABOUT 25 SLICES

225 g (8 oz) currants	2.5 ml (½ level tsp) ground cinnamon
225 g (8 oz) sultanas	225 g (8 oz) butter
225 g (8 oz) seedless raisins, chopped	225 g (8 oz) dark brown soft sugar
100 g (4 oz) glacé cherries, halved	finely grated rind of 1 lemon
100 g (4 oz) chopped mixed peel	4 eggs, beaten
50 g (2 oz) nibbed almonds	30 ml (2 tbsp) brandy
225 g (8 oz) plain white flour	60 ml (4 tbsp) apricot glaze (see page 328)
pinch of salt	900 g (2 lb) almond paste
2.5 ml (½ level tsp) ground mace	900 g (2 lb) royal icing (see page 328)

1 Grease a 20 cm (8 inch) round cake tin. Line with a double thickness of greaseproof paper, and tie a double band of brown paper round the outside.
2 Mix together the fruit, peel and almonds. Sift the flour, salt and spices together.
3 Cream the butter, sugar and lemon rind together until pale and fluffy. Beat in the eggs, a little at a time. Fold in half the flour, then fold in the rest with the brandy. Finally, fold in the fruit.
4 Spread in the tin, stand on a layer of brown paper and bake at 150°C (300°F) mark 2 for about 3¾ hours; cover with greaseproof paper after 1½ hours.
5 Cool in the tin, then turn out. Wrap in greaseproof paper, then in foil and store in an airtight tin for 1 month.
6 About 14 days before required, transfer cake to a board, brush with apricot glaze, then cover with almond paste. Leave to dry in a cool dry place for 4-5 days.
7 Flat ice the cake with royal icing and pipe decorative borders on the top and bottom. Finish with a ribbon and almond paste holly leaves or Christmas trees.

CHRISTMAS CAKE WITH GLACE FRUIT

MAKES ABOUT 10 SLICES

225 g (8 oz) butter or margarine	45 ml (3 tbsp) apricot glaze (see page 328)
225 g (8 oz) caster sugar	50 g (2 oz) glace cherries, halved
4 eggs, beaten	50 g (2 oz) blanched almonds
100 g (4 oz) ground almonds	25-40 g (1-1½ oz) angelica, cut into diamonds
125 g (4 oz) self-raising flour, sifted with a pinch of salt	
225 g (8 oz) can pineapple slices, drained and roughly chopped	

1 Grease and base line a deep 20 cm (8 inch) loose-bottomed round cake tin. Tie a double thickness of brown paper round the outside.
2 Cream the butter and sugar together until light and fluffy. Beat in the eggs a little at a time. Fold in the ground almonds and flour.
3 Fold in the pineapple, then add 15-30 ml (1-2 tbsp) warm water to give a soft dropping consistency. Spread in the prepared cake tin.
4 Bake in the oven at 170°C (325°F) mark 3 for 1½ hours, covering the top with a double thickness of greaseproof paper after 1 hour to prevent overbrowning.
5 Leave in the tin for 5-10 minutes, then turn out and stand on a wire rack. Brush the top with apricot glaze while still warm and press on the cherries, nuts and angelica in a decorative design. Glaze the decoration.
6 Finish with festive ribbon. Store in an airtight tin for up to 2 weeks.

YULE LOG

3 eggs	caster sugar, to dredge
100 g (4 oz) caster sugar	1 quantity chocolate butter cream (see page 328)
100 g (4 oz) plain flour	icing sugar, to decorate

1 Grease a 30 x 20 cm (12 x 8 inch) Swiss roll tin. Line with greaseproof paper and grease the paper. Dust with caster sugar and flour.

2 Put the eggs and sugar in a large bowl, place over a pan of hot water and whisk until pale and creamy and thick enough to leave a trail on the surface of the mixture when the whisk is lifted.

3 Sift half the flour over the mixture and fold in very lightly with a metal spoon. Sift and fold in the remaining flour, then lightly stir in 15 ml (1 tbsp) hot water.

4 Pour the mixture into the prepared tin. Bake in the oven at 220°C (425°F) mark 7 for 8-12 minutes until golden brown, well risen and firm to the touch.

5 Meanwhile, place a sheet of greaseproof paper over a damp tea towel. Dredge the paper with a little caster sugar.

6 Quickly turn out the cake on to the paper, trim off the crusty edges and roll up with the paper inside. Leave to cool on a wire rack.

7 When cold, unroll and remove the paper. Spread one third of the butter cream over the surface and re-roll. Refrigerate for 30 minutes until the roll is firm.

8 Coat with the remaining butter cream and mark lines with a fork to resemble tree bark.

9 Chill for 1 hour before serving. Dust lightly with icing sugar and decorate with a sprig of real or artificial holly.

STOLLEN

15 g (½ oz) fresh yeast or 7.5 ml (1½ tsp) dried plus a pinch of sugar	grated rind of 1 small lemon
100 ml (4 fl oz) tepid milk	50 g (2 oz) chopped mixed peel
225 g (8 oz) strong plain flour	50 g (2 oz) currants
1.25 ml (¼ level tsp) salt	50 g (2 oz) sultanas
25 g (1 oz) butter or margarine	25 g (1 oz) blanched almonds, chopped
	½ a beaten egg
	icing sugar, to dredge

1 Grease a large baking sheet.

2 Crumble the fresh yeast into a bowl and cream with the milk until smooth. If using dried yeast, sprinkle on to the milk with the sugar and leave in a warm place for 15 minutes or until the surface is frothy.

3 Put the flour and salt into a bowl and rub in the butter. Add the lemon rind, peel, fruit and nuts. Add the yeast mixture and the egg and mix thoroughly to a soft dough.

4 Turn on to a lightly floured working surface and knead for about 10 minutes until smooth. Cover with a clean cloth and leave to rise in a warm place for about 1 hour until doubled in size.

5 Knead the dough for 2-3 minutes, then roll into an oval shape measuring about 23 x 18 cm (9 x 7 inches). Mark a line lengthways with the rolling pin.

6 Carefully fold the dough in half along the marked line. Place on the baking sheet, cover with a clean cloth and leave in a warm place for about 40 minutes until doubled in size.

7 Bake in the oven at 200°C (400°F) mark 6 for about 30 minutes until well risen and golden brown. Transfer to a wire rack to cool. When cold, dredge the stollen all over with icing sugar to serve.

PANETTONE

MAKES ABOUT 10 SLICES

350 g (12 oz) plain white flour	50 g (2 oz) caster sugar
20 g (¾ oz) fresh yeast or 15 g (2¼ tsp) dried	75 g (3 oz) candied peel, chopped
225 ml (8 fl oz) tepid milk	50 g (2 oz) sultanas
100 g (4 oz) butter, softened	pinch of grated nutmeg
2 egg yolks	egg yolk, to glaze

1 Sift the flour into a large bowl and make a well in the centre. Blend the fresh yeast with the milk. If using dried yeast, sprinkle it on to the milk and leave in a warm place for 15 minutes or until frothy. Add the yeast liquid to the flour and mix well together, gradually drawing in the flour from the sides of the bowl. Leave to stand in a warm place for 45 minutes or until doubled in size.

2 Add the softened butter to the dough with the egg yolks, sugar, candied peel, sultanas and nutmeg. Mix well together. Leave to stand again in a warm place for a further 45 minutes or until doubled in bulk.

3 Meanwhile, cut 3 strips of baking parchment, each one measuring 56 x 25 cm (22 x 10 inches). Fold each piece over lengthways.

4 Stand the 3 pieces of parchment together on a greased baking sheet to make a 17 cm (6½ inch) circle and secure with staples. Place the dough inside the paper and leave in a warm place for about 1 hour or until risen to the top of the paper.

5 Cut the top of the dough in the shape of a cross, then brush with egg yolk, to glaze. Bake on the lowest shelf of the oven at 200°C (400°F) mark 6 for 20 minutes, then lower the temperature to 180°C (350°F) mark 4 for a further 40 minutes or until a fine warmed skewer inserted in the centre comes out clean. Leave to cool in the paper. Panettone may be stored in an airtight tin for a maximum of 1 week.

SCOTTISH BLACK BUN

MAKES ABOUT 12 SLICES

1 quantity shortcrust pastry (see page 327)	450 g (1 lb) seedless raisins
FOR THE FILLING	450 g (1 lb) currants
225 g (8 oz) plain flour	50 g (2 oz) chopped mixed peel
5 ml (1 level tsp) ground cinnamon	100 g (4 oz) chopped almonds
5 ml (1 level tsp) ground ginger	100 g (4 oz) dark brown soft sugar
5 ml (1 level tsp) ground allspice	1 egg, beaten
5 ml (1 level tsp) cream of tartar	150 ml (¼ pint) whisky
5 ml (1 level tsp) bicarbonate of soda	about 60 ml (4 tbsp) milk
	beaten egg, to glaze

1 Grease a deep 20 cm (8 inch) round cake tin.

2 Roll out two thirds of the pastry on a lightly floured surface to a round, 35 cm (14 inches) in diameter. Line the tin with the pastry, making sure it overhangs the sides.

3 Sift together the flour, spices, cream of tartar and bicarbonate of soda. Mix in the raisins, currants, peel, almonds and sugar.

4 Add the egg, whisky and milk and stir until the mixture is evenly moistened. Pack the filling into the pastry case and fold the top of the pastry over the filling.

5 On a lightly floured surface, roll out the remaining dough to a 20 cm (8 inch) round. Moisten the edges of the pastry case, put the pastry round on top and seal firmly.

6 With a skewer, make four or five holes right down to the bottom of the cake, then prick all over the top with a fork and brush with egg.

7 Bake in the oven at 180°C (350°F) mark 4 for 2½-3 hours or until a fine warmed skewer inserted in the centre comes out clean. Cover with greaseproof paper if it is becoming too brown. Turn out on to a wire rack to cool.

CHEESECAKES

Few can resist a creamy rich, velvety smooth cheesecake, and there is a wide variety to choose from in this chapter. From traditional baked cheesecakes to light gelatine-set cheesecakes with tangy citrus and berry fruit toppings, you will find a recipe to suit everyone.

RICOTTA CHEESECAKE

SERVES 4

350 g (12 oz) Ricotta or curd cheese	50 g (2 oz) ground almonds
3 egg yolks, beaten	40 g (1½ oz) chopped candied peel
100 g (4 oz) sugar	grated rind of 1 lemon
50 ml (2 fl oz) rum or brandy	caster sugar, to decorate

1 Grease and flour a 20 cm (8 inch) cake tin and set aside until required.
2 Push the Ricotta or curd cheese through a sieve into a bowl and beat in the egg yolks and sugar.
3 Add the rum, beat well, then fold in the ground almonds, candied peel and lemon rind.
4 Pour into the prepared tin and bake in the oven at 180°C (350°F) mark 4 for 30-40 minutes or until firm and slightly shrunken from the sides of the tin.
5 Open the door of the oven and switch off. Leave the cheesecake inside the oven for about 2-3 hours to cool with the door ajar.
6 To serve, carefully remove the cheesecake from the tin and dredge with sugar.

CALCIONI ALL'ASCOLANA

SERVES 16

225 g (8 oz) plain flour	25 g (1 oz) caster sugar
pinch of salt	1 egg yolk
2 eggs, beaten	finely grated rind of 1 lemon
30 ml (2 tbsp) olive oil	50 g (2 oz) candied peel, finely chopped
FOR THE FILLING	beaten egg, to glaze
225 g (8 oz) ricotta cheese	icing sugar, for dusting
50 g (2 oz) ground almonds	

1 To make the pastry, put the flour and salt in a bowl. Make a well in the centre and stir in the eggs and olive oil. Using your fingertips, knead to a smooth dough.
2 Turn out on to a floured work surface and knead for about 5 minutes. Wrap and chill for 30 minutes.
3 To make the filling, mix the ingredients together.
4 Roll out the pastry very thinly on a lightly floured surface and cut out sixteen 10 cm (4 inch) rounds.
5 Divide filling between pastry rounds. Brush edges with beaten egg, then fold in half to enclose the filling. Brush with beaten egg to glaze. Transfer to baking sheets.
6 Bake in the oven at 190°C (375°F) mark 5 for 25-30 minutes. Serve cold, dusted with icing sugar.

CHEESECAKE WITH RED FRUIT SAUCE

SERVES 8

175 g (6 oz) digestive biscuits, crushed	grated rind and juice of 3 lemons
50 g (2 oz) ground almonds	100 g (4 oz) caster sugar
75 g (3 oz) butter, melted	FOR THE SAUCE
FOR THE FILLING	350 g (12 oz) strawberries
225 g (8 oz) full fat soft cheese	350 g (12 oz) raspberries
225 g (8 oz) cottage cheese	40 g (½ oz) icing sugar
60 ml (4 tbsp) double cream	90 ml (6 tbsp) orange-flavoured liqueur
2 eggs, separated	TO DECORATE
1 egg yolk	whipped cream
15 ml (1 tbsp) cornflour	icing sugar, for dusting

1 Grease the base and sides of a 20 cm (8 inch) spring-release cake tin and line with greaseproof paper.

2 To make the base, stir the crushed biscuits and ground almonds into the melted butter and blend well. Press half the mixture into the base of the prepared tin.

3 To make the filling, blend the cheeses, double cream, egg yolks, cornflour, lemon rind and 60 ml (4 tbsp) lemon juice together in a blender or food processor.

4 Whisk the egg whites until stiff but not dry. Whisk in 30 ml (2 tbsp) of the caster sugar, then whisk again until stiff and shiny. Fold in the remaining caster sugar. Gently fold the egg whites into the cheese mixture. Spoon into the tin. Sprinkle the remaining biscuit mixture on top.

5 Bake in the oven at 200°C (400°F) mark 6 for 30 minutes. Reduce temperature to 180°C (350°F) mark 4, cover with foil and bake for a further 45 minutes. Cool in the tin. Chill for at least 1 hour.

6 To make the sauce, blend the strawberries, raspberries, icing sugar and liqueur together in a blender or food processor. Sieve to remove pips. Chill.

7 Carefully remove cheesecake from tin. Decorate with cream. Dust with icing sugar and serve with the sauce.

RUM AND RAISIN CHEESECAKE

SERVES 8

FOR THE PASTRY	FOR THE FILLING
225 g (8 oz) self raising flour	75 g (3 oz) raisins
5 ml (1 level tsp) bicarbonate of soda	75 ml (5 tbsp) dark rum
5 ml (1 level tsp) cream of tartar	100 g (4 oz) cottage cheese
75 g (3 oz) butter	100 g (4 oz) full fat soft cheese
finely grated rind of 1 lemon	2 eggs, separated
150 ml (¼ pint) soured cream	50 g (2 oz) caster sugar
	150 ml (¼ pint) double cream
	15 ml (1 tbsp) icing sugar, for dusting

1 Grease a 25 cm (10 inch) flan dish.

2 To make the filling, put the raisins and rum in a saucepan and bring to the boil. Remove from the heat and leave to cool for 15 minutes.

3 Meanwhile, to make the pastry, sift the flour, bicarbonate of soda and cream of tartar into a bowl. Rub in the butter until the mixture resembles fine breadcrumbs. Add the lemon rind. Bind to a smooth dough with the soured cream. Roll out and use to line the prepared dish.

4 Beat the cottage and cream cheeses together in a bowl. Stir in the rum and raisins.

5 In a separate bowl, whisk the egg yolks and caster sugar together until pale and fluffy. Whisk in the double cream, and continue whisking until the mixture is the consistency of lightly whipped cream. Fold into the cheese, rum and raisin mixture. Whisk the egg whites until stiff, then fold into the mixture. Pour into the pastry case.

6 Bake in the oven at 180°C (350°F) mark 4 for about 1 hour. Turn off the heat and leave to cool in the oven for 15 minutes. Remove from the oven and cool for a further 45 minutes. Dust with icing sugar.

TRADITIONAL BAKED CHEESECAKE

SERVES 8

FOR THE BASE	
50 g (2 oz) self-raising flour	225 g (8 oz) caster sugar
2.5 ml (½ level tsp) baking powder	450 g (1 lb) full fat soft cheese
50 g (2 oz) butter, softened	40 g (1½ oz) plain flour
50 g (2 oz) caster sugar	grated rind and juice of 1 lemon
1 egg	300 ml (½ pint) soured cream
FOR THE FILLING	75 g (3 oz) sultanas
4 eggs, separated	pinch of grated nutmeg

1 Grease a 20 cm (8 inch) round spring-release cake tin and line the base with greaseproof paper; grease the paper.
2 To make the base, sift the self-raising flour and baking powder into a bowl. Add the butter, sugar and egg. Mix well and beat for 2-3 minutes. Spread the mixture evenly over the bottom of the prepared tin.
3 To make the filling, whisk the egg yolks with the sugar until the mixture is thick and creamy.
4 Beat the soft cheese lightly in a bowl. Add the whisked egg mixture and mix until smooth. Sift in the plain flour and stir in. Add the lemon rind and juice, 150 ml (¼ pint) of the soured cream and the sultanas.
5 Whisk the egg whites until stiff, then fold into the mixture. Pour on to the mixture in the tin.
6 Bake in the oven at 170°C (325°F) mark 3 for 1 hour or until firm but still spongy to the touch. Turn off the heat and leave in the oven for 1 hour with the door ajar.
7 Remove from the oven and cool for 2-3 hours. Carefully remove cheesecake from tin. To serve, spread the remaining cream over the top and sprinkle with nutmeg.

COOK'S TIP

Bake cheesecakes in spring-release cake tins to make turning out easy. If you do not own a spring-release tin, a cake tin with a loose base works almost as well.

EASTER CHEESECAKE

SERVES 8

FOR THE PASTRY	
225 g (8 oz) plain flour	2.5 ml (½ tsp) vanilla flavouring
125 g (4 oz) butter	200 ml (7 fl oz) double cream
45 ml (3 tbsp) caster sugar	150 ml (5 fl oz) soured cream
FOR THE FILLING	50 g (2 oz) caster sugar
400 g (14 oz) full fat soft cheese	1 ripe pear (optional)
	icing sugar, for dusting
2 eggs, separated	crystallized primroses, to decorate (optional)

1 To make the pastry, sift the flour into a bowl. Rub in the butter until the mixture resembles fine bread-crumbs. Stir in the caster sugar. Bind to a dough with about 60 ml (4 tbsp) water. Roll out on a lightly floured surface and use to line a 22 cm (8½ inch) deep, fluted loose bottomed flan tin. Chill for 15 minutes then bake blind at 200°C (400°F) mark 6 for 20-25 minutes or until pale golden brown and cooked through.
2 Beat together the soft cheese, egg yolks and vanilla flavouring. Gradually beat in the double and soured creams until thoroughly combined.
3 Whisk the egg whites until they just hold their shape. Fold in 25 g (1 oz) caster sugar and continue whisking until stiff. Whisk in a further 25 g (1 oz) sugar. Fold into the cheese mixture.
4 Peel, core and thinly slice the pear into the prepared flan case if using. Spoon over the cheese mixture. Place the tin on a baking sheet and bake at 220°C (425°F) mark 7 for 20 minutes. Reduce the oven temperature to 180°C (350°F) mark 4 and bake for a further 35-40 minutes or until the cheesecake is golden brown and just set. Cool in the tin.
5 Serve the cheesecake warm, dusted with icing sugar and decorated with crystallized primroses, if desired.

HOT CHOCOLATE CHEESECAKE

SERVES 10-12

FOR THE CHOCOLATE PASTRY	FOR THE FILLING
150 g (5 oz) plain flour	2 eggs, separated
75 g (3 oz) butter or margarine	75 g (3 oz) caster sugar
30 ml (2 level tbsp) cocoa powder, sifted	350 g (12 oz) curd cheese
30 ml (2 level tbsp) caster sugar	40 g (1½ oz) ground hazelnuts
25 g (1 oz) ground hazelnuts	150 ml (¼ pint) double cream
1 egg yolk	25 g (1 oz) cocoa powder, sifted
	10 ml (2 tsp) dark rum
	icing sugar, for dusting

1 Grease a 20 cm (8 inch) round loose-based cake tin.

2 To make the chocolate pastry, put the flour in a bowl and rub in the butter until the mixture resembles fine breadcrumbs. Stir in the cocoa powder, sugar and hazelnuts. Add the egg yolk and sufficient water to give a soft dough.

3 Roll out the pastry on a lightly floured work surface and use to line the prepared tin. Chill while making the filling.

4 To make the filling, whisk the egg yolks and sugar together in a bowl until thick enough to leave a trail on the surface when the whisk is lifted. Whisk in the curd cheese, nuts, cream, cocoa powder and rum until blended.

5 Whisk the egg whites until stiff, then fold into the cheese mixture. Pour into the pastry case and fold the edges of the pastry over the filling.

6 Bake in the oven at 170°C (325°F) mark 3 for 1½ hours until risen and just firm to the touch. Carefully remove from the tin and dust the top with icing sugar. Serve the cheesecake while it is still hot.

FROSTED MINT CHEESECAKE

SERVES 6

75 g (3 oz) butter or margarine	7.5 ml (1½ tbsp) mint-flavoured liqueur
150 g (5 oz) caster sugar	30 ml (2 tbsp) water
100 g (4 oz) plain flour	7.5 ml (1½ level tsp) powdered gelatine
225 g (8 oz) full fat soft cheese	1 egg white
150 ml (5 fl oz) natural yogurt	mint sprigs, to decorate

1 To make the shortbread base, cream the butter with 50 g (2 oz) caster sugar until smooth. Stir in the flour and knead the mixture until it is smooth.

2 Press the shortbread mixture into the base of a 20 cm (8 inch) flan ring, placed on a foil-lined baking sheet. Bake in the oven at 180°C (350°F) mark 4 for 18-20 minutes; cool in the ring.

3 Meanwhile, beat the cheese with a wooden spoon until smooth, then gradually whisk in the yogurt, 25 g (1 oz) sugar and the mint-flavoured liqueur.

4 Place the water in a bowl and sprinkle in the gelatine. Stand the bowl over a saucepan of hot water and heat gently until dissolved. Leave to cool slightly, then stir into the cheese mixture. Whisk the egg white until stiff, then fold into the cheesecake mixture.

5 Pour the mixture over the shortbread base. Open freeze for about 8 hours or overnight, then ease off the flan ring. Wrap in foil when firm and return to the freezer until required.

6 About 1 hour before serving, remove the cheesecake from the freezer, and place on a serving plate.

7 Warm the remaining sugar until it caramelises, then pour over the cheesecake in a lattice pattern. Place in the refrigerator for 45 minutes before serving. Decorate the cheesecake with mint sprigs.

GINGER AND BANANA CHEESECAKE

SERVES 6-8

FOR THE BASE	30 ml (2 tbsp) clear honey
225 g (8 oz) ginger biscuits, crushed	15 ml (1 tbsp) chopped preserved ginger (with syrup)
100 g (4 oz) unsalted butter, melted and cooled	15 ml (1 level tbsp) powdered gelatine
FOR THE FILLING	60 ml (4 tbsp) lemon juice
225 g (8 oz) full fat soft cheese	TO DECORATE
150 ml (¼ pint) soured cream	banana slices
3 bananas	preserved ginger slices

1 To make the base, mix the biscuits and melted butter together. Press the mixture over the base of a 20 cm (8 inch) spring-release tin or deep cake tin with a removable base. Chill for about 30 minutes.

2 To make the filling, beat the cheese and cream together in a bowl until well mixed. Peel and mash the bananas, then beat into the cheese mixture with the honey and ginger.

3 Sprinkle the gelatine over the lemon juice in a small bowl and leave to soak for 2-3 minutes. Place the bowl over a pan of simmering water and stir until dissolved.

4 Stir the dissolved gelatine slowly into the cheesecake mixture. Spoon on to the biscuit base. Chill for about 3-4 hours until the cheesecake is set.

5 To serve, remove the cheesecake carefully from the tin and place on a serving plate. Decorate around the edge with banana and ginger slices. Serve as soon as possible or the banana will discolour.

VARIATION

Use chocolate digestive biscuits for the base of this cheesecake instead of ginger biscuits, and omit the preserved ginger from the filling. Decorate the top with bananas slices arranged alternately with chocolate buttons.

COFFEE CHEESECAKE

SERVES 8

FOR THE BASE	30 ml (2 tbsp) coffee-flavoured liqueur
50 g (2 oz) butter, melted	150 g (5 oz) light brown soft sugar
175 g (6 oz) gingernut biscuits, finely crushed	450 g (1 lb) curd cheese
FOR THE FILLING	300 ml (½ pint) whipping cream
15 ml (1 level tbsp) powdered gelatine	coffee beans, to decorate
15 ml (1 level tbsp) instant coffee powder	

1 Lightly oil a 20 cm (8 inch) loose-based deep cake tin or spring-release cake tin.

2 To make the base, stir the butter and crushed biscuits together. Press firmly into the base of the prepared tin. Chill for 30 minutes until set.

3 To make the filling, sprinkle the gelatine over 45 ml (3 tbsp) water in a small bowl and leave to soak for 10 minutes. Place the bowl over a pan of simmering water and stir until dissolved. (Alternatively, microwave on HIGH for 30 seconds or until dissolved.)

4 Stir the coffee and coffee liqueur into 300 ml (½ pint) boiling water. Stir in the gelatine, then the sugar.

5 Put the coffee mixture and curd cheese into a blender or food processor and work until just smooth. Leave until beginning to set. Lightly whip the cream and fold half into the cheese mixture.

6 Turn the mixture into the prepared tin and chill for 2-3 hours or until set.

7 When set, carefully remove the cheesecake from the tin. Pipe whirls of the remaining cream around the cheesecake and decorate with coffee beans.

COOK'S TIP

If you can find them use sugar coffee beans, available from high class confectioners, to decorate.

LEMON CHEESECAKE

SERVES 6

FOR THE BASE	225 g (8 oz) cottage cheese, sieved
75 g (3 oz) butter or margarine	150 ml (5 fl oz) soured cream
175 g (6 oz) digestive biscuits, finely crushed	75 g (3 oz) caster sugar
FOR THE FILLING	2 eggs, separated
15 ml (1 level tbsp) powdered gelatine	TO DECORATE
finely grated rind and juice of 1 lemon	sliced strawberries or lemon slices

1 Melt the butter in a saucepan and mix in the biscuit crumbs. Press into the base of a 20 cm (8 inch) loose-bottomed or spring-release cake tin. Chill in the refrigerator for 30 minutes.

2 Sprinkle the gelatine in 60 ml (4 tbsp) water in a small bowl. Place over a pan of simmering water and stir until dissolved. Cool slightly.

3 Put the lemon rind, juice and cottage cheese into a bowl, then add the soured cream and sugar and mix well together. Stir in the egg yolks and gelatine.

4 Whisk the egg whites until stiff, then fold lightly into the mixture. Carefully pour into the tin and chill for several hours, preferably overnight until firm.

5 Remove the cheesecake from the tin and place on a flat serving plate. Decorate with strawberries or lemon slices.

VARIATION

Set the cheesecake in an oiled 25 cm (10 inch) fluted savarin mould as for Cranberry Cheesecake (opposite). Set the filling in the tin first, then cover with the base. Turn out to serve.

MINI GRAPE CHEESECAKES

SERVES 24

FOR THE PASTRY	2 eggs, beaten
275 g (10 oz) plain flour	25 g (1 oz) caster sugar
pinch of salt	10 ml (2 level tsp) plain flour
175 g (6 oz) butter or margarine, cut into pieces	finely grated rind and juice of ½ lemon
50 g (2 oz) caster sugar	TO DECORATE
FOR THE FILLING	175 g (6 oz) grapes, halved and seeded
225 g (8 oz) full fat soft cheese	150 ml (¼ pint) whipping cream, whipped

1 To make the pastry, put the flour and salt into a bowl. Rub in the butter until the mixture resembles bread-crumbs. Stir in the sugar and add sufficient water, about 60 ml (4 tbsp), to mix to a smooth dough.

2 Roll out the pastry on a lightly floured work surface and cut out twelve 7.5 cm (3 inch) rounds, using a fluted pastry cutter. Use to line 24 deep patty tins.

3 Bake blind in the oven at 200°C (400°F) mark 6 for 10 minutes. Remove the foil and baking beans, then return to the oven for a further 5 minutes.

4 Meanwhile to make the filling, beat the soft cheese, eggs, sugar, flour and lemon rind and juice together in a bowl until evenly mixed. Pour the filling into the pastry cases.

5 Lower the oven temperature to 150°C (300°F) mark 2 and bake the cheesecakes for 15 minutes until the fillings are set. Leave to cool on a wire rack for 30 minutes, then refrigerate the cheesecakes for at least 1 hour before serving.

6 Just before serving, decorate the top of each cheese-cake with the grapes and piped whipped cream.

CRANBERRY CHEESECAKE

SERVES 10

FOR THE FILLING	300 ml (½ pint) double cream
225 g (8 oz) full fat soft cheese	15 ml (1 level tbsp) powdered gelatine
2 eggs, separated	225 g (8 oz) cranberries
finely grated rind and juice of 2 lemons	10 ml (2 level tsp) arrowroot
225 g (8 oz) caster sugar	FOR THE BASE
300 ml (½ pint) natural yogurt	175 g (6 oz) digestive biscuits, crushed
	75 g (3 oz) butter, melted

1 Lightly oil a 25 cm (10 inch) fluted savarin spring release tin.
2 For the filling, beat the cheese, egg yolks, lemon rind, 50 g (2 oz) of the sugar and the yogurt together in a bowl. Whip the cream lightly and fold into the cheese mixture.
3 In a small bowl, mix 75 ml (5 tbsp) lemon juice with 30 ml (2 tbsp) water. Sprinkle in the gelatine and leave to soak for 2-3 minutes. Place the bowl over a pan simmering water and stir until dissolved. Stir into the cheese mixture and leave to cool.
4 Whisk the egg whites until standing in soft peaks, then fold into the cheese mixture until evenly incorporated. Pour the mixture into the prepared tin. Chill for 3-4 hours until completely set.
5 To make the base, mix the biscuits and melted butter together. Spoon the mixture over the set cheesecake and pat down firmly. Chill again for 1 hour until set.
6 Cook the cranberries with the remaining sugar and 150 ml (¼ pint) water in a pan for about 10 minutes until soft but still whole. Blend a little water with the arrowroot, stir into the cranberry mixture and slowly bring to boiling point. Cook for 2-3 minutes, then leave to cool for 30 minutes.
7 Invert the cheesecake on to a flat serving plate. Spoon the cranberry mixture into the centre before serving.

INDIVIDUAL RASPBERRY CHEESECAKES

SERVES 2

50 g (2 oz) cream cheese	15 g (½ oz) butter
5 ml (1 level tsp) caster sugar	2 digestive biscuits, finely crushed
75 g (3 oz) fresh or frozen raspberries, thawed	raspberries, to decorate
120 ml (4 fl oz) double cream	

1 In a small bowl, beat the cream cheese and 2.5 ml (½ tsp) of the sugar together until smooth. Add the raspberries and mix well.
2 Whip the cream until it just holds its shape, then fold into the cheese mixture until evenly incorporated.
3 Wet the insides of 2 ramekin dishes, to ensure that the mixture will turn out easily. Spoon in the cheese mixture, levelling it evenly.
4 Melt the butter in a saucepan and stir in the biscuits and remaining sugar.
5 Press the biscuit mixture on top of the cheese mixture and level the top. Chill in the refrigerator for at least 2 hours before serving.
6 To serve, loosen around the edges of the ramekins with a knife and turn the cheesecakes out on to serving plates. Decorate with raspberries and serve chilled.

SERVING SUGGESTION

Light and creamy, these cheesecakes make perfect summer desserts. Serve with crisp biscuits.

GOOSEBERRY CHEESECAKE

SERVES 6

450 g (1 lb) gooseberries, topped and tailed	125 g (4 oz) cottage cheese
75 ml (5 tbsp) water	225 g (8 oz) full fat soft cheese
125 g (4 oz) caster sugar	150 ml (5 fl oz) double cream
75 g (3 oz) shelled hazelnuts	2 eggs, separated
75 g (3 oz) butter	15 ml (1 tbsp) lemon juice
175 g (6 oz) digestive biscuits, finely crushed	7.5 ml (1½ level tsp) powdered gelatine

1 Put the gooseberries into a pan with 60 ml (4 tbsp) water and 75 g (3 oz) caster sugar. Cover and cook slowly for 20 minutes until mushy. Press through a nylon sieve into a bowl and let cool for 30 minutes.

2 Roughly chop 50 g (2 oz) hazelnuts and fry gently in the butter until golden. Stir in the crushed digestive biscuits. Press into the base of a 24 cm (9½ inch) deep fluted flan dish. Refrigerate to set.

3 Sieve the cottage cheese into a large bowl. Beat in the soft cheese, then the cream.

4 Whisk the egg yolks and remaining caster sugar until thick enough to leave a trail on the surface when the whisk is lifted. Stir into the cheese mixture.

5 Put the lemon juice in a small bowl with 15 ml (1 tbsp) water and sprinkle in the gelatine. Leave to soak for 10 minutes. Stand the bowl over a pan of gently simmering water until the gelatine dissolves, then stir into the cheese mixture with half the fruit purée.

6 Whisk one egg white until stiff and fold into the mixture then spoon into the lined flan dish. Refrigerate for 1-2 hours.

7 Spread remaining nuts on a baking sheet and brown in the oven at 200°C (400°F) mark 6 for 5-10 minutes. Put into a tea towel and rub off skins, then chop roughly.

8 Decorate the cheesecake with the nuts and remaining gooseberry pureé.

QUICK CHERRY CHEESECAKE

SERVES 4-6

65 g (2½ oz) unsalted butter, melted	60 ml (4 tbsp) icing sugar, sifted
150 g (5 oz) digestive biscuits, crushed	300 ml (10 fl oz) double cream
225 g (8 oz) full fat soft cheese	400 g (14 oz) can cherry pie filling
2.5 ml (½ tsp) vanilla flavouring	

1 Stir the melted butter into the crushed biscuits and mix well, then press into the base and sides of a 22 cm (8½ inch) fluted flan dish. Refrigerate for 30 minutes.

2 Put the cheese into a bowl and beat until soft and creamy, then beat in the vanilla flavouring and icing sugar.

3 Whip the cream until it holds its shape, then fold into the cheese mixture until evenly blended.

4 Spoon the mixture into the biscuit base and level the surface. Refrigerate for 30 minutes.

5 Spoon the pie filling over the top of the cheesecake. Refrigerate for 2-3 hours to set.

VARIATION

Use blackcurrant instead of cherry pie filling.

LEMON MUESLI CHEESECAKE

SERVES 6

FOR THE BASE	225 g (8 oz) low fat soft cheese
175 g (6 oz) muesli	150 ml (¼ pint) natural yogurt
75 g (3 oz) butter or margarine, melted	60 ml (4 tbsp) clear honey
FOR THE FILLING	2 egg whites
3 lemons	
15 ml (1 level tbsp) powdered gelatine	

1   Grease a 20 cm (8 inch) spring-release cake tin.
2   To make the base, mix the muesli and melted butter together. Press the mixture over the base of the prepared tin, using the back of a metal spoon. Chill to set while making the filling.
3   To make the filling, finely grate the rind of 2 of the lemons; set aside. Squeeze the juice from the 2 lemons and make up to 150 ml (¼ pint) with water.
4   Sprinkle the gelatine over the lemon juice and water in a bowl and leave to soak for 2-3 minutes. Place the bowl over a pan of simmering water and stir until dissolved. (Alternatively, microwave on HIGH for 30 seconds or until dissolved.) Leave to cool slightly.
5   Whisk the cheese, yogurt and honey together in a separate bowl. Stir in the grated lemon rind and dissolved gelatine until evenly incorporated. Whisk the egg whites until standing in stiff peaks. Fold into the cheesecake mixture until evenly incorporated. Spoon the mixture into the prepared tin and level the surface. Chill for at least 4 hours until set.
6   Coarsely grate the rind from the remaining lemon over the centre of the cheesecake, to decorate. As an alternative, slice the lemon thinly and arrange on top of the cheesecake. Remove the cheesecake from the tin and place on a serving plate. Serve chilled.

RASPBERRY RIPPLE CHEESECAKE

SERVES 12

FOR THE BASE	300 ml (½ pint) Greek yogurt
25 g (1 oz) blanched almonds	150 g (5 oz) low fat soft cheese
225 g (8 oz) almond butter biscuits, crushed	15 ml (1 level tbsp) powdered gelatine
100 g (4 oz) butter or margarine, melted	2 egg whites
few drops of almond flavouring	50 g (2 oz) icing sugar
FOR THE FILLING	mint leaves, to decorate
450 g (1 lb) raspberries	

1   Grease a 2.3 litre (4 pint) loose-based cake tin or spring-release cake tin.
2   To make the base, lightly toast the almonds, then finely chop. Mix with the biscuits and butter. Add a few drops of almond flavouring. Spoon the mixture into the base of the prepared tin and pack down with the back of a metal spoon. Chill while making the filling.
3   To make the filling, purée 225 g (8 oz) of the raspberries in a blender or food processor, then press through a sieve. Pour three-quarters of the purée into a bowl and reserve. Add the yogurt and cheese to the purée remaining in the blender and process until well blended.
4   Sprinkle the gelatine over 30 ml (2 tbsp) water in a small bowl and leave to soak for 2-3 minutes. Place the bowl over a pan of simmering water and stir until dissolved. Leave to cool, then add to the cheese mixture.
5   Whisk the egg whites with the icing sugar until very thick and shiny. Fold into the cheese mixture.
6   Arrange 100 g (4 oz) of the reserved raspberries over the biscuit base. Pour the cheese mixture into the tin. Sprinkle with the remaining raspberries. Spoon in the reserved purée and mark in a swirl with a knife to make a marbled pattern. Chill for 3-4 hours or until set.
7   To serve, unmould and decorate with mint leaves.

TROPICAL CHEESECAKE

SERVES 8

FOR THE BASE	150 ml (¼ pint) orange juice
75 g (3 oz) butter, melted	350 g (12 oz) full fat soft cheese
175 g (6 oz) plain chocolate digestive biscuits, finely crushed	100 g (4 oz) caster sugar
50 g (2 oz) desiccated coconut	2 eggs, separated
FOR THE FILLING	30 ml (2 tbsp) lemon juice
2 medium mangoes	300 ml (½ pint) double cream
30 ml (2 level tbsp) powdered gelatine	3 kiwi fruit, peeled and sliced, to decorate

1 Lightly oil a 22 cm (8½ inch) spring-release cake tin. Line the base with greaseproof paper and grease the paper.
2 To make the base, stir the melted butter into the biscuit crumbs and coconut. Mix well together. Press over the base of the prepared tin. Chill for 30 minutes.
3 To make the filling, peel the mangoes and cut the flesh from the stone. Discard the stone. Roughly chop or mash the flesh.
4 Sprinkle the gelatine over the orange juice in a bowl and leave to soak for 2-3 minutes. Place the bowl over a pan of simmering water and stir until dissolved. Leave the gelatine to cool for 5 minutes.
5 Beat the soft cheese and sugar together in a bowl until smooth, then beat in the egg yolks and lemon juice. Stir in the mango flesh and dissolved gelatine. Lightly whip the cream and fold into the mixture.
6 Whisk the egg whites until stiff, then carefully fold into the cheese mixture. Pour on to the biscuit base. Chill for 3-4 hours until firm. Carefully remove the cheesecake from the tin. Decorate with the kiwi fruit.

COOK'S TIP

Once the cheesecake has set, remove it from the tin to prevent any reaction between the metal tin and the acid in the cheesecake causing discolouration.

REDCURRANT CHEESECAKE

SERVES 4-6

65 g (2½ oz) butter, melted	40 g (1½ oz) caster sugar
150 g (5 oz) wheatmeal biscuits, finely crushed	150 ml (5 fl oz) natural yogurt
175 g (6 oz) redcurrants	150 ml (5 fl oz) double cream
15 ml (1 level tbsp) powdered gelatine	15 ml (1 level tbsp) redcurrant jelly
125 g (4 oz) cottage cheese	redcurrants, to decorate
1 egg, separated	

1 Mix together the butter and biscuit crumbs. Press the mixture into a 20 cm (8 inch) round loose-bottomed cake tin to line the base.
2 Put the redcurrants in a medium saucepan with 45 ml (3 tbsp) water and simmer gently for 5-6 minutes, until soft. Allow to cool.
3 Sprinkle the gelatine in 45 ml (3 tbsp) water in a small bowl and leave to soak. Place the bowl over a saucepan of simmering water and stir until dissolved. Leave until lukewarm.
4 Put the cottage cheese, egg yolk, sugar and yogurt in a food processor or blender and work together until smooth. Whip the cream until it just holds its shape. Fold the cooked redcurrants, redcurrant jelly, gelatine and most of the cream into the cheese mixture. Whisk the egg white until stiff and fold into the mixture.
5 Pour the mixture on to the biscuit base and chill in the refrigerator until set.
6 Carefully remove the cheesecake from the tin and decorate with the remaining whipped cream and sprigs of redcurrants to serve.

PIES, FLANS & PASTRIES

Traditional fruit pies, colourful glazed fruit and nut flans, and crisp light-textured pastries are featured here. Remember, the secret to successful pastry making is to keep everything cool – the kitchen, work surface, utensils, ingredients and yourself!

BAKEWELL PUDDING

SERVES 4

212 g (7½ oz) packet frozen puff pastry, thawed	100 g (4 oz) butter or margarine, melted
FOR THE FILLING	100 g (4 oz) caster sugar
2 eggs	50 g (2 oz) ground almonds
2 egg yolks	30 ml (2 level tbsp) raspberry jam

1 Roll out the pastry on a floured surface and use to line an 18 cm (7 inch) pie plate or loose-based flan tin.
2 Beat the eggs and extra yolks together, add the butter, sugar and ground almonds and mix well.
3 Spread the bottom of the pastry case with the jam and pour on the egg mixture.
4 Bake in the oven at 200°C (400°F) mark 6 for 30 minutes, until the filling is firm to the touch. Serve warm or cold, with cream or custard.

DEEP-DISH APPLE FLAN

SERVES 8

1½ quantity flan pastry (see page 327)	1 cinnamon stick
FOR THE FILLING	75 g (3 oz) caster sugar
1.4 kg (3 lb) cooking apples	beaten egg, for glazing
50 g (2 oz) butter	flaked almonds
5 ml (1 level tsp) ground mixed spice	demerara sugar
	icing sugar, for dusting

1 Roll out the pastry and use to line a deep 22 cm (8½ inch) loose-based fluted flan tin. Chill the trimmings.
2 To make the filling, peel, quarter, core and thickly slice the apples. Put half in a saucepan with the butter, mixed spice, cinnamon and caster sugar. Cook, stirring, over a high heat until the apples are soft. Off the heat, remove cinnamon, then add the remaining apples. Cool slightly.
3 Spoon the apple mixture into the pastry case. Make pastry leaves from the trimmings. Arrange attractively interlocking over the apple filling and brush lightly with beaten egg. Sprinkle with almonds and demerara sugar.
4 Bake in the oven at 180°C (350°F) mark 4 for 35 minutes or until golden and crisp. Leave for 10 minutes before removing from tin. Serve warm dusted with icing sugar.

BANBURY APPLE PIE

SERVES 6

350 g (12 oz) plain flour	75 g (3 oz) soft brown sugar
pinch of salt	pinch of ground cinnamon
175 g (6 oz) butter	pinch of freshly grated nutmeg
15 ml (1 tbsp) caster sugar	grated rind and juice of 1 orange
1 egg, lightly beaten	milk, to glaze
700 g (1½ lb) cooking apples	caster sugar for sprinkling
juice of ½ lemon	
100 g (4 oz) sultanas	

1 To make the pastry, put the flour and salt in a bowl and rub in the butter until the mixture resembles fine breadcrumbs. Stir in the caster sugar, then stir in the egg and enough water to bind the mixture together.
2 Knead lightly on a lightly floured surface, then roll out two-thirds of the pastry and use to line a shallow 900 ml (1½ pint) pie dish.
3 Peel, core and thinly slice the apples. Put in a bowl and sprinkle with lemon juice.
4 Layer the apples, sultanas, brown sugar, spices and orange rind in the pie dish. Sprinkle with the orange juice.
5 Roll out the remaining pastry to form a lid, pressing the edges together. Scallop the edges, then make a slit in the centre of the pie.
6 Brush the top with milk to glaze, then bake at 200°C (400°F) mark 6 for 30 minutes, until golden brown. Sprinkle the top with caster sugar and serve hot or cold.

COOK'S TIP

Despite the mystique attached to making pastry, the only secrets to success are patience, practice and care. Unless making choux or filo (strudel) pastry, the golden rule is keep everything cool – kitchen, work surface, utensils, ingredients and yourself.

TARTE TATIN

SERVES 8 .

150 g (5 oz) butter or block margarine	1 egg yolk
175 g (6 oz) plain flour	15 ml (1 tbsp) water
65 g (2½ oz) caster sugar	450 g (1 lb) crisp eating apples

1 Rub 125 g (4 oz) fat into the flour until the mixture resembles fine breadcrumbs. Add 15 g (½ oz) caster sugar. Blend the egg yolk with the water and stir into the mixture. Knead the dough lightly, then refrigerate while making the filling.
2 In a saucepan, melt the remaining fat and add the remaining caster sugar. Heat until caramelised and golden brown. Remove from the heat and pour into a 20 cm (8 inch) round sandwich tin.
3 Peel, core and halve the apples and slice them into 1 cm (½ inch) pieces. Pack them tightly to fill the bottom of the tin, leaving no gaps.
4 Roll out the pastry on a floured work surface to a round slightly larger than the tin. Place on top of the apples and tuck in around the edges of the tin. Refrigerate for 30 minutes.
5 Place the tin on a baking sheet and bake in the oven at 200°C (400°F) mark 6 for 30-35 minutes until the pastry is golden. Turn out, apple side uppermost, on to a serving dish. Serve hot, with cream.

COOK'S NOTE

Correctly called Tarte des Demoiselles Tatin in French, this famous upside-down apple tart is named after the sisters Tatin, hoteliers in the nineteenth century who originated the recipe. There are now numerous versions of the original recipe, which has become something of a classic in French cookery. Most recipes use shortcrust pastry as here, although some use puff. In all versions the pastry is baked on the top so that the apples are completely sealed in with their juices, then the tart turned out upside down for serving.

PEACH PIE

SERVES 6

FOR THE PASTRY	2 egg yolks
225 g (8 oz) plain flour	FOR THE FILLING
50 g (2 oz) walnuts, finely chopped	900 g (2 lb) peaches
100 g (4 oz) softened butter or margarine, cut into pieces	1 egg white, for glazing
	caster sugar, for dredging
75 g (3 oz) caster sugar	

1 To make the pastry, place the flour on a work surface and sprinkle the walnuts over the top. Make a well in the centre and add the butter, sugar, egg yolks and 30 ml (2 tbsp) water.

2 Using the fingertips of one hand only, work the well ingredients together until evenly blended. Using a palette knife, gradually draw in the flour, then knead lightly until just smooth.

3 Roll out two thirds of the pastry on a floured work surface and use to line a 23 cm (9 inch) loose-based fluted flan tin. Chill for 30 minutes.

4 To make the filling, quarter the peaches and easy away from the stone. Peel off the skins carefully and divide each quarter in two lengthways.

5 Arrange the peaches in the pastry case. Roll out the remaining pastry and use to cover the pie, sealing well. Make a small hole in the centre to let steam escape.

6 Bake in the oven at 200°C (400°F) mark 6 for about 20-25 minutes or until just beginning to brown.

7 Brush the top of the pie with lightly beaten egg white and dredge with caster sugar. Return to the oven for a further 10 minutes or until well browned and crisp. Cool for 15 minutes in the tin before removing. Serve while still slightly warm, with cream.

VARIATION

Use firm, ripe nectarines in place of the peaches.

APRICOT AND CARDAMOM FLAN

SERVES 6

100 g (4 oz) no-soak dried apricots	150 ml (¼ pint) single cream
6 green cardamom pods, split	1 egg
2 bay leaves	1 egg yolk
1½ quantity pâte sucrée (see page 327)	25 g (1 oz) caster sugar
	60 ml (4 level tbsp) apricot jam

1 Place the apricots, cardamoms and bay leaves in a medium bowl. Completely cover with cold water and leave to soak overnight in the refrigerator.

2 Roll out the pastry on a lightly floured work surface and use to line a 34 x 11 cm (13½ x 4½ inch) loose-based fluted tranche tin. Chill for 10-15 minutes. Place on a flat baking sheet.

3 Bake blind in the oven at 190°C (375°F) mark 5 for about 20 minutes.

4 Drain the apricots, discard the bay leaves and cardamoms. Cut the apricots in half and pat dry with absorbent kitchen paper.

5 Whisk the cream, eggs and sugar together. Arrange the apricots, cut-side down, in the pastry case. Pour over the cream mixture.

6 Reduce the oven temperature to 180°C (350°F) mark 4 and bake for 35 minutes or until just set. Brown under the grill. Cool before removing the flan case.

7 Melt the apricot jam with 15 ml (1 tbsp) water over a gentle heat in a pan. Bring to the boil. Brush evenly over the warm flan. Serve warm or cold.

COOK'S TIP

Soaking the apricots with cardamoms and bay leaves gives them a delicious aromatic flavour.

FRENCH APPLE FLAN

SERVES 6

2 x quantity flan pastry (see page 327)	finely grated rind of ½ lemon
900 g (2 lb) cooking apples	30 ml (2 tbsp) Calvados or brandy
50 g (2 oz) butter or margarine	225 g (8 oz) eating apples
120 ml (9 level tbsp) apricot jam	about 30 ml (2 tbsp) lemon juice
50 g (2 oz) sugar	5 ml (1 level tsp) caster sugar

1   Roll out the pastry on a floured surface and use to line a 20 cm (8 inch) loose-based fluted flan tin placed on a baking sheet. Chill in the refrigerator for 30 minutes.
2   Bake blind in the oven at 200°C (400°F) mark 6 for 10-15 minutes, then remove paper and beans and bake for a further 5 minutes until the base is set.
3   Cut the cooking apples into quarters, core and roughly chop the flesh. Melt the butter in a saucepan and add the apples with 30 ml (2 tbsp) water. Cover the pan tightly and cook gently for about 15 minutes until soft and mushy.
4   Rub the apples through a sieve into a large clean pan. Add half the apricot jam with the sugar, lemon rind and brandy. Cook over a high heat for about 15 minutes, stirring, until all excess liquid has evaporated and the mixture is thickened.
5   Spoon the thick apple purée into the flan case and smooth the surface. Peel, quarter, core and slice the dessert apples very thinly. Arrange in an overlapping circle over the apple purée. Brush lightly with lemon juice; sprinkle with the caster sugar.
6   Return the flan to the oven and bake for a further 25-30 minutes, or until the pastry and apples are lightly coloured. Transfer to a plate. Cool for 10 minutes.
7   Gently warm the remaining jam with 15 ml (1 tbsp) lemon juice, then sieve. Brush over the top and sides of the flan. Serve warm or cold.

GLAZED NUT FLAN

SERVES 6-8

1 quantity pâte sucrée (see page 327)	25 g (1 oz) butter, melted
FOR THE FILLING	pinch of grated nutmeg
50 g (2 oz) hazelnuts	60 ml (4 level tbsp) golden syrup
25 g (1 oz) pistachio nuts	15 ml (1 level tbsp) plain flour
1 egg	
25 g (1 oz) caster sugar	75 g (3 oz) walnut pieces
grated rind and juice of 1 lemon	75 g (3 oz) Brazil nuts
	50 g (2 oz) pecan nuts

1   Roll out the pastry on a floured surface and use to line a 22 cm (8½ inch) loose-based fluted flan tin. Chill for 15 minutes.
2   Bake blind in the oven at 200°C (400°F) mark 6 for 10-12 minutes. Remove the beans and paper, then reduce the oven temperature to 180°C (350°F) mark 4 and bake for a further 10 minutes until pale golden.
3   Meanwhile to make the filling, brown the hazelnuts under a hot grill. Place in a clean tea towel and rub well to remove the skins. Dip the shelled pistachio nuts in boiling water for 1 minute. Drain and remove the skins.
4   Using an electric whisk, beat the egg and sugar together in a bowl until very thick and pale – about 5 minutes. Quickly stir in the lemon rind, melted butter, nutmeg and 30 ml (2 tbsp) of the golden syrup. Fold in the flour and finally all the nuts.
5   Spoon the nut mixture into the pastry case. Bake in the oven at 180°C (350°F) mark 4 for about 35 minutes or until golden brown and firm to the touch. Leave to cool for 10-15 minutes.
6   Heat the remaining golden syrup and 30 ml (2 tbsp) lemon juice together in a pan. Boil for 2-3 minutes until syrupy. Brush over the warm flan. Leave in the tin for 10-15 minutes before removing to a wire rack to cool. Serve warm or cold.

FUDGY NUT PIE

SERVES 8

225 g (8 oz) shortcrust pastry (see page 327)	100 ml (4 fl oz) milk
FOR THE FILLING	75 g (3 oz) corn syrup or golden syrup
50 g (2 oz) plain chocolate, broken into small pieces	5 ml (1 tsp) vanilla flavouring
50 g (2 oz) butter or margarine	1.25 ml (¼ tsp) salt
175 g (6 oz) caster sugar	3 eggs
75 g (3 oz) light soft brown sugar	100 g (4 oz) chopped mixed nuts
	icing sugar, to decorate

1   Roll out the pastry on a floured work surface and use to line a 23 cm (9 inch) flan dish or fluted flan ring placed on a baking sheet. Bake blind in the oven at 200°C (400°F) mark 6 for 10-15 minutes until set. Set aside to cool.
2   While the pastry case is cooling, put the chocolate and fat in a large heatproof bowl standing over a pan of simmering water. Heat gently until melted.
3   Remove the bowl from the pan and add the remaining ingredients, except the chopped nuts. Beat with a wooden spoon until well mixed, then stir in the nuts.
4   Pour the filling into the pastry case and bake in the oven at 180°C (350°F) mark 4 for 45-60 minutes or until puffy and golden. Dredge with icing sugar. Serve hot or cold, with ice cream.

COOK'S NOTE

Rich and nutty, this pie has a definite 'American' flavour. Corn syrup is a popular ingredient in American pies and desserts. A by-product of sweetcorn, it is similar to golden syrup but has a thinner consistency and lighter flavour. Look for it in delicatessens and large supermarkets if you want to give your pie an authentic flavour.

RIPE CHERRY TART

SERVES 8

225 g (8 oz) plain flour	FOR THE FILLING
pinch of salt	450 g (1 lb) cherries, stoned
25 g (1 oz) cornflour	2 eggs
100 g (4 oz) plus 10 ml (2 tsp) icing sugar	75 g (3 oz) ground almonds
100 g (4 oz) butter	few drops of almond flavouring
1 egg yolk	

1   Sift the flour, salt, cornflour and 10 ml (2 tsp) icing sugar into a bowl, then rub in the butter until the mixture resembles fine breadcrumbs. Add the egg yolk and 30 ml (2 tbsp) cold water and stir to bind together.
2   Knead lightly on a lightly floured surface, then roll out. Use to line a 23 cm (9 inch) fluted flan tin. Bake blind in the oven at 200°C (400°F) mark 6 for 10-15 minutes, until set.
3   Arrange the cherries in the flan case. Mix 100 g (4 oz) icing sugar with the eggs, almonds and flavouring, then pour over cherries.
4   Bake at 170°C (325°F) mark 3 for 50-60 minutes, until the top is firm and golden. Serve hot or cold.

COOK'S TIP

Baking Blind is the term used to describe the cooking of pastry cases without any filling. The pastry may be partially prebaked to be cooked for a further period when filled, or completely cooked if the filling requires no further cooking.
Cut out a piece of greaseproof paper or foil larger than the pastry case. Prick the pastry base, lay the paper or foil in the pastry case and fill with baking beans.
For partially prebaked cases, bake in the oven at 200°C (400°F) mark 6 for 10-15 minutes until the pastry is just 'set'. Remove the paper and beans, then bake for a further 5 minutes until lightly coloured. Pastry cases which need complete baking should be returned to the oven for a further 15 minutes or until pale golden brown.

YORKSHIRE CURD TART

SERVES 8-10

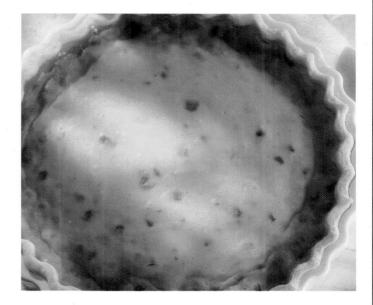

FOR THE PASTRY	FOR THE FILLING
225 g (8 oz) plain flour	450 g (1 lb) curd cheese
pinch of salt	3 eggs, beaten
150 g (5 oz) butter or block margarine	75 g (3 oz) currants
1 egg yolk	100 g (4 oz) demerara sugar
about 30 ml (2 tbsp) cold water	finely grated rind of 1 lemon

1 To make the pastry, place the flour and salt in a bowl, add 125 g (4 oz) of the fat and rub in until the mixture resembles fine breadcrumbs. Stir in the egg yolk and enough water to bind the mixture together. Form into a ball.

2 Roll out the pastry on a floured work surface. Use to line a 20 cm (8 inch) fluted flan dish or sandwich tin, then refrigerate while making the curd cheese filling.

3 Put the curd cheese in a bowl and stir in the eggs, followed by the currants, sugar and lemon rind. Melt the remaining fat and stir in until evenly mixed.

4 Pour the filling into the pastry case, place on a preheated baking sheet and bake in the oven at 190°C (375°F) mark 5 for 45 minutes or until the filling is golden and set. Serve the tart warm or cold.

OLD-FASHIONED TREACLE TART

SERVES 4-6

¾ quantity shortcrust pastry (see page 327)	finely grated rind and juice of 1 lemon
FOR THE FILLING	75 g (3 oz) fresh breadcrumbs
225 g (8 oz) golden syrup	beaten egg, to glaze

1 Roll out the pastry on a floured surface and use to line a 20 cm (8 inch) fluted flan dish. Reserve trimmings. Chill for 30 minutes.

2 Meanwhile, to make the filling, warm the golden syrup in a saucepan with the lemon rind and juice. Sprinkle the breadcrumbs evenly over the pastry base, then slowly pour in the syrup.

3 Make strips from the reserved pastry trimmings and place these over the tart in a lattice pattern, brushing the ends with water to stick them to the pastry case. Glaze with a little egg.

4 Bake in the oven at 190°C (375°F) mark 5 for about 25 minutes until the filling is just set. Serve warm.

COOK'S TIP

You may wonder why recipes for treacle tart always contain golden syrup rather than treacle. The explanation is quite simple. Treacle is the syrup which is left in the sugar refining process when the sugar has been crystallized. In the seventeenth century, when West Indian sugar cane was first refined to make sugar, treacle was unrefined and recipes for treacle tart such as this one would have used black treacle rather than syrup. It was not until the late nineteenth century that treacle was refined to make the golden syrup which is so popular today. As tastes changed, recipes which originally used treacle began to specify syrup instead.

FRESH
PEAR SHORTCAKE

SERVES 6

FOR THE SHORTCAKE	FOR THE FILLING
150 g (5 oz) self-raising flour	3 ripe large, even-sized pears, about 450 g (1 lb) total weight
25 g (1 oz) ground rice	
grated rind of 1 lemon	125 g (4 oz) full fat soft cheese
50 g (2 oz) dark soft brown sugar	
	1 egg
150 g (5 oz) butter or block margarine	few drops of almond flavouring

1 Lightly grease a 20 cm (8 inch) loose-based fluted flan tin and set aside. In a mixing bowl, stir together the flour, ground rice and lemon rind. Sieve the sugar into the bowl.
2 Rub in the butter and continue lightly kneading the mixture until it forms a dough.
3 Press the dough into the prepared tin with floured fingertips. Mark into six portions and prick well with a fork.
4 Bake in the oven at 190°C (375°F) mark 5 for 30-35 minutes until golden brown and cooked through. Leave in the tin to cool slightly.
5 Using a sharp knife, peel and halve the pears. Scoop out the cores using a teaspoon or corer.
6 Cut each pear half crossways into 3 mm (⅛ inch) slices, keeping them together at one edge. Place a sliced pear half on each portion of shortcake, fanning out the slices a little.
7 Beat together the soft cheese, egg and almond flavouring until smooth, then spoon over the pears, completely covering fruit and shortcake.
8 Bake in the oven at 180°C (350°F) mark 4 for about 40 minutes until golden. Ease the shortcake out of the tin and serve warm or cold.

WALNUT
AND HONEY TART

SERVES 6

FOR THE PASTRY	FOR THE FILLING
175 g (6 oz) plain wholemeal flour	60 ml (4 tbsp) clear honey
pinch of salt	75 g (3 oz) fresh wholemeal breadcrumbs
75 g (3 oz) butter	45 ml (3 tbsp) dark soft brown sugar
finely grated rind and juice of 1 orange	
	3 eggs
	100 g (4 oz) walnut pieces, roughly chopped

1 To make the pastry, put the flour and salt in a bowl and rub in the butter until the mixture resembles fine breadcrumbs. Stir in the orange rind and enough orange juice to bind the mixture together.
2 Roll out the pastry on a lightly floured surface and use to line a 20 cm (8 inch) fluted flan dish or tin. Bake blind at 200°C (400°F) mark 6 for 10-15 minutes, until set.
3 Mix the honey, breadcrumbs and the sugar together. Gradually beat in the eggs, one at a time, and any remaining orange juice.
4 Sprinkle the walnuts in the bottom of the pastry case and pour over the filling. Bake at 200°C (400°F) mark 6 for 20-25 minutes, until set. Cover the tart with greaseproof paper if it browns too quickly. Serve warm or cold with clotted or double cream.

BUTTERSCOTCH CREAM PIE

SERVES 6

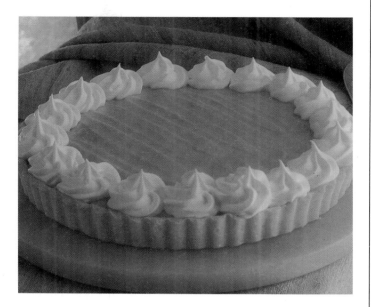

175 g (6 oz) plain flour	150 ml (¼ pint) milk
1.25 ml (¼ tsp) salt	170 ml (6 fl oz) evaporated milk
165 g (5½ oz) butter or block margarine	50 g (2 oz) dark soft brown sugar
10 ml (2 tsp) caster sugar	15 ml (1 tbsp) cornflour
5 egg yolks and 1 egg white	150 ml (5 fl oz) double cream

1 Put the flour into a bowl with half the salt. Add 100 g (4 oz) fat in pieces and rub in with the fingertips until the mixture resembles fine breadcrumbs.

2 Stir in the sugar and 1 egg yolk and draw the dough together to form a ball. Add a few drops of cold water if the dough is too dry.

3 Press the dough gently into a 20 cm (8 inch) loose-bottomed fluted flan tin or ring placed on a baking sheet. Refrigerate for 30 minutes.

4 Prick the base of the pastry case and bake blind in the oven at 200°C (400°F) mark 6 for 10 minutes. Remove the foil and beans, brush the pastry with the egg white, then return to the oven and bake for a further 10 minutes until crisp and lightly coloured. Leave to cool.

5 To make the filling, put the milk and evaporated milk in a saucepan and bring to boiling point. Put the brown sugar, cornflour, remaining butter, egg yolks and salt in a saucepan. Heat gently until the butter has melted and sugar dissolved, then gradually stir in the scalded milk.

6 Cook over gentle heat, whisking constantly until the custard is thick. Don't worry if the mixture is lumpy at first – keep whisking vigorously with a balloon whisk and it will become smooth.

7 Remove from the heat and cool slightly, then pour into the baked pastry case. Leave until cold.

8 To serve, whip the cream until stiff, then pipe on top of the pie. Chill before serving.

OLDE ENGLISH EGG-NOG PIE

SERVES 6

175 g (6 oz) flour	1.25 ml (¼ level tsp) ground nutmeg
125 g (4 oz) butter	2 eggs separated
45 ml (3 level tbsp) ground almonds	15 ml (3 level tsp) powdered gelatine
90 ml (6 level tbsp) caster sugar	45 ml (3 tbsp) rum
300 ml (½ pint) milk plus 30 ml (2 tbsp)	90 ml (6 tbsp) double cream
	grated chocolate, to decorate

1 Put the flour into a bowl. Rub the butter into the flour, then stir in the ground almonds with 45 ml (3 level tbsp) sugar. Add about 30 ml (2 tbsp) milk to bind the mixture to a soft dough.

2 Roll out the pastry and use to line a deep 20 cm (8 inch) loose-bottomed flan tin. Bake blind in the oven at 200°C (400°F) mark 6 for 10-15 minutes. Leave to cool.

3 Gently heat the milk and nutmeg in a saucepan. Beat the egg yolks, 1 egg white and remaining sugar together. Pour on the heated milk, return to the pan and cook gently, stirring, until it thickens. Do not allow the mixture to boil.

4 Soak the gelatine in the rum. Stir into the hot custard to dissolve. Allow to cool until beginning to set.

5 Whip the cream until softly stiff. Whisk the remaining egg white until stiff. Fold the cream, then the egg white into the cool, half-set custard. Turn into a flan case and refrigerate to set.

6 Remove from the flan tin and leave for 30 minutes at room temperature. Decorate with grated chocolate.

PANADE

SERVES 6-8

175 g (6 oz) butter or margarine	700 g (1½ lb) ripe pears
225 g (8 oz) plain flour	grated rind and juice of 1 large orange
large pinch of ground cinnamon	beaten egg and caster sugar, for glazing
700 g (1½ lb) sweet eating apples	

1 Rub 125 g (4 oz) butter into the flour and cinnamon until the mixture resembles fine breadcrumbs. Add enough chilled water, about 90 ml (6 tbsp), to bind to a soft paste. Wrap and refrigerate for 10 minutes.
2 On a lightly floured surface, roll the dough out thinly and line a 24 cm (9½ inch) loose-based fluted flan tin. Re-roll the excess pastry and cut into 1 cm (½ inch) wide strips. Cover and chill until required. Bake the flan blind in the oven at 200°C (400°F) mark 6 for about 20 minutes.
3 Meanwhile, peel, core and grate the apples and pears. Melt the remaining butter in a large non-stick frying pan and stir in the grated apples and pears, the grated orange rind and 45 ml (3 tbsp) orange juice.
4 Cook over a high heat, stirring constantly, until all excess moisture has evaporated and the mixture is quite dry. Spoon into the warm flan case.
5 Quickly lattice the pastry strips over the fruit mixture. Brush with beaten egg and dust with caster sugar. Bake at 200°C (400°F) mark 6 for about 20 minutes, or until golden brown and crisp.

COOK'S NOTE

The boulangeries of Provence provide wonderful fruit tarts but there are local specialities to make at home too. Panade is unusual: apples and pears are grated, cooked together with orange juice, then enclosed in pastry or dough. The origins of this recipe are not hard to trace, with so many fruit trees covering the valleys.

ROLY-POLY WITH HOT JAM SAUCE

SERVES 4

FOR THE SUETCRUST PASTRY	little milk, for brushing
175 g (6 oz) self-raising flour	FOR THE SAUCE
1.25 ml (½ level tsp) salt	45 ml (3 level tbsp) red jam
75 g (3 oz) shredded suet	finely grated rind of 1 orange
about 100 ml (32 fl oz) chilled water	10 ml (2 tsp) arrowroot
FOR THE FILLING	150 ml (¼ pint) fresh orange juice
90 ml (6 tbsp) red jam	

1 To make the suetcrust pastry, mix the flour, salt and suet together in a bowl. Using a round-bladed knife, stir in enough water to give a light elastic dough. Knead lightly until smooth.
2 Roll out the pastry on a floured work surface to a 25 x 20 cm (10 x 8 inch) oblong. Spread the jam over the pastry to 5 mm (¼ inch) of the edges. Brush edges with milk.
3 Roll up the pastry evenly like a Swiss roll, starting from one short side.
4 Place the roll, seam side down, on a sheet of greased foil measuring at least 30 x 23 cm (12 x 9 inches). Wrap the foil loosely around the roll to allow room for expansion during cooking. Seal well.
5 Place the roly-poly in the top of a steamer over a pan of boiling water and steam for 1½-2 hours, topping up the water as necessary.
6 Just before serving, make the sauce. Put the jam and orange rind in a heavy-based saucepan. Mix the arrowroot to a paste with a little of the orange juice, then stir the remaining orange juice into the pan. Heat gently until the jam has melted, then stir in the arrowroot paste and bring to the boil. Simmer until thickened, stirring constantly.
7 Unwrap the poly-poly and place on a warmed serving plate. Pour over the hot jam sauce and serve immediately.

APPLE AND BLACKBERRY TART

SERVES 6

½ quantity shortcrust pastry (see page 327)	25 g (1 oz) sultanas
450 g (1 lb) cooking apples, peeled, cored and sliced	225 g (8 oz) blackberries, or 200 g (7 oz) can blackberries, drained
50 g (2 oz) butter	2.5 ml (½ level tsp) ground cinnamon
1 egg, separated	150 ml (5 fl oz) double cream
50 g (2 oz) soft brown sugar	

1 Roll out the pastry on a lightly floured surface and use to line a 20 cm (8 inch) flan ring. Arrange the apples in the flan case.

2 Melt the butter, remove from heat and cool. Beat in the egg yolk and add the sugar, sultanas, blackberries, cinnamon and butter. Mix well together and place in the flan case.

3 Bake in the oven at 200°C (400°F) mark 6 for 30-35 minutes. Allow to cool.

4 Whip the cream until softly stiff. Whip the egg white until stiff and fold into the cream. Pile on top of the tart to serve.

SERVING SUGGESTION

Apples and blackberries are two delicious fruits which are traditionally cooked together in old-fashioned tarts and pies. Topped with a delicious creamy swirl, this lovely pudding, with a hint of cinnamon, makes a mouthwatering end to a late summer or early autumn meal.

LIME MERINGUE PIE

SERVES 6

1 quantity shortcrust pastry (see page 327)	45 ml (3 tbsp) cornflour
finely grated rind and juice of 2 limes	2 eggs, separated
75 g (3 oz) granulated sugar	knob of butter
	125 g (4 oz) caster sugar
	lime slices, to decorate

1 Roll out the pastry on a lightly floured work surface and use to line a 20 cm (8 inch) flan ring. Refrigerate for 30 minutes.

2 Bake blind in the oven at 200°C (400°F) mark 6 for 10-15 minutes.

3 Put the lime rind into a small saucepan. Strain the juice, make up to 300 ml (½ pint) with water and add to the pan with the granulated sugar. Heat gently to dissolve the sugar.

4 Blend the cornflour with 30 ml (2 tbsp) water to a smooth paste. Add some of the heated liquid and stir. Return to the pan and boil for 2 minutes, stirring all the time. Cool slightly, then beat in the egg yolks and butter. Pour into the warm pastry case.

5 Whisk the egg whites until stiff, then fold in the caster sugar. Spread a thin layer of meringue over the pie, then pipe the rest around the edge.

6 Bake in the oven at 150°C (300°F) mark 2 for about 45 minutes until the meringue is crisp and lightly browned.

7 Decorate with lime slices. Serve warm, with cream.

PINEAPPLE TARTE TATIN

SERVES 6

50 g (2 oz) caster sugar	60 ml (4 tbsp) double cream
175 g (6 oz) butter or margarine	900 g (2 lb) pineapple, peeled, cored and thinly sliced
2 egg yolks	15 ml (1 tbsp) kirsch (optional)
125 g (4 oz) self-raising flour	
125 g (4 oz) granulated sugar	mint sprigs, to decorate

1 Beat the caster sugar with 50 g (2 oz) of the butter until pale and light. Beat in the egg yolks, then fold in the flour and knead lightly together to form a smooth dough. Wrap and chill in the refrigerator for 30 minutes.

2 Melt the remaining 125 g (4 oz) butter with the granulated sugar in a small saucepan over a low heat. Bring to the boil, then simmer for 3-4 minutes, beating continuously until the mixture is smooth, dark and fudge-like. (Do not worry if the mixture separates at this stage.)

3 Take off the heat, allow to cool for 1 minute, then stir in the cream, beating until smooth. If necessary, warm gently, stirring, until completely smooth. Spoon into a shallow 22 cm (8½ inch) round non-stick sandwich tin.

4 Arrange the pineapple neatly in overlapping circles on the fudge mixture. Drizzle over the kirsch if wished.

5 Roll out the prepared pastry to a 25 cm (10 inch) round. Place over the pineapple, tucking and pushing the edges down the side of the tin. Trim off any excess pastry. Stand the tin on a baking sheet.

6 Bake in the oven at 200°C (400°F) mark 6 for about 20 minutes or until the pastry is a deep golden brown. Run the blade of a knife around the edge of the tin to loosen the pastry. Leave to cool for 2-3 minutes, then turn out onto a heatproof serving dish and place under a hot grill for 2-3 minutes to caramelize the top.

7 Decorate with mint sprigs and serve with thick yogurt, or cream.

LEMON MERINGUE PIE

SERVES 4-6

¾ quantity shortcrust pastry (see page 172)	125 g (4 oz) granulated sugar
	75 ml (5 level tbsp) cornflour
finely grated rind and juice of 2 lemons	2 eggs, separated
	75 g (3 oz) caster sugar

1 Roll out the pastry on a floured surface and use to line a 20 cm (8 inch) loose-based flan tin or fluted flan dish. Chill in the refrigerator for 30 minutes.

2 Bake blind in the oven at 200°C (400°F) mark 6 for 10-15 minutes, then remove the paper and beans and bake for a further 5 minutes until the base is firm.

3 Put the lemon rind and juice, granulated sugar and 300 ml (½ pint) water in a saucepan. Heat gently until the sugar dissolves.

4 Mix the cornflour to a smooth paste with 90 ml (6 tbsp) water and stir into the saucepan until well blended. Bring to the boil, stirring and cook for 1 minute, until thickened.

5 Cool slightly, then beat in the egg yolks, one at a time.

6 Pour the warm lemon filling into the pastry case, levelling the surface.

7 Whisk the egg whites until stiff. Whisk in half the caster sugar a little at a time, then carefully fold in the remainder.

8 Spoon the meringue on to the filling and swirl with a palette knife. The filling must be completely covered, but the meringue should not overlap the edge of the flan tin. Bake in the oven at 150°C (300°F) mark 2 for about 35 minutes. Allow to cool before serving.

RASPBERRY
AND APPLE TORTE

SERVES 8

450 g (1 lb) eating apples	225 g (8 oz) plain flour
150 g (5 oz) butter or block margarine	10 ml (2 level tsp) ground cinnamon
450 g (1 lb) raspberries, hulled	25 g (1 oz) icing sugar
65 g (2½ oz) demerara sugar	1 egg, separated
5 ml (1 tsp) lemon juice	45 ml (3 tbsp) water
	few raspberries (optional)

1 Peel, core and roughly chop the apples. Melt 25 g (1 oz) butter in a medium saucepan, then add the apples, raspberries and 50 g (2 oz) demerara sugar. Heat gently until the sugar dissolves. Increase the heat and cook, stirring, for about 10 minutes or until the apples are soft.
2 Turn the mixture into a bowl, stir in the lemon juice and cool for 30 minutes.
3 Meanwhile, sift the flour and cinnamon into a mixing bowl. Rub in the remaining butter until the mixture resembles fine breadcrumbs. Stir in the icing sugar. Mix the egg yolk with the water and stir into the pastry mixture; knead lightly.
4 Roll out two-thirds of the pastry and use to line a 23 cm (9 inch) fluted flan dish. Spoon in the raspberry and apple mixture.
5 Roll out the remaining pastry and cut into 1 cm (½ inch) wide strips long enough to make a lattice. Place over the filling and trim to fit.
6 Place on a baking sheet and bake in the oven at 200°C (400°F) mark 6 for about 15 minutes or until the pastry is set but not browned.
7 Lightly whisk the egg white and brush over the lattice; sprinkle with remaining demerara sugar.
8 Return to the oven for a further 15-20 minutes or until browned. Chill for 2-3 hours before serving. Decorate with a few raspberries, if wished.

PLUM
AND ALMOND TORTE

SERVES 8

1 quantity shortcrust pastry (see page 327)	2. 5 ml (½ tsp) almond flavouring
125 g (4 oz) butter	125 g (4 oz) self-raising flour
125 g (4 oz) caster sugar	30 ml (2 tbsp) lemon juice
1 egg, separated, plus 1 egg yolk	30 ml (2 tbsp) milk
	90 ml (6 level tbsp) plum jam
25 g (1 oz) ground almonds	25 g (1 oz) flaked almonds

1 Base-line a 22 cm (8½ inch) straight-sided sandwich tin with greaseproof paper. Roll out the pastry and use to line the tin; prick well with a fork. Bake blind in the oven at 200°C (400°F) mark 6 for 10-15 minutes until just set.
2 Ceam the butter and sugar until pale and fluffy. Gradually beat in the egg yolks one by one, then stir in the ground almonds and flavouring.
3 Fold in the flour, lemon juice and milk. Whisk one egg white and gently fold into the mixture.
4 Spread the jam over the pastry base. Spoon over the cake mixture, level the surface and sprinkle with flaked almonds.
5 Bake in the oven at 180°C (350°F) mark 4 until golden brown and firm to the touch, about 30 minutes. Cool in the tin. Serve cold.

COOK'S TIP

When rolling out pastry, dust the work surface and the rolling pin, never the pastry, with as little flour as possible. Roll the dough lightly and evenly in one direction only. Always roll away from you, rotating the pastry frequently to keep an even shape. Use light but firm strokes. Over-rolled pastry will shrink dramatically when baked.

STRAWBERRY CUSTARD FLAN

SERVES 6-8

1½ quantity flan pastry (see page 327)	2 eggs, separated
FOR THE FILLING	75 g (3 oz) caster sugar
	few drops of vanilla essence
40 g (1½ oz) cornflour	350 g (12 oz) strawberries, hulled
450 ml (¾ pint) milk	

1 Roll out the pastry on a floured work surface and use to line a 23 cm (9 inch) flan dish. Chill for 30 minutes. Prick the base of the flan.

2 Bake blind in the oven at 200°C (400°F) mark 6 for 20 minutes or until pale golden and cooked through. Cool in the dish for 30-40 minutes.

3 To make the filling, mix the cornflour to a smooth paste with a little of the milk. Mix the egg yolks with the cornflour paste.

4 Put the rest of the milk in a saucepan with the sugar and vanilla essence. Bring to the boil. Remove from the heat and pour on to the cornflour mixture. Return to the pan, then bring to the boil, stirring, and boil for 2 minutes until thickened. Cover with damp greaseproof paper and leave to cool for 30 minutes.

5 Thinly slice the strawberries into the base of the pastry case, reserving a few for decoration. Whisk the egg whites until stiff, then fold into the cold custard mixture. Smooth the custard mixture evenly over the strawberries. Chill for 1 hour until set.

6 Serve the flan decorated with the reserved strawberry slices, preferably within 2 hours of completion.

SWISS FLAN

SERVES 6-8

1 quantity pâte sucrée (see page 327)	FOR THE MERINGUE
FOR THE FILLING	3 egg whites
225 g (8 oz) granulated sugar	175 g (6 oz) caster sugar
juice of 1 lemon	30 ml (2 tbsp) redcurrant jelly or seedless raspberry jam
900 g (2 lb) dessert apples	

1 Roll out the pastry on a lightly floured work surface to a round 2.5 cm (1 inch) larger than a 23 cm (9 inch) fluted flan tin. Line the tin with the pastry, pressing it well into the flutes. Trim the edge, then prick the pastry well, all over, with a fork. Chill for 30 minutes.

2 Bake blind in the oven at 220°C (425°F) mark 7 for 20- 25 minutes until cooked and lightly browned. Cool. Reduce the temperature to 140°C (275°F) mark 1.

3 To make the filling, put the sugar and lemon juice into a saucepan with the water. Heat gently until the sugar has dissolved, bring to the boil and simmer for 5 minutes.

4 Peel, quarter, core and slice the apples about 5 mm (¼ inch) thick. Add the apples slices, in batches, to the sugar syrup and poach until just tender. Lift out with a slotted spoon and drain on absorbent kitchen paper.

5 Arrange the apple slices neatly inside the flan case.

6 To make the meringue, put the egg whites and sugar into a bowl standing over a pan of simmering water. Whisk until stiff. Remove from the heat and continue whisking until the meringue forms stiff peaks.

7 Put the meringue into a piping bag fitted with a large star nozzle, then pipe stars over the top of the apple flan.

8 Bake in the oven for 1 hour until the meringue is set, but not browned – it must remain as white as possible.

9 Put the redcurrant jelly into a small paper piping bag and cut a small hole in the tip of the bag. Pipe a small bead of jelly on the tip of every meringue star. Serve the flan warm or cold.

HAZELNUT CARTWHEEL

SERVES 8

212 g (7½ oz) packet frozen puff pastry, thawed	75 g (3 oz) hazelnuts, chopped
25 g (1 oz) butter	50 g (2 oz) raisins
25 g (1 oz) light soft brown sugar	finely grated rind of 1 lemon
1 egg, beaten	1 egg, beaten, to glaze
75 g (3 oz) plain cake crumbs	caster sugar, to dredge

1 Roll out the pastry on a lightly floured surface to a rectangle about 40 x 25 cm (16 x 10 inches). Cream the butter and sugar together until pale and fluffy, then beat in the egg and stir in the cake crumbs, hazelnuts, raisins and lemon rind. Spread the mixture over the pastry to within 5 mm (¼ inch) of the edges.
2 Roll up like a Swiss roll starting from the narrow end. Trim the ends, if necessary.
3 Place on a dampened baking sheet and curl round into a circle. Seal the ends together.
4 Snip all round the ring at 4 cm (1½ inch) intervals so the cuts come to within about 2 cm (¾ inch) of the ring's inner edge. Brush with beaten egg to glaze. Bake at 220°C (425°F) mark 7 for 25-30 minutes, until golden brown.
5 Dredge with caster sugar and serve warm.

SPICED PEAR STRUDEL

SERVES 8

75 g (3 oz) fresh white breadcrumbs	450 g (1 lb) pears, peeled, cored and sliced
150 g (5 oz) unsalted butter	4 large sheets of filo pastry
50 g (2 oz) light soft brown sugar	50 g (2 oz) blanched almonds, toasted and chopped
50 g (2 oz) sultanas	15 ml (1 tbsp) redcurrant jelly (optional)
2.5 ml (½ level tsp) ground mixed spice	icing sugar, for dusting
2.5 ml (½ level tsp) ground cinnamon	

1 Fry the breadcrumbs in 50 g (2 oz) of the butter, stirring frequently until crisp and golden. Mix together the brown sugar, sultanas, mixed spice, cinnamon and pear slices.
2 Melt remaining butter. Brush one sheet of filo pastry with a little of the melted butter. Cover with a second sheet of pastry and brush with a little more melted butter.
3 Cover the pastry with half of the fried crumbs, leaving a 5 cm (2 inch) border on all sides. Arrange half the pear mixture over the crumbs and sprinkle with half of the almonds. Dot with half of the redcurrant jelly, if using.
4 Fold the edges over the filling and brush with a little melted butter. Roll up, like a Swiss roll, starting from a long side. Place the strudel on a lightly greased baking sheet (with raised edges) and brush with melted butter.
5 Make a second strudel in the same way using the remaining ingredients.
6 Bake at 190°C (375°F) mark 5 for 35 minutes until crisp and golden, covering with foil during cooking if necessary, to prevent over-browning. Brush halfway through cooking, with butter from the baking sheet.
7 Allow the strudels to cool slightly, then sprinkle liberally with sifted icing sugar. Serve warm or cold, cut into chunky slices, with yogurt or cream.

CARAMELIZED APPLE WAFER

SERVES 6

212 g (7½ oz) packet frozen puff pastry, thawed	75 g (3 oz) butter or margarine, melted
6 small Granny Smith apples, total weight about 450-700 g (1-1½ lb)	60 ml (4 level tbsp) demerara sugar

1 Cut the pastry into two equal pieces. Roll out each half very thinly on a lightly floured work surface to a rectangle measuring about 20 x 10 cm (8 x 4 inches). Trim the edges. Place on a baking sheet.
2 Peel, halve and core the apples. Thinly slice the apple halves but not quite through to the base; the apples should still keep their shape.
3 Evenly space six halves flat side down on each pastry base. Cut each pastry base into three.
4 Brush the apple with the butter and sprinkle over the sugar.
5 Bake in the oven at 230°C (450°F) mark 8 for about 20 minutes or until the pastry is risen and golden. The apples should be quite soft and caramelized. Serve immediately with soured cream, Greek yogurt or crème fraîche.

COOK'S TIP

The richest of all the pastries, puff gives the most even rising, the most flaky effect and the crispest texture, but because of the time it takes, most people make it only occasionally. Bought puff pastry, either chilled or frozen, is very satisfactory, but remember to only roll it out to a maximum thickness of 3 mm (⅛ inch), as it rises very well.
'First rollings' are used where appearance is important. 'Second rollings' (usually the trimmings) can be used where appearance is not so important.

CLEMENTINE BISCUITS WITH APRICOT SAUCE

SERVES 6

75 g (3 oz) plain flour	drop of vanilla essence
pinch of salt	10 ml (2 tsp) brandy
2 egg whites, lightly whisked	30 ml (2 level tbsp) ground almonds
75 g (3 oz) icing sugar, sifted	150 ml (¼ pint) double cream, whipped
57g (2¼ oz) unsalted butter, melted	6-9 clementines peeled, seeded and segmented
icing sugar, for dusting	
FOR THE FILLING	FOR THE APRICOT SAUCE
65 ml (2½ fl oz) milk	50 g (2 oz) sugar
2.5 ml (½ tsp) cornflour	225 g (8 oz) dried apricots, soaked overnight
1 egg yolk	
20-25 g (¾-1 oz) caster sugar	squeeze of lemon juice

1 To make the biscuits, mix flour, salt, egg whites and icing sugar together in a bowl. Stir in the melted butter.
2 Spoon the mixture in 12 equal rounds, spaced a little way apart on lined and greased baking sheets.
3 Bake in the oven at 180°C (350°F) mark 4 for about 10 minutes until light golden. Leave to cool on a wire rack.
4 To make the filling, heat milk to boiling point in a pan. Blend the cornflour with the egg yolk, then stir in the hot milk. Pour into a pan and cook over a low heat, stirring, until the sauce thickens. Remove from the heat and stir in the sugar, vanilla, brandy and ground almonds.
5 Cover and leave to cool. When cold, fold in the cream.
6 To make the sauce, dissolve the sugar in about 60 ml (4 tbsp) water in a pan. Add the drained apricots and lemon juice, then simmer until soft. Purée in a blender or food processor, then leave to cool. Chill.
7 To assemble the dessert, place 6 biscuits on 6 plates. Cover with the filling, then top with clementine segments. Place the remaining biscuits on top and dust with icing sugar. Score with a hot skewer and surround with the apricot sauce to serve.

APPLE AND HAZELNUT LAYER

SERVES 8

75 g (3 oz) hazelnuts, shelled	15 ml (1 tbsp) apricot jam or marmalade
75 g (3 oz) butter	grated rind of 1 lemon
45 ml (3 level tbsp) caster sugar	15 ml (1 level tbsp) candied peel, chopped
115 g (4½ oz) plain flour	30 ml (2 level tbsp) currants
pinch of salt	30 ml (2 level tbsp) sultanas
450 g (1 lb) Cox's apples, peeled, cored and sliced	icing sugar, whipped cream and hazelnuts, to decorate

1 Cut out two 20 cm (8 inch) circles of greaseproof paper. Reserve 8 nuts and finely chop the remainder.
2 Cream the butter and sugar until pale and fluffy. Stir in the flour, salt and chopped nuts, then form into a ball and chill for 30 minutes.
3 Put the apples in a saucepan with the jam and lemon rind and cook over a low heat for 5 minutes, until soft. Add the candied peel and dried fruit and simmer for 5 minutes.
4 Divide the pastry in half, place on the sheets of greaseproof paper and roll out into two circles. Transfer to greased baking sheets.
5 Bake at 190°C (375°F) mark 5 for 7-10 minutes, until light brown. Cut one circle into 8 triangles while warm. Leave to cool.
6 Just before serving, place the complete circle on a serving plate and cover with the apple mixture. Arrange the triangles on top. Dust with icing sugar, pipe cream on top and decorate with hazelnuts.

ECLAIRS

MAKES 12

FOR THE CHOUX PASTRY	FOR THE FILLING AND TOPPING
65 g (2½ oz) plain or strong white flour	300 ml (10 fl oz) double cream
50 g (2 oz) butter or block margarine	125 g (4 oz) plain chocolate
150 ml (¼ pint) water	
2 eggs, lightly beaten	

1 Sift the flour on to a plate or piece of paper. Put the fat and water together in a saucepan, heat gently until the fat has melted, then bring to the boil. Remove the pan from the heat. Tip the flour at once into the hot liquid. Beat thoroughly with a wooden spoon.
2 Continue beating the mixture until it is smooth and forms a ball in the centre of the pan (take care not to overbeat or the mixture will become fatty). Leave the mixture to cool for 1-2 minutes.
3 Beat in the eggs a little at a time, adding just enough to give a piping consistency. It is important to beat vigorously at this stage to trap in as much air as possible.
4 Dampen a baking sheet. Put the choux pastry into a piping bag fitted with a medium plain nozzle and pipe 9 cm (3½ inches) lengths on to the baking sheet. Trim with a wet knife.
5 Bake in the oven at 200°C (400°F) mark 6 for about 35 minutes, until crisp and golden.
6 Make a slit down the side of each bun with a sharp, pointed knife to release the steam, then transfer to a wire rack and leave for 20-30 minutes to cool completely.
7 Just before serving, whip the double cream until stiff and use it to fill the éclairs.
8 Break the chocolate into a bowl and place over simmering water. Stir until melted. Pour into a wide shallow bowl. Dip in the tops of the filled éclairs, drawing each one across the surface of the chocolate to coat evenly.

MINCE PIES

1 quantity shortcrust pastry (see page 327)	icing or caster sugar, for dusting
350-450 g (12 oz-1 lb) mincemeat	

1 Roll out the pastry on a floured surface to about 3 mm (⅛ inch) thickness.
2 Cut out about 20 rounds with a 7.5 cm (3 inch) fluted cutter and 20 smaller rounds with a 5.5 cm (2¼ inch) fluted cutter.
3 Line 6 cm (2½ inch) patty tins with the larger rounds and fill with mincemeat. Dampen the edges of the small rounds with water and place firmly on top. Make a small slit in each top.
4 Bake in the oven at 220°C (425°F) mark 7 for 15-20 minutes, until light golden brown. Leave to cool on a wire rack. Serve dusted with sugar.

VARIATION

Puff Pastry Mince Pies
Mince pies can be made using a 368 g (13 oz) packet puff pastry. Roll out the pastry to 3 mm (⅛ inch) thickness. Cut 16 rounds with a 6 cm (2½ inch) cutter. Re-roll trimmings; cut another 16 rounds to use for the bases.
Place the bases on a dampened baking sheet. Put a heaped 5 ml (1 tsp) mincemeat on each and dampen the pastry edges. Cover with the remaining rounds and press the edges lightly together; glaze with beaten egg. Bake in the oven at 230°C (450°F) mark 8 for about 20 minutes.

FRESH FRUIT TARTLETS

2 x quantity pâte sucrée pastry (see page 327)	125 g (4 oz) green grapes, halved and seeded
300 ml (½ pin) crème pâtissière (see page 327)	2 kiwi fruit, peeled and sliced
125 g (4 oz) strawberries, sliced	FOR THE APRICOT GLAZE
	225 g (8 oz) apricot conserve
125 g (4 oz) raspberries	15 ml (1 tbsp) kirsch
125 g (4 oz) black grapes, halved and seeded	FOR THE REDCURRANT GLAZE
	125 g (4 oz) redcurrant jelly

1 Roll out the pastry on a lightly floured surface and cut out twelve 12 cm (5 inch) circles with a plain cutter. Use to line twelve 10 cm (4 inch) tartlet tins. Trim the edges and prick the base of each tartlet with a fork, then place the lined tins on baking sheets and chill for at least 30 minutes.
2 Bake blind in the oven at 200°C (400°F) mark 6 for 20-25 minutes until very lightly browned. Allow the cases to cool a little in their tins, then carefully transfer to a wire rack to cool.
3 To make the apricot glaze, put the jam and kirsch in a saucepan and heat gently until softened, then simmer for 1 minute. Sieve, then brush evenly over the inside of each pastry case. Reserve the remaining glaze.
4 Divide the crème pâtissière equally between the pastry cases and spread it evenly. Arrange the fruit in the pastry cases.
5 Reheat the remaining apricot glaze until boiling, then carefully brush it over the green grapes and the kiwi fruit to glaze them evenly. Heat the redcurrant jelly until boiling, then carefully brush it over the strawberries, raspberries and black grapes. Serve as soon as possible.

VARIATION
Sprinkle the glazed tartlets with finely chopped nuts or a few toasted almonds.

FRUIT DESSERTS

Make the most of flavourful fresh fruits in season with these delicious recipes. Refreshing fruit salads, tangy fruit jellies and light, creamy mousses are perfect for summer days. Sustaining steamed puddings and crumbles will satisfy winter appetites.

FRUDITES

SERVES 6

2 crisp eating apples	juice of 1 lemon
2 bananas	FOR THE DIP
225 g (8 oz) apricots, stoned	150 ml (¼ pint) double cream
175 g (6 oz) black or green grapes, seeded	150 ml (¼ pint) soured cream
225 g (8 oz) strawberries	30 ml (2 tbsp) icing sugar, sifted

1 To make the dip, whip the two creams and icing sugar together in a bowl until standing in soft peaks. Pipe or spoon into six individual dishes.
2 Quarter and core the apples, but do not peel them. Peel the bananas and cut into 4 cm (1½ inch) chunks.
3 Arrange the fruit on individual serving plates and sprinkle immediately with lemon juice to prevent discoloration.
4 Place the dishes of cream dip next to the fruit and serve immediately. Use fingers or small fondue forks to dunk the fruit into the cream dip.

THREE FRUIT SALAD

SERVES 8

50 g (2 oz) granulated sugar	1 pineapple, weighing about 1.1 kg (2½ lb)
15 ml (1 tbsp) lemon juice	225 g (8 oz) black grapes
15 ml (1 tbsp) kirsch	4 kiwi fruit

1 Put the sugar in a heavy-based saucepan with 150 ml (¼ pint) water. Heat gently until the sugar has dissolved, then bring to the boil and bubble for 2 minutes. Remove from the heat, stir in the lemon juice and kirsch, then set aside to cool.
2 Prepare the pineapple. With a sharp knife, cut off the leafy top and discard. Cut the pineapple into 1 cm (½ inch) pieces. Cut off the skin and dig out the 'eyes' with the tip of the knife. Cut out the core from each slice with an apple corer or small biscuit cutter. Cut the flesh into chunks.
3 Wash and dry the grapes, then halve. Remove the pips by flicking them out with the point of a sharp knife.
4 Peel the kiwi fruit using a potato peeler or sharp knife, then slice the flesh thinly.
5 Stir the prepared fruits into the syrup, cover and chill well in the refrigerator before serving.

INDIAN FRUIT SALAD

SERVES 6-8

3 ripe peaches	5 ml (1 level tsp) cumin seeds, dry fried
2 ripe guavas	30 ml (2 tbsp) lemon or lime juice
2 ripe bananas	pinch of cayenne
45 ml (3 tbsp) caster sugar	mint sprigs, to decorate

1 To skin the peaches, plunge them into a bowl of boiling water, leave for 30 seconds, then remove the skins.
2 Cut the skinned peaches in half and remove the stones. Slice the peach flesh thinly and place in a serving bowl.
3 Cut the guavas in half, scoop out the seeds and discard them. Peel the halved guavas, then slice them neatly and add to the peaches in the bowl.
4 Peel the bananas, cut into chunks, then mix carefully with the peaches, guavas and remaining ingredients. Serve immediately, decorated with sprigs of mint.

COOK'S TIP

Fresh guavas are available at specialist greengrocers, Indian stores and larger supermarkets. Guavas are a tropical fruit, originally from South America, with a pretty cream-pink skin. The flesh has a delicately scented aroma and a most delicious flavour. The seeds in the centre are not edible and should be removed before serving the fruit.

SPICED DRIED FRUIT COMPOTE

SERVES 4

15 ml (1 level tbsp) jasmine tea	100 g (4 oz) dried prunes, soaked overnight, drained and stoned
2.5 ml (½ level tsp) ground cinnamon	100 g (4 oz) dried apple rings
1.25 ml (¼ level tsp) ground cloves	150 ml (¼ pint) dry white wine
300 ml (½ pint) boiling water	50 g (2 oz) sugar
100 g (4 oz) dried apricots, soaked overnight, drained	toasted flaked almonds, to decorate

1 Put the tea, cinnamon and cloves in a bowl; pour in the boiling water. Leave for 20 minutes.
2 Put the dried fruit in a saucepan, then strain in the tea and spice liquid. Add the wine and sugar; heat gently until the sugar has dissolved.
3 Simmer for 20 minutes until tender, then cover and leave for 1-2 hours until cold.
4 Turn the compote into a serving bowl and chill for at least 2 hours. Sprinkle with almonds just before serving.

AUTUMN COMPOTE

SERVES 6-8

225 g (8 oz) granulated sugar	450 g (1 lb) dessert apples, such as Cox or Russet
juice of 1 lemon	
450 g (1 lb) small ripe, but firm pears	450 g (1 lb) Victoria plums, skinned and stoned

1 To make the sugar syrup, put the sugar, lemon juice and 300 ml (½ pint) cold water in a saucepan. Heat very gently until the sugar has completely dissolved. Bring to the boil and boil the syrup for 1 minute.
2 Thinly peel the pears, cut into half and remove the centre core (if only large pears are available, cut the pears into quarters). Add the pears to the syrup and cook very gently for about 10-15 minutes until barely tender.
3 Meanwhile core the apples. Cut the apples into halves, then cut into slices across the halves. Add the apple slices to the pan and cook for about 5 minutes until the apple slices are just tender. Add the plums and cook for a further 5 minutes.
4 Carefully transfer the fruits and syrup to a serving bowl, taking care not to break up the fruit. Serve hot or cold, with yogurt or cream if desired.

COOK'S TIP

Select very small pears for this compote. Lemon juice added to the syrup prevents the pears and apples discolouring, and adds a tangy flavour.

SUMMER CURRANT COMPOTE

SERVES 6

50-75 g (2-3 oz) granulated sugar	pared rind and juice of 1 medium orange
225 g (8 oz) blackcurrants, stalks removed	30 ml (2 tbsp) honey
450 g (1 lb) redcurrants, stalks removed	350 g (12 oz) strawberries, hulled and sliced

1 Dissolve the sugar in 150 ml (¼ pint) water in a pan. Boil for 1 minute. (Alternatively, microwave on HIGH for 3 minutes, stirring frequently. Continue to microwave on HIGH for 1 minute.)
2 Add the currants and orange rind and simmer until the fruits are just beginning to soften – about 1 minute only. (If cooking in the microwave, microwave on HIGH for 1-2 minutes or until beginning to soften.)
3 Carefully transfer the fruits and syrup to a serving bowl. Stir in the honey and leave to cool.
4 Mix in the orange juice, cover and chill well.
5 Just before serving, stir the sliced strawberries into the compote.

COOK'S TIP

Compotes are mixtures of fruits cooked in sugar syrup, which can be served hot or cold. The syrup may be flavoured with spices or with orange and lemon rind, but the fruits, being quite highly flavoured themselves, require little or no extra flavouring. Hot compotes make perfect desserts for the winter, not only because they are warming, but also because they are full of vitamins. Chilled compotes will keep well for up to a week in the refrigerator.

STRAWBERRIES WITH RASPBERRY SAUCE

SERVES 6

900 g (2 lb) small strawberries	450 g (1 lb) raspberries
	50 g (2 oz) icing sugar

1 Hull the strawberries and place them in individual serving dishes.
2 Purée the raspberries in a blender or food processor until just smooth, then work through a nylon sieve into a bowl to remove the pips.
3 Sift the icing sugar over the bowl of raspberry purée, then whisk in until evenly incorporated. Pour over the strawberries. Chill in the refrigerator for at least 30 minutes before serving.

COOK'S TIP

Freshly picked raspberries freeze successfully (unlike strawberries which tend to lose texture and shape due to their high water content). If you have raspberries which are slightly overripe or misshapen, the best way to freeze them is as a purée; this takes up less space in the freezer and is immensely useful for making quick desserts and sauces at the last minute. For this recipe, for example, you can freeze the purée up to 12 months in advance, then it will only take minutes to assemble the dessert after thawing the purée.

AMARETTI STUFFED PEACHES

SERVES 4

4 yellow peaches, skinned	25 g (1 oz) butter
50 g (2 oz) Amaretti or macaroons	25 g (1 oz) sugar
1 egg yolk	150 ml (¼ pint) dry white wine

1 Lightly grease an ovenproof dish.
2 Cut the peaches in half and carefully ease out the stones. Make the hollows in the peaches a little deeper with a sharp-edged teaspoon and reserve the removed flesh.
3 Crush the macaroons and mix them with the reserved peach flesh, the egg yolk, butter and 15 g (½ oz) of the sugar.
4 Use this mixture to stuff the hollows of the peach halves, mounding the filling slightly. Place the peaches in the prepared ovenproof dish and sprinkle with the rest of the sugar. Pour the white wine over and around the peaches.
5 Bake in the oven at 180°C (350°F) mark 4 for 25-30 minutes or until tender. (Alternatively, arrange around the edge of a large shallow dish, cover and microwave on HIGH for 3-5 minutes or until tender. Leave to stand, covered, for 5 minutes.) Serve hot or cold.

COOK'S TIP

Amaretti are almond macaroons made in Italy. They are available at Italian delicatessens, both in boxes and individually wrapped in tissue paper. Amaretti are delicious served with coffee and liqueurs at the end of a meal. If you cannot find them, use shop bought or home-made macaroons instead.

WHISKY MARINATED GRAPES

SERVES 6

350 g (12 oz) black grapes	45 ml (3 tbsp) clear honey
350 g (12 oz) green grapes	5 ml (1 tsp) lemon juice
30 ml (2 tbsp) whisky	

1   Wash the grapes, drain well and dry with absorbent kitchen paper.
2   Cut the grapes carefully in half lengthways, then ease out the pips with the point of a knife.
3   In a large mixing bowl, stir together the whisky, honey and lemon juice. Add the grapes and stir well. Cover and leave in a cool place (not the refrigerator) to marinate for at least 4 hours, preferably overnight.
4   Spoon into a serving dish and chill in the refrigerator for 30 minutes before serving. Serve with yogurt or cream.

COOK'S TIP

When choosing grapes for eating, avoid fruit which is shiny; fresh grapes should have a powdery whitish bloom on their skin. For this recipe, try to buy the seedless green grapes, which will save you time on preparation.

RØDGRØD

SERVES 4-6

450 g (1 lb) redcurrants or blackcurrants, stalks removed	100-175 g (4-6 oz) caster sugar
450 g (1 lb) raspberries or strawberries, hulled, or cherries, stoned	TO DECORATE whipped cream mint sprigs
30 ml (2 tbsp) arrowroot	

1   Place the currants and 60 ml (4 tbsp) water in a saucepan. Cover and simmer gently for about 20 minutes or until really soft. Leave to cool.
2   Meanwhile, purée half of the berries in a blender or food processor until smooth, then press through a nylon sieve.
3   Blend a little of the purée with the arrowroot. Put the rest into a pan and bring slowly to the boil. Stir into the blended mixture, then return it all to the pan. Bring to the boil again, cook for 4-5 minutes and sweeten to taste. Leave to cool for 10 minutes. Stir in the cooked currants and the remaining raspberries, strawberries or cherries.
4   Pour the Rødgrød into individual glasses and chill for 30 minutes. Top with whipped cream and mint sprigs just before serving.

COOK'S TIP

Rødgrød is a Danish dessert which essentially is a thick fruit soup. It is always made with fresh soft summer fruit, depending on what is available. An important point to remember is to mix at least two fruits together to provide good flavour and colour. In Russia, it is known as Kisel.

BOOZY BANANA

15 g (½ oz) butter or margarine	30 ml (2 tbsp) sherry
15 ml (1 tbsp) soft brown sugar	1.25 ml (¼ level tsp) ground cinnamon
30 ml (2 tbsp) freshly squeezed orange juice	1 banana
	orange twist, to decorate (optional)

1   Melt the butter in a heavy-based frying pan. Add the remaining ingredients, except the banana. Heat gently, stirring, until the sugar has dissolved.

2   Peel the banana, then cut in half lengthways. Place in the pan and cook over gentle heat for about 10 minutes until tender. Baste the banana frequently with the sauce and turn the pieces over once during cooking. Serve hot, decorated with an orange twist, if liked.

SERVING SUGGESTION

Serve with chilled cream or vanilla ice cream. Alternatively, if you prefer the combination of sweet and tart flavours, serve with Greek yogurt, Quark or fromage frais.

PLUM CROUTE

1 large slice of white bread	25 g (1 oz) demerara sugar
15 g (½ oz) butter or margarine, melted	1.25 ml (½ level tsp) ground cinnamon
2 ripe red plums, eg Victoria	

1   Cut the crusts off the slice of bread and discard. Brush both sides of the bread with the melted butter, making sure the bread is coated right to the edges.

2   Place the bread in an individual Yorkshire pudding tin, pressing it down well, but leaving the corners protruding over the edge.

3   Bake the croûte in the oven at 200°C (400°F) mark 6 for 15-20 minutes until crisp and golden brown.

4   Meanwhile, halve and stone the plums, then place in a pan with the sugar and cinnamon. Sprinkle in 5-10 ml (1-2 tsp) water, then cook gently for about 5 minutes until the plums are tender and juicy but still retaining their shape.

5   When the croûte is cooked, transfer to a serving plate. Spoon the plums in the centre and serve immediately, with chilled cream or thick Greek yogurt.

PEARS
IN RED WINE

SERVES 4

4 large firm Comice pears	50 g (2 oz) caster sugar
25 g (1 oz) blanched almonds, split in half	300 ml (½ pint) red wine
	2 cloves

1 Peel the pears, leaving the stalks on. Spike the pears with the almond halves.

2 Put the sugar, wine and cloves in a saucepan just large enough to hold the pears and heat gently until the sugar has dissolved. Add the pears, standing them upright in the pan. Cover and simmer gently for about 15 minutes until the pears are just tender. Baste them from time to time with the liquid. (Alternatively, put the sugar, wine and cloves in a bowl and microwave on HIGH for 3-4 minutes until boiling, stirring occasionally. Add the pears, cover and microwave on HIGH for 8-10 minutes until the pears are tender.)

3 Using a slotted spoon, transfer the pears to a serving dish. Boil the syrup in the pan until the liquid is reduced by half. (If cooking in the microwave, uncover and cook on HIGH for 10 minutes or until reduced by half.)

4 Pour the wine syrup over the pears. Serve hot or cold with thick natural yogurt or clotted cream.

VARIATION

Use medium dry cider in place of the red wine.

POIRES
BELLE HELENE

SERVES 6

100 g (4 oz) sugar	225 g (8 oz) plain chocolate, broken into pieces
900 ml (1½ pints) water	60 ml (4 tbsp) orange-flavoured liqueur
thinly pared rind and juice of 2 oranges	orange slices, to decorate
6 cooking pears (preferably Conference)	

1 Put the sugar, water and half the orange rind in a large heavy-based saucepan and heat gently, without stirring, until the sugar has dissolved.

2 Meanwhile, peel the pears quickly (to prevent discoloration), leaving the stalks on. Cut out the cores from the bottom and level them so that the pears will stand upright.

3 Stand the pears in the syrup, cover the pan and simmer gently for 20 minutes or until tender. Remove from the heat and leave to cool, covered tightly. Spoon the syrup over the pears occasionally during cooling.

4 Meanwhile, make the decoration. Cut the remaining orange rind into thin matchstick julienne strips. Blanch in boiling water for 2 minutes, then drain and immediately refresh under cold running water. Leave to drain on absorbent kitchen paper.

5 Make the chocolate sauce. Put the chocolate and liqueur in a heatproof bowl standing over a pan of gently simmering water Heat gently until the chocolate melts.

6 Remove the pears from the syrup, stand on a large serving dish, or 6 individual dishes and chill for 2 hours. Discard the orange rind from the syrup. Stir the melted chocolate into 150 ml (¼ pint) of the syrup with the orange juice, then slowly bring to the boil, stirring constantly. Simmer, stirring, until the sauce is thick and syrupy.

7 To serve, pour the hot chocolate sauce over the cold pears and sprinkle with the orange julienne. Decorate with orange slices and serve immediately.

ORANGES IN CARAMEL

SERVES 6

8 medium juicy oranges	30 ml (2 tbsp) Grand Marnier or other orange-flavoured liqueur
225 g (8 oz) caster sugar	

1 Thinly pare the rind from half the oranges and cut into very thin julienne strips. Place in a small saucepan and cover with water. Cover the pan and cook for 5 minutes until tender. Drain and rinse under cold water.

2 Cut away the pith from the oranges and both rind and pith from the four remaining oranges.

3 Slice the orange flesh into rounds, reserving any juice and discarding pips; arrange in a serving dish. (If liked, the orange rounds can be reassembled in the shape of oranges and secured with wooden cocktail sticks.)

4 Place the sugar and 300 ml (½ pint) water in a saucepan and heat gently until the sugar has dissolved. Bring to the boil and boil until the syrup is caramel coloured.

5 Remove the pan from the heat, carefully add 45 ml (3 tbsp) water and return it to a low heat to dissolve the caramel. Add the reserved orange juice and the liqueur.

6 Leave the caramel syrup to cool for 10 minutes, then pour over the oranges. Top with the julienne strips. Chill in the refrigerator for 2-3 hours, turning the oranges occasionally.

STUFFED FIGS

SERVES 8

225 g (8 oz) ricotta cheese, at room temperature	16 ripe fresh figs
150 ml (¼ pint) double or whipping cream	fig or vine leaves and rose petals, to serve (optional)
few drops of almond extract or rose water	

1 Beat the ricotta cheese in a bowl until softened. Whip the cream in another bowl until just standing in soft peaks, then fold into the ricotta, with almond extract or rose water according to taste.

2 With a sharp knife, cut a cross in each fig at the top (stem end). Continue cutting down almost to the base of the fig, but keeping the fruit whole. With your fingers, gently prise the four 'petals' of each fig apart, to allow room for the filling.

3 Spoon the ricotta mixture into a piping bag fitted with a large rosette nozzle and pipe into the centre of each fig. Chill in the refrigerator until serving time.

4 To serve, place the figs on individual serving plates. Alternatively arrange fig or vine leaves decoratively over a flat serving platter, place the stuffed figs on top and scatter rose petals around. Serve chilled.

COOK'S TIP

Ricotta, a soft Italian cheese, can be bought in tubs or loose by the kg (lb) at large supermarkets and Italian delicatessens. Made from the whey of sheep's or cow's milk, depending on the region where it is produced, it is mild in flavour, yet delightfully rich and creamy. If you are unable to obtain it, curd cheese is the best alternative.

MOCK FRUIT BRULEES

SERVES 6

6 large ripe peaches	30 ml (2 tbsp) almond-flavoured liqueur or a few drops of almond essence
30 ml (2 tbsp) lemon juice	
150 ml (¼ pint) double cream	150 ml (¼ pint) soured cream
30 ml (2 tbsp) icing sugar	90-120 ml (6-8 tbsp) demerara sugar

1 To skin the peaches, dip them in a bowl of boiling water for 30 seconds, then drain and plunge immediately into a bowl of cold water. Carefully peel off the skins.
2 Cut the peaches in half. Twist them to separate and remove the stones. Thinly slice the flesh. Toss in lemon juice.
3 Whip the double cream with the icing sugar until it just holds its shape. Gradually whisk in the liqueur or almond essence. Fold in the soured cream and peach slices.
4 Divide the mixture equally between six 150 ml (¼ pint) ramekin dishes. Cover and chill in the refrigerator overnight.
5 Sprinkle the demerara sugar evenly on top of each ramekin, to completely cover the peaches and cream mixture. Place under a preheated hot grill for 3-4 minutes until the sugar becomes caramelised. Chill thoroughly in the refrigerator for at least 1 hour before serving.

PINEAPPLE AND BANANA FLAMBE

SERVES 6-8

1 medium pineapple	125 g (4 oz) demerara sugar
900 g (2 lb) firm bananas	45 ml (3 tbsp) lemon juice
125 g (4 oz) dried figs	2.5 ml (½ level tsp) ground mixed spice
50 g (2 oz) butter or margarine	60 ml (4 tbsp) dark rum

1 Slice the pineapple into 1 cm (½ inch) pieces. Snip off the skin and cut the flesh into chunks, discarding the core.
2 Peel and thickly slice the bananas into the bottom of a shallow ovenproof dish; spoon the pineapple on top.
3 Cut the figs into coarse shreds and scatter over the fruit. Then put the butter, sugar, strained lemon juice and spice together in a saucepan and heat until well blended; pour over the prepared fruit.
4 Cover tightly and bake in the oven at 200°C (400°F) mark 6 for 25 minutes until the fruit is tender.
5 Heat the rum gently in a small saucepan, remove from the heat and ignite with a match. Pour immediately over the fruit and bring the dish to the table while still flaming.

SERVING SUGGESTION

For a special occasion, you can serve this dessert in the pineapple shells. Any mixture which will not fit into the pineapple shells can be served separately in a fruit bowl.

To make two pineapple shells from one pineapple: with a large sharp knife, slice the pineapple in half lengthways, cutting right through the crown and base. Insert the blade of a long, serrated knife into the flesh of one pineapple half, about 5 mm (¼ inch) in from the edge of the shell, and cut all around the inside. Cut through the flesh in parallel lines, first lengthways and then crossways to produce squares of flesh (take care not to cut through the skin at the base). Scoop out the flesh with a sharp-edged teaspoon. Repeat with the second pineapple half, then turn both shells upside-down and leave to drain before filling.

BRANDIED CHERRIES

SERVES 8

450 g (1 lb) cherries, washed	1 cinnamon stick
225 g (8 oz) sugar	about 150 ml (¼ pint) brandy

1 Prick the cherries all over with a fine skewer or darning needle.

2 Make a light syrup by dissolving 100 g (4 oz) of the sugar in 300 ml (½ pint) water. Add the cherries and cinnamon stick and poach gently for 4-5 minutes.

3 Remove the pan from the heat and drain the cherries, reserving the syrup but removing the cinnamon stick. Cool, then arrange the fruit in small sterilized jars.

4 Add the remaining sugar to the reserved syrup and dissolve it slowly. Bring to the boil and boil to 110°C (230°F), then allow to cool.

5 Measure the syrup and add an equal quantity of brandy. Pour over the cherries. Cover and store in a cool, dry place for 2-3 weeks before eating.

6 Serve with thick yogurt or cream.

SPICED FRUIT WAFERS

SERVES 8

FOR THE WAFERS	pared rind and juice of 1 orange
75 g (3 oz) butter, softened	6 fresh peaches, stoned and sliced
75 g (3 oz) caster sugar	225 g (8 oz) redcurrants
few drops of vanilla flavouring	225 g (8 oz) strawberries
pinch of grated nutmeg	300 ml (½ pint) double cream, whipped
2 egg whites	150 ml (5 fl oz) Greek-style yogurt
75 g (3 oz) plain flour	icing sugar for dusting
FOR THE FILLING	
175 g (6 oz) caster sugar	
1 cinnamon stick	

1 To make the wafers, cream together the butter and sugar until very soft and light. Add the vanilla flavouring and nutmeg. Gradually beat in the lightly whisked egg whites. Fold in the flour.

2 Drop heaped teaspoons of the mixture onto greased baking sheets allowing space to spread. Bake at 200°C (400°F) mark 6 for 6-7 minutes or until set and pale golden around the edges. Remove from the baking sheet and cool on a wire rack.

3 To make the filling, place the caster sugar, cinnamon and orange rind in a saucepan with 300 ml (½ pint) water over a low heat until the sugar has dissolved. Bring to the boil, bubble for 2 minutes then add the peaches and redcurrants. Simmer for 2-3 minutes or until just tender. With a slotted spoon, transfer the fruit to a bowl and add the strawberries.

4 Return the liquid to the heat, bring to the boil and bubble for 4-5 minutes or until reduced and syrupy. Add the strained orange juice and cool.

5 Mix the cream with the yogurt. Layer up the wafers with the cream and spiced fruits. Dust the top with icing sugar to serve.

WILD STRAWBERRY AND CHAMPAGNE JELLY

SERVES 6

100 g (4 oz) caster sugar	450 ml (¾ pint) pink champagne
pared rind and juice of 1 lemon	175 g (6 oz) Alpine strawberries or frais du bois
20 ml (4 level tsp) powdered gelatine	edible flowers or mint sprigs, to decorate

1 Put the sugar, lemon rind and 300 ml (½ pint) water in a saucepan. Heat gently until the sugar has dissolved. (Alternatively, microwave on HIGH for 3 minutes or until dissolved, stirring occasionally.) Leave to cool.

2 Sprinkle the gelatine over the lemon juice in a small bowl and leave to soak for 2-3 minutes. Place the bowl over a pan of simmering water and stir until dissolved. (Alternatively, microwave on HIGH for 30 seconds or until dissolved.)

3 Mix the sugar syrup with the dissolved gelatine and the champagne. Divide most of the strawberries between six champagne flutes. Carefully pour over a little of the jelly and chill until set. When the jelly has set, pour over the remaining jelly. Chill until set.

4 Decorate with the reserved strawberries and edible flowers or mint sprigs.

COOK'S TIP

The Alpine strawberry is a version of the rare wild strawberry, that is now cultivated in France. Also known as frais du bois, these deliciously flavoured baby strawberries do not need to be hulled before they are eaten.

LAYERED FRUIT TERRINE

SERVES 6

FOR THE JELLY	200 g (7 oz) small green seedless grapes
30 ml (6 level tsp) powdered gelatine	FOR THE SAUCE
450 ml (¾ pint) clear grape or apple juice	225 g (8 oz) fresh raspberries, hulled, or frozen, thawed
275 g (10 oz) small even-sized strawberries, hulled	icing sugar, to taste
200 g (7 oz) small black seedless grapes	lemon juice
	dash of kirsch (optional)
4 large oranges, peeled, segmented and well drained	TO DECORATE
	few strawberries
	mint sprigs

1 To make the jelly, sprinkle the gelatine over 150 ml (¼ pint) of the grape juice in a small bowl and leave to soak for 2-3 minutes. Place the bowl over a pan of simmering water and stir until dissolved. (Alternatively, microwave on HIGH for 30 seconds or until dissolved.) Stir the dissolved gelatine into the remaining juice and mix well.

2 Pour a 5 mm (¼ inch) layer of jelly into the base of a 750 ml (1¼ pint) non-stick (or non-corrosive) loaf tin or mould. Chill until set.

3 Arrange the whole strawberries in a tightly packed layer over the set jelly. Arrange the black grapes in a thick layer over the strawberries, followed by the oranges, then the green grapes. Slowly pour the fruit jelly over the fruit until it just covers the final layer. Tap the mould very lightly on the work surface to remove any air bubbles. Chill for at least 4 hours or until completely set.

4 To make the sauce, purée the raspberries in a blender or food processor until smooth. Press through a sieve if liked, and add sugar and lemon juice to taste. Stir in the liqueur, if using. Cover and chill.

5 To serve, dip the tin or mould in a bowl of lukewarm water for 10 seconds and invert on to a flat plate. Decorate with strawberries and mint. Serve with the sauce.

RHUBARB AND ORANGE FOOL

SERVES 6

450 g (1 lb) rhubarb	300 ml (½ pint) whipping cream
grated rind and juice of 1 orange	5 ml (1 tsp) orange flower water
pinch of ground cinnamon	shredded orange rind, to decorate
25-50 g (1-2 oz) sugar	

1 Chop the rhubarb into 2.5 cm (1 inch) pieces, discarding the leaves and the white ends of the stalks.
2 Put the rhubarb, orange rind, juice, cinnamon and sugar into a pan. Cover and cook gently for about 15 minutes.
3 Uncover and boil rapidly for 10 minutes, stirring frequently, until the mixture becomes a thick purée. Leave to cool for 1 hour.
4 When cool, whip the cream until stiff. Fold into the mixture with the orange flower water to taste.
5 Spoon the fool into glasses and chill for 1-2 hours until required. Decorate with orange rind and serve with sponge fingers.

COOK'S TIP

Serve this fool well chilled with sponge fingers or crisp biscuits. Follow the basic recipe to make other fruit fools of your choice.

GOOSEBERRY MACAROON CRUNCH

SERVES 6

450 g (1 lb) gooseberries, topped and tailed	100 g (4 oz) French almond macaroons (ratafias), crumbled
30 ml (2 tbsp) water	150 ml (¼ pint) whipping cream
100 g (4 oz) caster sugar	
30 ml (2 tbsp) kirsch	3 macaroons or 6 ratafias, to decorate

1 Cook the gooseberries with the water and sugar for 10-15 minutes until the fruit is soft and well reduced, then sieve it. Stir in the kirsch. Chill for 30 minutes.
2 Arrange the macaroon crumbs and gooseberry purée in alternate layers in 6 tall glasses. Chill in the refrigerator for several hours for the flavours to mellow.
3 Whip the cream until it barely holds its shape. Spoon some of the soft cream over each portion and top each with a halved macaroon or whole ratafias. Serve immediately.

VARIATIONS

According to seasonal availability, you can use different fruit from the gooseberries and an alternative liqueur to the kirsch. For example, cherries and kirsch would go well together; strawberries or raspberries and an orange-flavoured liqueur (in which case you can use the fruit raw); stewed apples and calvados or brandy; banana with rum; peaches or apricots go well with the Italian almond-flavoured liqueur Amaretto, which would also complement the flavour of the almond macaroons. For a less rich (and less fattening) dessert, natural yogurt can be used instead of the whipping cream.

PRUNE AND PORT FOOL

SERVES 4

100 g (4 oz) stoned prunes, soaked overnight	150 ml (¼ pint) thick custard, cooled
50 g (2 oz) caster sugar	150 ml (¼ pint) double cream
60 ml (4 tbsp) port	orange twists, to decorate
finely grated rind and juice of 1 orange	

1 Drain the prunes, then put in a saucepan with the sugar, port, orange rind and juice. Simmer for about 15 minutes until soft. (Alternatively, microwave, covered, on HIGH for 8 minutes or until soft.)

2 Leave to cool slightly, then purée in a blender or food processor. Leave to cool completely.

3 Fold the cooled custard into the puréed prunes. Whip the cream until standing in soft peaks, then fold into the prune custard until evenly blended.

4 Divide the mixture between four individual glasses. Chill for about 2 hours until firm. Decorate with orange twists and serve chilled, with sweet biscuits.

COOK'S TIP

Because the flavours in this fool are so strong you can get away with using canned custard instead of home-made.

BANANA WHIPS

SERVES 4

2 egg whites	60 ml (4 level tbsp) soft brown sugar
300 ml (½ pint) natural set yogurt	2 medium bananas
finely grated rind and juice of ½ orange	50 g (2 oz) crunchy breakfast cereal

1 Whisk the egg whites until standing in stiff peaks. Put the yogurt in a bowl and stir until smooth. Fold in the egg whites until evenly incorporated.

2 In a separate bowl, mix together the orange rind and juice and the sugar. Peel the bananas and slice thinly into the juice mixture. Fold gently to mix.

3 Put a layer of the yogurt mixture in the bottom of 4 individual glasses. Cover with a layer of cereal, then with a layer of the banana mixture. Repeat these 3 layers once more. Serve immediately..

COOK'S TIP

A quickly made dessert that appeals particularly to children of all ages.

CREAM CROWDIE

SERVES 4

50 g (2 oz) medium oatmeal	45 ml (3 tbsp) whisky
300 ml (½ pint) double cream	350 g (12 oz) raspberries, hulled
60 ml (4 tbsp) clear honey	

1 Place the oatmeal in a grill pan (without the rack) and toast until golden brown, stirring occasionally with a spoon. Leave for 15 minutes until cool.

2 Whip the cream until just standing in soft peaks. Stir in the honey, whisky and cooled toasted oatmeal.

3 Reserve a few raspberries for decoration, then layer up the remaining raspberries and cream mixture in 4 tall glasses. Cover and chill for at least 1 hour.

4 Allow to come to room temperature for 30 minutes before serving. Decorate each glass with the reserved raspberries.

COOK'S TIP

In Scotland, crowdie can mean a cream cheese or a kind of porridge. This recipe for cream crowdie is so called because it contains oatmeal, which the Scots use for making porridge.

PASKHA

SERVES 8-10

175 g (6 oz) unsalted butter	100 g (4 oz) raisins, chopped
finely grated rind of 1 lemon	50 g (2 oz) blanched almonds, chopped
finely grated rind of 1 orange	50 g (2 oz) glacé cherries, chopped
175 g (6 oz) caster sugar	50 g (2 oz) glacé pineapple, chopped
2 eggs	
5 ml (1 tsp) vanilla essence	TO DECORATE
900 g (2 lb) curd cheese	citron peel, glacé cherries, glacé pineapple and flaked almonds
150 ml (¼ pint) double cream	
25 g (1 oz) each candied citron, lemon and orange peel, chopped	

1 Beat the butter with the lemon and orange rind and sugar in a bowl until very light and fluffy. Beat in the eggs, one at a time, beating well after each addition. Add the vanilla essence and curd cheese and beat until smooth.

2 Beat in the cream, then mix in the candied peels, raisins, nuts, cherries and pineapple. Set aside.

3 Line a 12 cm (5 inch) deep, 16 cm (6½ inch) wide clay flower pot smoothly with a large square of muslin.

4 Fill the flower pot with the paskha mixture, then bring the overhanging muslin up and over the mixture to enclose it completely. Place a small flat plate on top of the paskha, then weight down, to compress the mixture. Stand the flower pot on a plate, then refrigerate overnight.

5 To unmould the paskha, open out the muslin on the top, then place a flat serving plate on top of the paskha. Invert the plate and the flower pot together. Remove the flower pot, then very carefully peel away the muslin.

6 Decorate the paskha attractively with strips of citron peel, cherries, pineapple and almonds. Keep the paskha refrigerated until ready to serve.

DANISH PEASANT GIRL IN-A-VEIL

SERVES 4

50 g (2 oz) butter or margarine	juice of ½ lemon
175 g (6 oz) fresh rye or brown breadcrumbs	sugar, to taste
75 g (3 oz) light soft brown sugar	150 ml (¼ pint) double or whipping cream
700 g (1½ lb) cooking apples	50 g (2 oz) grated chocolate, to decorate

1 Melt the butter in a frying pan. Mix the breadcrumbs and sugar together. Add to the pan and fry until crisp, stirring frequently with a wooden spoon to prevent the crumbs from catching and burning.

2 Peel, core and slice the apples. Put them in a saucepan with 30 ml (2 tbsp) water, the lemon juice and sugar to taste. Cover and cook gently for 10-15 minutes until they form a purée. (Alternatively, put the apples, lemon juice and sugar in a bowl. Cover and microwave on HIGH for 7-10 minutes until they form a pulp, stirring frequently.) Leave to cool, then taste for sweetness and add more sugar if required.

3 Put alternate layers of the fried crumb mixture and apple purée into a glass serving dish, finishing with a layer of crumbs. Chill for 2-3 hours.

4 Whip the cream until stiff. Pipe around the top of the crumb mixture and decorate with grated chocolate. Serve chilled.

COOK'S TIP

This simple but delicious pudding of stewed apples layered with fried breadcrumbs and sugar is very similar to an apple charlotte. In Denmark, where it is called *bondepige med slør*, it takes its name from the fact that the apple and crumbs are 'veiled' or covered with cream.

MANGO MOUSSE

SERVES 6

2 ripe mangoes, about 350 g (12 oz) each	15 ml (1 level tbsp) powdered gelatine
finely grated rind and juice of 1 orange	300 ml (10 fl oz) double cream
3 whole eggs, plus 1 egg yolk	shredded orange rind, to decorate (optional)
40 g (1½ oz) caster sugar	

1 Stand the mangoes on a board on their long rounded edges. Cut a thick slice down either side of the mango keeping the knife as close to the stone as possible.

2 Scrape the mango flesh out of the skin. Purée in a blender or food processor. Rub through a nylon sieve. Add the orange rind.

3 Place the whole eggs and egg yolk in a large bowl, add the caster sugar and whisk until the mixture is very pale, thick and creamy.

4 Whisk the mango purée, a little at a time, into the mixture, whisking well after each addition.

5 Sprinkle the gelatine over the orange juice in a small bowl and leave to soak. Place the bowl over a pan of simmering water and stir until dissolved.

6 Meanwhile, pour half the cream into a bowl and lightly whip, then, using a metal spoon, lightly fold the cream into the mango mixture. Pour the gelatine in a thin stream into the mango mixture, stirring gently.

7 Pour the mixture into a 2 litre (3½ pint) shallow serving dish. Chill in the refrigerator for about 1 hour until beginning to set, then cover and chill for several hours, or overnight, until set.

8 Lightly whisk the remaining cream until it just holds its shape. Spoon the cream into a piping bag fitted with a star nozzle and pipe small rosettes around the edge of the mousse. Decorate with shredded orange rind if desired.

STRAWBERRY AND ORANGE MOUSSE

SERVES 6

700 g (1½ lb) strawberries, hulled	125 g (4 oz) caster sugar
finely grated rind and juice of 1 large orange	15 ml (1 level tbsp) powdered gelatine
45 ml (3 level tbsp) icing sugar	300 ml (10 fl oz) double cream
3 egg yolks and 2 egg whites	150 ml (5 fl oz) single cream

1 Thinly slice enough strawberries to form a ring around the side of a 2.3 litre (4 pint) shallow glass dish.

2 Purée half the remainder in a blender or food processor with the orange rind, 75 ml (5 tbsp) juice and the icing sugar. Pass through a nylon sieve to give a very smooth texture. Reserve the remaining strawberries for decoration.

3 Whisk the egg yolks and caster sugar until thick and light. Then gradually whisk in the strawberry purée.

4 Sprinkle the gelatine in 45 ml (3 tbsp) water in a small bowl and leave to soak. Place the bowl over a saucepan of simmering water and stir until dissolved. Leave to cool, then stir into the mousse mixture.

5 Lightly whip the creams together. Fold one third into the mousse and keep the rest covered in the refrigerator. Whisk the two egg whites until stiff and fold into the mixture. Pour into the strawberry-lined dish, and chill in the refrigerator for 2-3 hours, until set.

6 Decorate with piped cream and strawberries.

STRAWBERRY YOGURT MOULD

SERVES 6

3 eggs	20 ml (4 level tsp) powdered gelatine
50 g (2 oz) caster sugar	150 ml (5 fl oz) natural yogurt
finely grated rind and juice of 1 lemon	150 ml (5 fl oz) strawberry yogurt
450 g (1 lb) strawberries	

1 Put the eggs, sugar and lemon rind in a large bowl. Using an electric mixer, whisk together until the mixture is pale, thick and creamy and leaves a trail when the whisk is lifted from the bowl.

2 Hull half of the strawberries and place in a blender or food processor with half of the lemon juice. Purée until smooth.

3 Gradually whisk the purée into the mousse mixture, whisking well to keep the bulk.

4 Sprinkle the gelatine over the remaining lemon juice in a small bowl and leave to soak for 5 minutes. Place the bowl over a saucepan of simmering water and stir until dissolved. Leave until lukewarm, then gradually add to the mousse mixture with the natural and strawberry yogurts. Stir carefully but thoroughly to mix. Pour into a greased 1.7 litre (3 pint) ring mould and chill for 4-5 hours or until set.

5 To serve, dip the mould briefly in hot water, then invert on to a serving plate. Hull most of the remaining strawberries, but leave a few of the green hulls on for decoration. Fill the centre of the ring with the fruit. Serve with extra natural yogurt, if liked.

SUMMER PUDDING

SERVES 4-6

700 g (1½ lb) mixed summer fruit, such as redcurrants, blackcurrants, raspberries, prepared	8-10 thin slices of day-old bread, crusts removed
about 25 g (1 oz) light soft brown sugar	fruit and mint sprigs, to decorate

1 Stew the fruit gently with 60-90 ml (4-6 tbsp) water and the sugar until soft but still retaining their shape. The exact amounts of water and sugar depend on the ripeness and sweetness of the fruit.

2 Meanwhile, cut a round from one slice of bread to neatly fit the bottom of a 1.1 litre (2 pint) pudding basin and cut 6-8 slices of the bread into fingers about 5 cm (2 inches) wide. Put the round at the bottom of the basin and arrange the fingers around the sides, overlapping them so there are no spaces.

3 When the fruit is cooked, and still hot, pour it gently into the basin, being careful not to disturb the bread framework. Reserve about 45 ml (3 tbsp) of the juice. When the basin is full, cut the remaining bread and use to cover the fruit so a lid is formed.

4 Cover with a plate or saucer which fits just inside the bowl and put a weight on top. Leave the pudding until cold, then put into the refrigerator and chill overnight.

5 To serve, run a knife carefully round the edge to loosen, then invert the pudding on to a serving dish. Pour the reserved juice over the top. Decorate with fruit and mint sprigs. Serve cold with cream.

VARIATION

Autumn Pudding

Replace the summer fruits with a selection of autumn fruits, such as apples or pears, blackberries and plums.

CABINET PUDDING

SERVES 4

425 ml (15 fl oz) milk	25 g (1 oz) caster sugar
1 vanilla pod	2 trifle sponge cakes, diced
25 g (1 oz) glacé cherries, halved	40 g (1½ oz) ratafias, crushed
25 g (1 oz) angelica, chopped	25 g (1 oz) large raisins, chopped, or sultanas
3 eggs	

1 Put the milk and the vanilla pod in a saucepan and bring slowly to the boil. Remove from the heat, cover and leave for 15 minutes.

2 Arrange some of the cherries and angelica in a buttered 750 ml (1¼ pint) charlotte mould or other plain mould.

3 Lightly whisk the eggs and sugar together. Remove the vanilla pod from the milk then stir the milk into the eggs.

4 Mix the sponge cakes, ratafias, raisins or sultanas and remaining cherries and angelica together and spoon into the mould. Strain in the egg and milk and leave to soak for 15 minutes.

5 Place the mould in a deep baking tin, surround with boiling water and cover with greaseproof paper. Bake in the oven at 170°C (325°F) mark 3 for about 1 hour until just set.

6 Remove the mould from the tin and leave to stand for 2-3 minutes before unmoulding.

COOK'S TIP

This type of custard-based pudding was very popular in the eighteenth century. Richer versions use single, even double, cream instead of milk, a higher proportion of ratafias, and sometimes brandy is added as well.

EVE'S PUDDING

SERVES 4

450 g (1 lb) cooking apples, peeled and cored	75 g (3 oz) caster sugar
75 g (3 oz) demerara sugar	1 egg, beaten
grated rind of 1 lemon	150 g (5 oz) self-raising flour
75 g (3 oz) butter or block margarine	a little milk, to mix

1 Grease a 900 ml (1½ pint) ovenproof dish. Slice the apples and place in the dish. Sprinkle over the sugar and lemon rind.
2 Cream the fat and caster sugar together until pale and fluffy. Add the egg, a little at a time, beating well after each addition.
3 Fold in the flour with enough milk to give a smooth dropping consistency and spread the mixture over the apples.
4 Bake in the oven at 180°C (350°F) mark 4 for 40-45 minutes, until the apples are tender and the sponge mixture golden brown.

VARIATION

Add 25 g (1 oz) ground almonds with the flour and sprinkle 25 g (1 oz) flaked almonds over the top of the pudding.

BLACKBERRY AND PEAR COBBLER

SERVES 4

FOR THE FILLING	FOR THE TOPPING
450 g (1 lb) blackberries	225 g (8 oz) self-raising flour
450 g (1 lb) ripe cooking pears, such as Conference	pinch of salt
finely grated rind and juice of 1 lemon	50 g (2 oz) butter or margarine
2.5 ml (½ level tsp) ground cinnamon	25 g (1 oz) caster sugar
	about 150 ml (¼ pint) milk, plus extra to glaze

1 To make the filling, pick over the blackberries and wash them. Peel and core the pears, slice thickly.
2 Put the blackberries and pears into a saucepan with the lemon rind and juice and the cinnamon. Poach for 15-20 minutes until the fruit is tender. Cool.
3 To make the topping, place the flour and salt in a bowl. Rub in the butter until the mixture resembles fine breadcrumbs, then stir in the sugar. Gradually add the milk to mix to a fairly soft dough.
4 Roll out the dough on a floured work surface until 1 cm (½ inch) thick. Cut out rounds using a fluted 5 cm (2 inch) pastry cutter.
5 Put the fruit in a pie dish and top with overlapping pastry rounds, leaving a gap in the centre.
6 Brush the top of the pastry rounds with milk. Bake in the oven at 220°C (425°F) mark 7 for 10-15 minutes until the pastry is golden brown. Serve hot.

COOK'S TIP

Recipes with the strange-sounding title of 'cobbler' are invariably American in origin, although very little is known for certain about the meaning behind the word in culinary terms. Cobblers always have a scone dough topping which is stamped into small rounds.

CRANBERRY
UPSIDE DOWN CAKE

SERVES 8

FOR THE TOPPING	large pinch of salt
25 g (1 oz) butter, melted	1 egg
350 g (12 oz) cranberries	finely grated rind and juice of 1 large orange
75 g (3 oz) caster sugar	50 ml (2 fl oz) milk
60 ml (4 tbsp) cranberry sauce	100 g (4 oz) butter or margarine, softened
FOR THE CAKE	100 g (4 oz) caster sugar
225 g (8 oz) self-raising flour	
5 ml (1 level tsp) baking powder	

1 Grease a 23 cm (9 inch) round spring-release cake tin.
2 To make the topping, pour the melted butter into the prepared cake tin. Mix the cranberries, sugar and cranberry sauce together. Spoon the cranberry mixture evenly over the base of the cake tin.
3 To make the cake, put all the ingredients into a large bowl and beat until smooth and glossy. Carefully pour over the cranberries and level the surface.
4 Bake in the oven at 180°C (350°F) mark 4 for about 1 hour or until well risen and firm to the touch. Cover the top with a double sheet of greaseproof paper after 40 minutes to prevent overbrowning.
5 Leave to cool in the tin for 5 minutes, then turn the cake out on to a serving plate. Serve warm with ice cream or whipped cream.

BLUEBERRY
OAT CRUMBLE

SERVES 6-8

FOR THE FILLING	FOR THE CRUMBLE TOPPING
900 g (2 lb) blueberries	100 g (4 oz) butter
45 ml (3 level tbsp) light soft brown sugar	100 g (4 oz) plain flour
30 ml (2 level tbsp) plain flour	100 g (4 oz) light soft brown sugar
15 ml (1 tbsp) lemon juice	75 g (3 oz) rolled oats
	50 g (2 oz) pecan or walnut halves, chopped and toasted
	grated nutmeg (optional)

1 To make the filling, mix the blueberries with the sugar, flour and lemon juice in a 1.4 litre (2½ pint) pie dish.
2 To make the crumble topping, rub the butter into the flour in a bowl. Stir in the sugar, oats and nuts. Flavour with grated nutmeg, if liked. Spoon the crumble mixture on top of the berries and lightly press down.
3 Bake in the oven at 190°C (375°F) mark 5 for about 30-35 minutes or until golden brown. Serve warm or cold with custard or cream.

RHUBARB BROWN BETTY

SERVES 6

450 g (1 lb) rhubarb	2.5 ml (½ level tsp) ground ginger
225 g (8 oz) fresh wholewheat breadcrumbs	50 ml (2 fl oz) fresh orange juice
50 g (2 oz) muscovado sugar	

1 Trim the rhubarb and cut the stalks into short lengths. Put in a greased 900 ml (1½ pint) ovenproof dish.
2 Mix the breadcrumbs, sugar and ground ginger together and sprinkle over the fruit. Spoon the orange juice over the crumbs.
3 Bake in the oven at 170°C (325°F) mark 3 for 40 minutes or until the fruit is soft and the topping browned. Serve hot or cold, with natural yogurt.

COOK'S TIP

Rhubarb Brown Betty is equally good served hot or cold, with natural yogurt. Any leftover will also reheat well.

SPICED APPLE AND PLUM CRUMBLE

SERVES 6

450 g (1 lb) plums	7.5 ml (1½ level tsp) ground mixed spice
700 g (1½ lb) cooking apples	175 g (6 oz) plain wholemeal flour
100 g (4 oz) butter or margarine	50 g (2 oz) blanched hazelnuts, toasted and chopped
100 g (4 oz) sugar	

1 Using a sharp knife, cut the plums in half, then carefully remove the stones.
2 Peel, quarter, core and slice the apples. Place the apples in a medium saucepan with 25 g (1 oz) of the butter, 50 g (2 oz) of the sugar and about 5 ml (1 tsp) of the mixed spice. Cover and cook gently for 15 minutes until the apples begin to soften.
3 Stir in the plums. Transfer the fruit mixture to a 1.1 litre (2 pint) shallow ovenproof dish. Leave to cool for about 30 minutes.
4 Stir the flour and remaining mixed spice well together. Rub in the remaining butter until the mixture resembles fine breadcrumbs. Stir in the rest of the sugar with the hazelnuts. Spoon the crumble over the fruit.
5 Bake in the oven at 180°C (350°F) mark 4 for about 40 minutes or until the top is golden, crisp and crumbly.

COOK'S TIP

All plums can be cooked, but dessert varieties tend to be more expensive, so it makes good sense to look for cooking plums. Whether you cook with red or yellow plums is entirely a matter of personal choice but cooking plums worth looking for are Czars, small red cherry plums, Pershore Yellow Egg, Purple Pershore and Belle de Loutain. Greengages and damsons come from the plum family and can be used in any recipe for plums, although extra sugar may be required.

WALNUT AND ORANGE PUDDING

SERVES 6

125 g (4 oz) soft tub margarine	5 ml (1 tsp) vanilla essence
50 g (2 oz) walnut pieces, chopped	75 g (3 oz) self-raising flour
75 g (3 oz) caster sugar	5 ml (1 level tsp) baking powder
15 ml (1 level tbsp) golden syrup	grated rind of 1 orange
2 eggs	60 ml (4 tbsp) fresh orange juice

1 Grease six ovenproof ramekins.
2 Place all the ingredients together in a large bowl and beat thoroughly until smooth.
3 Two-thirds fill the ramekins with the mixture. Place on a baking tray and bake in the oven at 180°C (350°F) mark 4 for 20-25 minutes or until firm to the touch.
4 Turn out or leave in the ramekins if preferred, and serve warm with custard.

BLACKBERRY UPSIDE DOWN PUDDING

SERVES 8

FOR THE TOPPING	5 ml (1 level tsp) baking powder
90 ml (6 tbsp) raspberry jam	
350 g (12 oz) blackberries	large pinch of salt
1 large eating apple, peeled, cored and roughly chopped	1 egg
	finely grated rind and juice of 1 large orange
FOR THE CAKE	30 ml (2 tbsp) milk
75 g (3 oz) self-raising flour	75 g (3 oz) butter or soft tub margarine
75 g (3 oz) self-raising wholemeal flour	75 g (3 oz) caster sugar

1 Grease a 23 cm (9 inch) round spring-release cake tin.
2 To make the topping, gently heat the jam in a small saucepan and pour into the prepared cake tin. Arrange the blackberries and apple evenly over the base of the cake tin.
3 To make the cake, put all the ingredients into a large bowl and beat until smooth and glossy. Carefully spread over the fruit and level the surface.
4 Bake in the oven at 190°C (375°F) mark 5 for about 1 hour or until well risen and firm to the touch. Cover the top with a double sheet of greaseproof paper after 40 minutes to prevent overbrowning.
5 Leave the pudding to cool in the tin for 5 minutes, then turn out and serve.

BAKED APPLE AND COCONUT PUDDING

SERVES 6

finely grated rind and juice of 1 lemon	100 g (4 oz) plain wholemeal flour
100 g (4 oz) soft light brown sugar, plus 30 ml (2 tbsp)	7.5 ml (1½ tsp) baking powder
6 medium eating apples, each weighing about 100 g (4 oz), peeled, cored and sliced	25 g (1 oz) desiccated coconut
100 g (4 oz) butter	about 60 ml (4 tbsp) apricot jam, warmed
2 eggs, separated	shredded coconut, toasted, to decorate

1 Pour the lemon juice into a large bowl; stir in the 30 ml (2 tbsp) sugar and add the apples, making sure they are well coated.

2 Gradually beat the 100 g (4 oz) sugar into the butter until well blended. Add the lemon rind, then beat in the egg yolks one at a time. Stir in the flour, baking powder and desiccated coconut.

3 Whisk the egg whites until stiff but not dry, then fold into the creamed ingredients. Spoon into a lightly greased 24-25 cm (9½-10 inch) fluted flan dish. Press the apples into the mixture, spooning any juices over them.

3 Stand the dish on a baking sheet and bake in the oven at 170°C (325°F) mark 3 for 1-1¼ hours or until well browned and firm to the touch, covering lightly with greaseproof paper if necessary.

4 Cool for about 15 minutes, then brush with the apricot jam and scatter over the toasted shredded coconut. Serve while still warm with custard.

DAMSON AND APPLE TANSY

SERVES 4

2 large Cox's apples, peeled, cored and thinly sliced	40 g (1½ oz) sugar
	pinch of ground cloves
225 g (8 oz) damsons, halved, stoned and quartered	pinch of ground cinnamon
	4 eggs, separated
15 g (½ oz) butter	45 ml (3 tbsp) soured cream

1 Put the apples, damsons, butter and half of the sugar in a large frying pan. Cook over a gentle heat until the fruit is softened, stirring continuously. Stir in the cloves and cinnamon, then remove from the heat.

2 Beat the egg yolks and cream together and stir into the fruit. Whisk the egg whites until stiff, then fold in.

3 Cook over a low heat until the mixture has set. Sprinkle the top with the remaining sugar, then brown under a hot grill. Serve immediately, straight from the pan, with soured cream.

COOK'S TIP

Tansies originally always included the bitter-sweet herb called tansy, which still lends its name to many custard and omelette-type puddings. This sweet/tart combination with Cox's apples traditionally used the Witherslack damsons which grow south of Lake Windermere.

STEAMED FRUIT PUDDING

SERVES 4

450 g (1 lb) fresh fruit, prepared and stewed, or drained canned fruit	2 eggs, beaten
	few drops of vanilla essence
100 g (4 oz) butter or margarine	175 g (6 oz) self-raising flour
	little milk, to mix
100 g (4 oz) caster sugar	

1 Half-fill a steamer or large saucepan with water and put it on to boil. Grease a 900 ml (1½ pint) pudding basin and spoon the fruit into the bottom.
2 Cream the butter and sugar together in a bowl until pale and fluffy. Add the eggs and vanilla essence, a little at a time, beating well after each addition.
3 Using a metal spoon, fold in half the flour, then fold in the rest, with enough milk to give a smooth dropping consistency.
4 Pour the mixture into the prepared pudding basin. Cover with greased greaseproof paper and foil and secure with string. Steam for 1½ hours. Serve with custard.

VARIATIONS

Syrup or Jam Pudding
Put 30 ml (2 tbsp) golden syrup or jam into the bottom of the basin instead of the fruit.

Individual Dried Fruit Puddings
Add 75g (3 oz) dried mixed fruit to the basic mixture. Omit the stewed fruit. Spoon into greased individual pudding moulds filling them two-thirds full. Cover each mould with greased foil and secure with string. Steam for 30-45 minutes depending on size. (Illustrated above.)

RICH CHRISTMAS PUDDING

SERVES 8

100 g (4 oz) prunes	75 g (3 oz) fresh breadcrumbs
175 g (6 oz) currants	100 g (4 oz) shredded suet
175 g (6 oz) seedless raisins	100 g (4 oz) dark soft brown sugar
175 g (6 oz) sultanas	25 g (1 oz) blanched almonds, chopped
100 g (4 oz) plain flour	finely grated rind of ½ lemon
1.25 ml (¼ level tsp) grated nutmeg	150 ml (¼ pint) brown ale
1.25 ml (¼ level tsp) ground cinnamon	2 eggs, beaten
2.5 ml (½ level tsp) salt	

1 Snip the prunes into small pieces, discarding the stones.
2 Half-fill a steamer or large saucepan with water and put it on to boil. Grease a 1.3 litre (2½ pint) pudding basin.
3 Place the prunes in a large mixing bowl and stir in the remaining ingredients. Stir well until evenly mixed.
4 Put the mixture into the prepared basin, pushing down well. Cover with greased, pleated greaseproof paper and foil. To cook, steam for about 8 hours.
5 Leave the greaseproof paper in position, allow to cool, then cover with a clean dry cloth or foil and store in a cool place for at least 2 weeks before serving.
6 To reheat, steam for 2½ hours. Turn out on to a warmed serving plate and serve with brandy butter.

INDIVIDUAL PLUM PUDDINGS

SERVES 4

8 prunes, stoned and chopped	2.5 ml (½ level tsp) ground mixed spice
45 ml (3 tbsp) seedless raisins	pinch of salt
45 ml (3 tbsp) currants	30 ml (2 tbsp) fresh breadcrumbs
45 ml (3 tbsp) sultanas	30 ml (2 tbsp) shredded suet
12 whole blanched almonds, chopped	30 ml (2 tbsp) soft brown sugar
finely grated rind and juice of 1 tangerine	1 egg, size 4, beaten
30 ml (2 level tbsp) plain flour	30 ml (2 tbsp) brown ale
	30 ml (2 tbsp) brandy

1 Place the dried fruits in a bowl with the nuts and tangerine rind and juice. Mix well.

2 In a separate bowl, sift together the flour, mixed spice and salt. Add the breadcrumbs, suet and sugar and mix well together.

3 Pour in the beaten egg and brown ale, beat well, then stir in the dried fruit mixture. Cover and leave in a cool place for 24 hours.

4 The next day, add the brandy, stirring well. Butter 4 dariole moulds or ramekins and pack in the pudding mixture tightly.

5 Cover the moulds with pleated greaseproof paper and foil and secure tightly with string.

6 Place the moulds in a large saucepan, then pour in enough boiling water to come halfway up the sides of the moulds. Steam the puddings for about 1 hour, topping up with boiling water when necessary.

7 Remove the puddings from the pan and allow to cool.

8 Uncover the puddings, then re-cover in fresh greaseproof paper and foil. Store in a cool, dry place for at least 1 month before serving.

9 To serve, steam in the same way for 1 hour. Turn out on to warmed individual plates. Serve with custard.

SPOTTED DICK

SERVES 4

100 g (4 oz) fresh breadcrumbs	175 g (6 oz) currants
75 g (3 oz) self-raising flour	finely grated rind of 1 lemon
75 g (3 oz) shredded suet	75 ml (5 tbsp) milk
50 g (2 oz) caster sugar	lemon slices, to decorate

1 Half-fill a preserving pan or large saucepan with water and put on to boil.

2 Place the breadcrumbs, flour, suet, sugar, currants and lemon rind in a bowl and stir well until thoroughly mixed.

3 Pour in the milk and stir until well blended. Using one hand, bring the ingredients together to form a soft, slightly sticky dough.

4 Turn the dough on to a floured surface and knead gently until just smooth. Shape into a neat roll about 15 cm (6 inches) in length.

5 Make a 5 cm (2 inch) pleat across a clean tea towel or pudding cloth. Or pleat together sheets of greased greaseproof paper and strong foil. Encase the roll in the cloth or foil, pleating the open edges tightly together.

6 Tie the ends securely with string to form a cracker shape. Make a string handle across the top. Lower the suet roll into the pan of boiling water and boil for about 2 hours.

7 Lift the spotted dick out of the water using the string handle. Place on a wire rack standing over a plate and allow excess moisture to drain off.

8 Snip the string and gently roll the pudding out of the cloth or foil on to a warmed serving plate. Cut into slices and decorate with lemon slices. Serve with custard.

SOUFFLES & MERINGUES

Impress your guests with a sensational soufflé or an elaborate meringue gâteau. Choose a cold soufflé or meringue concoction for a prepare-ahead dessert; a hot soufflé must be served immediately for maximum effect. Meringues have the added advantage that they can be made well in advance and stored in an airtight container.

ORANGE SEMOLINA SOUFFLES

SERVES 6

5 large juicy oranges	3 eggs, separated
25 g (1 oz) granulated sugar	icing sugar, for dusting
25 g (1 oz) semolina	orange slices, to decorate

1 Finely grate the rind and squeeze the juice from 2 of the oranges into a measuring jug. You will need 300 ml (½ pint) juice. Make up with juice from one of the remaining oranges if there is not enough.

2 Halve the remaining oranges. Scoop out any loose flesh still attached to the skins and eat separately or use in another recipe. You need six clean orange halves to serve the soufflés in. Cut a thin slice from the bottom of each so that they stand flat.

3 Place the orange juice and rind, sugar and semolina in a pan and simmer until thickened, stirring all the time.

4 Cool slightly, then stir in the egg yolks. Whisk the egg whites until stiff and fold into the mixture. Spoon into the reserved orange shells and stand on a baking sheet.

5 Bake in the oven at 200°C (400°F) mark 6 for 15-20 minutes or until risen and golden brown. Dust with icing sugar and serve immediately, surrounded by orange slices.

HOT APRICOT SOUFFLE

SERVES 4

450 g (1 lb) fresh apricots, halved and stoned	150 ml (¼ pint) milk
40 g (1½ oz) butter or margarine	50 g (2 oz) caster sugar
60 ml (4 level tbsp) plain flour	4 eggs, size 2, separated
	15 ml (1 tbsp) apricot brandy
	icing sugar, for dusting

1 Grease a 2 litre (3½ pint) soufflé dish. Put the apricots in a saucepan with 30 ml (2 tbsp) water and cook until soft. Purée the fruit in a blender or food processor; seive to remove the skins.

2 Melt the butter in a saucepan, stir in the flour and cook for 1 minute, stirring. Remove from the heat and gradually stir in the milk and apricot purée. Bring to the boil, and cook, stirring, until the sauce thickens. Remove from the heat.

3 Stir in the sugar, egg yolks and brandy. Whisk the egg whites until stiff, then fold into the mixture.

4 Pour into the soufflé dish and bake in the oven at 180°C (350°F) mark 4 for 45 minutes, until well risen. Dust with icing sugar and serve immediately.

HOT CHOCOLATE CINNAMON SOUFFLE

SERVES 4

50 g (2 oz) butter or margarine, plus extra for greasing	40 g (1½ oz) plain flour
75 g (3 oz) plain chocolate	2.5 ml (½ level tsp) ground cinnamon
300 ml (½ pint) plus 15 ml (1 tbsp) milk	5 eggs, separated
	25 g (1 oz) caster sugar
	icing sugar, for dusting

1 Tie a double strip of greaseproof paper around a 1.4 litre (2½ pint) soufflé dish to make a 7.5 cm (3 inch) collar. Brush the inside of the dish and the paper with melted butter.

2 Break the chocolate into small pieces. Place in a heatproof bowl with the 15 ml (1 tbsp) milk. Stand the bowl over a pan of simmering water and heat gently until the chocolate melts. Remove from the heat.

3 Melt the butter in a large heavy-based saucepan. Add the flour and cook for 1 minute, then blend in the remaining milk and the cinnamon. Bring to the boil, stirring all the time, and cook for about 1 minute.

4 Cool slightly, then beat in the egg yolks, sugar and chocolate.

5 Whisk the egg whites until stiff but not dry. Beat one spoonful into the sauce mixture to lighten it, then carefully fold in the remaining egg whites.

6 Gently pour the soufflé mixture into the prepared dish. Level the top with a palette knife and make a few cuts through the outer edges of the mixture – this helps it to rise evenly. Stand the dish on a baking sheet.

7 Bake in the oven at 190°C (375°F) mark 5 for about 35-40 minutes or until well risen, just set and well browned. Remove the paper and dust lightly with icing sugar. Serve straight away.

INDIVIDUAL CHOCOLATE SOUFFLES

SERVES 6

75 g (3 oz) plain chocolate or chocolate dots	knob of butter or margarine
150 ml (¼ pint) milk	3 egg yolks
50 g (2 oz) caster sugar	4 egg whites
60 ml (4 level tbsp) flour	icing sugar for dusting

1 Lightly grease six 150 ml (¼ pint) ramekin dishes. Dust them out with icing sugar.

2 Put the chocolate in a bowl with 30 ml (2 tbsp) water and melt over a pan of simmering water.

3 Heat the milk, reserving a little, with the sugar, then pour on to the melted chocolate.

4 Blend the flour to a smooth paste with the remaining milk, and stir in the chocolate mixture. Return to the pan, bring to the boil, stirring, then cook for 2 minutes, stirring occasionally. Add the butter, in small pieces, then leave until lukewarm.

5 Stir in the egg yolks. Whisk the egg whites until stiff and fold into the mixture. Divide between the prepared ramekin dishes so that each is three-quarters full.

6 Bake in the oven at 180°C (350°F) mark 4 for about 30 minutes or until just set and golden brown. Dust quickly with icing sugar. Serve straight away with single cream.

COOK'S TIP

Make sure that the temperature in the oven remains constant and that there are no draughts while the soufflé is baking – which means no peeking! A hot soufflé is cooked when it is risen and golden, and just firm to the touch. Test it in the oven, in case it needs more time. The creamy middle should be a little gooey – if it is dry it tastes like overcooked scrambled egg.

INDIVIDUAL APPLE SOUFFLES

SERVES 6

icing sugar, for dusting	30 ml (2 level tbsp) plain flour
350 g (12 oz) cooking apples	150 ml (¼ pint) milk
50 g (2 oz) butter or margarine	3 eggs, separated
25 g (1 oz) caster sugar	30 ml (2 tbsp) apple brandy

1   Lightly grease six 150 ml (¼ pint) ramekin dishes. Dust them out with icing sugar.

2   Peel, quarter, core and roughly chop the apples. Place in a small saucepan with 25 g (1 oz) of the butter and the sugar. Cover tightly and cook gently until the apples are very soft. Uncover and cook over a moderate heat, stirring frequently until all excess moisture evaporates. (Alternatively, cover and microwave on high for 5 minutes, or until really soft, stirring.) Mash or beat until smooth; cool slightly.

3   Melt the remaining butter in a pan, add the flour and cook for 2 minutes. Remove from the heat and stir in the milk. Cook, stirring, for 2-3 minutes. (Alternatively, put everything in a bowl and microwave on HIGH for 3-4 minutes or until boiling and thickened, whisking.)

4   Remove from the heat, cool slightly, then stir in the apple purée and egg yolks. Gently mix in the apple brandy. Whisk the egg whites until stiff but not dry. Stir one large spoonful into the apple mixture, then gently fold in the remaining egg whites. Divide between the prepared ramekin dishes so that each is three-quarters full.

5   Bake in the oven at 180°C (350°F) mark 4 for about 30 minutes or until just set and golden brown. Dust quickly with icing sugar. Serve straight away with cream.

CHILLED CHOCOLATE MINT CHIP SOUFFLE

SERVES 4

450 ml (¾ pint) milk	75 g (3 oz) caster sugar
50 g (2 oz) plain chocolate	15 ml (3 level tsp) powdered gelatine
113 g (4 oz) packet chocolate mint sticks, roughly chopped	300 ml (10 fl oz) whipping cream
3 eggs, separated, plus 1 egg white	

1   Prepare a 900 ml (1½ pint) soufflé dish with a paper collar (as for Citrus Soufflé, page 280).

2   Heat the milk, chocolate and 25 g (1 oz) chocolate mint sticks until melted, then bring to the boil, whisking. Remove from the heat.

3   Beat the egg yolks with the sugar until light. Pour on the flavoured milk, return to the pan and cook over a gentle heat, without boiling, until the custard coats the back of a spoon. Pour into a bowl; cool.

4   Soak the gelatine in 45 ml (3 tbsp) water in a small bowl. Dissolve by standing the bowl over a pan of gently simmering water. Stir into the custard and chill.

5   Whip the cream until softly stiff. Stir half into the custard when it is on the point of setting. Stir 50 g (2 oz) chocolate mint sticks into the custard.

6   Whisk the four egg whites until stiff then fold into the mixture. Spoon into a soufflé dish; refrigerate to set.

7   Remove the paper. Decorate soufflé with remaining cream and chocolate mint sticks.

COOK'S TIP

Cold soufflés are very light mixtures set high above a soufflé dish, as imitations of hot soufflés. They are not true soufflés but mousses set with gelatine. The preparation of the dish is all important. Do not tie the paper collar so tightly as to flute the paper and spoil the final appearance of the soufflé. To remove the paper from the cold soufflé once it has set, rinse a round bladed knife in hot water and slip it, upright between the paper and the soufflé, peeling away the paper.

CITRUS SOUFFLE

SERVES 6-8

finely grated rind and juice of 1 lemon	4 eggs, separated
finely grated rind and juice of 1 orange	100 g (4 oz) caster sugar
juice of 1 grapefruit	300 ml (10 fl oz) double cream
15 ml (3 level tsp) powdered gelatine	crushed sweet biscuits and crystallised oranges and lemons, to decorate

1 Prepare an 18 cm (6 inch) soufflé dish. Cut a double thickness of greaseproof paper long enough to go around the outside of the dish and 5-7.5 cm (2-3 inches) deeper. Secure around the outside with paper clips and string.
2 Pour the fruit juices into a heatproof bowl and sprinkle in the gelatine. Stand the bowl over a saucepan of hot water and heat gently until dissolved. Remove the bowl from the water and set aside to cool slightly.
3 Put the fruit rinds, egg yolks and sugar in a large heatproof bowl and stand over the pan of gently simmering water. Whisk until the mixture is thick and holds a ribbon trail.
4 Remove the bowl from the pan and whisk in the gelatine liquid. Leave until beginning to set, whisking occasionally.
5 Whip the cream until it will stand in soft peaks. Whisk the egg whites until stiff. Fold the cream into the soufflé, then the egg whites, until evenly blended.
6 Pour the mixture into the prepared soufflé dish and level the surface. Chill in the refrigerator for at least 4 hours until set.
7 Carefully remove the paper from the edge of the soufflé. Press the crushed biscuits around the edge, then decorate the top with crystallised fruit. Serve chilled.

CHILLED APRICOT SOUFFLE

SERVES 6-8

225 g (8 oz) dried apricots, soaked overnight	4 eggs, separated
175 g (6 oz) caster sugar	300 ml (10 fl oz) double cream
30 ml (2 tbsp) almond-flavoured liqueur	ratafia biscuits and whipped cream, to decorate
15 ml (3 level tsp) powdered gelatine	

1 Prepare a 15 cm (6 inch) soufflé dish. Cut a double thickness of greaseproof paper long enough to go around the outside of the dish and 5-7.5 cm (2-3 inches) deeper. Secure around the outside with paper clips and string.
2 Drain the apricots, then put them in a saucepan with 120 ml (8 tbsp) water and 50 g (2 oz) of the sugar. Heat gently until the sugar has dissolved, then cover and simmer for about 30 minutes until tender. Leave to cool slightly, then rub through a sieve or purée in a blender. Stir in the liqueur and leave to cool for about 30 minutes.
3 Meanwhile, place 60 ml (4 tbsp) water in a small heatproof bowl and sprinkle in the gelatine. Stand the bowl over a saucepan of hot water and heat gently until dissolved. Remove and cool slightly.
4 Put the egg yolks and remaining sugar in a large heat-proof bowl and stand over the pan of gently simmering water. Whisk until the mixture is thick and holds a ribbon trail, then remove and cool, whisking occasionally.
5 Whip the cream until it will stand in soft peaks. Whisk the egg whites until stiff.
6 Stir the gelatine liquid into the apricot purée, then fold into the egg yolk mixture until evenly blended. Fold in the whipped cream, then the egg whites.
7 Put the mixture into the prepared soufflé dish. Level the surface, then chill for at least 4 hours until set.
8 Carefully remove the paper from the edge of the soufflé. Press the crushed ratafias around the exposed edge. Decorate top with apricots and whipped cream.

CREAM MERINGUES

SERVES 8-10

FOR THE MERINGUE	FOR THE FILLING
3 egg whites, size 2	150 ml (¼ pint) double cream
75 g (3 oz) granulated sugar and 75 g (3 oz) caster sugar, or 175 g (6 oz) caster sugar	

1 Line two baking sheets with non-stick baking parchment.

2 Whisk egg whites until stiff. Gradually whisk in half the sugar, whisking after each addition until thoroughly incorporated, then fold in the remaining sugar very lightly with a metal spoon.

3 Spoon the meringue into a piping bag fitted with a large star nozzle and pipe small rounds on to the prepared baking sheets. Alternatively, spoon the mixture into fingers.

4 Bake in the oven at 110°C (225°F) mark ¼ for about 2½-3 hours, until firm and crisp, but still white. If they begin to brown, prop the oven door open a little. Transfer to a wire rack to cool.

5 To serve, whip the cream until thick. Sandwich the meringues together in pairs with cream.

COOK'S TIP

The secret of these delicious melt-in-the-mouth meringues, sandwiched lavishly with fresh cream, is to let them 'dry out' rather than bake, in a very slow oven.

Historians of cookery say that meringues were invented in 1720 by a Swiss pastry-cook called Gasparini. They have been a popular sweet for royalty for centuries and legend has it that Marie-Antoinette, the doomed Queen of France, used to make them herself.

MERINGUE BASKET

SERVES 6-8

FOR THE MERINGUE	FOR THE FILLING
4 egg whites	300 ml (½ pint) whipping cream
225 g (8 oz) icing sugar	about 450 g (1 lb) prepared fruit, eg strawberries, raspberries, bananas

1 Line three baking sheets with non-stick baking parchment and draw a 19 cm (7½ inch) circle on each. Turn the paper over.

2 To make the meringue, place three of the egg whites in a large bowl standing over a pan of simmering water. Sift in 175 g (6 oz) of the icing sugar. Whisk the egg whites and sugar until the mixture stands in very stiff peaks. Do not allow the bowl to get too hot.

3 Spoon one third of the meringue mixture into a piping bag fitted with a large star nozzle. Pipe rings of meringue, about 1 cm (½ inch) thick, inside two of the circles on the paper. Fill the bag with the remaining meringue and, starting from the centre, pipe a continuous coil of meringue on the third sheet of paper to make the base of the basket.

4 Bake all in the oven at 110°C (225°F) mark ¼ for 2½-3 hours until dry. Swap the positions of the meringues during this time so that they cook evenly.

5 Use the remaining egg white and sugar to make meringue as before and put into the piping bag. Remove the cooked meringue rings from the paper and layer up on the base, piping a ring of fresh meringue between each. Return to the oven for a further 1½-2 hours.

6 Leave to cool, then slide on to a wire rack and peel off the base paper. Just before serving, stand the meringue shell on a flat serving plate.

7 To make the filling, lightly whip the cream and spoon half into the base of the meringue basket; top with fruit. Cover with the remaining cream and top with fruit.

MERINGUE MEDLEY

MAKES 44 SMALL MERINGUES

FOR THE MERINGUE	15 ml (1 tbsp) orange-flavoured liqueur
6 egg whites	25 g (1 oz) pecans, walnuts or hazelnuts, finely chopped
350 g (12 oz) caster sugar	
15 ml (1 tbsp) finely chopped pistachio nuts	15 ml (1 tbsp) raspberry purée
FOR THE FILLING	75 g (3 oz) plain chocolate, melted
300 ml (¼ pint) double cream	

1 Line several baking sheets with non-stick baking parchment.

2 To make the meringue, whisk the egg whites and sugar together in a large bowl standing over a large pan of simmering water until very stiff and shiny. Remove from the heat and continue whisking until the meringue will hold unwavering peaks; do not let the meringue become too hot.

3 Fill a large piping bag fitted with a large star nozzle with meringue. Pipe into 7.5 cm (3 inch) plain and wavy lengths and into small whirls on the prepared baking sheets. Sprinkle the plain fingers with chopped pistachios.

4 Bake in the oven at 140°C (275°F) mark 1 for 2-2½ hours until dry. Change the sheets around in the oven during cooking to ensure that they all dry evenly. Allow the meringues to cool, then remove from the paper.

5 Whisk 150 ml (¼ pint) of the double cream with the liqueur until it will hold soft peaks, then fold in the chopped nuts. Sandwich the meringue whirls together, in pairs, with the nut cream.

6 Whisk the remaining cream until thick, then fold in the raspberry purée. Put the cream into a piping bag fitted with a large star nozzle. Sandwich the wavy meringue fingers together, in pairs, with the raspberry cream.

7 Dip the base of each pistachio meringue in the melted chocolate to coat evenly. Place on a sheet of greaseproof paper and leave until set.

BROWN SUGAR AND HAZELNUT MERINGUES

MAKES ABOUT 20

FOR THE MERINGUE	FOR THE FILLING
25 g (1 oz) hazelnuts	ice cream or whipped cream
3 egg whites	
175 g (6 oz) light brown soft sugar	

1 Line two large baking sheets with non-stick baking parchment.

2 Toast the hazelnuts under the grill until golden brown. Tip on to a clean tea towel and rub off the loose skins. Chop roughly.

3 Whisk the egg whites in a bowl until stiff. Whisk in the sugar, 15 ml (1 tbsp) at a time. Spoon the meringue mixture into a piping bag fitted with a large star nozzle and pipe about 40 small swirls on to the prepared baking sheets. Sprinkle with the hazelnuts.

4 Bake in the oven at 110°C (225°F) mark ¼ for about 2-3 hours or until dry. If the baking sheets are on different shelves, swap them halfway through cooking to ensure even browning. Leave to cool.

5 Sandwich the meringues together in pairs with a little ice cream or whipped cream to serve.

ROSE PETAL MERINGUES

SERVES 8

FOR THE MERINGUE	FOR THE FILLING
3 egg whites	300 ml (½ pint) double or whipping cream, whipped
175 g (6 oz) caster sugar	few drops of rose water (optional)
	crystallised rose petals (see below)

1 Mark eight 6 cm (2½ inch) circles on a sheet of non-stick baking parchment. Place on a baking sheet pencil side down.

2 Whisk the egg whites until stiff but not dry. Add half of the sugar and whisk until thick and glossy. Fold in the remaining sugar.

3 Transfer the meringue to a piping bag fitted with a 1 cm (½ inch) plain or star-shaped nozzle. Starting at the centre of each circle pipe the meringue in a spiral out to the edge of the marked circles. Pipe another ring around the edge of each round to form small nest shapes.

4 Bake at 140°C (275°F) mark 1 (or at your ovens lowest setting) for about 1-1½ hours or until firm and dried out. Leave to cool on the baking sheet.

5 Flavour the cream with a few drops of rose water, if wished and use to fill the meringues. Sprinkle with crystallised rose petals.

COOK'S TIP

To crystallise rose petals, carefully break off the petals, brush with egg white and dip in caster sugar. Arrange on a sheet of greaseproof paper and leave to set.

Unfilled meringue nests keep well in an airtight container for several weeks. To prevent meringues softening, serve the cream separately and allow guests to help themselves. Once filled, meringues should be eaten right away.

ALMOND RUM MERINGUE

SERVES 8

75 g (3 oz) ground almonds	16 flaked almonds
4 eggs, separated	15 ml (1 tbsp) dark rum
250 g (9 oz) caster sugar	50 g (2 oz) unsalted butter
10 ml (2 level tsp) cornflour	150 ml (5 fl oz) double cream
10 ml (2 tsp) white vinegar	225 g (8 oz) raspberries

1 Spread the ground almonds out on a baking sheet and brown in the oven at 200°C (400°F) mark 6 for 5-10 minutes. Remove from the oven and leave for about 15 minutes to cool.

2 Line a large baking sheet with non-stick baking parchment. Lower the oven temperature to 150°C (300°F) mark 2.

3 Whisk the egg whites until stiff. Add 100 g (4 oz) sugar, the cornflour and vinegar. Whisk again until very stiff and shiny. Fold in a further 100 g (4 oz) sugar and the ground almonds.

4 With a palette knife, spread one third of the meringue in a 20 cm (8 inch) square on the non-stick paper.

5 Spoon the remaining meringue into a piping bag fitted with a large star nozzle. Pipe lines to make a square at each corner of the meringue and then pipe a square in the centre to form nine boxes. Decorate with flaked almonds.

6 Put into the oven and immediately lower it to 140°C (275°F) mark 1. Bake for about 1½ hours or until well dried out. Slide on to a wire rack and cool.

7 Put the egg yolks, rum and remaining sugar into a bowl. Melt the butter gently in a small pan and pour over the egg yolks, whisking constantly until thick.

8 Lightly whip the double cream until it just holds its shape and fold into the egg mixture. When the meringue is cold, carefully peel off the paper and place on a flat plate.

9 Spoon the cream into the meringue boxes and decorate with the raspberries. Refrigerate for 20 minutes before serving.

PAVLOVA

SERVES 8

FOR THE MERINGUE	FOR THE FILLING
3 egg whites	2 passion fruit
175 g (6 oz) caster sugar	2 kiwi fruit
5 ml (1 tsp) cornflour	225 g (8 oz) strawberries
5 ml (1 tsp) vinegar	225 g (8 oz) fresh pineapple
2.5 ml (½ tsp) vanilla essence	450 ml (¾ pint) double cream
	walnuts, pecans or almonds, to decorate

1 Line a baking sheet with greased foil or non-stick baking parchment.

2 To make the meringue, whisk the egg whites in a large bowl until very stiff. Add 50 g (2 oz) of the sugar and whisk until very stiff. Add another 50 g (2 oz) sugar and whisk once more until the mixture returns to its stiff texture. Spoon in the remaining sugar and whisk again until shiny and standing in stiff peaks.

3 Fold in the cornflour, vinegar and vanilla essence.

4 Pile or pipe the meringue in a 23 cm (9 inch) round or oval on to the prepared baking sheet, making sure there is a substantial dip or hollow in the centre to hold the filling.

5 Bake in the oven at 130°C (250°F) mark ½ for 1¼-1½ hours or until pale brown and dry but a little soft in the centre. Press lightly with a finger to test if the meringue is cooked. Leave to cool slightly, then peel off the foil or paper and place on a serving dish to cool completely. At this stage the meringue will probably crack and sink a little – this is to be expected with a Pavlova.

6 To make the filling, halve the passion fruit and scoop out the pulp. Peel and slice the kiwi fruit. Halve the strawberries. Slice the pineapple, discard skin and core, and roughly chop the flesh. Whip the cream until it just holds its shape. Either fold the fruit into the cream and spoon into the Pavlova or fill the centre with cream. Scatter with nuts and serve immediately.

HAZELNUT MERINGUE GATEAU

SERVES 6-8

FOR THE MERINGUE	FOR THE FILLING
3 egg whites	300 ml (½ pint) double cream
175 g (6 oz) caster sugar	350 g (12 oz) raspberries, hulled
50 g (2 oz) hazelnuts, skinned, toasted and finely chopped	icing sugar, for dusting
	finely chopped pistachio nuts, to decorate

1 Line two baking sheets with non-stick baking parchment, then draw a 20 cm (8 inch) circle on each one. Invert the paper.

2 To make the meringue, whisk the egg whites in a bowl until very stiff, but not dry. Gradually add the caster sugar, a little at a time, whisking well between each addition until stiff and very shiny. Carefully fold in the chopped hazelnuts.

3 Divide the meringue equally between the prepared baking sheets, then spread neatly into rounds. With a palette knife, mark the top of one of the rounds into swirls – this will be the top meringue.

4 Bake in the oven at 140°C (275°F) mark 1 for about 1½ hours until dry. Change the positions of the baking sheets during cooking so that the meringues dry out evenly. Turn the oven off, and allow the meringues to cool in the oven.

5 To make the filling, whip the cream until it will hold soft peaks. Carefully remove the meringues from the paper. Place the smooth meringue round on a large flat serving plate, then spread with the cream. Arrange the raspberries on top of the cream, then place the second meringue on top. Sift icing sugar over the top of the gâteau, then sprinkle with the nuts. Serve the gâteau as soon as possible.

RASPBERRY AND LAVENDER PAVLOVA

SERVES 8

3 egg whites	300 ml (½ pint) Greek-style yogurt
190 g (6½ oz) lavender sugar (see below)	450 g (1 lb) fresh raspberries
5 ml (1 level tsp) cornflour	150 ml (¼ pint) double cream
5 ml (1 tsp) raspberry vinegar	a few lavender flowers, to decorate

1 Draw a 23 cm (9 inch) oval on a piece of non-stick baking parchment and place on a baking sheet.
2 To make the meringue, whisk the egg whites in a large bowl until very stiff. Add 50 g (2 oz) of the sugar and whisk until stiff. Add another 50 g (2 oz) sugar and whisk again. Add a further 50 g (2 oz) sugar and continue whisking until the meringue forms soft peaks. Fold in the cornflour and vinegar.
3 Pile or pipe the meringue into the oval marked on the baking sheet. Make a dip in the middle to hold the filling.
4 Bake in the oven at 180°C (350°F) mark 4 for 5 minutes, then at 130°C (250°F) mark ½ for a further 45-50 minutes or until set but still soft in the middle.
5 Leave to cool slightly, then carefully peel off the paper. Don't worry if the meringue cracks at this stage.
6 When completely cold, whip the cream with the remaining sugar until it just holds its shape, then fold in the yogurt. Roughly crush half of the raspberries and fold into the cream mixture. Pile on top of the Pavlova.
7 Push the remaining raspberries through a sieve to make a raspberry sauce. Drizzle the sauce over the Pavlova. Decorate with lavender flowers.

COOK'S TIP

To make the lavender sugar, put a few sprigs of fresh or dried lavender in a screw topped jar filled with caster sugar. Leave for at least two weeks. Shake well then discard the lavender and use as required.

STRAWBERRY MERINGUE

SERVES 4

FOR THE MERIGUE	FOR THE FILLING
3 egg whites	300 ml (10 fl oz) double cream
pinch of salt	350 g (12 oz) strawberries, sliced
250 g (9 oz) caster sugar	
5 ml (1 tsp) vanilla flavouring	
5 ml (1 tsp) vinegar	

1 Draw a 23 cm (9 inch) circle on a piece of non-stick baking parchment and place on a baking sheet.
2 Whisk the egg whites with the salt until very stiff, then gradually whisk in the sugar. Beat until it forms stiff peaks again. Fold in the vanilla flavouring and vinegar.
3 Spread the meringue mixture over the circle and bake in the oven at 140°C (275°F) mark 1 for about 1 hour until firm.
4 Leave to cool. Then carefully remove the paper and place the meringue on a plate. Whip the cream until stiff then pile on to the meringue and decorate with the fruit.

COOK'S TIP

The light, crisp texture of meringues is the perfect foil to creamy fillings and slices of soft fruit. To make the meringue filling lower in calories, use a mixture of half natural yogurt and half cream or fromage frais.

BAKED ALASKA

SERVES 6-8

225 g (8 oz) plus 10 ml (2 level tsp) caster sugar	225 g (8 oz) fresh or frozen raspberries
50 g (2 oz) plus 5 ml (1 level tsp) plain flour	30 ml (2 tbsp) orange-flavoured liqueur
2 eggs, size 2	4 egg whites, at room temperature
finely grated rind of 1 orange	450 ml (15 fl oz) vanilla ice cream

1 Grease a 20 cm (8 inch) non-stick flan tin. Sprinkle over 10 ml (2 level tsp) caster sugar and tilt the tin to give an even coating of sugar. Add 5 ml (1 level tsp) plain flour and coat similarly.

2 Place the eggs and 50 g (2 oz) caster sugar in a bowl and whisk until the mixture is very thick. Fold in the orange rind and sifted flour.

3 Pour the mixture into the tin and level the surface. Bake in the oven at 180°C (350°F) mark 4 for 20-25 minutes, until golden. Turn out on to a wire rack to cool.

4 Place the raspberries in a shallow dish and sprinkle over the liqueur. Cover and leave in a cool place for 2 hours turning occasionally.

5 Place the cold sponge flan on a large ovenproof serving dish and spoon the raspberries with the juice into the centre of the flan.

6 Stiffly whisk the egg whites. Whisk in half the remaining sugar, then carefully fold in the rest.

7 Fit a piping bag with a large star nozzle and fill with the meringue mixture. Place the ice cream on top of the raspberries. Pipe the meringue on top; start from the base and pipe the meringue around and over the ice cream to cover completely.

8 Immediately bake in the oven at 230°C (450°F) mark 8 for 3-4 minutes, until the meringue is tinged with brown; do not allow to burn. Serve immediately.

FLOATING SPICE ISLANDS

SERVES 6-8

FOR THE SAUCE	FOR THE MERINGUE
350 g (12 oz) blackcurrants, stalks removed	2 egg whites
75 g (3 oz) granulated sugar	50 g (2 oz) caster sugar
30 ml (2 tbsp) blackcurrant-flavoured liqueur	grated nutmeg
	pinch of salt

1 To make the sauce, place the blackcurrants, granulated sugar and 60 ml (4 tbsp) water in a small saucepan. Cover tightly and cook gently until the fruit softens. Rub through a nylon sieve, then leave to cool. Stir in the liqueur. Cover and chill.

2 Meanwhile to make the meringue, whisk the egg whites in a bowl until stiff, but not dry. Gradually whisk in the caster sugar, keeping the mixture stiff. Fold in 1.25 ml (¼ tsp) grated nutmeg.

3 Pour 2 cm (¾ inch) water into a large frying pan and bring to a gentle simmer. Add the salt.

4 Shape the meringue into small egg shapes, using two spoons as moulds. Slide about six or eight at a time into the liquid and poach gently for 2-3 minutes. The meringue will pull up then shrink back a little. When cooked, it will be firm if lightly touched. Remove with a fish slice and drain on absorbent kitchen paper. Poach the remaining mixture. Store in a cool place for not more than 2 hours.

5 To serve, spoon a little blackcurrant sauce on to individual serving dishes. Float a few 'islands' on top and sprinkle with nutmeg.

LIGHT BATTERS & OMELETTES

Quick and easy fruit-filled pancakes, classic French flambéed crêpes, crisp light fritters and soufflé omelettes are included in this chapter. For a special occasion, try one of the desserts based on a yeast batter – savarin, strawberry babas or blueberry blinis.

PANCAKES

MAKES 8 PANCAKES OR CRÊPES

100 g (4 oz) plain flour	300 ml (½ pint) milk
pinch of salt	oil for frying
1 egg	

1 Sift the flour and salt into a bowl and make a well in the centre. Break in the egg and beat well with a wooden spoon. Gradually beat in the milk, drawing in the flour from the sides to make a smooth batter.
2 Heat a little oil in an 18 cm (7 inch) heavy-based frying pan, running it around the base and sides of the pan, until hot. Pour off any surplus.
3 Pour in just enough batter to thinly coat the base of the pan. Cook for 1-2 minutes until golden brown. Turn or toss and cook the second side until golden.
4 Transfer the pancake to a plate and keep hot. Repeat with the remaining batter to make eight pancakes. Pile the cooked pancakes on top of each other with greaseproof paper in between each one and keep warm in the oven while cooking the remainder.
5 Serve as soon as they are all cooked, sprinkled with sugar and lemon juice.

CHERRY AND ALMOND PANCAKES

SERVES 4

425 g (15 oz) can cherry pie filling	8 pancakes (see left)
225 g (8 oz) can Morello cherries pitted	50 g (2 oz) flaked almonds, toasted
15 ml (1 tbsp) kirsch or cherry brandy	150 ml (¼ pint) double cream

1 Heat the pie filling and cherries with the kirsch or cherry brandy.
2 Spread the mixture evenly over four pancakes, place on a large ovenproof plate or dish, cover with the four remaining pancakes and sprinkle the tops with flaked almonds.
3 Cover lightly with foil and bake in the oven at 180°C (350°F) mark 4 for 25-30 minutes. Serve with the cream.

COOK'S TIP

An essential for pancake and omelette making is a good heavy-based frying pan. Ideally it should be kept solely for this purpose and should never be scrubbed, just wiped out with absorbent kitchen paper after use. Choose a pan with a base area of about 20-23 cm (8-9 inches), with or without a non-stick coating.

PANCAKES CREOLE

SERVES 4

8 pancakes (see page 287)	60 ml (4 tbsp) dark rum
finely grated rind and juice of 1 lime	2.5 ml (½ level tsp) ground cinnamon
50 g (2 oz) butter or margarine	3-4 bananas
50 g (2 oz) demerara sugar	orange and lime, to decorate

1 As they are cooked, slide each pancake out of the pan on to a warm plate and stack with greaseproof paper in between.

2 Put the lime rind and juice in a saucepan with the fat, sugar, rum and cinnamon. Heat gently until the fat has melted and the sugar dissolved, stirring occasionally.

3 Peel the bananas and slice thinly into the sauce. Cook gently for 5 minutes until tender.

4 Remove the banana slices from the sauce with a slotted spoon. Place a few slices in the centre of each pancake, then fold the pancakes into 'envelopes' around the cooked bananas.

5 Place in a warmed serving dish and pour over the hot sauce. Decorate with orange and lime twists and serve with cream, if liked.

CLAFOUTIS

SERVES 6

45 ml (3 tbsp) kirsch	pinch of salt
450 g (1 lb) black cherries, stoned	25 g (1 oz) butter, melted
FOR THE BATTER	300 ml (½ pint) creamy milk
75 g (3 oz) plain flour	3 eggs, beaten
50 g (2 oz) icing sugar	icing sugar, for dusting

1 Generously grease a shallow ovenproof dish or tin.

2 Pour the kirsch over the cherries and leave to macerate for at least 30 minutes.

3 To make the batter, mix the flour, icing sugar and salt together in a bowl, then make a well in the centre. Pour in the butter, milk and eggs. Beat together to make a smooth batter. Pour a very thin layer of batter into the prepared dish.

4 Bake in the oven at 220°C (425°F) mark 7 for 5-10 minutes or until just set.

5 Drain the cherries, reserving the liquid, and arrange in a layer over the batter. Stir the reserved liquid into the remaining batter, pour evenly over the cherries. Return to the oven and bake for a further 40-45 minutes or until risen and golden brown.

6 Leave to cool for 5 minutes, then dust generously with icing sugar and serve while still warm with single cream.

COOK'S TIP

A Clafoutis is a baked batter pudding popular throughout France. It is usually made with black cherries. Traditionalists insist that the cherries must not be stoned; we found that with stoned cherries it was much easier and daintier to eat! The choice is yours.

CREPES SUZETTE

MAKES 8

50 g (2 oz) butter or margarine	30 ml (2 tbsp) Grand Marnier or other orange-flavoured liqueur
25 g (1 oz) caster sugar	45 ml (3 tbsp) brandy or rum
finely pared rind and juice of 1 large orange	8 freshly cooked pancakes (see page 287)

1 Melt the butter in a large frying pan. Remove from the heat and add the sugar, shredded orange rind and juice, and the liqueur. Heat gently to dissolve the sugar.
2 Fold each pancake in half and then in half again to form a fan shape. Place the pancakes in the frying pan in overlapping lines.
3 Warm the brandy, pour it over the pancakes and set alight. Shake gently, then serve at once with cream.

CREPES ANNETTE

SERVES 6

FOR THE CREPES	25 g (1 oz) butter, melted
250 g (9 oz) plain flour	2 eggs, beaten
5 ml (1 level tsp) baking powder	oil for frying
2.5 ml (½ level tsp) bicarbonate of soda	FOR THE FILLING
pinch of salt	425 g (15 oz) can black cherries
135 ml (9 tbsp) kirsch	175 g (6 oz) full fat soft cheese
600 ml (1 pint) milk	50 g (2 oz) caster sugar

1 To make the crêpes, sift the flour, baking powder, bicarbonate of soda and salt into a bowl. Add 90 ml (6 tbsp) of the kirsch, the milk, butter and eggs, then beat until smooth.
2 Heat a little oil in a heavy-based frying pan. Pour in 30 ml (2 tbsp) batter. Swirl around the pan and cook until golden underneath. Turn over and cook on the other side. Make 12 crêpes.
3 Stack the crêpes with greaseproof paper in between and keep warm in the oven.
4 To make the filling, drain the cherries; reserve the juice and a few cherries. Stone the cherries, if necessary. Beat the soft cheese and sugar together until soft and fluffy. Chop the remaining cherries roughly and fold them into the cheese mixture.
5 Spread a little filling on each crêpe and fold into triangles; or put the filling in the centre and roll up the crêpes. Arrange in a serving dish and keep warm.
6 Heat the reserved cherries and syrup in a pan. Gently warm the remaining kirsch. Drizzle the cherries and syrup over the crêpes, then add the kirsch and set alight. Serve immediately.

ORANGE AND NECTARINE CREPES

SERVES 4-6

8 pancakes (see page 287)	4 large ripe nectarines
finely grated rind and juice of 2 oranges	30 ml (2 tbsp) orange-flavoured liqueur
50 g (2 oz) caster sugar	45 ml (3 tbsp) brandy

1 Grease an ovenproof dish.

2 Stack the crêpes with greaseproof paper in between and keep warm in the oven.

3 Make the orange juice up to 150 ml (¼ pint) with water. Place the rind and juice in a saucepan with the sugar. Warm gently until the sugar dissolves, then boil for 1 minute.

4 Meanwhile, quarter each nectarine, skin and roughly chop the flesh. Place the flesh in the syrup and simmer gently for 3-4 minutes.

5 Remove from the heat and stir in the liqueur. Strain off the syrup and reserve.

6 Fill the pancakes with the nectarines, then fold each pancake into a fan shape. Place, slightly overlapping, in the prepared ovenproof dish. Pour over the syrup and cover tightly with greased foil.

7 Bake in the oven at 190°C (375°F) mark 5 for about 25 minutes or until thoroughly hot.

8 Place the brandy in a small saucepan. Warm slightly, then set alight with a match and immediately pour over the crêpes. Serve straight away, with cream or yogurt.

VARIATION

Use peaches instead of nectarines for the crêpe filling.

BEIGNETS DE FRUITS

SERVES 8

225 g (8 oz) plain flour	2 large eating apples, peeled, cored and cut into rings
large pinch of salt	2 firm nectarines, stoned and cut into quarters
15 ml (1 tbsp) icing sugar	
300 ml (½ pint) beer	2 bananas, peeled and cut into chunks
2 eggs, separated	
15 ml (1 tbsp) oil	caster sugar, for sprinkling
oil for deep-frying	

1 To make the batter, mix the flour, salt and icing sugar together in a bowl, then make a well in the centre. Add the beer and egg yolks. Beat together to make a smooth batter. Add the oil. Whisk the egg whites until stiff, then fold into the batter.

2 Heat the oil in a deep-fryer to 190°C (375°F). Dip the prepared fruits in the batter and deep-fry in batches. The apple will take about 4 minutes and the nectarine and banana about 3 minutes.

3 Drain on absorbent kitchen paper and keep warm while frying the remainder. Serve hot, sprinkled with caster sugar.

COOK'S TIP

Most fruits make delicious beignets. Remember that soft fruits like apricots or peaches will require a much shorter cooking time than fruits such as apples and pears.

FRUIT AND RUM SAVARIN

SERVES 6

15 g (½ oz) fresh yeast	225 g (8 oz) granulated sugar
45 ml (3 tbsp) tepid milk	120 ml (8 tbsp) dark rum
100 g (4 oz) strong plain flour, sifted with a pinch of salt	2 bananas, peeled and sliced
	450 g (1 lb) black grapes, halved and seeded
30 ml (2 tbsp) caster sugar	2 kiwi fruit, peeled and sliced
2 eggs, beaten	2 small oranges, skinned and segmented
50 g (2 oz) unsalted butter	

1   Grease and flour a 1.1 litre (2 pint) savarin mould.
2   Cream the yeast in a small bowl with the milk. Add 25 g (1 oz) of the flour and beat well with a fork. Leave in a warm place for 10-15 minutes until frothy.
3   Put remaining flour in a warmed large bowl with 5 ml (1 tsp) of the caster sugar and the eggs. Add the frothy yeast mixture, then beat until an elastic dough is formed. Cover and leave in a warm place until doubled in size.
4   Beat the softened butter into the dough a little at a time until evenly incorporated.
5   Put the dough in the prepared mould. Cover with a floured tea towel and leave to prove in a warm place until it has risen to the top of the mould. Uncover the mould.
6   Bake in the oven at 200°C (400°F) mark 6 for 25-30 minutes until risen and golden brown.
7   Meanwhile, make the rum syrup. Put the granulated sugar and 200 ml (7 fl oz) water in a heavy-based saucepan and heat gently until the sugar has dissolved. Bring to the boil and boil steadily for 5 minutes until syrupy. Remove from the heat and stir in 90 ml (6 tbsp) of the rum.
8   Turn the savarin out on to a wire rack placed over a large plate. Prick all over with a fine skewer, then slowly spoon over the warm syrup. Leave until cold.
9   Toss the fruits together with the remaining caster sugar and rum. Place the savarin on a serving plate and pile the fruits in the centre. Serve immediately, with cream.

STRAWBERRY BABAS

SERVES 6

15 g (½ oz) fresh yeast or 7.5 ml (1½ tsp) dried	25 g (1 oz) desiccated coconut
45 ml (3 tbsp) tepid milk	90 ml (6 tbsp) redcurrant jelly or sieved strawberry jam
2 eggs, lightly beaten	
50 g (2 oz) butter, melted and cooled	75 ml (5 tbsp) lemon juice
100 g (4 oz) plain flour	450 g (1 lb) strawberries, hulled
15 ml (1 tbsp) caster sugar	

1   Lightly oil six 9 cm (3½ inch) individual ring moulds and turn upside down on absorbent kitchen paper to drain off the excess oil.
2   Blend the fresh yeast with the milk. If using dried yeast, sprinkle it on to the milk and leave in a warm place for 15 minutes or until frothy. Gradually beat the eggs and butter into the yeast liquid.
3   Mix the flour, sugar and coconut together in a bowl. With a wooden spoon, gradually stir in the yeast mixture to form a thick smooth batter. Beat together.
4   Turn the batter into the prepared moulds, cover and leave in a warm place for about 30 minutes or until the moulds are nearly two-thirds full.
5   Bake in the oven at 190°C (375°F) mark 5 for 15-20 minutes until golden. Turn out on to a wire rack placed over a large plate.
6   Put the jelly and lemon juice into a small pan over a low heat. (Alternatively, microwave on HIGH for 1-2 minutes.) When the jelly has melted, spoon over the warm babas until well glazed, allowing any excess to collect on the plate under the wire rack. Transfer to individual serving plates.
7   Return the excess jelly mixture to the pan and add the strawberries; stir to coat. Remove from heat and cool for 15-20 minutes or until almost set. Spoon into the centre of the babas. Serve warm or cold, with cream.

BLUEBERRY AND BUTTERMILK BLINIS

SERVES 8

125 g (4 oz) plain flour	450 ml (¾ pint) buttermilk
125 g (4 oz) buckwheat flour	1 egg, separated
30 ml (2 tbsp) caster sugar	vegetable oil for frying
2.5 ml (½ level tsp) salt	225 g (8 oz) blueberries
2.5 ml (½ level tsp) fast action dried yeast	raspberry sauce and soured cream or maple syrup, to serve

1 Put the flours, sugar, salt and yeast into a bowl and mix well. Gradually beat in the buttermilk to make a smooth batter. Cover and leave in a warm place for about 40 minutes or until doubled in size.

2 Beat in the egg yolk. Whisk the egg white until stiff, then fold into the batter with the blueberries.

3 Heat a griddle or large flat, heavy-based frying pan. Brush generously with oil and heat until the oil is hot.

4 Using a measuring jug or a ladle, drop three or four small 'pools' of batter onto the hot griddle.

5 Cook over medium heat for 2-3 minutes until bubbles rise to the surface and burst, then turn the blinis over with a palette knife. Continue cooking for a further 2-3 minutes until golden brown on the other side.

6 Keep the blinis warm, wrapped in a clean tea towel in a low oven while you cook the remainder. Re-grease the griddle or frying pan in between cooking each batch. Serve warm with raspberry sauce and soured cream or maple syrup.

RUM SOUFFLE OMELETTE

SERVES 1

2 eggs, separated	15 g (½ oz) butter
5 ml (1 tsp) caster sugar	5 ml (1 tbsp) apricot jam, warmed
15 ml (1 tbsp) dark rum	30 ml (2 tbsp) icing sugar

1 Mix the egg yolks, caster sugar and rum together in a bowl.

2 Whisk the egg whites until stiff and standing in peaks.

3 Melt the butter in a heavy-based omelette pan until foaming. Fold the egg whites quickly into the egg yolk mixture, then pour into the foaming butter.

4 Cook over moderate heat for 2-3 minutes until the underside of the omelette is golden brown. Place the pan under a preheated hot grill and cook for a few minutes more until the top is golden brown.

5 Slide the omelette on to a sheet of foil placed on a warmed serving plate. Spread with the warmed jam, then tip the foil to fold over the omelette.

6 Sift the icing sugar thickly over the top of the omelette, then mark in a criss-cross pattern with hot metal skewers, if liked. Carefully remove the foil and serve immediately.

VARIATIONS

Fruit Soufflé Omelette
Replace the apricot jam with sliced fresh fruit or berries, such as raspberries or strawberries.

Chocolate Soufflé Omelette
Omit the jam and drizzle the omelette with 40 g (1½ oz) melted chocolate (in step 5). Add a few chopped nuts. Sprinkle the soufflé omelette with a mixture of icing sugar and ground cinnamon.

CUSTARDS & CREAM DESSERTS

From fragrant custards and syllabubs – delicately flavoured with vanilla, subtle spices and herbs – to sophisticated bavarois and classic Italian tiramisu, here you will find smooth, creamy desserts to tempt every palate. Childhood favourites such as blancmange are included too.

CREME CARAMEL

SERVES 4

125 g (4 oz) sugar plus 15 ml (1 level tbsp)	600 ml (1 pint) milk
4 eggs	1.25 ml (¼ tsp) vanilla flavouring

1 Place the 125 g (4 oz) sugar in a small saucepan and carefully pour in 150 ml (¼ pint) water. Heat gently until all the sugar has dissolved, stirring occasionally.
2 Bring the syrup to a fast boil and cook rapidly until the caramel is a golden brown. Remove from the heat and leave for a few seconds to darken. Pour into a 15 cm (6 inch) soufflé dish and cool.
3 Whisk the eggs and remaining sugar in a bowl. Warm the milk and pour on to the egg mixture. Whisk in the vanilla, then strain the custard on to the cool caramel.
4 Stand the dish in a roasting tin containing enough hot water to come halfway up the sides of the dish. Bake in the oven at 170°C (325°F) mark 3 for about 1 hour. The custard should be just set and firm to the touch.
5 When cold, cover the dish and leave in the refrigerator for several hours, preferably overnight. Take out of the refrigerator 30 minutes before serving. Carefully invert on to plates, allowing the caramel to run down the sides.

CREME BRULEE

SERVES 6

600 ml (1 pint) double cream	4 egg yolks
1 vanilla pod	125 g (4 oz) caster sugar

1 Pour the cream into the top of a double boiler or into a mixing bowl placed over a pan of simmering water. Add the vanilla pod and warm gently until almost boiling, then remove from the heat. Remove the vanilla pod.
2 Beat together the egg yolks and 50 g (2 oz) of the caster sugar until light in colour. Gradually pour on the cream, stirring until evenly mixed.
3 Stand 6 individual ramekin dishes in a roasting tin containing enough hot water to come halfway up the sides of the dishes. Pour the custard mixture slowly into the ramekins, dividing it equally between them.
4 Bake in the oven at 150°C (300°F) mark 2 for about 1 hour until set. Do not allow the skin to colour. Remove from the tin and leave to cool, then refrigerate overnight.
5 Sprinkle the remaining sugar evenly over the top of each and put under a preheated hot grill for 2-3 minutes until the sugar turns to a caramel. Leave to cool, then chill before serving.

TANGERINE BRULEES

SERVES 2

150 ml (¼ pint) double cream	45 ml (3 tbsp) caster sugar
few drops of vanilla flavouring	1 tangerine, peeled and segmented
2 egg yolks, size 6	20 ml (4 tsp) orange-flavoured liqueur

1 Pour the cream into a small saucepan and heat until almost boiling, then remove from the heat. Add the vanilla flavouring.
2 In a medium bowl, beat together the egg yolks and 15 ml (1 tbsp) of the caster sugar until light in colour.
3 Pour the cream gradually on to the egg yolk and sugar mixture, stirring well.
4 Strain the mixture into the saucepan and cook, stirring over a gentle heat for about 10 minutes, or until the mixture coats the back of a spoon. Cover with greaseproof paper and allow to cool for 20 minutes.
5 Lay the segments of tangerine in the bottom of two 150 ml (¼ pint) ramekins and add 10 ml (2 tsp) liqueur to each one. Spoon the cooled custard mixture evenly into the ramekins, dividing it equally between them.
6 Cover and chill in the refrigerator for at least 3 hours or overnight.
7 Sprinkle the remaining sugar evenly over the top of each ramekin and put under a preheated hot grill for 2-3 minutes until the sugar turns to a caramel. Leave to cool for 15 minutes, then chill for at least 2 hours before serving.

MINTED STRAWBERRY CUSTARDS

SERVES 6

450 ml (¾ pint) milk	20 ml (4 level tsp) powdered gelatine
4 large sprigs mint	700 g (1½ lb) strawberries, hulled
1 egg	
2 egg yolks	15 ml (1 tbsp) icing sugar
45 ml (3 tbsp) caster sugar	strawberries, to decorate

1 Oil six 150 ml (¼ pint) ramekin dishes.
2 Place the milk and mint sprigs in a saucepan. Bring slowly to the boil, cover and leave to infuse for about 30 minutes.
3 Whisk the egg and yolks with the caster sugar in a bowl. Strain over the milk. Return to the pan and cook gently, stirring, until the custard just coats the back of the spoon; do not boil. Leave to cool.
4 Sprinkle the gelatine over 45 ml (3 tbsp) water in a small bowl and leave to soak for 2-3 minutes. Place the bowl over a pan of simmering water and stir until dissolved. (Alternatively, microwave on HIGH for 30 seconds or until dissolved.) Stir the gelatine into the custard.
5 Purée and sieve the strawberries. Whisk about two thirds into the cold, but not set, custard. Pour the custard into the dishes and chill to set – about 3 hours.
6 Meanwhile, whisk the icing sugar into the remaining strawberry purée. Chill.
7 To serve, turn out the custards. Surround with strawberry sauce, then decorate with strawberries.

VARIATION

Replace the mint sprigs with a few lemon geranium leaves.

COEURS
A LA CREME

225 g (8 oz) curd or ricotta cheese	few drops of vanilla essence
300 ml (½ pint) crème fraîche	25 g (1 oz) caster sugar
	2 egg whites

1 Line four small heart-shaped perforated moulds with muslin.
2 Press the cheese through a nylon sieve into a bowl. Lightly whip the cream, vanilla essence and sugar together. Mix into the cheese.
3 Whisk the egg whites until stiff, then fold into the cheese mixture.
4 Turn the mixture into the prepared moulds. Leave to drain overnight in the refrigerator. Turn out and serve with strawberries and single cream.

COOK'S TIP

Light, delicate and refreshing, this may be eaten with cream, or with soft summer fruit, ideally, tiny wild strawberries. This dessert takes its name from the small heart-shaped white porcelain colanders in which it is made.

COCONUT CUSTARDS
WITH TROPICAL FRUITS

225 g (8 oz) granulated sugar	60 ml (4 tbsp) shredded or desiccated coconut
3 eggs	2 mangoes, peeled
2 egg yolks	1 large pawpaw, peeled
30 ml (2 tbsp) caster sugar	juice of 1-2 limes
600 ml (1 pint) thin coconut milk	2 passion fruit
300 ml (½ pint) evaporated milk	

1 Have ready eight warmed 150 ml (¼ pint) ramekins. Put the granulated sugar in a heavy saucepan, pour in 150 ml (¼ pint) cold water and heat gently, until dissolved. Increase the heat and boil, without stirring, until dark caramel in colour. Immediately pour into the ramekins, swirling the caramel around the sides quickly.
2 Put the eggs, egg yolks and caster sugar in a bowl and beat to mix. Pour the coconut and evaporated milks into a saucepan and heat to scalding point. Pour over the egg mixture, stirring all the time.
3 Strain the custard into the ramekins. Place the ramekins in a roasting pan and pour in enough hot water to come halfway up the sides. Cover with lightly oiled foil, then bake in the oven at 170°C (325°F) mark 3 for 50 minutes or until set, but still wobbly around the edges. Remove from the oven and leave to cool in the pan of hot water. Chill in the refrigerator overnight.
4 Meanwhile, dry fry the coconut in a wok or heavy frying pan over low heat for 5-6 minutes, stirring, until golden. Slice the mangoes and pawpaw lengthways.
5 To serve, run a knife around the edge of each custard, then carefully invert onto dessert plates, allowing the caramel to run down the sides. Arrange a few slices of mango and pawpaw to the side of each custard, then sprinkle with lime juice and squeeze the passion fruit pulp over the top. Sprinkle toasted coconut on top.

CAPPUCCINO CREAMS

SERVES 8

550 g (1¼ lb) fromage frais	175 g (6 oz) dark or bitter chocolate
15-30 ml (1-2 tbsp) finely ground espresso coffee	chocolate curls, to decorate
15-30 ml (1-2 tbsp) icing sugar (optional)	

1 Mix the fromage frais with the coffee and icing sugar, if liked.

2 Pulverise the chocolate in an electric blender or liquidiser until very fine. Alternatively grate finely.

3 Spoon half the fromage frais into eight individual ramekins or glass dishes. Sprinkle over most of the chocolate mixture. Top with the remaining fromage frais and sprinkle with the remaining chocolate mixture. Decorate with chocolate curls.

COOK'S TIP

These little desserts are light but creamy and can be made with low-fat fromage frais if preferred. Use a good dark chocolate – the flavour is so much better.

ALMOND CUSTARD TARTS

SERVES 10

1 quantity shortcrust pastry (see page 327)	50 g (2 oz) caster sugar
FOR THE FILLING	1.25 ml (¼ tsp) almond flavouring
200 ml (7 fl oz) milk	flaked almonds, toasted
2 eggs	icing sugar, for dusting

1 Grease ten 75 cm (3 inch) fluted brioche tins and place on a baking sheet.

2 Roll out the pastry thinly on a floured work surface and use to line the tins. Chill for 20 minutes.

3 Bake blind in the oven at 200°C (400°F) mark 6 for 15 minutes.

4 To make the filling, whisk the milk, eggs, caster sugar and almond flavouring together. Pour into the pastry cases. Scatter toasted almonds on top.

5 Reduce the oven temperature to 180°C (350°F) mark 4 and bake for a further 15-20 minutes until just set. Leave the tarts to cool before serving. Dust with icing sugar.

COFFEE BAVAROIS

SERVES 6

125 g (4 oz) well roasted coffee beans	20 ml (4 level tsp) powdered gelatine
900 ml (1½ pints) milk	300 ml (10 fl oz) double cream
6 egg yolks	grated chocolate and sugar coffee beans, to decorate
75 g (3 oz) caster sugar	

1 Put the coffee beans in a saucepan and place over a low heat; warm very gently for 2-3 minutes, shaking the pan frequently. Remove from the heat, pour the milk into the pan, return to the heat and bring to the boil. Remove from the heat, cover and leave to infuse for 30 minutes.

2 Place the egg yolks and caster sugar in a deep mixing bowl and beat until thick and light in colour. Strain the coffee infusion on to the egg yolks, stirring well.

3 Return the custard mixture to the rinsed-out saucepan and cook very gently, stirring, until the custard thickens slightly. Do not boil. Strain into a large bowl and cool.

4 In a small bowl, sprinkle the gelatine over 60 ml (4 tbsp) water. Place over a pan of hot water and stir until dissolved. Stir the gelatine into the cooled custard. Stand the custard in a roasting tin half-filled with water and surround with ice cubes. Stir the custard frequently while it cools to setting point.

5 Meanwhile, lightly whip half the cream and grease a 1.4 litre (2 pint) soufflé dish or mould.

6 When the custard is well chilled and beginning to thicken, fold in the whipped cream. Pour the setting custard into the dish and refrigerate until completely set.

7 With a dampened finger, gently ease the edges of the bavarois away from the dish. Moisten a flat plate and place over the dish. Invert the plate and shake gently. Ease off the dish and slide the bavarois on to the plate.

8 Whisk the remaining cream until it holds its shape. Decorate the bavarois with piped cream, grated chocolate and coffee beans.

CALEDONIAN CREAMS

SERVES 6

90 ml (6 level tbsp) thin shred marmalade	juice of 1 lemon
25 g (1 oz) caster sugar	300 ml (10 fl oz) double or whipping cream
60 ml (4 tbsp) whisky liqueur	

1 Mix together the marmalade, sugar, liqueur and lemon juice.

2 Whip the cream until softly stiff. Gently whisk in the marmalade mixture until the cream stands in soft peaks; take care not to overwhip. Serve in small glasses.

COOK'S TIP

Properly whipped cream is essential when a smooth, airy texture is required. Choose double or whipping cream for whipping. To achieve more volume, add 15 ml (1 tbsp) milk to each 150 ml (¼ pint) cream before starting. Chill the cream and all the utensils thoroughly beforehand. Whip quickly at first, using a balloon whisk or hand-held electric whisk, until the cream begins to look matt on the surface. Continue whipping, a little more slowly until it stands in soft peaks and does not fall off the upturned whisk. Extra care is needed if using an electric whisk.

If overwhipped, the cream will look granular and the flavour will be affected. It is impossible to rescue if this happens. Overwhipped cream will not fold smoothly into mousses, bavarois and other creamy desserts.

DAMASK CREAM

SERVES 4

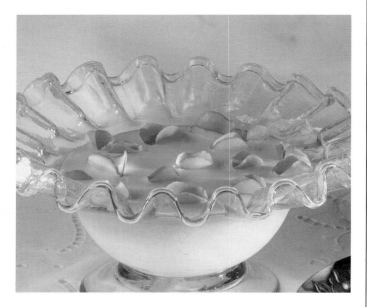

600 ml (1 pint) single cream	15 ml (1 tbsp) brandy
45 ml (3 tbsp) caster sugar	60 ml (4 tbsp) clotted or double cream
10 ml (2 tsp) rennet essence	5 ml (1 tsp) rose water
large pinch of grated nutmeg	rose petals, to decorate (optional)

1 Put the cream and 30 ml (2 tbsp) of the sugar in a saucepan. Heat gently until tepid, stirring until the sugar dissolves. (When the mixture is tepid it will register 36.9°C (98.4°F) on a sugar thermometer, or not feel hot or cold if you put your finger in it.)

2 Stir in the rennet, nutmeg and brandy, then pour into a serving dish. Leave for 2-3 hours until set. It is important not to disturb the junket during this time or it will not set.

3 When the junket is set, mix the remaining sugar, the cream and rose water together and spoon carefully over the top. Decorate with rose petals, if liked.

COOK'S TIP

This subtly flavoured dish, also known as Devonshire junket, is a far cry from a junket that comes from a packet. Do not serve it until you are ready to eat, as once it is cut the shape will disintegrate. Rose petals make a pretty decoration.

TEA CREAM

SERVES 4

300 ml (½ pint) milk	30 ml (2 tbsp) caster sugar
15 g (½ oz) Earl Grey tea leaves	15 ml (1 level tbsp) powdered gelatine
2 eggs, separated	150 ml (¼ pint) double cream

1 Put the milk into a saucepan, add the tea and bring to the boil. Remove from the heat and leave to infuse for 10-15 minutes or until the milk is well coloured with the tea.

2 Beat the egg yolks and sugar together, then strain on the milk and mix well. Return to the pan and cook gently for 10 minutes, stirring all the time, until the custard thickens slightly and just coats the back of the spoon.

3 Sprinkle the gelatine over 45 ml (3 tbsp) water in a small bowl and leave to soak for 2-3 minutes. Place the bowl over a pan of simmering water and stir until dissolved. (Alternatively, microwave on HIGH for 30 seconds or until dissolved.)

4 Mix the dissolved gelatine into the tea mixture. Leave for about 2 hours until beginning to set. Stir the mixture occasionally.

5 Whip the cream until thick but not stiff, then fold into the custard. Finally, whisk the egg whites until stiff, then fold into the mixture.

6 Pour the cream mixture into a dampened 600 ml (1 pint) mould. Chill for about 2-3 hours until set. Turn out on to a chilled dish and decorate with grapes and crisp biscuits, if liked.

SERVING SUGGESTION

Smooth puddings such as fools, bavarois, syllabubs and creams are best served with crisp biscuits to give a contrast in texture.

ZABAGLIONE

SERVES 6

4 egg yolks	100 ml (4 fl oz) Marsala
65 g (2½ oz) caster sugar	

1 Beat the egg yolks and sugar together in a large bowl. Add the Marsala and beat until mixed.
2 Place the bowl over a saucepan of simmering water and heat gently, whisking the mixture until it is very thick and creamy.
3 To serve, pour the zabaglione into six glasses and serve immediately, with sponge fingers.

COOK'S TIP

A classic, rich Italian dessert to serve after a light main course. It should be served as soon as it is made so that it remains light, fluffy and slightly warm. Serve with sponge fingers or crisp dessert biscuits.

LEMON BALM SYLLABUB

SERVES 6-8

30 ml (2 tbsp) finely chopped lemon balm leaves	5 ml (1 tsp) caster sugar, or to taste
600 ml (1 pint) double cream	TO DECORATE
150 ml (¼ pint) sweet white wine	nutmeg, lemon shreds and sprigs of lemon balm
grated rind and juice of 2 lemons	

1 Whisk together all the ingredients until the mixture is the consistency of custard.
2 Leave in the refrigerator for 2-3 hours to chill. To serve, spoon the syllabub into tall glasses, grate a little nutmeg on the top and garnish with lemon shreds and sprigs of lemon balm.

OLD ENGLISH SYLLABUB

SERVES 4

1 clove	finely grated rind and juice of 1 lemon
1 allspice	90 ml (6 tbsp) pale cream sherry
2.5 cm (1 inch) cinnamon stick	300 ml (½ pint) double cream
little grated nutmeg	24 ratafia biscuits
50 g (2 oz) caster sugar	

1 Very finely grind the clove, allspice and cinnamon stick with a pestle and mortar, then sift through a fine sieve.

2 Put the ground spices, nutmeg, sugar, lemon rind, lemon juice and sherry into a bowl. Stir well until the sugar dissolves, then cover and leave to stand for 1 hour.

3 Strain the sherry mixture through a fine nylon sieve into a clean bowl. Pour in the cream in a continuous stream, whisking all the time. Whip the cream mixture until it is just thick enough to hold a trail when the whisk is lifted.

4 Place four ratafias in each of four serving glasses, then fill each glass with the spicy syllabub. Chill for about 1 hour. Decorate with the remaining ratafias.

COOK'S TIP

Bring out the full fragrance of the spices by grinding them just before use. Decorate the syllabub with fresh edible flower petals such as nasturtium, geranium and rose, or with borage flowers.

WINE JELLY CREAM

SERVES 4

300 ml (½ pint) white wine	15 ml (1 tbsp) cornflour
45 ml (3 tbsp) sugar	2. 5 ml (½ tsp) vanilla flavouring
15 g (½ oz) powdered gelatine	150 ml (5 fl oz) whipping cream
450 ml (¾ pint) milk	
2 egg yolks	strawberries, to decorate

1 Heat half the wine, 30 ml (2 tbsp) of the sugar and the gelatine in a small saucepan. Dissolve over a gentle heat, then mix with remaining wine and set aside to cool.

2 Pour into 4 wine glasses. Place in the refrigerator to set at a 45° angle.

3 Pour the milk into a medium saucepan and heat almost to boiling point. In a medium bowl, blend together the egg yolks, cornflour, remaining sugar and vanilla flavouring until pale, then pour on the hot milk, stirring continuously.

4 Strain the mixture into a medium heavy-based or double saucepan and stir over a gentle heat until the custard thickens enough to coat the back of a wooden spoon; this takes about 20 minutes. Cool. Whip the cream until stiff, then fold into the cooled custard.

5 When the wine jelly is set, stand the glasses upright and pour in the custard. Return to the refrigerator to chill. Decorate with strawberries and serve with dessert biscuits.

HONEY MOUSSE

SERVES 6

3 eggs, separated	300 ml (10 fl oz) whipping cream
100 g (4 oz) caster sugar	30 ml (2 tbsp) clear honey
finely grated rind of 2 lemons	pistachio nuts or coarsely grated chocolate, to decorate
90 ml (6 tbsp) lemon juice	
10 ml (2 level tsp) powdered gelatine	

1 Whisk together the egg yolks, sugar and lemon rind until thick. Add 45 ml (3 tbsp) lemon juice and place over a pan of simmering water until thick and mousse-like. Remove from the heat and whisk occasionally until cold.
2 Soak the gelatine in the remaining lemon juice in a small bowl. Place the bowl over a pan of hot water and stir until dissolved.
3 Whip the cream until softly stiff. Whisk the egg whites until stiff. Fold half the cream into the mousse with the gelatine, honey and whisked egg whites. Turn into a 1.1 litre (2 pint) glass bowl.
4 Decorate with the remaining whipped cream and chopped pistachio nuts.

GOOSEBERRY CHARLOTTE

SERVES 6

450 g (1 lb) gooseberries, topped and tailed	2 egg yolks
75 g (3 oz) caster sugar	300 ml (½ pint) milk
10 ml (2 level tsp) powdered gelatine	300 ml (½ pint) double cream
	20 langue de chat biscuits, trimmed to size

1 Oil a 15 cm (6 inch) soufflé dish and line the base with greaseproof paper.
2 Place the gooseberries in a small saucepan with 60 ml (4tbsp) water. Cover and simmer for about 10 minutes until the fruit softens to a pulpy consistency.
3 Purée the gooseberries in a blender or food processor, then sieve to remove pips. Stir in 50 g (2 oz) of the sugar.
4 Sprinkle the gelatine over 30 ml (2 tbsp) water in a small bowl and leave to soak for 2-3 minutes. Place the bowl over a pan of simmering water and stir until dissolved. (Alternatively, microwave on HIGH for 30 seconds or until dissolved.)
5 Meanwhile, make the custard. Beat the egg yolks and remaining sugar together in a bowl until light in colour. In a small saucepan, warm the milk, and pour over the eggs and sugar, stirring until blended.
6 Return to the pan and cook over a low heat, stirring all the time, until the custard thickens sufficiently to lightly coat the back of the spoon – do not boil.
7 Remove from the heat and add the dissolved gelatine. Pour the custard out into a large bowl and mix in the gooseberry purée. Leave to cool for 45 minutes.
8 Lightly whip the cream. When the gooseberry mixture is cold, but not set, stir in half the cream until evenly blended. Pour the gooseberry mixture into the prepared dish. Chill for 1-2 hours to set. When firm, turn out on to a flat serving plate.
9 Spread a thin covering of the remaining cream around the side of the charlotte and press on the biscuits. Decorate with the remaining cream.

BOODLE'S ORANGE FOOL

SERVES 6

4-6 trifle sponge cakes, cut into 1 cm (½ inch) thick slices	25-50 g (1-2 oz) sugar
grated rind and juice of 2 oranges	300 ml (10 fl oz) double cream
grated rind and juice of 1 lemon	orange slices or segments, to decorate

1 Use the sponge cake slices to line the bottom and halfway up the sides of a deep dish or individual bowls.
2 Mix the orange and lemon rinds and juice with the sugar and stir until the sugar has completely dissolved.
3 In another bowl, whip the cream until it just starts to thicken, then slowly add the sweetened fruit juice, continuing to whip until the cream is light and thickened and the juice all absorbed.
4 Pour the mixture over the sponge cakes and refrigerate for at least 2 hours. Decorate with orange slices, or segments to serve.

CHILLED BLACKBERRY SNOW

SERVES 6

450 g (1 lb) blackberries, fresh or frozen, thawed	300 ml (10 fl oz) double cream
2 egg whites	few blackberries, to decorate
50 g (2 oz) caster sugar	

1 Rub the blackberries through a nylon sieve. Pour the purée into a rigid container and freeze for about 2 hours or until mushy.
2 Whisk the egg whites until stiff, then add the sugar gradually, whisking until the mixture stands in soft peaks. Whip the cream until it just holds its shape.
3 Remove the frozen blackberry purée from the freezer and mash to break down the large ice crystals, being careful not to break it down completely.
4 Fold the cream and egg white mixture together, then quickly fold in the semi-frozen blackberry purée to form a 'swirled' effect. Spoon into tall glasses and decorate with blackberries. Serve immediately, with crisp wafers.

COOK'S TIP

The swirled layers of iced fruit purée and creamy egg white are very effective in this recipe but do finish it off just before it is needed and serve immediately. If really necessary, it can be kept refrigerated for a couple of hours, but it will start to lose some volume.

BLANCMANGE

SERVES 4

60 ml (4 level tbsp) cornflour	strip of lemon rind
600 ml (1 pint) milk	45 ml (3 level tbsp) sugar

1 Blend the cornflour to a smooth paste with 30 ml (2 tbsp) of the milk.
2 Put the remaining milk in a saucepan with the lemon rind, bring to the boil, then strain it on to the blended mixture, stirring well.
3 Return the mixture to the pan and bring to the boil, stirring until the mixture thickens; cook for a further 3 minutes. Add sugar to taste.
4 Pour into a 600 ml (1 pint) dampened jelly mould and leave for several hours until set. Turn out to serve.

VARIATIONS

Omit the lemon rind and add 50 g (2 oz) melted chocolate or 15-30 ml (1-2 tbsp) coffee essence to the cooked mixture.

ZUPPA INGLESE

SERVES 6-8

600 ml (1 pint) milk	150 ml (¼ pint) water
1 vanilla pod	16 trifle sponge cakes
4 eggs	300 ml (10 fl oz) double cream
50 g (2 oz) caster sugar	glacé cherries and angelica, to decorate
225 ml (8 fl oz) Marsala	

1 To make the custard, bring the milk to the boil with the vanilla pod added and immediately remove from the heat. Leave to infuse for 20 minutes, then strain.
2 Put the eggs and sugar in a heatproof bowl and lightly whisk together. Slowly pour in the milk, whisking all the time.
3 Stand the bowl over a pan of gently simmering water and stir until thick enough to coat the back of a spoon. (Be patient – this can take as long as 20 minutes.)
4 Remove the bowl from the 4 heat, cover the surface of the custard closely with greaseproof paper and leave until cold.
5 Mix the Marsala and water together in a shallow dish. Dip a few of the trifle sponges in the liquid, then use them to line the bottom of a glass serving bowl.
6 Pour one third of the cold custard over the sponges. Dip a few more trifle sponges in the liquid and place on top of the custard. Cover with another third of the custard.
7 In a separate bowl, whip the cream until thick, then spread half over the custard.
8 Finish with a layer each of the remaining sponges and liquid, the custard and cream. Chill in the refrigerator for at least 4 hours, preferably overnight. Decorate with glacé cherries and angelica just before serving.

OLDE ENGLISH TRIFLE

SERVES 6-8

4 trifle sponges	450 ml (¾ pint) milk
60 ml (4 tbsp) cherry jam	3 eggs
15 ratafia biscuits	50 g (2 oz) caster sugar
60 ml (4 tbsp) sherry	150 ml (5 fl oz) double cream
2 bananas, peeled and sliced	few cherries, to decorate
grated rind and juice of ½ lemon	25 g (1 oz) chopped nuts, toasted, to decorate
225 g (8 oz) cherries, stoned	

1   Cut the trifle sponges in half and spread with jam, then sandwich together. Arrange in the base of a glass serving dish.

2   Cover with ratafias and sprinkle with sherry. Coat the bananas in lemon juice. Arrange the bananas and cherries on top of the ratafias.

3   Heat the milk in a medium saucepan until almost boiling. In a large bowl, whisk together the eggs, lemon rind and sugar until pale, then pour on the hot milk, stirring continuously.

4   Return to the saucepan and heat gently, stirring continuously, until the custard thickens enough to coat the back of a wooden spoon; do not allow to boil. This takes about 20 minutes. Set aside to cool.

5   Pour the custard over the trifle and leave until cold.

6   Whip the cream until softly stiff and spread on the top of the trifle. Decorate with cherries and nuts.

TIRAMISU

SERVES 8

four 250 g (9 oz) cartons mascarpone cheese	425 ml (14 fl oz) very strong cold black coffee
40 g (1½ oz) caster sugar	about 30 savoiardi (Italian sponge fingers)
3 eggs, separated	cocoa powder, for sprinkling
250 ml (8 fl oz) kahlua or other coffee-flavoured liqueur	

1   Put the mascarpone cheese, sugar and egg yolks in a bowl and beat with an electric mixer until evenly blended and creamy.

2   Whisk the egg whites until standing in stiff peaks. Fold into the mascarpone mixture until evenly incorporated. Spoon a quarter of the mixture into the base of a glass serving bowl.

3   Mix the liqueur and coffee together in a shallow dish. One at a time, dip one third of the savoiardi in this mixture for 10-15 seconds, turning once so they become soaked through but do not lose their shape. After each one has been dipped, place it on top of the mascarpone in the bowl, making a single layer of savoiardi that covers the mascarpone completely.

4   Cover the savoiardi with one third of the remaining mascarpone, then dip another third of the savoiardi in the liqueur and coffee mixture and layer them in the bowl as before.

5   Repeat with another layer of mascarpone and savoiardi, then spread the remaining mascarpone over the top and swirl with a palette knife. Sift cocoa powder liberally all over the top. Cover the bowl and chill in the refrigerator for 24 hours. Serve chilled.

KHEER

SERVES 4-6

seeds of 4 green cardamoms	100 g (4 oz) caster sugar
4 whole cloves	1.25 ml (¼ tsp) orange flower water
2.5 cm (1 inch) stick cinnamon	split pistachio nuts or almonds, to decorate
1.2 litres (2 pints) milk	
75 g (3 oz) short grain pudding rice	

1 Grind the cardamom seeds, whole cloves and cinnamon stick in a small electric mill or with a pestle and mortar to a coarse powder.
2 Pour the milk into a heavy-based saucepan, add the rice, sugar and crushed spices and bring slowly to the boil, stirring.
3 Lower the heat and simmer very gently, uncovered, for 1 hour or until the rice is tender. Stir frequently during this time to prevent the rice sticking to the bottom of the pan.
4 Remove the pan from the heat and pour the Kheer into a bowl. Add the orange flower water and stir well to mix.
5 Cover the bowl with cling film. Leave until cold, then chill for at least 2 hours before serving.
6 To serve, pour the Kheer into 4-6 individual glasses or glass dishes and decorate with pistachios or almonds. Serve well chilled.

BAKED SAFFRON YOGURT

SERVES 8

300 ml (½ pint) milk	383 g (13.5 oz) can condensed milk
pinch of saffron threads	300 ml (½ pint) natural yogurt
6 green cardamoms	1 large ripe mango, to decorate
2 eggs	
2 egg yolks	

1 Pour the milk into a heavy-based sausepan, add the saffron and cardamoms and bring slowly to the boil. Remove from the heat, cover and infuse for 10-15 minutes.
2 Put the eggs, egg yolks, condensed milk and yogurt in a bowl and beat together.
3 Strain in the milk, stirring gently to mix. Divide between 8 ramekin dishes.
4 Place the ramekins in a roasting tin. Add hot water to come halfway up the sides. Bake in the oven at 180°C (350°F) mark 4 until firm to the touch.
5 Cool the baked yogurt desserts completely, then chill for at least 2 hours before serving.
6 To serve, run a blunt-edged knife around the edge of each yogurt, then turn out on to individual dishes.
7 Peel the mango and slice thinly on either side of the central stone. Serve with the saffron yogurts.

SERVING SUGGESTION

These individual, golden-tinted yogurts make an attractive finale to an Indian meal. They are also excellent for children at tea-time, served with fresh fruit.

QUEEN OF PUDDINGS

SERVES 4

4 eggs	45-60 ml (3-4 level tbsp) raspberry jam
600 ml (1 pint) milk	75 g (3 oz) caster sugar
100 g (4 oz) fresh breadcrumbs	

1 Separate 3 eggs and beat together the 3 egg yolks and 1 whole egg. Add to the milk and mix well. Stir in the breadcrumbs.
2 Spread the jam on the bottom of a pie dish. Pour over the milk mixture and leave for 30 minutes.
3 Bake in the oven at 150°C (300°F) mark 2 for 1 hour, until set.
4 Whisk the egg whites until stiff, then fold in the sugar. Pile on top of the custard and return to the oven for a further 15-20 minutes until the meringue is set.

OSBORNE PUDDING

SERVES 4

4 thin slices day-old wholemeal bread	2 eggs
butter for spreading	15 ml (1 tbsp) brandy or rum (optional)
orange marmalade for spreading	finely grated rind of 1 orange
50 g (2 oz) currants or sultanas	15 ml (1 tbsp) light soft brown sugar
450 ml (¾ pint) milk	grated nutmeg

1 Spread the bread with butter and marmalade, then cut into triangles. Arrange, buttered side up, in a buttered ovenproof serving dish, sprinkling the layers with the fruit.
2 Heat the milk, but do not boil. Beat the eggs with the brandy, if using, and the orange rind, then gradually pour on the warm milk, stirring continuously. Pour over the bread and leave to stand for at least 15 minutes to allow the bread to absorb the milk.
3 Sprinkle the sugar and nutmeg on top of the pudding and bake at 180°C (350°F) mark 4 for 30-40 minutes, until set and lightly browned. Serve hot with custard or cream.

CHOCOLATE DESSERTS

These unashamedly rich desserts are guaranteed to satisfy all chocolate addicts. Choose from smooth creamy mousses, rich gooey puddings and a mouth-watering selection of luxurious chocolate gâteaux. Elaborate concoctions for special occasions include a sensational truffle cake, chocolate chestnut vacherin and an irresistible roulade.

CHOCOLATE LACE BASKETS

SERVES 6

150 g (5 oz) plain chocolate-flavoured cake covering	¼ fresh pineapple
1 small mango	12 strawberries
	1 passion fruit

1 Break the cake covering into small pieces. Place in a heatproof bowl standing over a pan of simmering water and heat gently until it melts.
2 Invert six 8.5 cm (3½ inch) ring moulds and stretch cling film over the rounded bases to cover completely.
3 Spoon half the melted chocolate cake covering into a greaseproof paper piping bag and snip off the point. Pipe three of the ring moulds with a lacy pattern of cake covering.
4 Fill a second bag with melted cake covering and pipe the remaining three moulds. Chill until set.
5 Meanwhile, peel the mango and chop the flesh. Cut the pineapple flesh into pieces. Hull the strawberries. Halve the passion fruit and scoop out the pulp.
6 Carefully lift the chocolate baskets with the cling film, then remove the cling film from the shells. Fill the baskets with the fruit. Serve with whipped cream.

PROFITEROLES

SERVES 4

1 quantity choux pastry (see page 251)	15 g (½ oz) butter or margarine
FOR THE CHOCOLATE SAUCE AND FILLING	30 ml (2 tbsp) golden syrup
	2-3 drops of vanilla essence
100 g (4 oz) plain chocolate	150 ml (¼ pint) double cream

1 Put the choux pastry in a piping bag fitted with a 1 cm (½ inch) plain nozzle. Pipe about 20 small bun shapes on two dampened baking sheets.
2 Bake in the oven at 220°C (425°F) mark 7 for about 20-25 minutes until well risen and golden brown. Reduce the oven temperature to 180°C (350°F) mark 4. Remove the choux buns from the oven and make a hole in the side of each bun with a knife. Return to the oven for 5 minutes to dry out completely. Leave to cool on a wire rack.
3 For the chocolate sauce, melt the chocolate, butter, 30 ml (2 tbsp) water, the golden syrup and vanilla essence in a small saucepan over a very low heat. Stir until smooth.
4 Whip the cream until it just holds its shape. Spoon into a piping bag, fitted with a medium plain nozzle and use to fill the choux buns through the hole in the sides.
5 Serve with the chocolate sauce spooned over.

CHOCOLATE MOUSSE CUPS

SERVES 6

3 large sheets filo pastry, about 25 x 50 cm (10 x 20 inches)	2 eggs, separated
	150 ml (¼ pint) double cream, lightly whipped
25 g (1 oz) butter	
100 g (4 oz) plain chocolate	toasted flaked almonds, to decorate
30 ml (2 tbsp) brandy	icing sugar, for dusting
15 ml (1 level tbsp) instant coffee powder	

1 Cut each filo pastry sheet into 12 squares. Line 12 deep bun tins with three overlapping squares, brushing with melted butter between each layer.
2 Bake blind in the oven at 200°C (400°F) mark 6 for 10-12 minutes or until the pastry is crisp, golden brown and cooked through. Turn out on to a wire rack to cool.
3 Break the chocolate into small pieces. Place in a heatproof bowl with the brandy, coffee powder and 15 ml (1 tbsp) water. Stand the bowl over a pan of simmering water and heat gently until the chocolate melts. Stir the mixture until smooth. (Alternatively, microwave on LOW for 4-6 minutes or until melted, stirring occasionally.)
4 Stir in the egg yolks, cool slightly, then mix in the cream. Whisk the egg whites until stiff but not dry, then fold into the chocolate mixture. Leave to set until the consistency of thick cream. Spoon the mousse into the pastry cups and chill for 1 hour.
5 Sprinkle the mousse cups with the toasted flaked almonds and dust heavily with icing sugar before serving.

COOK'S TIP

Melting Chocolate
Many of the recipes require melted chocolate and it is important to do this gently. Stand the bowl of chocolate over a saucepan of just simmering water and stir until the chocolate is smooth and creamy. Alternatively, melt chocolate in the microwave on LOW, stirring frequently.

CHOCOLATE AND LIME MOUSSE

SERVES 2

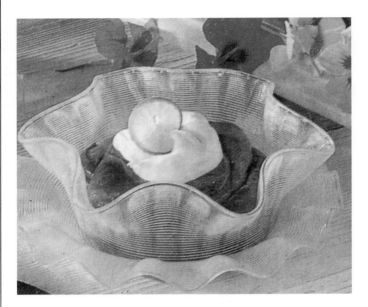

75 g (3 oz) plain chocolate	150 ml (¼ pint) double cream
2 eggs, separated	2.5 ml (½ level tsp) powdered gelatine
15 ml (1 tbsp) caster sugar	
finely grated rind and strained juice of 1 small lime	chocolate caraque or twists of lime, to decorate

1 Break the chocolate into small pieces. Place in a small heatproof bowl standing over a pan of simmering water and heat gently until the chocolate melts. (Alternatively, microwave on LOW for 4-5 minutes or until melted, stirring occasionally.) Cool slightly.
2 Whisk the egg yolks, sugar and lime rind in a bowl, using an electric whisk, until thick and mousse-like. Whisk in the chocolate, then 30 ml (2 tbsp) of the cream.
3 Sprinkle the gelatine over the lime juice in a small bowl and leave to soak for 2-3 minutes. Place the bowl over a saucepan of simmering water and stir until dissolved. (Or, microwave on HIGH for 30 seconds or until melted.) Whisk into the chocolate mixture.
4 Whisk the egg whites until stiff but not dry, then fold into the chocolate mixture.
5 Divide the mousse between two glasses and chill until set. Whip the remaining cream and use to decorate the desserts, with chocolate caraque or twists of lime. Leave at cool room temperature for 30 minutes before serving.

COOK'S TIP

Chocolate Caraque
Melt at least 100 g (4 oz) chocolate in a bowl over a pan of simmering water. Pour it in a thin layer on to a marble slab or cold baking sheet and leave to set until it no longer sticks to your hand when you touch it. Holding a large knife with both hands, push the blade across the surface of the chocolate to roll pieces off in long curls. Adjust the angle of the blade to get the best curls.

BAKED CHOCOLATE MARBLE SPONGE

SERVES 8

	CHOCOLATE FUDGE SAUCE
75 g (3 oz) plain chocolate	75 ml (5 tbsp) single cream
175 g (6 oz) butter or margarine	25 g (1 oz) cocoa powder
175 g (6 oz) light soft brown sugar	100 g (4 oz) caster sugar
3 eggs, beaten	175 g (6 oz) golden syrup
200 g (7 oz) self-raising flour	25 g (1 oz) butter or margarine
45 ml (3 tbsp) milk	pinch of salt
50 g (2 oz) macaroons	2.5 ml (½ tsp) vanilla essence

1 Grease a 1.3 litre (2¼ pint) loaf dish.
2 Break the chocolate into small pieces. Place in a small heatproof bowl standing over a pan of simmering water and heat until the chocolate melts. (Alternatively, microwave on LOW for 3-4 minutes or until melted, stirring occasionally.) Leave to cool.
3 Cream the butter and sugar together in a bowl until pale and fluffy. Gradually beat in the eggs. Using a metal spoon, fold in the flour and milk.
4 Divide the mixture in two and flavour half with the cooled chocolate, folding it evenly through the mixture.
5 Place alternate spoonfuls of the mixtures in two layers in the prepared dish and zig-zag a knife through the mixture to make a marbled pattern. Roughly crush the macaroons and scatter over the top. Cover with foil.
6 Bake in the oven at 180°C (350°F) mark 4 for about 1¼ hours or until firm to the touch.
7 Meanwhile, combine all the ingredients for the fudge sauce, except the vanilla essence, in a saucepan over low heat and mix well. Slowly bring to the boil, stirring occasionally. Boil for 5 minutes, then add the vanilla essence.
8 Turn out the pudding and serve thickly sliced with the hot chocolate fudge sauce.

AMERICAN CHOCOLATE CUSTARD PIE

SERVES 8

1 quantity shortcrust pastry (see page 327)	3 egg yolks
FOR THE FILLING	40 g (1½ oz) butter or margarine
100 g (4 oz) sugar	5 ml (1 tsp) vanilla essence
50 g (2 oz) plain flour	225 ml (8 fl oz) double or whipping cream
pinch of salt	
450 ml (¾ pint) milk	chocolate curls or grated chocolate, to decorate
50 g (2 oz) plain chocolate	

1 Roll out the pastry on a lightly floured work surface and use to line a 23 cm (9 inch) loose-based fluted flan tin or ring placed on a baking sheet. Crimp the edges. Chill for 30 minutes. Prick the base of the pastry case.
2 Bake blind in the oven at 200°C (400°F) mark 6 for 10-15 minutes until set. Remove the paper and beans and bake for a further 5-10 minutes. Leave to cool.
3 To make the filling, mix the sugar, flour and salt in a large saucepan and stir in the milk.
4 Break the chocolate into small pieces and add to the pan. Heat gently until the chocolate has melted, stirring continuously.
5 Whisk until the chocolate and milk are blended, then increase the heat and cook for about 10 minutes, stirring constantly. Remove the pan from the heat.
6 Beat the egg yolks and whisk in a small amount of the hot chocolate sauce. Slowly pour the egg mixture into the saucepan, stirring rapidly. Cook over low heat stirring, for 10-15 minutes, until the mixture is very thick and creamy. Do not allow to boil.
7 Remove from the heat. Stir in the butter and vanilla essence, then pour into the cold pastry case. Cover to prevent a skin forming and chill for 3-4 hours until set.
8 Just before serving, whip the cream lightly and spread evenly over the chocolate filling. Decorate the top with chocolate curls or grated chocolate. Serve chilled.

MISSISSIPPI MUD PIE

SERVES 12-16

FOR THE BASE	FOR THE FILLING
100 g (4 oz) ginger biscuits, crushed	225 g (8 oz) butter or margarine
100 g (4 oz) digestive biscuits, crushed	175 g (6 oz) plain chocolate
75 g (3 oz) butter, melted	120 ml (8 tbsp) golden syrup
25 g (1 oz) soft light brown sugar	4 eggs, beaten
	50 g (2 oz) pecan nuts, chopped

1 Grease a 23 cm (9 inch) loose-based cake tin.

2 To make the base, mix the biscuits with the butter and sugar. Press into the bottom and 4 cm (1½ inches) up the sides of the prepared tin. Chill while making the filling.

3 To make the filling, put the butter, chocolate and syrup in a saucepan and heat very gently until melted, stirring all the time. (Alternatively, put the ingredients in a bowl and microwave on LOW for 4-6 minutes or until melted, stirring frequently.) Cool, then beat in the eggs and pecans. Pour the mixture into the biscuit crust.

4 Bake in the oven at 180°C (350°F) mark 4 for 1¼ hours or until just firm to the touch but still soft in the centre. Serve warm or cold.

COOK'S TIP

This rich and sticky pie originated in the United States, where it is served warm with hot fudge sauce or cold topped with whipped cream and grated chocolate. Either way, a small portion is all that is needed.

GOOEY CHOCOLATE BROWNIES

MAKES 24 SQUARES

550 g (1¼ lb) plain chocolate	225 g (8 oz) caster sugar
225 g (8 oz) butter, cut into pieces	75 g (3 oz) self-raising flour
3 eggs	2.5 ml (½ level tsp) salt
30 ml (2 tbsp) freshly made strong coffee	175 g (6 oz) walnut halves, chopped
	5 ml (1 tsp) vanilla essence

1 Grease and line a baking tin measuring 22 x 29 cm (8½ x 11½ inches) across the top and 19 x 26 cm (7½ x 10½ inches) across the base.

2 Using a very sharp knife, roughly chop 225 g (8 oz) of the chocolate. Break the remaining chocolate into small pieces and place in a heatproof bowl with the butter. Stand the bowl over a pan of simmering water and heat gently until the chocolate melts, stirring. (Alternatively, microwave on LOW for 10 minutes or until melted, stirring occasionally.) Leave to cool.

3 Mix the eggs, coffee and sugar together in a bowl, then gradually beat in the chocolate mixture. Fold in the flour, salt, walnuts, vanilla essence and chopped chocolate. Pour the mixture into the prepared tin.

4 Bake in the oven at 190°C (375°F) mark 5 for 45 minutes or until just firm to the touch in the centre. Leave to cool in the tin.

5 When the cake is completely cold, turn out on to a board and trim the edges. Cut into 24 squares. Serve on their own or with ice cream.

DARK CHOCOLATE TRUFFLE CAKE

SERVES 24

225 g (8 oz) plain chocolate	FOR THE FILLING
100 g (4 oz) butter	350 g (12 oz) plain chocolate, in pieces
350 g (12 oz) caster sugar	175 g (6 oz) butter
2 eggs, separated	75 ml (5 tbsp) brandy
150 ml (¼ pint) soured cream	FOR THE ICING
350 g (12 oz) self-raising flour	200 g (7 oz) plain chocolate, in pieces
5 ml (1 tsp) bicarbonate of soda	200 ml (7 fl oz) double cream

1 Grease a 25 cm (10 inch) spring-release cake tin and line the base with greaseproof paper.

2 Break the chocolate into small pieces. Place in a large heatproof bowl with the butter and 150 ml (¼ pint) water, over a pan of simmering water and heat gently until the chocolate melts. Beat in the sugar, then leave to cool.

3 Beat in the egg yolks, then fold in the soured cream, flour and soda. Whisk the egg whites until stiff, then fold into the mixture. Pour into the prepared tin.

4 Bake in the oven at 180°C (350°F) mark 4 for 1 hour or until risen and firm. Turn out and cool on a wire rack.

5 To make the filling, place the chocolate in a large heatproof bowl with the butter, over a pan of simmering water and heat gently until melted, stirring. Stir in 45 ml (3 tbsp) of the brandy. Leave until slightly thickened.

6 Cut the cake into two layers and sprinkle with the remaining brandy. Place the top half in the base of the tin, cut side up. Pour in the truffle filling. Top with the second sponge. Chill until set. Unmould and stand on a wire rack.

7 To make the icing, put the chocolate in a large heatproof bowl with the cream, stand over a pan of simmering water and heat gently until the chocolate melts.

8 Cool until the icing coats the back of a spoon. Pour the icing over the cake, using a palette knife to cover the sides. Leave until set.

CHOCOLATE BOX GATEAU

SERVES 9

3 eggs	300 ml (½ pint) double cream
100 g (4 oz) caster sugar	700 g (1½ lb) mandarin oranges or tangerines, peeled and segmented
75 g (3 oz) plain flour	
30 ml (2 tbsp) cocoa powder	1 quantity apricot glaze (see page 328)
FOR THE FILLING AND DECORATION	
150 g (5 oz) plain chocolate	

1 Grease and flour an 18 cm (7 inch) square cake tin, then line the base with greaseproof paper.

2 To make the sponge, using an electric whisk, whisk the eggs and sugar together in a bowl until very thick and pale, and the mixture leaves a trail when the whisk is lifted. Sift the flour and cocoa over the mixture, then fold in using a large metal spoon. Transfer to the prepared tin.

3 Bake in the oven at 190°C (375°F) mark 5 for 30-35 minutes or until firm to the touch and shrunken from the sides of the tin. Turn out and cool on a wire rack.

4 Break the chocolate into small pieces. Place in a heatproof bowl standing over a pan of simmering water and heat gently until the chocolate melts.

5 Meanwhile, spread a sheet of foil on a baking sheet and mark a 22 cm (8½ inch) square. Spread the chocolate evenly over the square marked on the foil. Leave until set. When set, trim the edges and cut into 24 squares, measuring about 5 cm (2 inches).

6 Whip the cream until it just holds its shape. Cut the cake in half horizontally, then sandwich together with half of the cream and a few of the mandarins.

7 Arrange the rest of the fruit evenly all over the top of the cake and brush with warm apricot glaze.

8 Spread the remaining cream round the sides of the cake. Press on the chocolate squares, overlapping each one slightly. Decorate with flowers if desired.

CHOCOLATE ROULADE

SERVES 8-10

100 g (4 oz) plain chocolate	15 ml (1 tbsp) icing sugar
4 eggs, separated	150 ml (¼ pint) Greek yogurt
100 g (4 oz) caster sugar	few drops of rose water (optional)
FOR THE FILLING AND DECORATION	350 g (12 oz) raspberries
300 ml (½ pint) double cream	icing sugar, for dusting

1   Grease a 23 x 33 cm (9 x 13 inch) Swiss roll tin, line with greaseproof paper and grease the paper.
2   To make the roulade, break the chocolate into small pieces. Place in a heatproof bowl standing over a pan of simmering water and heat gently until the chocolate melts.
3   Whisk the egg yolks and sugar together in a bowl until very thick and pale in colour. Beat in the chocolate. Whisk the egg whites until stiff, then fold carefully into the chocolate mixture. Pour the mixture into the prepared tin and spread out evenly.
4   Bake in the oven at 180°C (350°F) mark 4 for 20-25 minutes until well risen and firm to the touch.
5   Lay a piece of greaseproof paper on a flat surface and sprinkle generously with caster sugar. When the roulade is cooked, turn it out on to the paper. Carefully peel off the lining paper. Cover the roulade with a warm, damp tea towel and leave to cool.
6   To make the filling, whip the cream with the icing sugar until it forms soft peaks. Set aside half for decoration. Fold the yogurt into the other half, with a few drops of rose water. Spread over the roulade and sprinkle with two thirds of the raspberries. Starting from one of the narrow ends, carefully roll it up, using the paper to help. Transfer the roulade to a serving plate and dust generously with icing sugar.
7   Decorate with the remaining cream and raspberries.

WHISKY MOCHA FLAN

SERVES 6-8

1 quantity shortcrust pastry (see page 327)	3 egg yolks
	15 ml (1 tbsp) caster sugar
FOR THE FILLING	150 ml (¼ pint) double cream
75 g (3 oz) plain chocolate, melted	FOR THE TOPPING
10 ml (2 level tsp) powdered gelatine	200 ml (7 fl oz) double cream
150 ml (¼ pint) milk	15-30 ml (1-2 tbsp) whisky
	15 ml (1 tbsp) caster sugar
15 ml (1 level tbsp) instant coffee granules	chocolate caraque, to decorate

1   Roll out the pastry on a lightly floured work surface and use to line a 23 cm (9 inch) fluted flan tin. Trim the edges, then prick with a fork. Chill for 30 minutes.
2   Bake blind in the oven at 220°C (425°F) mark 7 for 20-25 minutes. Leave to cool. Remove flan from tin.
3   Using a pastry brush, brush half of the melted chocolate evenly all over the inverted pastry case. Leave in a cool place until set. Turn the flan case over and brush the inside with the remaining chocolate; leave to set.
4   Sprinkle the gelatine over 30 ml (2 tbsp) water in a small bowl and leave to soak for 2-3 minutes. Place over a pan of simmering water and stir until dissolved.
5   Put the milk and coffee in a small saucepan. Heat gently until the coffee dissolves and the milk comes almost to the boil. Very lightly whisk the egg yolks and sugar in a bowl. Stir in the coffee-flavoured milk. Place bowl over a pan of hot water and cook, stirring, until thick enough to coat the back of the spoon. Strain into a clean bowl. Stir in the dissolved gelatine. Leave to cool.
6   Whip the cream until it will just hold soft peaks, then gently fold into the coffee custard. Spoon into the chocolate coated flan case. Chill until set.
7   To make topping, whip the cream with the whisky and sugar. Spread an even layer over the top of the flan. Decorate with the remaining cream and caraque. Chill.

CHOCOLATE PRALINE RING

SERVES 4-6

50g (2 oz) plain or milk chocolate	50 g (2 oz) caster sugar
200 ml (7 fl oz) milk	2.5 ml (½ level tsp) cornflour
15 ml (1 level tbsp) powdered gelatine	50 g (2 oz) praline, finely crushed (see page 221)
75 ml (5 tbsp) cold black coffee	75 ml (5 tbsp) double cream
	TO DECORATE
3 eggs, separated	whipped cream
	marrons glacés (optional)

1 Lightly oil a 1.1 litre (2 pint) ring mould.
2 Break the chocolate into small pieces. Place in a medium saucepan and add the milk. Heat gently until the chocolate melts. Bring to the boil, stirring all the time, until the chocolate mixture is smooth – about 2-3 minutes.
3 Sprinkle the gelatine over the coffee in a small bowl and leave to soak for 2-3 minutes. Place the bowl over a saucepan of simmering water and stir until dissolved.
4 Whisk the egg yolks, 25 g (1 oz) of the caster sugar and the cornflour together in a bowl until very thick and pale. Slowly whisk in the hot chocolate mixture.
5 Return the mixture to the rinsed-out pan and stir over a very gentle heat until it thickens enough to coat the back of a wooden spoon. Do not boil. Pour into a bowl.
6 Stir the dissolved gelatine into the chocolate mixture with 30 ml (2 tbsp) of the praline powder. Leave to cool.
7 When the custard is cool and just beginning to set, whip the cream until it just begins to hold its shape. Fold into the mixture. Whisk egg whites until stiff but not dry. Whisk in the remaining sugar, then fold into the custard.
8 Pour into the prepared ring mould and chill for about 3 hours to set.
9 To serve, dip the mould briefly into hot water and invert the ring on to a serving plate. Decorate with the remaining praline, whipped cream and marrons glacés.

CHOCOLATE CHESTNUT VACHERIN

SERVES 8

6 egg whites	500 g (1.1 lb) can sweetened chestnut purée
350 g (12 oz) caster sugar	300 ml (½ pint) double cream
75 g (3 oz) hazelnuts, skinned, toasted and finely chopped	a little icing sugar for dusting
175 g (6 oz) plain chocolate, in pieces	whipped cream and cocoa powder, to decorate

1 Line 3 baking sheets with non-stick baking parchment and draw a 20 cm (8 inch) circle on each. Invert the paper.
2 To make the meringue, whisk the egg whites in a bowl until very stiff, but not dry. Gradually whisk in the caster sugar a little at a time, whisking well between each addition until the meringue is smooth and shiny. Very lightly fold in the chopped hazelnuts.
3 Either spread the mixture over the marked circles, or transfer to a piping bag fitted with a plain 1 cm (½ inch) nozzle and pipe the meringue in a spiral over the marked circles, starting from the centre.
4 Bake at 140°C (275°F) mark 1 for 1-1½ hours or until dried out. Change the positions of the baking sheets during cooking so that the meringues dry out evenly. Remove from the oven and leave to cool, then carefully remove the lining papers.
5 Melt the chocolate in a heatproof bowl set over a pan of hot water. Soften the chestnut purée in a bowl and stir in the melted chocolate. Lightly whip the cream until soft peaks form and fold into the chestnut mixture.
6 To assemble the vacherin, sandwich the meringues together with a little of the chestnut cream. Cover the top and sides with the remainder and decorate with whipped cream and cocoa powder.

FROZEN DESSERTS

Nothing can compare with the superb flavour of homemade ices, whether you choose to make a simple refreshing sorbet, a rich velvety ice cream or an elaborate iced dessert. The choice of flavourings is endless – vanilla, coffee, chocolate, liqueurs, nuts and all kinds of fruits.

RASPBERRY REDCURRANT FREEZE

SERVES 4-6

350 g (12 oz) fresh or frozen raspberries	300 ml (½ pint) soured cream
225 g (8 oz) jar redcurrant jelly	

1 Put the raspberries and redcurrant jelly in a saucepan and heat gently, stirring frequently, until the fruit is soft. (Alternatively, microwave on HIGH for 4-5 minutes, stirring occasionally.)
2 Purée in a blender or food processor, then sieve to remove the seeds. Chill for about 1 hour until cold.
3 Whisk in the soured cream. Freeze by hand or in an ice cream machine (see page 316).
4 Leave at cool room temperature for 20-30 minutes to soften before serving.

COOK'S NOTE

The knack of successfully making smooth frozen desserts largely involves making sure that no large ice crystals form during freezing. This means that it is necessary to periodically whisk the freezing mixture by hand, if you do not own an ice cream machine which will do the job for you.

PEACH ICE CREAM

SERVES 6

350 g (12 oz) fresh ripe peaches	300 ml (10 fl oz) whipping cream
300 ml (½ pint) milk	peach slices and fan wafers, to decorate (optional)
grated rind and juice of 1 lemon	

1 Using a sharp knife, quarter the peaches and remove the skins, discarding the stones.
2 Roughly slice the peaches into a blender or food processor, add the milk, lemon rind and juice and the cream. Blend well until the mixture is quite smooth.
3 Pour the mixture into a shallow freezer container. Freeze for about 2 hours until mushy in texture.
4 Turn into a large, chilled basin and mash with a fork. Return to the freezer for 3-4 hours to become firm.
5 About 30 minutes before serving, remove from the freezer and leave the ice cream to soften at room temperature. Serve decorated with peach slices and a fan wafer, if wished.

COOK'S TIP

Refer to instructions on page 316 for freezing in an ice cream machine.

VANILLA ICE CREAM

SERVES 4-6

1 vanilla pod	50-75 g (2-3 oz) caster sugar
300 ml (½ pint) milk	300 ml (10 fl oz) double cream
3 egg yolks	

1 Split the vanilla pod to reveal the seeds. Put the milk and vanilla pod into a heavy-based saucepan and bring almost to the boil. Remove from the heat, cover and leave to infuse for about 20 minutes.

2 Beat the egg yolks and sugar together in a bowl until well blended. Stir in the milk and strain back into the pan. Cook the custard over a gentle heat, stirring all the time, until it thickens very slightly. (Alternatively, cook the custard in a bowl standing over a pan of simmering water.) It is very important not to let the custard boil or it will curdle. Pour out into a bowl and leave to cool.

3 Whisk the cream into the cold custard mixture.

4 Freeze the ice cream mixture by hand or in an ice cream machine (see right). Leave at cool room temperature for 20-30 minutes to soften before serving.

VARIATIONS

Coffee Ice Cream

Add 150 ml (¼ pint) strong fresh cooled coffee to the cooled custard or 10 ml (2 level tsp) instant coffee granules to the milk. Omit the vanilla.

Chocolate Ice Cream

Put the milk in a saucepan with 125 g (4 oz) plain chocolate. Heat gently until the chocolate melts, then bring almost to the boil. Continue as left.

Fruit Ice Cream

Add 300 ml (½ pint) fruit purée, sweetened to taste, to the cooled custard.

MANGO ICE CREAM

SERVES 4-6

450 ml (¾ pint) milk	2 ripe mangoes, skinned, sliced and stoned, or two 425 g (15 oz) cans mango slices, drained
1 vanilla pod	
4 egg yolks	juice of 1 lime
75 g (3 oz) sugar	300 ml (½ pint) double cream
	twists of fresh lime, to decorate (optional)

1 Pour the milk into a large, heavy-based saucepan. Add the vanilla pod and bring almost to the boil. Remove from the heat, cover and leave to infuse for at least 15 minutes. Remove the vanilla pod.

2 Put the egg yolks and sugar in a large bowl and beat together. Stir in the milk, then strain back into the pan.

3 Cook the custard gently, stirring until it coats the back of a wooden spoon. Do not boil. Cool completely for at least 1 hour.

4 Purée the mangoes in a blender or food processor until smooth. Stir the mango purée and lime juice into the cool custard. Whip the cream lightly, then fold into the mixture. Pour into a shallow freezer container.

5 Freeze the mixture for about 2 hours until mushy in texture. Turn into a large, chilled bowl and mash with a fork. Freeze for 3-4 hours until firm.

6 Soften in the refrigerator for about 1 hour before serving, decorated, if liked.

COOK'S TIP

Refer to instructions on page 316 for freezing in an ice cream machine.

BLACKBERRY
ICE CREAM

SERVES 6-8

450 g (1 lb) blackberries, fresh or frozen	150 ml (¼ pint) whipping cream
30 ml (2 tbsp) thick honey	30 ml (2 tbsp) orange-flavoured liqueur
410 g (14 oz) can evaporated milk, chilled	45 ml (3 tbsp) lemon juice

1 Place the blackberries and honey in a small saucepan. Cover and cook gently until the fruit is soft and pulpy. Purée in a blender or food processor, then rub through a nylon sieve. Leave to cool.
2 Whip evaporated milk until thickened slightly. Whip cream to the same consistency, then fold gently together. Stir in the cold fruit purée, liqueur and lemon juice.
3 Freeze by hand or in an ice cream machine.
4 Leave at cool room temperature for 20-30 minutes to soften before serving. Scoop into individual glass dishes.

COOK'S TIP

To Freeze Ice Cream by Hand
Suggested freezing times are based on 900 ml (1½ pint) ice cream. If making a larger quantity, increase them.
1 Set the freezer to maximum or fast freeze about 1 hour before you intend to freeze the mixture.
2 Make the ice cream as directed in the recipe.
3 Pour the mixture into a shallow non-metal, freezer container. Cover and freeze for about 3 hours or until just frozen all over. It will have a mushy consistency.
4 Spoon into a bowl and mash with a fork or flat whisk to break down the ice crystals. Work quickly so that the ice cream does not melt completely.
5 Return the mixture to the shallow container and freeze again for about 2 hours or until mushy.
6 Mash again as step 4. If any other ingredients are to be added, such as nuts, then fold in at this stage.
7 Return to the freezer and freeze for about 3 hours or until firm.

PISTACHIO AND
ALMOND ICE CREAM

SERVES 6

1.4 litres (2½ pints) milk	50 g (2 oz) ground almonds
15 ml (1 level tbsp) rice flour	few drops of rose water
175 g (6 oz) granulated sugar	150 ml (¼ pint) double cream
25 g (1 oz) pistachio nuts	shredded pistachio nuts, to decorate

1 Pour the milk into a large, heavy-based saucepan. Bring to the boil, then simmer gently for about 45 minutes or until the milk reduces by half. Cool slightly.
2 Mix the rice flour with a little of the cooled milk until smooth. Return to the pan and bring to the boil, stirring. Cook for 15 minutes, stirring frequently until the consistency of thin batter. Strain, add the sugar and stir until dissolved. Leave to cool.
3 Soak the pistachio nuts in boiling water for 1-2 minutes, then drain. Ease off the skins, then shred finely.
4 Stir the pistachios, ground almonds and rose water into the milk mixture. Whip the cream lightly, then fold in.
5 Freeze by hand or in an ice cream machine.
6 Leave at cool room temperature for 20-30 minutes to soften before serving. Serve, decorated with pistachios.

COOK'S TIP

Using an Ice Cream Machine
An ice cream machine will freeze an ice cream or sorbet mixture and churn it at the same time, thus eliminating the physical effort. The results will be smooth and even textured. There are several types of ice cream machine available, some use a salt solution and others a disc which needs to be frozen before use. Always follow manufacturer's instructions.
Generally speaking, the cooled mixture should be poured into the machine when the paddles are moving, otherwise it tends to freeze on to the base and sides of the bowl, stopping the paddles working. When making ice cream this way, if the recipe calls for whipped cream, it should be ignored. The cream can simply be added from the carton with the custard.

COFFEE AND HAZELNUT ICE CREAM

SERVES 4-6

100 g (4 oz) shelled hazelnuts	300 ml (½ pint) double cream
50 ml (2 tbsp plus 4 tsp) coffee-flavoured liqueur	300 ml (½ pint) single cream
15 ml (1 tbsp) coffee and chicory essence	75 g (3 oz) icing sugar, sifted

1 Toast the hazelnuts under the grill for a few minutes, shaking the grill pan constantly so that the nuts brown evenly.

2 Tip the nuts into a clean tea-towel and rub to remove the skins. Chop finely.

3 Mix 30 ml (2 tbsp) coffee liqueur and the essence together in a bowl. Stir in the chopped nuts, reserving a few for decoration.

4 In a separate bowl, whip the creams and icing sugar together until thick. Fold in the nut mixture, then turn into a shallow freezerproof container. Freeze for 2 hours until ice crystals form around the edge of the ice cream.

5 Turn the ice cream into a bowl and beat thoroughly for a few minutes to break up the ice crystals. Return to the freezer container, cover and freeze for at least 4 hours, preferably overnight (to allow enough time for the flavours to develop).

6 To serve, transfer the ice cream to the refrigerator for 30 minutes to soften slightly, then scoop into individual glasses. Spoon 5 ml (1 tsp) coffee liqueur over each serving and sprinkle with the remaining nuts. Serve immediately.

COOK'S TIP

Refer to instructions on page 316 for freezing in an ice cream machine.

RASPBERRY ROSE ICE CREAM

SERVES 6-8

300 ml (½ pint) milk	450 g (1 lb) raspberries
2 large handfuls of fragrant pink rose petals	15 ml (1 tbsp) rosewater
3 egg yolks	300 ml (½ pint) double cream
75 g (3 oz) caster sugar	raspberries and rose petals, to decorate

1 Put the milk and rose petals in a heavy-based saucepan and bring almost to the boil. Remove from the heat and leave to infuse for at least 30 minutes.

2 Beat the egg yolks and sugar together until well blended. Stir in the milk and rose petals, then strain back into the pan, discarding the rose petals. Cook over a gentle heat, stirring all the time until it thickens very slightly. Do not let the custard boil or it will curdle. Pour into a bowl and leave to cool.

3 While the custard is cooling, mash the raspberries then push through a nylon sieve to make a purée. Stir in the rosewater.

4 Whisk the cream into the cold custard mixture, then stir in the raspberry purée. Pour into a shallow non-metallic freezer container. Cover and freeze on fast freeze for about 3 hours or until just frozen.

5 Spoon into a bowl and mash with a fork to break down the ice crystals. Work quickly so that the ice cream does not melt completely.

6 Return the mixture to the container and freeze again for about 2 hours until mushy.

7 Mash again as step 4, then return to the freezer for a further 3 hours or until firm.

8 Remove from the freezer and leave at room temperature for about 20-30 minutes to soften. Serve sprinkled with a few raspberries and rose petals.

LEMON GERANIUM ICE CREAM

SERVES 4-6

300 ml (½ pint) milk	100 g (4 oz) icing sugar
10-12 lemon-scented geranium leaves, crushed	300 ml (10 fl oz) whipping cream
3 egg yolks	lemon-scented geranium leaves, to decorate

1 Bring the milk and geranium leaves almost to the boil. Remove from the heat and leave to infuse for 30 minutes. Remove the geranium leaves.

2 Whisk the egg yolks and icing sugar together in a medium bowl until pale and frothy. Stir in the milk, then strain back into the pan.

3 Cook the custard gently over a low heat, stirring continuously, until it coats the back of a wooden spoon. Do not boil. This takes about 20 minutes.

4 Pour into a shallow freezer container, cool, then cover and freeze for 2 hours, until mushy.

5 Spoon into a bowl and beat to break down the ice crystals. Whip the cream until stiff, then fold into the mixture. Return to the freezer container and freeze for a further 2 hours.

6 Turn into a chilled bowl and beat well again. Return to the freezer and freeze until firm.

7 Transfer to the refrigerator to soften for 30 minutes before serving. Decorate with geranium leaves.

COOK'S TIP

Refer to instructions on page 316 for freezing in an ice cream machine.

TUTTI FRUTTI ICE CREAM

SERVES 8-10

90 ml (6 tbsp) dark rum	600 ml (1 pint) milk
50 g (2 oz) sultanas	1 vanilla pod or few drops of vanilla essence
50 g (2 oz) stoned dates	
50 g (2 oz) glacé cherries	6 egg yolks
50 g (2 oz) no-soak dried apricots	175 g (6 oz) caster sugar
	600 ml (1 pint) double cream, whipped

1 Pour the rum into a bowl. Add the sultanas, then roughly snip the dates, cherries and apricots into the bowl. Make sure all the fruit is coated with rum. Cover and leave to macerate for 2-3 hours, tossing occasionally.

2 Put the milk and vanilla pod or essence into a heavy-based saucepan and bring almost to the boil. Remove from the heat, cover and leave to infuse for 15 minutes.

3 Beat the egg yolks and sugar together in a bowl until pale and thick. Stir in the milk and strain back into the pan. Cook the custard over a gentle heat, stirring all the time, until it coats the back of a wooden spoon. Do not boil. Cover and leave to cool.

4 Pour into a chilled, shallow freezer container and freeze by hand to the end of step 5 (see page 316).

5 Whip the cream. Mash the ice cream, then fold in the cream and macerated fruit. Freeze until firm. (If using an ice cream machine, put the custard, cream and macerated fruit into the machine together.)

6 Leave at cool room temperature for 20-30 minutes to soften before serving.

VARIATION

For a short-cut version of this ice cream, use a 425 g (15 oz) can custard instead of making the egg custard. With vanilla flavouring added and the heady flavour of fruit macerated in rum, no-one will guess the custard came out of a can!

PRUNE AND BRANDY ICE CREAM

SERVES 8

225 g (8 oz) no-soak dried prunes	5 egg yolks
90 ml (6 tbsp) brandy	40 g (1½ oz) butter
30 ml (2 tbsp) lemon juice	50 g (2 oz) fresh brown breadcrumbs
100 g (4 oz) caster sugar	30 ml (2 tbsp) demerara sugar
450 ml (¾ pint) milk	450 ml (¾ pint) whipping cream, whipped
1 vanilla pod	

1 Cut all the prune flesh off the stones, then snip into small pieces. Place in a bowl with the brandy, lemon juice and 25 g (1 oz) of the caster sugar. Stir well to mix, then cover and leave to soak.

2 Put the milk and vanilla pod into a heavy-based pan and bring almost to the boil. Remove from the heat, cover and leave to infuse for 10 minutes.

3 Beat the egg yolks and remaining caster sugar together in a bowl until pale and frothy. Stir in the milk and strain back into the pan. Cook the custard over a gentle heat, stirring all the time, until thickened slightly. Do not boil. Leave to cool.

4 Melt the butter in a small frying pan, add the breadcrumbs and demerara sugar and cook over a moderate heat, stirring frequently until the crumbs turn golden brown and become crisp. Immediately, spoon the mixture out on to a plate. Leave to cool.

5 Freeze the ice cream mixture by hand to the end of step 5 (see page 316). Mash the ice cream, then fold in the whipped cream, the soaked prunes with any juices, and the crumb mixture. Freeze until firm.

6 Leave at cool room temperature for 20-30 minutes to soften before serving.

VARIATION

Use 225 g (8 oz) no-soak dried figs in place of the prunes and 90 ml (6 tbsp) port in place of the brandy.

CHRISTMAS PUDDING ICE CREAM

SERVES 4-6

100 g (4 oz) mixed no-soak dried fruit	450 ml (15 fl oz) single cream
60 ml (4 tbsp) light or dark rum	3 egg yolks
30 ml (2 tbsp) port	100 g (4 oz) caster sugar
grated rind and juice of 1 orange	150 ml (5 fl oz) whipping cream
	5 ml (1 level tsp) ground mixed spice

1 Mix the dried fruit, rum, port and orange rind and juice together, then set aside to macerate overnight.

2 Gently heat the single cream in a small saucepan to simmering point.

3 Whisk the egg yolks and sugar together in a medium bowl until pale and thick. Gradually pour on the hot cream, stirring continuously.

4 Strain the mixture into a medium heavy-based saucepan or double boiler and cook over a gentle heat, stirring continuously, until it coats the back of a wooden spoon; do not boil. This takes about 20 minutes. Set aside to cool.

5 Whip the cream until stiff, then fold into the cold custard with the dried fruit mixture and mixed spice.

6 Pour into a shallow freezer container, then cover and freeze for about 3 hours until mushy.

7 Turn into a chilled bowl and beat well. Return to the freezer container and freeze for a further 2 hours.

8 Beat the mixture again, then turn into a 1.1 litre (2 pint) bombe mould, cover and freeze for a further 2 hours until firm.

9 Transfer to the refrigerator to soften for 30 minutes before serving. Turn out on to a cold serving plate.

COOK'S TIP

Refer to instructions on page 316 for freezing in an ice cream machine.

FROZEN BRANDY CREAMS

SERVES 4

4 egg yolks	150 ml (¼ pint) double cream
150 g (5 oz) caster sugar	coffee dragees, to decorate
90 ml (6 tbsp) brandy	

1 Mix the egg yolks, sugar and brandy together in a medium bowl, stirring well.

2 Place the bowl over a pan of simmering water. Stir the mixture all the time for about 15 minutes until it thickens slightly and will just coat the back of the spoon. Do not overheat or the eggs may curdle. Remove from the heat and leave to cool for 30 minutes. (Alternatively, microwave on LOW for 4-6 minutes or until thickened. Cool.)

3 Lightly whip the cream and stir half into the cold brandy mixture. Pour into four small freezerproof soufflé or ramekin dishes. Cover and freeze for at least 5 hours until firm.

4 To serve, decorate each ramekin with a whirl of the remaining whipped cream, then top with a coffee dragee. Serve immediately.

COOK'S TIP

This works equally well with other liqueur flavours, such as almond or coffee.

FROZEN PASSION FRUIT SOUFFLE

SERVES 8

16 passion fruit	175 g (6 oz) caster sugar
6 egg yolks	600 ml (1 pint) double cream

1 Tie a double strip of greaseproof paper around a 900 ml (1½ pint) soufflé dish to make a 7.5 cm (3 inch) collar. Lightly brush the inside of the paper with oil.

2 Cut each passion fruit in half and scoop out the flesh and seeds into a nylon sieve, placed over a small bowl. Press with a spoon to extract all of the juice – about 150 ml (¼ pint).

3 Whisk the egg yolks in a large bowl with an electric mixer until very thick.

4 Put 60 ml (4 tbsp) of the passion fruit juice into a small saucepan with the caster sugar. Stir over a low heat until the sugar has dissolved. Bring to the boil and boil until the temperature reaches 110°C (230°F) on a sugar thermometer.

5 Whisk the syrup in a steady stream into the egg yolks, then continue whisking until the mixture cools and thickens. Gradually whisk in the remaining passion fruit juice, whisking until the mixture is thick and mousse-like.

6 Whip the cream until it just holds its shape. Fold the cream into the passion fruit mixture until no trace of white remains. Pour into the prepared dish, then freeze until firm. Once frozen, cover the top of the soufflé.

7 Remove the soufflé from the freezer 20-30 minutes before serving and carefully ease away the paper collar. Decorate with whipped cream and pistachios, if liked.

COOK'S TIP

This velvety smooth soufflé should be made the day before. The soufflé can be decorated with whipped cream and pistachio nuts, but as its impressive qualities are in the texture and fresh flavour, it doesn't necessarily need to be dressed-up.

FROZEN CHESTNUT BOMBE

SERVES 8-10

FOR THE BOMBE	TO DECORATE
1 quantity vanilla ice cream (see page 315)	300 ml (½ pint) whipping cream
285 g (10 oz) can whole chestnuts, drained	15 ml (1 tbsp) rum
30 ml (2 tbsp) icing sugar	marrons glacés or dragees and herb leaves
150 ml (¼ pint) soured cream	
100 g (4 oz) macaroons	
45 ml (3 tbsp) rum	

1 To make the bombe, remove the ice cream from the freezer and leave at cool room temperature for 45 minutes to soften.

2 Purée the chestnuts, icing sugar and soured cream in a blender or food processor until smooth. Add the ice cream and purée.

3 Roughly crush the macaroons and sprinkle with the rum. Fold into the ice cream mixture.

4 Pour into a 1.1 litre (2 pint) bombe mould or pudding basin. Cover and freeze for at least 5 hours or until firm.

5 To serve, dip the mould or bowl briefly in hot water, then unmould on to a serving plate. Return to the freezer for 10 minutes.

6 To make the decoration, whip the cream and rum until stiff. Spoon into a piping bag fitted with a large star nozzle. Pipe around the base of the bombe and up and over the sides. Decorate with marrons glacés or dragées and herb leaves. Leave in the refrigerator for 1 hour to soften before serving.

FROZEN CHOCOLATE AND MANGO CAKE

SERVES 8-10

	TO DECORATE
1 chocolate Swiss roll sponge, made with 2 eggs (see page 326)	chocolate caraque or curls and mango slices
½ quantity mango ice cream (see page 315)	
¼ quantity chocolate ice cream (see page 315)	

1 Trim the Swiss roll sponge and cut into three pieces the width and length of a 1.1 litre (2 pint) loaf tin.

2 Take the ice creams out of the freezer and leave at room temperature for 30 minutes or until soft enough to spread. Spread half the mango ice cream into the loaf tin and level the surface.

3 Place one piece of sponge on top of the mango ice cream in the loaf tin. Spread with the chocolate ice cream. Return to the freezer for 15 minutes to firm.

4 Place a second piece of sponge on top of the chocolate ice cream. Spread with the remaining mango ice cream. Top with the last piece of sponge. Cover and freeze for at least 3 hours or until firm.

5 One hour before serving, dip the tin briefly in hot water then unmould on to a serving plate. Leave in the refrigerator for 1 hour before serving. Decorate with chocolate caraque or curls and slices of mango.

COOK'S TIP

Use this as a basic recipe to make other ice cream cakes of your choice.

ORANGES EN SURPRISE

SERVES 6

6 large oranges	90 ml (6 tbsp) chunky orange marmalade
300 ml (½ pint) double cream	bay leaves or chocolate leaves, to decorate
50 g (2 oz) icing sugar	
90 ml (6 tbsp) orange-flavoured liqueur	

1 Cut a slice off the top of each orange and reserve. Scoop out all the flesh, pips and juice from the oranges and discard (the juice can be used for drinking or in other recipes). Wash, then dry thoroughly. Set aside.

2 Whip the cream and icing sugar together in a bowl until standing in stiff peaks. Mix the liqueur and marmalade together, then fold into the cream until evenly distributed.

3 Spoon the cream mixture into the orange shells, mounding it up over the top. Freeze for at least 4 hours, preferably overnight (to allow the flavours to develop).

4 Serve straight from the freezer, decorated with the reserved orange lids, bay leaves or chocolate leaves.

COOK'S TIP

Chocolate Leaves
To make these, using a small paintbrush, thinly spread melted chocolate on the undersides of clean, dry, undamaged rose leaves. Leave to set. Gently peel off chocolate.

ORANGE SHERBET

SERVES 8

178 ml (6¼ oz) carton frozen orange juice	600 ml (1 pint) milk
175 g (6 oz) caster sugar	300 ml (½ pint) single cream
45 ml (3 tbsp) golden syrup	shredded orange rind and mint sprigs, to decorate
45 ml (3 tbsp) lemon juice	

1 Tip the frozen undiluted orange juice into a deep bowl. Leave until beginning to soften, then add the sugar, golden syrup and lemon juice. Whisk until smooth.

2 Combine the orange mixture with the milk and cream and pour into a deep rigid container. Cover and freeze for 4-5 hours. There is no need to whisk the mixture during freezing.

3 Transfer to the refrigerator to soften 45 minutes or 1 hour before serving. Serve scooped into individual glasses or orange shells, decorated with orange shreds and sprigs of mint.

COOK'S TIP

There is always some confusion over the term 'sherbet' when used to describe a dessert. The word 'sherbet' is in fact the American term for a sorbet, although it is often mistakenly used to describe a water ice. Water ices are simple concoctions of sugar syrup and fruit purée or fruit juice, sometimes with liqueur or other alcohol added. Sorbets are a smoother version of water ices. They are made in the same way, with sugar syrup and fruit, but at the half-frozen stage they have whisked egg whites or other ingredients folded into them.

ORANGE WATER ICE

SERVES 6

175 g (6 oz) sugar	10 large oranges
450 ml (¾ pint) water	1½ lemons

1 To make the sugar syrup, place the sugar and water in a medium saucepan. Heat gently until the sugar dissolves, then boil gently for 10 minutes without stirring.

2 Meanwhile, using a potato peeler, thinly pare the rind from four oranges and the lemons. Add the orange and lemon rind to the sugar syrup and leave until cold.

3 Squeeze the juice from the four oranges and the lemons. Strain into a measuring jug – there should be 450 ml (¾ pint).

4 Strain the cold syrup into a shallow freezer container and stir in the fruit juices. Mix well. Cover and freeze for about 4 hours until mushy in texture.

5 Remove from the freezer and turn the frozen mixture into a bowl. Beat well with a fork to break down the ice crystals. Return to the freezer container and freeze for at least 4 hours or until firm.

6 Meanwhile, using a serrated knife, cut away the peel and pith from the remaining oranges.

7 Slice the oranges down into thin rings, ease out and discard any pips. Place the oranges in a serving bowl, cover tightly and refrigerate until serving time.

8 Place the water ice in the refrigerator for 45 minutes to soften before serving. Serve with the fresh orange slices.

VARIATIONS

Lemon Water Ice

With 6-8 lemons as a basis, follow the recipe using the pared rind of four lemons and enough juice to give 450 ml (¾ pint).

Coffee Granita

Put 30 ml (2 tbsp) sugar and 50 g (2 oz) finely ground Italian coffee in a jug. Pour over 600 ml (1 pint) boiling water and leave to stand for 1 hour. Strain the coffee through a filter paper or muslin, then freeze as in steps 4-5.

GERANIUM GRAPE SORBET

SERVES 6

100 g (4 oz) sugar	90 ml (6 tbsp) dry white vermouth
300 ml (½ pint) water	2 egg whites
15 ml (½ tbsp) chopped rose- or lemon-scented geranium leaves	rose- or lemon-scented geranium leaves, to decorate
700 g (1½ lb) seedless green grapes	

1 To make the sugar syrup, dissolve the sugar in the water over a low heat. Bring to the boil and boil gently for 10 minutes without stirring. Add the geranium leaves, cover and leave to cool.

2 Purée the grapes in a blender or food processor and then work through a sieve. There should be 600 ml (1 pint) purée. Add the vermouth and the strained sugar syrup, mix well and pour this mixture into a shallow freezer container. Freeze for about 1 hour until half frozen and mushy.

3 Turn the half frozen mixture into a large bowl and break up with a fork.

4 Whisk the egg whites until stiff and fold into the grape mixture. Return to the container and freeze for about 2-3 hours until firm. Serve straight from the freezer, decorated with geranium leaves.

COOK'S TIP

Using a Sorbetière

A sorbetière or ice cream machine will freeze a sorbet and churn it at the same time, to give a smooth, even textured result. When making sorbet, any egg white should be lightly whisked with a fork and added at the start of the churning process. Freezing time is usually about 20-30 minutes. The sorbet should then be transferred to the freezer and frozen for 1-2 hours to allow the flavours to develop. Soften slightly at room temperature before serving.

LEMON SORBET

SERVES 3-4

350 ml (12 fl oz) Stock syrup (see below)	pared rind and juice of 3 lemons
	1 egg white

1 Prepare the stock syrup as far as dissolving the sugar. Add the lemon rinds and simmer gently for about 10 minutes. Leave to cool completely.

2 Stir in the lemon juice and strain into a shallow freezer container. Cover and freeze for about 3 hours until mushy.

3 Whisk the egg white until stiff. Turn the sorbet into a bowl and beat gently to break down the ice crystals. Fold in the egg white.

4 Return to the freezer container, cover and freeze for 4 hours or until firm.

5 Leave in the refrigerator for about 40 minutes to soften slightly before serving. To freeze in an ice cream machine, see page 316.

VARIATION

Orange or Lime Sorbet

Make as above, using the pared rind and juice of 2 oranges or 5 limes instead of the lemons.

COOK'S NOTE

Stock Syrup

Put 100 g (4 oz) granulated sugar in a heavy-based saucepan. Add 300 ml (½ pint) water and heat gently until the sugar dissolves. Do not stir the ingredients but occasionally loosen the sugar from the base of the pan to help it dissolve. Bring to the boil and boil for 2 minutes. Cool and use as required in these sorbet recipes. Makes about 350 ml (12 fl oz).

KIWI FRUIT SORBET

SERVES 6

50 g (2 oz) sugar	kiwi fruit slices, to decorate
150 ml (¼ pint) water	orange-flavoured liqueur and wafers, to serve
6 kiwi fruit	
2 egg whites	

1 Place the sugar in a saucepan with the water. Heat gently until the sugar dissolves, then simmer for 2 minutes. Cool for 30 minutes.

2 Halve the kiwi fruit and peel thinly, using a potato peeler.

3 Place the fruit in a blender or food processor with the cool syrup. Work to a smooth purée, then pass through a nylon sieve to remove the pips. Pour into a chilled shallow freezer container. Freeze for 2 hours until mushy.

4 Beat the mixture with a fork to break down any ice crystals.

5 Whisk the egg whites until stiff, then fold through the fruit mixture until evenly blended. Return to the freezer for 4 hours.

6 Scoop into individual glass dishes, decorate with kiwi fruit and spoon over some liqueur. Serve with wafers.

APRICOT AND MINNEOLA SORBET

SERVES 8

two 420 g (15 oz) cans apricot halves in syrup	pared rind and juice of 1 minneola
	2 egg whites

1 Drain the apricots, reserving the syrup. Simmer the minneola rind in the apricot syrup for 2-3 minutes. Leave to cool, then strain.
2 Purée the apricots with 60 ml (4 tbsp) minneola juice in a blender or food processor. Press through a nylon sieve. Add the apricot syrup.
3 Freeze as for Lemon sorbet, adding the egg whites as directed (see page 324).

MELON AND GINGER SORBET

SERVES 6

1 medium green or orange-fleshed melon, such as Ogen, Galia or Canteloupe	30 ml (2 tbsp) lemon juice
	350 ml (12 fl oz) Stock syrup (see page 324)
50 g (2 oz) stem ginger	2 egg whites

1 Purée the melon flesh, ginger and lemon juice in a blender or food processor. Press through a nylon sieve.
2 Add the stock syrup. Freeze as for Lemon sorbet, adding the egg whites as directed (see page 324).

CHAMPAGNE SORBET

SERVES 4-6

350 ml (12 fl oz) Stock syrup (see page 324)	350 ml (12 fl oz) champagne
	1 egg white
juice of 1 lemon	

1 Mix the stock syrup, lemon juice and champagne together.
2 Freeze as for Lemon sorbet, adding the egg white as directed (see page 324).

RASPBERRY SORBET

SERVES 6

450 g (1 lb) raspberries	350 ml (12 fl oz) Stock syrup (see page 324)
30 ml (2 tbsp) lemon juice	
30 ml (2 tbsp) kirsch	2 egg whites

1 Purée the raspberries with the lemon juice and kirsch in a blender or food processor. Press through a nylon sieve.
2 Add to the stock syrup. Freeze as for Lemon sorbet, adding the egg whites as directed (see page 324).

BASIC RECIPES

You can't beat a light-as-a-feather sponge to create a mouth-watering dessert. Lots of gâteaux are based on a basic Genoese or whisked sponge. These are delicious enough simply to split and fill with fruit and cream, or can be transformed into decadent desserts with nuts, liqueurs and praline.

WHISKED SPONGE

MAKES TWO 18 CM (7 INCH) SPONGES

3 eggs

75 g (3 oz) caster sugar

75 g (3 oz) plain flour

1 Grease two 18 cm (7 inch) sandwich tins, line with greaseproof paper, then dust with a mixture of flour and caster sugar.
2 Put the eggs and sugar in a large heatproof bowl standing over a pan of hot water. Whisk until doubled in volume and thick enough to leave a thin trail on the surface when the whisk is lifted.
3 Remove from the heat and continue whisking for a further 5 minutes until the mixture is cool.
4 Sift half the flour over the mixture and fold in very lightly, using a large metal spoon. Sift and fold in the remaining flour in the same way.
5 Pour the mixture into the prepared tins, tilting the tins to spread the mixture evenly. Do not use a palette knife or spatula as this will crush out the air bubbles.
6 Bake in the oven at 190°C (375°F) mark 5 for 20-25 minutes until well risen, firm to the touch and beginning to shrink away from the sides of the tins. Turn out on to a wire rack and leave to cool.

COOK'S TIP

To make two 20 cm (8 inch) sponges, use 4 eggs, 100 g (4 oz) caster sugar and 100 g (4 oz) plain flour.

SWISS ROLL

1 Line a 33 x 23 cm (13 x 9 inch) Swiss roll tin with greaseproof paper.
2 Make the sponge as above but use 100 g (4 oz) plain flour and fold in with 15 ml (1 tbsp) hot water. Pour into the prepared tin. Tilt the tin backwards and forwards to spread the mixture in an even layer.
3 Bake in the oven at 200°C (400°F) mark 6 for 10-12 minutes until golden brown, well risen and firm.
4 Meanwhile, place a sheet of greaseproof paper over a damp tea towel. Dredge the paper with caster sugar.
5 Quickly turn out the cake on to the paper, trim off the crusty edges and spread with jam. Roll up the cake with the aid of the paper. Make the first turn firmly so that the whole cake will roll evenly and have a good shape when finished, but roll more lightly after this turn. Place seam-side down on a wire rack and dredge with caster sugar.

CHOCOLATE SWISS ROLL

Make the sponge as for Swiss roll (left) but replace 15 ml (1 tbsp) plain flour with 15 ml (1 tbsp) sifted cocoa powder. Turn out the cooked sponge, trim, then cover with a sheet of greaseproof paper and roll with the paper inside. When cold, unroll and remove the paper. Spread with whipped cream and re-roll. Dust with icing sugar.

GENOESE CAKE

MAKES ONE 23 CM (9 INCH) CAKE

75 g (3 oz) butter

6 eggs

75 g (3 oz) caster sugar

150 g (5 oz) plain flour

30 ml (2 tbsp) cornflour

1 Grease a 23 cm (9 inch) spring-release cake tin and line with greaseproof paper.
2 Put the butter into a saucepan and heat gently until melted, then remove from the heat and leave for a few minutes to cool slightly.
3 Put the eggs and sugar in a heatproof bowl standing over a pan of hot water. Whisk until pale and creamy and thick enough to leave a trail on the surface when the whisk is lifted. Remove from the heat and whisk until cool.
4 Sift the flours together into a bowl. Fold half the flour into the egg mixture with a metal spoon.
5 Pour half the cooled butter around the edge of the mixture. Gradually fold in the remaining butter and flour alternately. Fold in very lightly or the butter will sink and result in a heavy cake. Pour the mixture into the prepared tin.
6 Bake in the oven at 180°C (350°F) mark 4 for 35-40 minutes until well risen, firm to the touch and beginning to shrink away from the sides of the tin. Turn out on to a wire rack and leave to cool.

CHOCOLATE GENOESE CAKE

Substitute 25 g (1 oz) of the plain flour with cocoa powder. Sift the cocoa with the flours and proceed as above.

COOK'S TIP

Like the whisked sponge, a Genoese cake is made by the whisking method, but melted butter is added with the flour. This gives a delicate sponge with a moister texture than the plain whisked sponge and a richer buttery taste.

SHORTCRUST PASTRY

MAKES 225 G (8 OZ) PASTRY

This plain short pastry is probably the most widely used of all pastries. For shortcrust pastry, the proportion of flour to fat is 2:1, or twice the quantity. Therefore, for a recipe using quantities of shortcrust pastry other than 225 g (8 oz) simply use half the quantity of fat to the flour weight specified.

This quantity, is approximately equivalent to one 368 g (13 oz) packet ready-made shortcrust pastry.

225 g (8 oz) plain flour

pinch of salt

50 g (2 oz) butter or block margarine, chilled and diced

50 g (2 oz) lard, chilled and diced

chilled water, to mix

1 Place the flour and salt in a bowl and add the fat.
2 Using both hands, rub the fat lightly into the flour until the mixture resembles fine breadcrumbs.
3 Add 45-60 ml (3-4 tbsp) water, sprinkling it evenly over the surface. (Uneven addition may cause blistering when the pastry is cooked.)
4 Stir in with a round-bladed knife until the mixture begins to stick together in large lumps.
5 With one hand, collect the dough mixture together to form a ball. Knead lightly for a few seconds to give a firm, smooth dough. Do not overhandle the dough.
6 To roll out, sprinkle a very little flour on a working surface and the rolling pin (not on the pastry) and roll out the dough evenly in one direction only, turning it occasionally. The usual thickness is 3 mm (⅛ inch). Do not pull or stretch the pastry.
7 The pastry can be baked straight away, but it is better if allowed to 'rest' for about 30 minutes in the tin or dish, covered with foil or greaseproof paper, in the refrigerator.

PATE SUCREE

MAKES 100 G (4 OZ) PASTRY

100 g (4 oz) flour

pinch of salt

50 g (2 oz) caster sugar

50 g (2 oz) butter (at room temperature)

2 egg yolks

1 Sift the flour and salt on to a working surface. Make a well in the centre and add the sugar, butter and egg yolks.
2 Using the fingertips of one hand, pinch and work the sugar, butter and egg yolks together until well blended.
3 Gradually work in all the flour to bind the mixture together.
4 Knead lightly until smooth. Wrap the pastry in foil or greaseproof paper and leave to 'rest' in the refrigerator or a cool place for about 1 hour, or overnight if possible.

FLAN PASTRY

MAKES 100 G (4 OZ) PASTRY

100 g (4 oz) flour

pinch of salt

75 g (3 oz) butter or block margarine and lard, diced

5 ml (1 level tsp) caster sugar (optional)

1 egg, beaten

1 Place the flour and salt in a bowl. Rub the fat into the flour as for shortcrust pastry, until the mixture resembles fine breadcrumbs. Stir in the sugar if using.
2 Add the egg, stirring with a round-bladed knife until the ingredients begin to stick together in large lumps.
3 With one hand, collect the mixture together and knead lightly for a few seconds to give a firm, smooth dough. Wrap the pastry in greaseproof paper or foil and chill in the refrigerator for at least 30 minutes before use. Roll out as for shortcrust pastry.

CREME PATISSIERE

MAKES 600 ML (1 PINT)

600 ml (1 pint) milk

1 vanilla pod

4 eggs

75 g (3 oz) caster sugar

60 ml (4 level tbsp) plain flour

75 ml (5 level tbsp) cornflour

1 Put the milk and the vanilla pod in a heavy-based saucepan and heat gently until just boiling. Remove from the heat and leave to infuse for 30 minutes.
2 Cream the eggs and sugar together in a bowl until really pale and thick.
3 Sift the flour and cornflour into a bowl, then gradually add a little of the milk to make a smooth paste. Gradually beat the flour mixture into the egg mixture.
4 Remove the vanilla pod from the milk, then reheat until just boiling. Pour onto the egg mixture, in a steady stream, stirring all the time.
5 Strain the mixture back into the saucepan. Reheat gently, stirring all the time until the custard coats the back of a spoon. Pour into a clean bowl, cover the top with a piece of damp greaseproof paper and leave to cool.

BUTTER CREAM

MAKES 250 G (9 OZ)

75 g (3 oz) butter, softened

175 g (6 oz) icing sugar

few drops of vanilla flavouring

15-30 ml (1-2 tbsp) milk or warm water

1 Put the butter in a bowl and cream until soft. Sift and gradually beat in the icing sugar, then add the vanilla flavouring and milk or water. Beat until smooth.

VARIATIONS

Orange or Lemon
Replace the vanilla flavouring with a little finely grated orange or lemon rind. Add a little juice from the fruit instead of the milk, beating well to avoid curdling the mixture.

Coffee
Replace the vanilla flavouring with 10 ml (2 level tsp) instant coffee granules dissolved in some of the hot liquid; cool before adding to the mixture. Or replace 15 ml (1 tbsp) of the liquid with the same amount of coffee essence.

Chocolate
Dissolve 15 ml (1 level tbsp) cocoa powder in a little hot water and cool before adding to the mixture.

Mocha
Dissolve 5 ml (1 level tsp) cocoa powder and 10 ml (2 level tsp) instant coffee granules in a little hot water taken from the measured amount. Cool before adding to the mixture.

GLACE ICING

MAKES ABOUT 100 G (4 OZ)

100 g (4 oz) icing sugar

few drops of vanilla or almond flavouring (optional)

colouring (optional)

1 Sift the icing sugar into a bowl. Add a few drops of vanilla or almond flavouring if wished.

1 Gradually mix in 15 ml (1 tbsp) warm water. The icing should be thick enough to coat the back of a spoon. If necessary, add more water or sugar to adjust consistency. Add colouring, if liked, and use at once.

VARIATIONS

Orange or Lemon
Replace the water with 15 ml (1 tbsp) strained orange or lemon juice.

Chocolate
Dissolve 10 ml (2 level tsp) cocoa powder in the 15 ml (1 tbsp) hot water.

Coffee
Flavour the glacé icing with 5 ml (1 tsp) coffee essence or dissolve 10 ml (2 level tsp) instant coffee granules in the 15 ml (1 tbsp) hot water.

APRICOT GLAZE

MAKES 150 ML (¼ PINT)

100 g (4 oz) apricot jam

1 Put the jam and 30 ml (2 tbsp) water in a saucepan and heat gently, stirring, until the jam softens. Bring to the boil and simmer for 1 minute.
2 Sieve the glaze and use while still warm.

ROYAL ICING

MAKES ABOUT 900 G (2 LB)

4 egg whites

900 g (2 lb) icing sugar

15 ml (1 tbsp) lemon juice

10 ml (2 tsp) glycerine

1 Whisk the egg whites in a bowl until slightly frothy. Then sift and stir in about a quarter of the icing sugar with a wooden spoon. Continue adding more sugar gradually, beating well after each addition, until about three-quarters of the sugar has been added.
2 Beat in the lemon juice and continue beating for about 10 minutes, until the icing is smooth.
3 Beat in the remaining sugar until the required consistency is achieved.
4 Finally, stir in the glycerine to prevent the icing hardening. Cover and keep for 24 hours before using to allow air bubbles to rise to the surface.

FLAT ICING
1 Always apply royal icing over a layer of almond paste rather than directly on to the cake. Keep the bowl of icing covered with a damp cloth, to prevent it developing a crusty surface. Spoon almost half the icing on to the top of the cake and spread it evenly with a palette knife, using a padding action to remove any air bubbles.
2 Using an icing ruler or palette knife longer than the width of the cake, draw it steadily, without applying any pressure, across the top of the cake at an angle of 30°. Neaten the edges. Leave to dry for 24 hours before icing the sides.
3 To ice the sides, place the board on an icing turntable or on an upturned plate. Spread the remaining icing on the side of the cake and smooth it roughly with a small palette knife. Hold the palette knife or an icing comb upright and at an angle of 45° to the cake. Starting at the back, slowly rotate the turntable while moving the knife or comb slowly and evenly towards you to smooth the surface.
4 For a really smooth finish, let dry for 1-2 days, then apply a second thinner coat of icing. Use a piece of fine sandpaper to sand down any imperfections in the first coat. Allow to dry before piping on decorations.

INDEX

330